Corporate Wellness Programs

Corporate Wellness Programs

Linking Employee and Organizational Health

Edited by

Ronald J. Burke

Emeritus Professor, Schulich School of Business, York University, Canada

Astrid M. Richardsen

Professor, BI Norwegian Business School, Norway

Edward Elgar

Cheltenham, UK • Northampton, MA, USA

Published by
Edward Elgar Publishing Limited
The Lypiatts
15 Lansdown Road
Cheltenham
Glos GL50 2JA
UK

Edward Elgar Publishing, Inc.
William Pratt House
9 Dewey Court
Northampton
Massachusetts 01060
USA

A catalogue record for this book
is available from the British Library

Library of Congress Control Number: 2014943901

This book is available electronically in the ElgarOnline.com
Business Subject Collection, E-ISBN 978 1 78347 170 6

ISBN 978 1 78347 169 0

Typeset by Servis Filmsetting Ltd, Stockport, Cheshire
Printed and bound in Great Britain by T.J. International Ltd, Padstow

Contents

Figures

Tables

Contributors

David R. Anderson, StayWell Health Management, USA

Tessa S. Bailey, University of South Australia, Australia

David W. Ballard, American Psychological Association, USA

William B. Baun, MD Anderson Cancer Center, USA

Caroline Biron, Laval University, Canada

Ronald J. Burke, York University, Canada

Quan Campbell, Lifewellness Institute, USA

Marie-Eve Caouette, Laval University, Canada

Melondie Carter, University of Alabama, USA

Sarah Dawkins, University of Tasmania, Australia

Maureen F. Dollard, University of South Australia, Australia

Jessica Grossmeier, StayWell Health Management, USA

Lisa M. Holland, StayFit Plan, USA

Adam Kaufman, DPS Health, USA

Rebecca K. Kelly, University of Alabama, USA

Gerjo Kok, Maastricht University, Netherlands

Angela Martin, University of Tasmania, Australia

Chad D. Morris, University of Colorado, Denver, USA

Cindy W. Morris, University of Colorado, Denver, USA

Ronald J. Ozminkowski, Optum, USA

Marie-Esther Paradis, Laval University, Canada

Silvia Pignata, University of South Australia, Australia

Astrid M. Richardsen, BI Norwegian Business School, Norway

Robert A.C. Ruiter, Maastricht University, Netherlands

Jonathan Spero, InHouse Physicians, USA

Paul E. Terry, StayWell Health Management, USA

Fred R.H. Zijlstra, Maastricht University, Netherlands

Acknowledgements

One thread that runs through much of my research and writing is the link between individual well-being and health and organizational performance and success. Corporate wellness initiatives have emerged as a practical way to realize both of these important outcomes. I have worked with Astrid for several years but this is our first editorial project. Astrid did a terrific job in working with our contributors and Edward Elgar Publishing Ltd. I also thank our international authors for their important contributions. The staff at Edward Elgar were always supportive, particularly Fran O'Sullivan. My contributions were supported in part by York University, Canada.

Ronald Burke, Schulich School of Business, York University,
Toronto, Canada

PART I

Introduction: setting the stage

1. Corporate wellness programs: an overview*

Ronald J. Burke

HIGH-PERFORMANCE WORKPLACES, HUMAN RESOURCE MANAGEMENT PRACTICES, EMPLOYEE WELL-BEING AND ORGANIZATIONAL PERFORMANCE

Organizations today are facing new and major challenges, including globalization, meeting the needs of customers, change and transformation, adopting new technologies, attracting and retaining the best talent, decreasing costs and increasing revenues, and building organizational capability. Organizations can copy the technology, manufacturing processes, products and strategies of their competitors but they cannot easily copy their human resource management processes (Pfeffer, 1998). Critical organizational assets reside in employees and human resource management practices. Research evidence has accumulated over the past 20 years showing that human resource management practices associated with high-performance workplaces are also associated with healthy employees and higher levels of productivity (Burke and Cooper, 2008; Lowe, 2010). Research has shown a positive relationship between human resource management practices and organizational financial performance (e.g., Becker and Huselid, 1998; Katzenbach, 2000; Becker et al., 2001).

Pfeffer (1994) identified 16 inter-related human resource management practices that were proposed to be effective and later condensed these to seven broader strategies (Pfeffer, 1998). These were: employment security, selective hiring, self-managed teams and decentralization, high compensation contingent on performance, training and development, reduction in status differences, and the sharing of information. O'Reilly and Pfeffer (2000) suggested six human resource management levers across eight high-performing organizations. These were: alignment of values, culture and strategy, hiring people for fit with the values and culture of the organization, investing in training and development of all employees, widespread sharing of information, the use of teams, and tying rewards and recognition to observed behaviors and results.

Other researchers and writers have demonstrated a link between human resource management practices and employee health and well-being, employee engagement and organizational performance (e.g., Sirota et al., 2005; Sisodia et al., 2007). Considerable evidence has emerged indicating the key role played by people in the performance of organizations (O'Reilly and Pfeffer, 2000; Lawler, 2003); people are responsible for every initiative an organization undertakes to provide a service or manufacture a product. In addition, there is evidence that healthy employees are associated with healthy organizations. For a long time organizations saw issues of employee health as being the employee's responsibility. More organizations today are taking an interest in not only their role in affecting employee health but a broader interest in improving employee health and well-being in the interests of becoming a more effective workplace (Berry et al., 2004, 2012). They are increasingly interested in enhancing employee health, not out of altruism, but as a key part of their business strategy. Healthy employees are more productive and also reduce health care costs of employing organizations.

This book focuses on what organizations can do to enhance the health and well-being of their employees. Organizations invest time and money in these efforts, in part because they will benefit in the long term from these investments. Health includes physical, mental and social well-being; it is more than the absence of disease and illness. Individuals' health is interlinked with the variety of environments in which they exist and function: their families, socioeconomic status, social networks, employing organizations, wider communities, and government policies and regulations. Individuals are embedded in a variety of levels, each lower level embedded in a higher level (Kok et al., 2008; Minkler and Wallerstein, 2008; Bartholomew et al., 2011).

HUMAN SUSTAINABILITY

Pfeffer (2010) recently noted that 'human sustainability', the capacity of humans to endure and remain productive over time, has received little attention. He cites examples of organizational actions and decisions that affect employees, their health and mortality, leading to a call for the management of human resources in ways that enhance human sustainability. Human health and mortality need to be added as important management criteria and research outcomes. A sample of workplace experiences affecting health and mortality includes the provision of health insurance, the effects of layoffs, work hours, work–family conflict and work stress. Human sustainability includes energy, vitality, joy, engagement, enthusiasm and feeling alive. Human energy helps organizations function more effectively.

FACTORS INFLUENCING EMPLOYEE HEALTH AND WELL-BEING

Individuals and families function within social, political and economic systems that influence their behaviors and resources, both of which affect their health and well-being. Most people work, and work within organizations of varying sizes in various sectors. Organizations also influence individual behaviors, resources and well-being (overload, fatigue, negative and positive emotions, support), thus it is not surprising that interventions to enhance individual and family well-being have been undertaken in, and by, organizations. Individual behavior and attitude change has also been encouraged and supported by various levels of government and professional associations (e.g., American Heart Association, the US National Institute for Occupational Safety and Health).

An increasing number of organizations have become interested in corporate wellness programs/worksite health promotion (McGinnis, 1993). Some of these efforts have focused on a single behavioral risk factor (e.g., smoking) while others have targeted several risk factors (e.g., smoking, diet, exercise). Most programs offered health education (Heaney and Goetzel, 1997), with significantly fewer changing their organizational policies and work environment (e.g., exercise facilities, on-site non-smoking regulations, healthier cafeteria food). Still fewer efforts have tackled more significant organizational factors such as culture, job design and technology. Yet the organizational context is critical to the success of corporate wellness initiatives. Efforts are increasingly being made to utilize employee participation in the design of these efforts, and enlisting the contribution of senior executives in supporting and role-modeling desired changes in employee health behaviors. Occupational safety and health programs support the potential benefits of corporate wellness initiatives by reducing exposure to health and safety risks (e.g., noise, chemicals, equipment safeguards and training). There is some evidence that increasing individual control and influence over work-related decisions has positive effects on employee health and well-being (Bakker and Demerouti, 2007). It is important to note, however, that while corporate wellness programs have been found to have benefits, efforts must also continue at the community and societal levels.

EMPLOYEE LIFESTYLES AFFECT EMPLOYEE HEALTH

Many deaths, perhaps as high as 40 percent, are 'premature' and due to unhealthy lifestyle choices (tobacco, poor diet, alcohol, lack of physical activity). Unhealthy lifestyles are a primary factor in the leading causes of death (e.g., heart disease, stroke, diabetes). People with healthier lifestyles live longer. Obesity has increased, reaching about 30 percent of adults; approximately two-thirds of US adults are obese or overweight. Obesity has also increased among young people. The United Nations Food and Agriculture Organization estimated that, as of 2008, 1.4 billion people were overweight and 500 million were obese (*Globe and Mail*, 2013). Both the American and Canadian Medical Associations have called obesity a disease. There is also a need to reduce the burden of health care costs in all countries.

Unhealthy people are tired, dissatisfied, work more slowly, make more errors, and have more accidents (Stewart et al., 2003). Healthy people work harder, are more satisfied with their jobs and work environments, are more productive, and more likely to help others (Wolfe et al., 1994). Other benefits include lower levels of job stress, fewer injuries and higher levels of commitment when employees see that their organization cares about its people.

FINANCIAL EFFECTS OF LIFESTYLE

Lifestyle-related chronic diseases account for 70 percent of a nation's medical care costs. Individuals with unhealthy habits have higher medical costs (Thorpe et al., 2004; Thorpe, 2005) and high health risks (high blood cholesterol, high blood pressure, etc.) account for about 25 percent of total medical costs. Lifestyle risk factors lower productivity and are costly to organizations. Unhealthy lifestyles lead to chronic diseases that cannot be cured and require years of costly treatments (Donaldson, 1993; Berry, 2008).

Over the past 20 years employee health and well-being have declined (Schroeder, 2007). Between 1994 and 2005 there were increases in diabetes (48 percent), hypertension (27 percent) and obesity (18 percent). Unfortunately there have also been increases in these diseases among younger employees. These can be attributed for the most part to unhealthy lifestyles. More than one-third of the US adult population are obese, more than twice the number of those who were obese 30 years ago.

A study by the International Heart and Stroke Foundation of Canada concluded that most Baby Boomers (80 percent) believed they were unhealthier than they were, and would likely spend their later/final years chronically ill, disabled or immobile (Boyle, 2013). Reasons for lost years included physical inactivity, poor diet, excessive stress, smoking, and excessive alcohol consumption; 85 percent did not eat enough fruit and vegetables; 46 percent did not get enough physical activity; 21 percent smoked; 12 percent were heavy drinkers; and 30 percent were often or always stressed.

In addition, more women and men in the workplace are now getting fewer hours of sleep. Chronic sleep deprivation was costing US employers $63.2 billion annually. Sleep-deprived employees are less productive and more likely to make errors and have accidents. Interestingly, women and men who sleep more are less likely to smoke, more likely to exercise, and consume less alcohol.

The economic recession in 2008 resulted in increased levels of job losses, with more women and men now in temporary, contract or casual jobs, and higher levels of job insecurity. The American Psychological Association surveyed levels of stress among US women and men (Clay, 2011). It found that 30 percent reported their levels of stress had increased in the past year, with 20 percent reporting very high levels of stress. The major causes of stress were: money (69 percent), work (65 percent), the economy (61 percent), family responsibilities (57 percent), relationships (56 percent), family health concerns (53 percent) and personal health issues (51 percent). Respondents often coped with these stresses in unhealthy ways too: 42 percent by smoking, 15 percent by overeating, and 13 percent by drinking alcohol. Job stressors for those having jobs included deadlines, workload, work methods, and relationships with managers, colleagues and customers.

Private sector organizations in Canada spend between $180 to $300 million in short-term disability benefits related to mental illness and $135 million for long-term disability benefits. Mental health has become the fastest-growing disability claim in Canadian organizations (Morrison and MacKinnon, 2008).

CORPORATE WELLNESS PROGRAMS

These concerns have spawned academic interest in the field of occupational health psychology, leading to ways in which organizations can implement programs to enhance employee health, often through stress-reducing interventions (Biron et al., 2012, 2014). Related to this body of work is the field of worksite wellness or corporate wellness programs. This field unfortunately has not been well integrated into occupational health psychology (Quick and Tetrick, 2011) but this book aims to do that by looking directly at contributions of corporate wellness programs to employee and organizational health. It also integrates writing on corporate wellness, occupational health psychology, stress interventions, and organizational development initiatives (see Sauter et al., 1996).

What do we mean by a corporate wellness program? Corporate wellness programs are long-term organizational activities designed to promote the adoption of organizational practices and personal behavior conducive to improving employee physiological, mental and social well-being (Wolfe and Parker, 1994). Berry et al. (2011, p. 4) define a corporate wellness program as 'an organized, employer-sponsored program that is designed to support employees (and sometimes their families) as they adopt and sustain behaviors that reduce health risks, improve quality of life, enhance personal effectiveness, and benefit the organization's bottom line'. Healthy employees are more likely to contribute to the achievement of healthy profits (Heaney and Goetzel, 1997; Pelletier et al., 2004; Pelletier, 2005; Goetzel and Ozminkowski, 2008)

Health insurance for employees ranks as one of the top expenses for many companies. Corporate wellness programs rest on the premise that most organizations would get a better return on their investment (ROI) by promoting and supporting employee wellness. Employee absenteeism, and employee presenteeism – employees coming to work when sick – cost companies significant amounts of money (Daley and Parfitt, 1996; Aldana, 2001; Chapman, 2005).

Company health almost always refers to an organization's financial health. Enlightened managers are increasingly seeing company health as also including the health of their employees (Carnethen et al., 2009). Organizations have considerable opportunities to affect employee behavior. Examples include: on-site medical clinics for employees and their families, weight loss and smoking cessation support initiatives, exercise breaks during the work day, health screening, healthy food options in the cafeteria, and stress reduction workplace audits.

Corporate wellness programs include disease prevention, but 'wellness' is more than the absence of disease. Organizations invest in programs that help employees create fuller work and family lives and experience higher levels of well-being (Hillier et al., 2005).

IMPORTANCE OF THIS TOPIC

Issues of talent management and development, and human resource management more broadly, are gaining currency as organizational and government leaders strive for greater understanding of how to leverage performance in an increasingly demanding and competitive international environment. Organizations cannot be successful without a healthy engaged workforce.

Organizational Interest in Corporate Wellness Programs

Academics and practitioners are interested in what makes one organization more competitive than another. Lencioni (2012) offers 'organizational health' as the key competitive advantage. Successful organizations are healthy organizations. For Lencioni, an organization is healthy when it is whole, consistent and complete, having a unified management, operations and culture. Healthy organizations support the development of satisfied, engaged and healthy employees.

Blanchard and Edington (2009) place the rising costs of health care as a key business priority in terms of organizational performance and employee health. Health and wellness must become an important business strategy. A 2011 study by Towers Watson and the non-profit National Business Group on Health reported that 23 percent of mid-sized and large US organizations had on-site health clinics and that another 12 percent planned to establish an on-site clinic in 2012. There are also several consulting firms offering services to help organizations of all sizes to develop corporate wellness programs.

Government Interest

Bensimon (2010) examined workplace wellness strategies and initiatives among 63 Canadian government departments and all 13 provincial and territorial Departments of Corrections. Four broad categories of intervention were observed: learning and development-educational initiatives that promoted individual well-being, employee wellness support of fitness-focused activities, health promotion and health screening initiatives such as addressing blood pressure and weight, and employee recognition programs. He concluded that there was increasing interest in the development of employer-sponsored wellness interventions that help employees increase their psychological and physical health.

In the USA, the Centers for Disease Control and Prevention has developed the National Healthy Worksite Program (NHWP) to help organizations implement prevention and wellness strategies. The NHWP will help up to 100 small, mid-sized and large organizations establish comprehensive workplace health programs. Expertise will be provided in developing programs, policies and interventions to support physical activity, good nutrition and tobacco-use cessation. Ongoing evaluation of these efforts will monitor changes in employee knowledge, behavior and productivity, and changes in the organizational health and safety culture. Young et al. (2011) describe initiatives started in North Carolina government departments.

   Corporate wellness programs that are only concerned with potential cost savings in terms of health and insurance claims are likely to fall short. Wellness programs should be more than just about cutting costs. Some corporate wellness programs failed and were ended (see Watson and Gauthier, 2003, for an example of one that failed due to lack of funding).

WHY STRONG LEADERSHIP AND ADMINISTRATION MATTERS

When organizations undertake the launch of a new service or product, they typically embark on a series of critical steps. The introduction of a significant corporate wellness program is no different as it also requires strong, committed leadership and considerable administrative support. Golaszewski et al. (2008) describe the following steps:

1. The CEO makes an announcement at a meeting of the Board of Directors, followed up by communications to all employees as well as meetings with managers of all departments to 'spread the word'.
2. An administrative task force of senior managers and influential members of all work groups is organized.
3. A respected and influential senior manager is appointed to head the initiative.
4. The task force creates a plan and a vision, what will happen and a timeline of events.
5. Individual and organizational goals are set within a one-year horizon, identifying criteria, and the determination of rewards for successful achievements.
6. Other important individuals representing relevant functions (occupation safety, Employee Assistance Program, nursing) are appointed to the task force to broaden participation and commitment to action.
7. Research on how to best communicate and inform employees is undertaken.
8. A communication and information strategy and communication media are developed and delivered to increase employee understanding, interest and participation.
9. The organization monitors progress and takes steps to continually increase commitment and participation and reward successes.

KEY STRATEGIC ELEMENTS OF SUCCESSFUL CORPORATE WELLNESS PROGRAMS

Key strategic elements include making the business case (Nicholson et al., 2005; NIHCM Foundation, 2011), developing a strategic plan that defines success (Bertera, 1990), creating a company culture that encourages and supports employees in practicing healthy behaviors and uses outcomes-based rewards (for not smoking, for making a weight target). Corporate wellness programs often include assessment and screening programs, behavior change interventions, reimbursement for costs of smoking cessation sessions, and weight loss programs. Most common initiatives include weight, cholesterol, blood pressure, and tobacco use. Company wellness goals need articulation. Developing a supportive workplace culture is key.

Berry et al. (2011) also describe a number of corporate wellness programs and their success. They identify six pillars common to these successes:

1. *Multilevel leadership.* Committed, passionate leaders are vital to creating a culture of health. There is a need for 'wellness' champions who model desired attitudes and behaviors.
2. *Alignment.* A corporate wellness program should flow from an organization's identity and goals. This culture should embody a health-supporting workforce culture. A central tenet of such cultures is that employee health and well-being is an important business priority. And building such a culture takes time and resources.
3. *Scope, relevance and quality.* Wellness programs must be comprehensive, relevant, engaging, fun, tailored to individual needs, contain some 'key' programs, be of high quality, and excellent.
4. *Accessibility.* Corporate wellness programs need to be low- or no-cost services and integrated into the organization and its facilities and resources so they are easy to access. This should include on-site programs, healthy food at work, smoking cessation at work and outside of work, as well as internet accessibility.
5. *Partnerships.* Corporate wellness programs need to collaborate with both internal and external partners and vendors (government agencies, non-profit organizations such as heart associations).
6. *Communications.* Wellness is a message to employees and the way this message is delivered matters. Messages work best if they are creative, sensitive and use a variety of media. Some messages should be targeted to specific employee groups or categories (e.g., high risk).

Building the Business Case

Before organizations embark on any change in or introduce new operating policies, procedures or programs, they usually think about the business case (or at least they tell us they do). Is there a business case to be made for the development of a corporate wellness program? What is the best currently available evidence on their value-added? Is this information clear-cut and compelling? Does the development and implementation of a corporate wellness program impact an organization's bottom line, their ROI?

At a general level, we know the following. First, employee lifestyle risk factors (e.g., smoking and drinking, physical fitness levels, levels of work and life stress) influence health directly (medical costs, morbidity and mortality). Second, we know that individual clinical risk factors (obesity, elevated levels of cholesterol and blood pressure) also directly affect health. We also know that levels of emotional and physical health have direct effects on employee absenteeism, health care costs to organizations, levels of job and life satisfaction, and job performance).

HERE'S WHAT A HEALTHY WORK ENVIRONMENT MIGHT LOOK LIKE

A health-fostering work environment makes it easier for employees to exhibit healthy behaviors. Some initiatives include: healthy food in the cafeteria, the presence of exercise/fitness centers or the financial support for using them, the creation of walking or running trails, space available for meditation, yoga, zumba and other movement or stretching classes, a tobacco-free work environment, support for employees taking part in Weight Watchers' programs, and providing a pedometer to encourage employees to walk so many steps each day. The key is to get employees involved. Since all employees are different in some ways, it is important to target individuals – what works best for a given person

Health-related Intervention Projects

A number of more narrowly focused stand-alone health-related intervention projects have been undertaken and evaluated. These are informative for organizations interested in introducing a comprehensive corporate wellness program. Dunn et al. (1997) compared two interventions (lifestyle physical activity, traditional structured exercise) on cardiovascular risk factors among healthy sedentary middle-aged women and men. Measures were taken at baseline and at six months. After the intervention, 78 percent of lifestyle participants and 85 percent of structured exercise participants met or exceeded recommended levels of physical activity. There was also increases in cardio-respiratory fitness in both groups, lower levels of total cholesterol, diastolic blood pressures and percentage of body fat.

Emmons et al. (1999) evaluated the Working Healthy Project, a worksite health promotion initiative targeting physical activity diet and smoking. Data were collected in 26 manufacturing worksites from 2055 people and involved three health behavior assessments in a matched-pair design. Participants in the intervention condition increased levels of their exercise behavior and ate more fruit, vegetables and fiber. However, the intervention had no effect of levels of smoking.

Sorensen et al. (2003) did find lower levels of smoking in a compre-hensive worksite cancer prevention intervention carried out in 15 manu-facturing worksites. They reported a considerable drop in smoking rates over a two-year period but no change in diet (consumption of fruit and vegetables).

A Corporate Wellness Program Example

Johnson & Johnson is just one example of a corporate wellness program that has proven to be effective. For every dollar invested in wellness, Johnson & Johnson reported a reduction of nearly $4 in reduced health care costs, lower absenteeism and improved productivity. Isaac and Ratzan (2013), from Johnson & Johnson, suggest that four critical leader-ship beliefs contribute to the effectiveness of a corporate wellness program:

1. *A definition of health that includes well-being.* Being fully engaged means being physically healthy, being sufficiently rewarded, having a work–family-life balance, and not being burdened by enduring job demands and stressors. Employees are more work engaged if healthy. Benefits include less employee turnover, lower health care costs, less presenteeism – workers coming to the organization when sick and not performing effectively as a result.
2. *Prevention-focused education.* When risk is found during a volun-tary health assessment, employees can meet with a health profes-sional in one-on-one sessions to address the risk. Health education means improving an employee's health literacy in subjects such as stress reduction, blood pressure, cholesterol, diabetes, cardiovascular disease, diversity skills, workplace bullying, and safe driving skills. Health news should be placed throughout the building, including e-mail health tips to those requesting them. Organizations should

have a variety of health and benefits publications available and allow employees access to websites to access online tests to indicate stress, work–family issues, nutrition and so on.

3. *Rewards for healthy behaviors.* Offer financial incentives for employees. These include taking opportunities for risk assessments for addressing identified health risks, for participating in sessions addressing weight/obesity, for taking part in a preventive colonoscopy program for employees over 50, for example.

4. *Creating a workplace environment supporting employees in engaging in healthy behaviors.* This means continuous leadership and commitment. Teach senior executives the link between good health and business success. Offer a number of integrated programs. Establish supportive policies and procedures. Improve engagement with employees through marketing of the corporate wellness program. Measure outcomes not effort.

EMPLOYEE PARTICIPATION

It is obviously critical to get high rates of employee participation if corporate wellness programs are to make a difference. Why don't employees participate in these potentially life-enhancing opportunities? Common factors for not taking part include: a lack of awareness of the program and its potential benefits, a lack of time, no perceived personal benefits, a lack of manager and organizational support, difficulty or inconvenience in accessing these initiatives, and concerns about one's privacy

Some Research Evidence

McGlynn et al. (2003) evaluated a comprehensive health program, LifeSteps, introduced in General Motors. In the 1990s, General Motors (GM) wanted to reduce rising health care costs by improving the health of its employees and their dependents. The United Auto Workers union successfully bargained for a comprehensive preventative health program, and working with GM, launched a corporate wellness program, LifeSteps, in April 1996. LifeSteps included quarterly newsletters on health topics, toll-free 24-hour telephone line access to nurses for health advice, and a health risk appraisal (a multi-item survey that assigned respondents a wellness score based on their responses), among other initiatives. The health risk assessment categorized individuals according to their likelihood of developing diseases (being overweight, smoking, drinking excessively, having high levels of cholesterol, a sedentary lifestyle, being under stress). Some

GM plants included on-site assessments of weight, blood pressure and cholesterol. High-risk employees, those with three of more risk factors, were encouraged to participate in counseling for behavioral change. High-risk employees could also have two visits to doctors paid for by GM. They found that LifeSteps increased both wellness scores overall and movement to low-risk from high-risk categories. They concluded that the program saved about $42 a person, a sizable amount in a company with 1.25 million employees and self-insured for health care costs.

Jackson et al. (2011) evaluated a program designed to reduce blood pressure (hypertension) among auto workers at Chrysler (n = 539) The intervention, lasting six months, included education, awareness, and support for moderate to high cardiovascular risk employees. At baseline, employees were tested for hypertension and cardiovascular disease risk. After six months, both systolic and diastolic blood pressure had dropped, 86 percent believed the intervention helped them better understand and control their blood pressure, and 84 percent said they now had better understanding of treatment options.

Byrne et al. (2011) reported an evaluation of seven-year trends (2003 to 2009) in employee health benefits from a worksite health promotion program at Vanderbilt University. The majority of risk factors improved over time, the most consistent being physical activity; the proportion of employees exercising one or more times a week increased from 73 percent to 83 percent. The largest gains occurred in the first two years but continued through the remaining years.

Liu et al. (2013) examined the effect of PepsiCo's corporate wellness program on medical costs and utilization. The sample included employees and dependents from 19 to 64 years of age and had two years of baseline date (2002 and 2003) and at least one year of data following the intervention (2004 to 2007). The first year showed an increase in cost per member per month but a reduction in these costs in the second and third years. Over the three years, costs per member had reduced, including a decrease in hospital admissions and a decrease in emergency room visits.

Davis et al. (2009) describe and evaluate a corporate wellness program introduced by Capital Metropolitan Transit Authority, the local transit authority in Austin, Texas. This corporate wellness program offered consultations with wellness coaches and personal trainers, a 24-hour company fitness center, personalized health assessments, preventative screenings, healthier food options, case incentives, health newsletters, workshops, dietary counseling, and smoking cessation programs. Participants in the corporate wellness program reported improvements in physical activity, healthier food consumption, weight loss and lowered blood pressure. The organization's total health care costs increased by increasingly smaller amounts from 2003 to 2006 then decreased from 2006 to 2007. Employee absenteeism decreased by 25 percent and the ROI was determined to be $2.43 for every dollar spent.

Merrill et al. (2011) evaluated a corporate wellness program in Lincoln Industries in 2009, a small business in Lincoln, Nebraska, comparing their employees with employees working in other organizations in Lincoln and Omaha, Nebraska. Four well-being indicators were included: physical health, emotional health, engaging in healthy behaviors, and access to health-related conditions and services. Employees at Lincoln Industries scored higher on the first three than employees in comparison sites.

Hochart and Lang (2011) examined the benefits of a comprehensive corporate wellness program introduced by Blue Cross Blue Shield in 2005 to impact employer culture and help healthy employees stay at low risk, and to move employees at moderate to high risk to lower-risk levels. They studied 15 employee groups (n = 9627) for three consecutive years (2006 to 2008). Health risk appraisals and biometric screening were used to examine the program's impact. Individuals at low risk remained at low risk (86 percent) and 40 percent at medium risk and 49 percent at high risk moved to lower-risk categories. There were improvements in blood pressure and total cholesterol but not in body weight.

Neville et al. (2011) studied health benefits of an eight-year participation in an employer-based wellness program focusing on chronic disease factors. Annual data collection included measures of weight, blood pressure, cholesterol and body fat percentage. Participants were categorized into risk levels at baseline. Levels of participation by individuals were also considered. Participants had smaller increases in body mass index (BMI) than the general population over the eight years. Long-term participation was associated with improved BMI, blood pressure and cholesterol, with greatest benefits found in the highest-risk group. They advocate a focus on retention of participants in general, the encouragement of higher levels of employee participation, and a greater focus on high-risk groups.

Short et al. (2010) examined the effects of a corporate wellness program at Prudential Financial using biometric measures of blood lipids and glucose. Physically active employees had higher levels of high-density lipoproteins and employees participating in a disease management program lowered both cholesterol and low-density lipoproteins during a one-year period, compared to a group of non-participants.

Naydeck et al. (2008) studied the return on investment of Highmark Inc.'s employee wellness programs based on medical claims of participants versus risk-matched non-participants. They compared medical claims over a four-year period (2001–04). The Highmark program included both health risk assessments, online programs in nutrition, smoking cessation, weight management, stress management, on-site nutrition and stress sessions, individual nutrition and smoking cessation coaching, campaigns to increase physical fitness participation, and information on disease prevention strategies. Highmark employees could also use state-of-the-art fitness centers. Employees had a health risk assessment (cholesterol, glucose, blood pressure) at the launch of the wellness program. In general, employee participation in various health promotion programs grew each year over the four-year period. Health care costs grew more slowly for participants than non-participants. Health care expenses per person per year were $176 lower for participants, with in-patient expenses lower by $182. Four-year savings compared to expenses yielded an ROI of $1.65 for every dollar spent on the program.

Berry et al. (2012) describe the corporate wellness program implemented by US software provider SAS Institute. SAS always ranks at the very top of best companies to work for. SAS has reported annual productivity savings in the millions as a result of its program. SAS operates its own on-site full-service health care center for employees and their families. This center started small in 1985 and now has a staff of 55, including four physicians and ten nurse practitioners, does not charge for services and collects no copays.[1] Same-day appointments are typical, and care is unhurried; clinicians spend 30 minutes or more with a patient. All services available in a primary care medical practice are offered, and more. These include allergy shots, consulting a dietician, obtaining physical therapy, getting blood work done, or seeing a psychotherapist. Employees create a relationship with a primary care physician – a medical home – which ensures continuity of care. The center offers a wide range of health-related educational materials and programming both on-site and online.

Golaszewski et al. (1998) introduced changes in the workplace environment in one US government department available to all employees (n = 2276) regardless of their health status over a three-year period (2005–07) Outcome measures included changes in sick time, employee health risks using health assessments, and changes in the work environment. Hours of sick leave decreased, there was an improved workplace environment, and employee risk status remained the same although employees were now older.

IS THE MEDIUM THE MESSAGE?

Improving individual health requires behavior change but behavior change is difficult; changing a lifetime habit is hard. To work, engagement programs must appeal to individuals (Pearson et al., 2010). They must present information that is relevant, useful, timely, educational, attention-grabbing and easily accessed. And people differ in terms of what kinds of information media they prefer. Information then must use various channels, from print to digital media; a multi-channel and multimedia approach. Information needs to be presented in ways that individuals feel comfortable with, be engaging and interesting, come from a credible source, and be tailored to the individual.

GLOBAL FACTORS AND CORPORATE WELLNESS PROGRAMS

Corporate wellness programs have been introduced and adopted in the USA more than in other countries over the past decade or more. Corporate wellness programs are still primarily a North American phenomenon, reflecting in part North America's health insurance programs. Different health care systems are a major factor in this. In many other countries the national or provincial governments assume the majority of health care costs (e.g., Canada, UK, France, Norway, Sweden, among others). Relevant work has also been carried out in the UK, Australia, and in Scandinavia, with emerging interest being shown in South Africa. Thus, another benefit of this book is to spread research and writing on corporate wellness initiatives to other countries.

Corporate wellness programs offer benefits to worldwide organizations, including higher levels of workforce engagement, less absenteeism and presenteeism, and higher productivity. Organizations should be concerned about the well-being of their employees for these and other benefits. As a consequence, workplace health promotion is growing internationally. This has resulted in part from increasing numbers of organizations having multinational workforces, more international joint ventures, and increasing global knowledge and understanding of potential individual and organizational benefits of corporate health promotion initiatives.

Corporate wellness programs are still also implemented primarily by large organizations. There is a need to encourage small businesses to consider them as well (Eakin et al., 2001; McPeck et al., 2009).

THE NEED FOR MORE RIGOROUS EVALUATION RESEARCH

Most studies evaluating corporate wellness programs report favorable results (e.g., Ozminkowski et al., 2000, 2002). Among the limitations of much evaluation research is the use of non-experimental designs that do not control for selection bias, and a failure to identify the most effective and cost-saving components of the corporate wellness program.

Grossmeier et al. (2010) address the thorny question of how best to evaluate corporate wellness programs. They raise and address the following questions:

- *What are the measures of success of corporate wellness programs?* They include the following: engagement or participation metrics, satisfaction metrics, health behavior changes, biometric health and clinical impact, population-level health risk reduction, productivity impacts, health care cost impacts, and return on investment.
- *How can program performance metrics be organized into a comprehensive evaluation framework?* They suggest a process evaluation (0–12 months) an impact evaluation (12–24 months), and an outcomes evaluation (2–5 years), and offer examples of each.
- *What kind of corporate wellness program is needed to achieve the best outcomes?* They note the following: program goals and purpose, senior management support, a comprehensive program design, multiple modalities to engage participation and deliver the program, a variety of programs, widespread communication, use of incentives, health screening, highly motivated and qualified staff, and relationships with internal and external partners.
- *What outcomes can be expected from a best-practice program?* These include high levels of employee participation, employee satisfaction, health risk reduction, of job performance and productivity assessments, low medical claim filings, and higher ROI.
- *How does a best-practice evaluation framework support assessment of economic impacts?* Assessing the indicators listed above provides an indication of how successful the corporate wellness program was and when future investments should be made.
- *How can the best-practice evaluation framework be used to foster and maintain stakeholder support for corporate wellness programs?* These measures include whether the corporate wellness program is on the right track and yielding expected benefits over the long term.

The development and implementation of a corporate wellness program represents a major cultural change in an organization. The success rate in bringing about such successful change efforts is mixed. It is important that organizations contemplating such an investment learn from the experiences of others (see Whitehead, 2001 for lessons learned from Chevron's efforts in this regard).

SOME ADDITIONAL CAUTIONS AND CONCERNS ABOUT CORPORATE WELLNESS PROGRAMS

We are concerned that corporate wellness programs might become another fad. This is likely to happen if corporate wellness programs are seen as a quick fix, are introduced poorly, have little top management support, and emerge as a stand-alone initiative separate from organizational strategy and business goals. While observing the potential contribution of corporate wellness programs to improve employee health and reduce costs of health care, the shortcomings in evaluation of the results of corporate wellness programs should be noted. Not only is implementing a corporate wellness program a demanding task, evaluating its effectiveness is also equally challenging. Studies need to be longitudinal in design, involve large matched groups of employees in treatment and control groups, adequate measures of critical concepts, and sophisticated analysis techniques.

There are also both ethical and legal concerns about the implementation of corporate wellness programs (Zoller, 2004; Mello and Rosenthal, 2008; Pearson and Liebert, 2009). These include the following:

- The tying of rewards and penalties to employees reaching the necessary standards of health status, particularly those that affect employee health insurance premiums; a concern that this shifts health care costs from healthy employees to 'sick' employees.
- Obviously an employee's health is the result of a number of factors, not all of which can an employee control (e.g., genetic factors influencing weight, blood pressure and cholesterol). Incentives are thus unfair because health issues may not be under the individual's control.
- Results-based and designed incentives may coerce women and men with a health condition to take part in activities without adequate medical supervision (Halpern et al., 2009).
- Concerns have been raised about the issue of maintaining medical privacy.
- Corporate wellness programs may discriminate against low-income employees who have greater obstacles to healthy living.(job stress, job insecurity, lack of access to healthy food).
- There are limits to how far organizations can keep asking employees to quit smoking or offering rewards to employees who lose weight.

CONCLUSIONS AND IMPLICATIONS

After examining a sample of the literature the following conclusions and implications seem warranted:

1. Interest in corporate wellness programs is high and growing. While starting primarily in the USA, corporate wellness initiatives are being implemented in a large number of countries today. More organizations, both private and public sectors, are implementing corporate wellness programs. Most employers plan to allocate more resources to their corporate wellness programs in the next few years.

2. Interest in corporate wellness programs comes from governments, organizations, professional health associations, and the academic and research communities. Corporate wellness has now become a multi-billion dollar industry.

3. Several previously separate research streams have come together to underpin interest in corporate wellness programs (occupational health psychology, human resource management and organizational performance, health and wellness researchers, health economics, epidemiology, organizational change expertise, among others).

4. Planning, developing and implementing a comprehensive corporate wellness program represents a major organizational/culture change, is difficult to carry out, requires considerable resources, is time-consuming, with no guarantee of success. There is no quick and easy fix.

5. Corporate wellness programs vary in comprehensiveness, with some focusing on one or two individual health behaviors and health risk outcomes (e.g., smoking cessation, weight reduction) while others address a wide array of individual and organizational outcomes (e.g., biometric measures, physical health assessments, absenteeism). There is low but increasing interest in employee mental health. Most common elements in corporate wellness programs include Employee Assistance Programs, seminars, health fairs and lunch-and-learn sessions, fitness programs, condition-targeted programs (e.g., diabetes), and individual physical health assessments.

6. We have considerable understanding of characteristics of 'successful' corporate wellness programs. Workplace wellness is increasingly seen as a strategic imperative. A business case is made for focusing on employee health. Top management support, involvement and ownership of their corporate wellness program are important for program success. Wellness is increasingly being integrated into work-site health centers. More efforts to change the workplace culture,

processes, procedures and systems need to be undertaken. There is still debate, however, on the best incentive and reward offerings, with more interest now in outcome-based incentives or rewards.

7. A continuing challenge for corporate wellness programs is participation and retention of participants. Employee participation in corporate wellness offerings remains low, typically less that 50 percent.

8. Another continuing challenge is to evaluate the benefits of corporate wellness programs. Many evaluations use research designs that limit understanding of their potential benefits (Lerner et al., 2013). Most employers are satisfied with the results of their corporate wellness programs. Employers see a greater benefit of their corporate wellness programs on the morale, engagement and productivity of employers than in health care cost savings. And the vast majority of employers believe they are getting value from this investment. But corporate wellness program success is increasingly being measured in more sophisticated ways.

9. Organizations need to be aware of ethical and legal issues in their development and implementation of corporate wellness initiatives.

10. The majority of evaluations of corporate wellness programs, while based sometimes on limited research designs, provide generally consistent findings on the benefits of these programs (see Baicker et al., 2010). I conclude that increasing implementation of corporate wellness programs is warranted and necessary, and if well designed and well implemented, likely to increase both individual and organizational health (Harris et al., 2001). And healthy employees lead to healthy organizations.

NOTES

*   Preparation of this chapter was supported in part by York University.
1. Copayment in the USA is a payment defined in the insurance policy and paid by the insured person each time a medical service is accessed.

REFERENCES

Aldana, S.G. (2001), 'Financial impact of health promotion programs: a comprehensive review of the literature', *American Journal of Health Promotion*, **15**(5), 296–320.

Baicker, K., D. Cutler and Z. Song (2010), 'Workplace wellness programs can generate savings', *Health Affairs*, **29**(2), 304–11.

Bakker, A.B. and E. Demerouti (2007), 'The job demands-resources model: state of the art', *Journal of Managerial Psychology*, **22**(3), 309–28.

Bartholomew, L.K., G.S. Parcel, G. Kok, N.H. Gottlieb and M.E. Fernandez (2011), *Planning Health Promotion Programs: An Intervention Mapping Approach*, San Francisco, CA: Jossey-Bass.

Becker, B.E. and M. Huselid (1998), 'High performance work systems and firm performance: synthesis of research and managerial implications', *Research in Personnel and Human Resources Management*, **16**, 53–101.

Becker, B.E., M.A. Huselid and D. Ulrich (2001), *The HR Scorecard: Linking People, Strategy and Performance*, Boston, MA: Harvard Business School Press.

Bensimon, P. (2010), *Wellness at Work: A Matter of Choice for a Better Future*, Ottawa: Correctional Services Canada.

Berry, L.L. (2008), 'Confronting America's healthcare crisis', *Business Horizons*, **51**(4), 273–89.

Berry, L.L., G. Adcock and A.M. Mirabito (2012), '"Do-it-yourself" employee health care', *MIT Sloan Management Review*, **53**(2), Winter.

Berry, L.L., A.M. Mirabito and W.B. Baun (2011), 'What's the hard return on employee wellness programs?', *Harvard Business Review*, **89**(3), 1–10.

Berry, L.L., A.M. Mirabito and D.M. Berwick (2004), 'A health care agenda for business', *Sloan Management Review*, **45**(4), 56–64.

Bertera, R.L. (1990), 'Planning and implementing health promotion in the work-place: a case study of the Du Pont company experience', *Health Education Quarterly*, **17**(3), 307–27.

Biron, C., R.J. Burke and C.L. Cooper (2014), *Creating Healthy Workplaces: Interventions that Reduce Stress, Improve Well-being and Organizational Effectiveness*, 2nd edition, Surrey, UK: Gower Publishing Co.

Biron, C., M. Karanika-Murray and C.L. Cooper (2012), *Organizational Stress and Well-being Interventions: Addressing Process and Content*, London: Routledge.

Blanchard, K. and D.W. Edington (2009), 'Averting the collision between rising health care costs and corporate survival', *Leader to Leader*, **53**(Summer), 24–30.

Boyle, T. (2013), 'Improve lifestyle choices now, boomers told: or face becoming ill, disabled, report writes', *Toronto Star*, 13 December, A2.

Burke, R.J. and C.L. Cooper (2008), *Building More Effective Organizations: HR Management and Performance in Practice*, Cambridge, UK: Cambridge University Press.

Byrne, D.W., R.Z. Goetzel, P.W. McGowan, M.S. Beckowski, M.J. Tabrizi, N. Kowlessar and M.I. Yarbrough, (2011), 'Seven-year trends in employee health habits from a comprehensive workplace health promotion program at Vanderbilt University', *Journal of Occupational and Environmental Medicine*, **53**(12), 1372–81.

Carnethen, M., L.P. Whitsel, B.A. Franken, P. Kris-Etherton, R. Milani, C.A. Pratt and G.R. Wagner (2009), 'Workplace wellness programs for cardiovascular disease prevention: a policy statement from the American Heart Association', *Circulation*, **120**(17), 1725–41.

Chapman, L. (2005), 'Meta-evaluation of worksite health promotion economic return studies: 2005 update', *American Journal of Health Promotion*, **19**(6), 1–11.

Clay, R.A. (2011), 'Stressed in America', *Monitor on Psychology*, **42**(1), 66–9.

Daley, A.J. and G. Parfitt (1996), 'Good health, is it worth it? Mood states, physical well-being, job satisfaction, and absenteeism in members and nonmembers of a British corporate health and fitness club', *Journal of Occupational and Organizational Psychology*, **69**(2), 121–34.

Davis, L., K. Loyo, A. Glowka, R. Schwertfeger, L. Danielson, C. Bres, A. Easton and S. Griffith-Blake (2009), 'A comprehensive worksite wellness program in Austin, Texas: partnership between Steps to a Healthier Austin and Capital Metropolitan Transportation Authority', *Preventing Chronic Disease*, **6**(2), 56–80.

Donaldson, S.J. (1993), 'Effects of lifestyle and stress on the employee and organization: implications for promoting health at work', *Anxiety, Stress and Coping: An International Journal*, **6**(3), 356–78.

Dunn, A.L., B.H. Marcus, J.B. Kampert, M.E. Garcia, H.W. Kohl and S.N. Blair (1997), 'Reduction in cardiovascular disease risk factors: 6-month results from Project Active', *Preventative Medicine*, **26**(6), 883–92.

Eakin, J.M., M. Cava and T.F. Smith (2001), 'From theory to practice: a determinants approach to workplace health promotion in small businesses', *Health Promotion Practice*, **2**(2), 172–81.

Emmons, K.M., L.A. Linnan, W.G. Shadel, B. Marcus and D.B. Abrams (1999), 'The Working Healthy Project: a worksite health-promotion trial targeting physical activity, diet and smoking', *Journal of Occupational and Environmental Medicine*, **41**(7), 545–55.

Globe and Mail (2013), 'Obesity is taking on epic proportions globally', 15 July, L3.

Goetzel, R.Z. and R.J. Ozminkowski (2008), 'The health and cost benefits of work site health-promotion programs', *Annual Review of Public Health*, **29**, 303–23.

Golaszewski, T., J. Allen and D. Edington (2008), 'The role of the environment in health management programs', *American Journal of Health Promotion: The Art of Health Promotion*, **22**, 1–10.

Golaszewski, T., D. Barr and S. Cochran (1998), 'An organization-based intervention to improve support for employee heart health', *American Journal of Health Promotion*, **13**(1), 26–35.

Grossmeier, J., P.E. Terry, A. Cipriotti and J.E. Burtaine (2010), 'Best practices in evaluation worksite health promotion programs', *The Art of Health Promotion*, January–February, 1–9.

Halpern, S.D., K.M. Madison and K.G. Volpp (2009), 'Patients as mercenaries: the ethics of using financial incentives in the war on unhealthy behaviors', *Circulation and Cardiovascular Qualitative Outcomes*, **2**(5), 514–16.

Harris, J.R., P.B. Holman and V.G. Carande-Kulis (2001), 'Financial impact of health promotion: we need to know much more but we know enough to act', *American Journal of Health Promotion*, **15**(5), 378–82.

Heaney, C. and R. Goetzel (1997), 'A review of health-related outcomes of multi-component worksite health promotion programs', *American Journal of Health Promotion*, **11**(4), 290–308.

Hillier, D., F. Fewell, W. Cann and W. Shephard (2005), 'Wellness at work: enhancing the quality of our working lives', *International Review of Psychiatry*, **17**(5), 419–31.

Hochart, C. and M. Lang (2011), 'Impact of a comprehensive worksite wellness program on health risk, utilization, and health care costs', *Population Health Management*, **14**(3), 111–16.

Isaac, F.W. and S.C. Ratzan (2013), 'Corporate wellness programs: why investing in employee health and well-being is an investment in the health of the company', in R.J. Burke and C.L. Cooper (eds), *The Fulfilling Workplace: The Organization's Role in Achieving Individual and Organizational Health*, Surrey, UK: Gower Publishing Co., pp. 301–14.

Jackson, J., K.A. Kohn-Parrott, C. Parker, N. Levine, S. Dyer, E.J. Hedalen, E. Frank, S. Bramer, D. Brandt and J.J. Doyle (2011), 'Blood pressure success zone: You Auto Know, a worksite-based program to improve blood-pressure control among auto workers', *Population Health Management*, **14**(5), 257–63.

Katzenbach, J.R. (2000), *Peak Performance: Aligning the Hearts and Minds of Your Employees*, Boston, MA: Harvard Business School Press.

Kok, G., N.H. Gottlieb, M. Commers and D. Smerecnik (2008), 'The ecological approach in health promotion programs: a decade later', *American Journal of Health Promotion*, **22**(6), 437–42.

Lawler, E.E. (2003), *Treat People Right*, San Francisco, CA: Jossey-Bass.

Lencioni, P. (2012), *The Advantage: Why Organizational Health Trumps Everything Else*, San Francisco, CA: Jossey-Bass.

Lerner, D., A.M. Rodday, J.T. Cohen and W.H. Rogers (2013), 'A systematic review of the evidence concerning the economic impact of employee-focused health promotion and wellness programs', *Journal of Occupational and Environmental Medicine*, **55**(2), 209–22.

Liu, H., K.M. Harris, S. Weinberger, S. Serxner, S. Mattke and E. Exum (2013), 'Effect of an employer-sponsored health and wellness program on medical cost and utilization', *Population Health Management*, **16**(1), 1–6.

Lowe, G. (2010), *Creating Healthy Organizations: How Vibrant Workplaces Inspire Employees to Achieve Sustainable Success*, Toronto: University of Toronto Press.

McGinnis, M. (1993), '1992 National Survey of Worksite Health Promotion activities: summary', *American Journal of Health Promotion*, **7**(6), 452–64.

McGlynn, E.A., T. McDonald, L. Champagne, B. Bradley and W. Walker (2003), *The Business Case for a Corporate Wellness Program: A Case Study of General Motors and the United Auto Workers Union*, New York: The Commonwealth Fund.

McPeck, W., M. Ryan and L.S. Chapman (2009), 'Bringing wellness to the small employer', *American Journal of Health Promotion*, **23**(5), 1–10.

Mello, M.M. and M.B. Rosenthal (2008), 'Wellness programs and lifestyle discrimination – the legal limits', *New England Journal of Medicine*, **359**(2), 192–9.

Merrill, R.M., S.G. Aldana, J.E. Pope, D.R. Anderson, C.R. Coberley, T.F. Vyhlidal, G. Howe and R.W. Whitmer (2011), 'Evaluation of a best-practice worksite wellness program in a small-employer setting using selected well-being indices', *Journal of Occupational and Environmental Medicine*, **53**(4), 448–54.

Minkler, M. and N. Wallerstein (2008), *Community-based Participatory Research for Health: From Process to Outcomes*, San Francisco, CA: Jossey-Bass.

Morrison, E. and N.J. MacKinnon (2008), 'Workplace wellness programs in Canada: an exploration of key issues', *Healthcare Management Forum*, **21**(1), 26–31.

Naydeck, B.L., J.A. Pearson, R.J. Ozminkowski, B.T. Dayu and R.Z. Goetzel (2008), 'The impact of the Highmark Employee Wellness Programs on 4-year healthcare costs', *Journal of Occupational and Environmental Medicine*, **50**(2), 146–56.

Neville, B.H., R.M. Merrill and K.L. Kumpfer (2011), 'Longitudinal outcomes of a comprehensive, incentivized worksite wellness program', *Evaluation & the Health Professions*, **34**(1), 103–23.

Nicholson, S., M.V. Pauly, D. Polsky, C.M. Baase, G.M. Billotti, R.J. Ozminkowski, M.L. Berger and C.E. Sharda (2005), 'How to present the business case for healthcare quality to employers', *Applied Health Economics and Health Policy*, **4**(4), 209–18.

NIHCM Foundation (2011), *Building a Stronger Evidence Base for Employee Wellness Programs*, Washington, DC: NIHCM Foundation.

O'Reilly, C.A, III and J. Pfeffer (2000), *Hidden Value: How Great Companies Achieve Extraordinary Results with Ordinary People*, Boston, MA: Harvard Business School Press.

Ozminkowski, R.J., R.Z. Goetzel, M.W. Smith, R.I. Cantor, A. Shaughnessy and M. Harrison (2000), 'The impact of the Citibank, NA, health management program on changes in employee health risks over time', *Journal of Occupational and Environmental Medicine*, **42**(5), 502–11.

Ozminkowski, R.J., D. Ling, R.Z. Goetzel, J.A. Bruno, R.R. Rutter, F. Isaac and W. Wang (2002), 'Long-term impact of Johnson & Johnson's Health & Wellness Program on health care utilization and expenditures', *Journal of Occupational and Environmental Medicine*, **44**(1), 21–9.

Pearson, A.L., S.E. Colby, J.A. Bulova and J.W. Eubanks (2010), 'Barriers to participation in workplace wellness programs', *Nutrition Research and Practice*, **4**(2), 149–54.

Pearson, S.D. and S.R. Liebert (2009), 'Financial penalties for the unhealthy? Ethical guidelines for holding employees responsible for their health', *Health Affairs*, **28**(3), 845–52.

Pelletier, K.R. (2005), 'A review and analysis of the clinical and cost-effectiveness studies of comprehensive health promotion and disease management programs at the worksite: Update VI 2000–2004', *Journal of Occupational and Environmental Medicine*, **47**(10), 1051–8.

Pelletier, B., M. Boles and W. Lynch (2004), 'Change in health risks and work productivity over time', *Journal of Occupational and Environmental Medicine*, **46**(7), 746–54.

Pfeffer, J. (1994), *Competitive Advantage Through People: Unleashing the Power of the Work Force*, Boston, MA: Harvard Business School Press.

Pfeffer, J. (1998), *The Human Equation: Building Profits by Putting People First*, Boston, MA: Harvard Business School Press.

Pfeffer, J. (2010), 'Building sustainable organizations', *Academy of Management Perspectives*, **24**(1), 34–45.

Quick, J.C. and L.E. Tetrick (2011), *Handbook of Organizational Health Psychology*, Washington, DC: American Psychological Association.

Sauter, S., S. Lim and L. Murphy (1996), 'Organizational health: a new paradigm for occupational stress research in NIOSH', *Japanese Journal of Occupational Mental Health*, **4**(4), 248–54.

Schroeder, S. (2007), 'We can do better – improving the health of the American people', *New England Journal of Medicine*, **357**, 1221–8.

Short, M.E., R.Z. Goetzel, J.S. Young, N.M. Kowlessar, C. Liss-Levinson, M.J. Tabrizi, E.C. Roemer, A.A. Sabatelli, K. Winick, M. Montes and K.A. Creighton (2010), 'Measuring changes in lipid and blood glucose values in the health and wellness program of Prudential Financial, Inc.', *Journal of Occupational and Environmental Medicine*, **52**(8), 797–806.

Sirota, D., L.A. Mischkind and M.L. Meltzer (2005), *The Enthusiastic Employee: How Companies Profit by Giving Workers What They Want*, Philadelphia, PA: Wharton School Publishing.

Sisodia, R., D.B. Wolfe and J. Sheth (2007), *Firms of Endearment: How World-class Companies Profit From Passion and Purpose*, Philadelphia, PA: Wharton School Publishing.

Sorensen, G., A.M. Stoddard, A.D. LaMontagne, K. Emmons, M.K. Hunt, R. Youngstrom, D. McLellan and D.G. Christiani (2003), 'A comprehensive worksite cancer prevention intervention: behavioral change results from a randomized controlled trial (United States)', *Journal of Public Health Policy*, **24**(1), 5–25.

Stewart, W.F., J.A. Ricci, E. Chee, D. Morganstein and R. Lipton (2003), 'Lost productive time and cost due to common pain conditions in the US workforce', *Journal of the American Medical Association*, **290**(18), 2443–54.

Thorpe, K.E. (2005), 'The rise in health care spending and what to do about it', *Health Affairs*, **24**(6), 1435–45.

Thorpe, K.E., C.S. Florence, D.H. Howard and P. Jeski (2004), 'The impact of obesity on rising medical spending', *Health Affairs*, 20 October, 480–85.

Towers Watson and National Business Group on Health (2011), *Pathway to Health and Productivity: 2011/2012 Staying@Work Survey Report*, New York: Towers Watson/NBGH.

Watson, W. and J. Gauthier (2003), 'The viability of organizational wellness programs: an examination of promotion and results', *Journal of Applied Social Psychology*, **33**(6), 1297–312.

Whitehead, D.A. (2001), 'A corporate perspective on health promotion: reflections and advice from Chevron', *American Journal of Health Promotion*, **15**(5), 367–9.

Wolfe, R.A. and D.F. Parker (1994), 'Employee health management: challenges and opportunities', *Academy of Management Executive*, **8**(2), 22–31.

Wolfe, R.A., D.F. Parker and N. Napier (1994), 'Employee health management and organizational performance', *Journal of Applied Behavioral Science*, **30**(1), 22–42.

Young, S., J. Halladay, M. Plescia, C. Herget and C. Dunn (2011), 'Establishing worksite wellness programs for North Carolina Government employees', *Preventing Chronic Diseases*, **8**(2), 48–63.

Zoller, H.M. (2004), 'Manufacturing health: employee perspectives on problematic outcomes in a workplace health promotion initiative', *Western Journal of Communications*, **68**(3), 278–301.

2. Changing environmental conditions impacting health – a focus on organizations

Gerjo Kok, Fred R.H. Zijlstra and Robert A.C. Ruiter

INTRODUCTION

Environmental factors impact heavily on individual well-being. A clear example of environmental influences on health is the relation between social economic status and health, which also constitutes a challenge when it comes to changing these influences to promote health. Indeed, the ecological approach to health education and health promotion (Green and Kreuter, 2005) views health, which is defined as a state of complete physical, mental, and social well-being and not merely the absence of disease (WHO, 1948, p. 100), not only as a function of individuals but also of the environments in which individuals are embedded, including family, social networks, organizations, community, and public policies. A focus on mental and physical well-being only at the level of the individual is therefore not sufficient; individuals live and act in social and physical environments. These environments can influence decision-making processes with regard to personal well-being, as evidenced, for example, in the role of social influence processes in making lifestyle choices. These environments can also contain direct threats to individual health, which becomes clear in epidemiological analyses of exposure to physical dangers in relation to safety and health issues, but also in psychological studies that assess the impact of work-related factors on stress and burnout, and the extent to which people have access to effective coping mechanisms.

At the same time, social and physical environments can be targeted to promote individual health, which is the focus of the present chapter. In particular, we will discuss the role of environmental conditions in the promotion of health, with a specific focus on the role of organizations. Healthy employees are important for organizations; sickness absence and incapacity to work represent huge costs for organizations. Although most organizations are aware of this, they are struggling with implementing programs that aim to increase the health of employees and create more sustainable employment, for example by increasing ease of access to health and fitness programs or by reducing the workload or work pressure for employees through focusing on continuous work participation of older people or the (re-)integration of people with disabilities in work situations.

In the present chapter we will present a systematic approach towards the development of health promotion programs in the context of organizations, called Intervention Mapping (Bartholomew et al., 2011). Intervention Mapping describes a step-by-step protocol for the systematic development of theory- and evidence-based health promotion programs. Intervention Mapping works from the ecological approach towards health and health promotion and makes use of different theories to explain and understand human behavior at the different ecological levels. We will therefore start with providing a brief outline of the ecological approach towards health promotion and relevant theories at the individual and organizational level for understanding and changing individual behavior. Finally, we will present a topic that combines health promotion and organizational change: sustainable organizations. We will illustrate this topic with insights on inclusive organizations and data on the integration of employees with disabilities in organizations.

HEALTH PROMOTION AT THE ORGANIZATIONAL LEVEL

Health education has evolved into health promotion (Green and Kreuter, 2005). Health education is any combination of learning experiences designed to facilitate voluntary actions conducive to health. Health promotion is the combination of educational and environmental supports for actions and conditions of living conducive to health, thereby including health education. Health promotion is characterized by the need for planning, the importance of evaluation, and the use of social and behavioral science theories in the development of health promotion interventions.

The central concern of health promotion is health behavior. However, health behavior refers not only to the individual's behavior but also to the behavior or actions of groups and organizations. Stress at work may be related to individual coping behavior, but also to the fit between the person and the environment (P-E fit), which also relates to organizational aspects, for instance, managers' decision-making behavior. Kok et al. (2008) describe the various environmental levels as embedded systems. They indicate that individuals function within groups, which are in turn embedded within organizations and higher-order systems. The individual is influenced by, and can influence directly or through groups and organizations, the higher-order systems. The picture that emerges is a complex web of causation as well as a rich context for interventions. In the stress example, the individual as well as the manager will both be targets for health promotion interventions. Moreover, at the society level, the intervention may target politicians' decision-making related to a healthier organization of labor. Bartholomew et al. (2011) see managers and politicians as *agents* in the environment who serve as targets for health promotion interventions.

The ecological approach to health promotions assumes that the individual is embedded within social networks, organizations, community and society; and each lower level is embedded within higher levels. A facilitating environment that makes the health-promoting behavior the easiest behavior to perform (Milio, 1981) is key to a change in the behavior of the at-risk population, as well as to a change of environmental conditions. Examples of environmental conditions include social influences (such as norms, social support, and reinforcement) and structural influences (such as access to resources, organizational policies). Barriers to performing a health behavior are often structural, such as lack of exercise, stress, high-fat food in restaurants at worksites, and unsafe working conditions.

For each environmental condition, human agents behave in ways that influence the existence or intensity of the environmental condition. A government allocates money to support companies to create opportunities to combine work and care for children. Legislators are environmental agents in this case, and their behaviors are proposing and voting to allocate funds. Note that agents and actions at different levels are directed at the same environmental condition in this example. Working to influence change at multiple ecological levels is synergistic in producing and sustaining changes in environmental conditions (Rosen, 1992; Chu et al., 2000; Paton et al., 2005). Once the agents and their behaviors have been identified, the planner can select determinants and methods to change them. In the next section, we will present theories at different ecological levels that describe determinants of behavior and strategies for behavior change.

THEORIES OF BEHAVIOR AND BEHAVIOR CHANGE AT INDIVIDUAL AND ORGANIZATION LEVEL

Theories are very important tools for professionals in health education and promotion. A health promotion program is most likely to benefit individuals and organizations when it is guided by social and behavioral science theories of health behavior and health behavior change (Glanz et al., 2008). Theory-driven health promotion programs require an understanding of the components of the theory as well as the operational or practical forms of these theories. Finding and applying relevant theories is a professional skill that health educators have to master (Bartholomew et al., 2011). On the one hand, theories have become available to health promotion practice through textbooks such as Glanz et al. (2008) or DiClemente et al. (2009). On the other hand, the application of theory has long been a challenge, for researchers as well as practitioners. Students of health education and health promotion learn of theories and learn how to apply theories to well-selected practical problems. However, in real life the order is reversed: the problem is given and the practitioner has to find theories that may be helpful for better understanding or changing behavior (Buunk and van Vugt, 2013; Ruiter et al., 2013).

The behavioral science theories that try to explain behavior and provide strategies for behavior change have two types of roots: health and health promotion in particular or behavior and behavior change in general (the last mainly being social psychological theories). Health and health promotion-oriented theories are often related to perceptions of health risks, for example, the health belief model (Champion and Skinner, 2008) or protection motivation theory (Norman et al., 2005). Some other theories were developed in a health setting, but have evolved into a general theory such as the transtheoretical model of stages of change (Prochaska et al., 2008) or relapse prevention theory (Marlatt and Donovan, 2005). Most general social psychological models were developed for a broad range of behaviors, but are easily applicable to health behavior and change. Some examples are learning theories (Kazdin, 2008), reasoned action approach/theory of planned behavior (Fishbein and Ajzen, 2010), social cognitive theory (McAlister et al., 2008), goal-setting (Latham and Locke, 2007), self-regulatory theories (Vohs and Baumeister, 2011), social networks and social support theories (Heaney and Israel, 2008), persuasion-communication model (Petty et al., 2009), and diffusion of innovations theory (Oldenburg and Glanz, 2008). Next to these so-called social cognitive theories there is an increase in applications of theories on automatic behavior (Hassin et al., 2005), impulsive behavior (Hofmann et al., 2009), and habits (Wood and Neal, 2007), resulting from dual process thinking about human behavior as being the result of either more associative, unconscious, cue-driven processes or more reflective, conscious, reasoning processes (Strack and Deutsch, 2004; Hofmann et al., 2008). All theories are potentially applicable to all ecological levels. For example, the reasoned action approach (Fishbein and Ajzen, 2010), formerly the theory of planned behavior, is often applied to individual health behavior but also to politicians' behavior and to program implementers' behavior.

At the individual level, theories assume that behavior is most directly influenced by the intention to perform the behavior, which can be defined as the individual's motivation to undertake the behavior. Intention, in turn, is determined by attitude, perceived social norm, and perceived behavioral control. Attitude represents a person's evaluation of the anticipated outcomes of the behavior (e.g., will it lead to valued outcomes?), in which a distinction can be made between three outcome expectancies: perceived benefits, perceived risk, and anticipated affect. Perceived benefits reflect beliefs about the positive consequences of performing the behavior. Risk perception accounts for the weighted result of the perceived susceptibility and severity of possible negative consequences of performing or not performing the behavior under consideration. Anticipated affect refers to positive and negative emotional reactions that individuals would expect to experience as a result of performing or not performing the behavior (e.g., worries about the side-effects of the vaccine). Perceived social norm reflects the social approval a person anticipates from significant others in response to performing (or not performing) a behavior. A distinction is made between what significant others think we should do (referred to as injunctive norms) and what others have done or are doing (descriptive norm). Finally, perceived behavioral control refers to the person's anticipated mastery of the behavior. Perceived behavioral control is closely related to Bandura's construct of self-efficacy, that is, people's expressed confidence in successfully performing the target behavior (Fishbein et al., 2001; Fishbein and Ajzen, 2010). Please note that perceived behavioral control and self-efficacy differ from the skills people have to successfully perform the target behavior. People might feel able to successfully perform the target behavior, but miss the skills to do so; or vice versa, people have the abilities but do not feel confident.

Skills, but also physical, financial, and social barriers (e.g., accessibility to resources, social norms) might thus result in insufficient or inadequate translation of intentions to corresponding behaviors. This phenomenon that has been termed the 'intention–behavior gap' (Sheeran, 2002) and relates to theories that distinguish between two stages of action control at the individual level: (1) a decisional or motivational stage that culminates in intention formation and (2) a post-decisional or volitional stage that involves self-regulatory activities directed towards the enactment of intentions (Schwarzer, 1992; Kuhl and Fuhrmann, 1998; Gollwitzer, 1999). This work suggests that social cognitive models of motivation do not adequately represent key aspects of action control. Gollwitzer (1993), for example, has demonstrated that forming 'implementation intentions', that is, specifying when and where an intention is to be enacted, can distinguish between intenders who do and do not act. He argues that such detailed plans create cues to action in relevant environments, which prompt intenders to act automatically when encountered (see also Gollwitzer and Sheeran, 2006).

Interventions to change behavior at the individual level are directed at determinants of behavior as described above. Behavior will change if an intervention succeeds in changing a determinant that is relevant for that behavior. In the next section we will describe methods for change as part of a systematic evidence-based approach: Intervention Mapping.

At the organizational level, theories are specifically targeting organizational-level analysis and change: organizational change theories (Schein, 2004), organizational development theories (Cummings and Worley, 2009), stage theory of organizational change (Butterfoss et al., 2008), and diffusion of innovations theory (Flaspohler et al., 2008). In health promotion, these organizational theories focus on the development of health-promoting organizational structures and culture. The environmental agents include upper and middle management, internal change consultants, and other organizational members. Their behaviors are adoption, implementation, and institutionalization of new policies, practices, structures, cultural beliefs, and norms. The determinants of agent behaviors include outcome expectations, attitudes and beliefs, skills, and resources. Strategies for behavior change are at the organizational level, such as sense-making, participatory problem-solving through organizational diagnosis and feedback, modeling, team-building or human relations training, technical assistance, and structural redesign. Additionally, stakeholder theory provides guidance to health promoters, working through their own organizations or through the community to change an organization's policies and practices (Den Hond and de Bakker, 2007; Foster-Fishman et al., 2007). The determinants of agent behaviors, that is, those of the focal organization's decision-makers, include outcome expectations, attitudes, and beliefs. Behavior change strategies include social influence, alliances, community development, and social action.

At the community and society level, theoretical input can be found in the classic models of community organization and community development and the current perspectives being used for health promotion (Minkler and Wallerstein, 2008). Issues of power, participation, and goals, for instance, have received much discussion among health educators in recent years. In selecting the constructs to use for community change, planners must clarify their assumptions and values about the nature of the change process and select and implement strategies congruent with these. Also, there are theories of policy-making that have been used primarily at the national, state, and governmental level, such as policy window theory (Kingdon, 2003).

Finally, some theories are applicable to all ecological levels, including the organizational level. Systems theory is used to define and address all levels of the environment as interrelated social systems (Green and Glasgow, 2006; National Cancer Institute, 2007). There are environmental agents at each level who can engage in activities to change the system to facilitate health. The environmental influences of these agents' behavior can include norms, regulatory processes, and resources, whereas methods address social change broadly and include dialogue, planning, organizing, evaluation, and feedback. Theories of power are applicable to all environmental levels, and agents at each level with power are able to exert their influence to make environmental changes (Rothman, 2004; Turner, 2005). The determinants of an agent's power include authority, charisma, legitimacy, group norms, and group identity. Methods for changing the behavior of others and the environmental conditions include persuasion, social influence, coercion, community organizing, and agenda-setting. Empowerment theories address the process by which community members (e.g., employees in an organization) become involved in their community and take action to gain power and control. Environmental conditions that enable and demonstrate empowerment in organizations include collective problem-solving, shared leadership and decision-making, accessible management, media and resources, and collective efficacy (Minkler et al., 2008). Methods by which community members become empowered include participation in decision-making, enactive mastery experiences and feedback, and modeling.

PLANNING HEALTH PROMOTION PROGRAMS: INTERVENTION MAPPING

Health promotion is a planned activity, which includes four major phases: diagnosis, development, implementation, and evaluation (Green and Kreuter, 2005). A protocol that describes a step-by-step process for developing theory-based and evidence-based health education programs is Intervention Mapping (Bartholomew et al., 2011). Intervention Mapping distinguishes six steps: (1) conduct the needs assessment, (2) define proximal program objectives, (3) select theoretical methods and practical strategies, (4) design the program, (5) anticipate adoption and implementation, and (6) anticipate process and effect evaluation (see Figure 2.1).

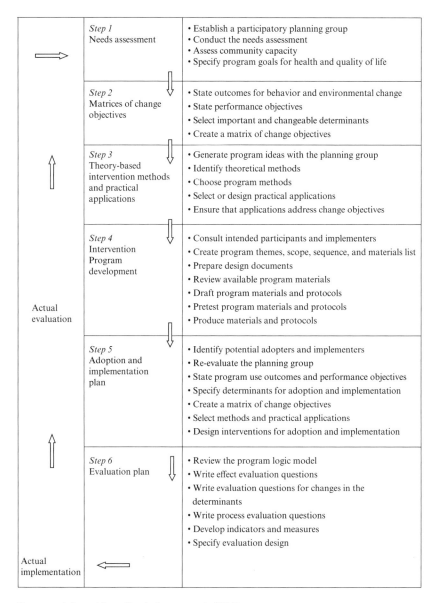

Source: Adapted from Bartholomew et al. (2011).

Figure 2.1   Intervention Mapping

Bartholomew et al. (2011) see planning as an iterative process: two steps forward and one step back. They describe three core processes for Intervention Mapping, that is, tools for the professional health promoter for applying theories and research: searching the literature for empirical findings, accessing and using theory, and collecting and using new data. From the literature search, a provisional list of answers is developed, which is often not adequate in finding solutions for the problem. The planner must go further to search for theory, using three approaches: topic, concept, and general theories approach (Buunk and van Vugt, 2013; Ruiter et al., 2013). The topic approach searches the literature for theoretical perspectives on the issue. The concept approach begins with the concepts in the provisional answers, linking these concepts to theoretical constructs and theories that may be useful. The general theory approach considers general theories that may be applicable. Finally, it is important to identify gaps in the information obtained and collect new data to fill these gaps.

Intervention Mapping has been applied in the development of worksite health promotion programs, with varying fidelity to the protocol and with varying success. McEachan et al. (2008, 2011) used Intervention Mapping to develop a worksite physical activity intervention to improve employees' health and reduce sickness absence. Munir et al. (2013) developed a work-related guidance tool for those affected by cancer to make decisions regarding work. Oude Hengel et al. (2010, 2012) developed a worksite prevention program for construction workers to promote work ability and prolong a healthy working life. Strijk et al. (2009, 2011) developed a lifestyle intervention to improve older workers' vitality. Van Oostrom et al. (2007, 2013) developed a workplace intervention for sick-listed employees with stress-related mental disorders. Vermeulen et al. (2009, 2011) developed a participatory return-to-work intervention for temporary agency workers and unemployed workers sick-listed due to musculoskeletal disorders. Verweij et al. (2012) applied Intervention Mapping for an occupational health guideline to reduce sedentary behavior and increase fruit intake at work. Van Scheppingen et al. (in press) conducted a Delphi procedure to determine what organization-specific factors are relevant to worksite health promotion. They showed that adaptation to external factors, adjustment to internal factors and involving the broad concerns of all stakeholders may be seen as three generic factors that are essential for meaningful intervention development and implementation.

INTERVENTION MAPPING: STEPS AND TASKS

Intervention Mapping Step 1

Before beginning to actually plan an intervention, the planner conducts a needs assessment. The needs assessment is Intervention Mapping Step 1 and encompasses two components: (1) an epidemiological, behavioral, and social analysis of the at-risk group or community and its problems and (2) an assessment of the strengths and capacity of the community and its target members as a part of intervention planning. The product of this step is a description of the problem and its impact on quality of life, followed by a theory- and evidence-based analysis of the proximal behavioral and environmental causes of the problem and the personal and situational factors (i.e., determinants) that contribute to these causes. In addition, the organization's experience with potential solutions is assessed and important internal and external players are identified (Bartholomew et al., 2011).

Intervention Mapping Step 2

Intervention Mapping Step 2 is the development of program objectives, a crossing of performance objectives, determinants, and target groups. For instance, one program objective for a stress intervention program in worksites would be: 'employees (target population) express their confidence (determinant) in successfully asking support from their colleagues (performance objective) when confronted with problems'. Performance objectives are the specific behaviors that we want the target group (or the environmental agents) to 'do' as a result of the program. For example, in the case of eating low-fat food, the performance objectives might be: read food labels, select low-fat food, prepare low-fat food, and avoid the use of fatty additives (Bartholomew et al. 2011, p. 256). At the organizational level, for example, performance objectives for reducing bullying at work might be: co-workers show disapproval when they notice that a colleague is being bullied and expressing empathy when interacting with persons being bullied; company managers develop policies against bullying and stigmatization and endorse providing information, training, and interventions (ibid., p. 262). Determinants of behavior can be personal or environmental. Personal determinants are, among others, outcome expectations, social influences, and self-efficacy expectations. Environmental determinants are, for instance, social norms and support, and barriers. Target groups can be subgroups of the total group, such as men or women, or people in different stages of change. Program objectives combine target,

performance objective, and determinant. Program objectives are numerous and should be ordered by determinant and by level. So, we end this
step with a series of lists, for instance, all program objectives that have to
do with skills training (determinant) of managers (organizational level).

Intervention Mapping Step 3

Intervention Mapping Step 3 is the selection of theoretical methods and
practical applications. A theoretical method, or behavior change technique, is a general technique or process for influencing changes in the
determinants of behavior of the target population or of behavior of the
environmental decision-maker (see Table 2.1 for examples). Practical
applications are specific techniques for practical use of theoretical methods
in ways that fit the intervention population and the context in which the
intervention will be conducted. For example, a change objective for an
intervention might be to increase workers' coping skills (and self-efficacy)
for dealing with high-stress situations at work. For the change objective
of increasing coping skills, theoretical methods might include modeling,
guided practice with feedback, and reinforcement. One application for
modeling could be a videotaped step-by-step demonstration by workers
of how to deal effectively with stressful situations at work. However, there
may be environmental conditions relevant in this example. An environmental condition of workers' coping with stress could be the high level of
stress at work due to a structural high workload, with an objective that the
managers would hire extra staff to help to systematically lower the stress
level for employees. A change objective for this might be to increase the
managers' positive outcome expectations, for example, that this approach
would lower absenteeism, be popular with the unions, and promote
productivity. The primary environmental theoretical method could be
advocacy, which might include methods of information, persuasion,
negotiation, and coercion. One practical application of advocacy might
be for union representatives to have a meeting with the Executive Board.
The union representatives might present detailed information on the frequency of stressful situations at work. If the manager does not respond to
this application, the union and workers might undertake, as an additional
method, media advocacy, with an exposé story in the media calling for
action by the company as the application. An important task in this step
is to identify the conditions or parameters that limit the effectiveness of
theoretical models. In Table 2.1, some examples are shown of methods by
determinant and by level, plus parameters and applications.

   Also, methods at the individual level seem to be frequently bundled
together as part of a change method at a higher ecological level. This is

Table 2.1 Examples of methods, parameters, and applications

Methods	Parameters for Use	Examples
Basic methods at the individual level		
Modeling		
Providing an appropriate model being reinforced for the desired action (McAlister et al., 2008)	Attention, remembrance, self-efficacy and skills, reinforcement of model, identification with model, coping model instead of mastery model	The health promoter finds a role model from the at-risk group who will encourage identification and serve as a coping model: 'I tried to quit smoking several times and was not successful, then I tried . . . Now I have been off cigarettes for . . .'
Facilitation		
Creating an environment that makes the action easier or reduces barriers to action (Bandura, 1986)	Requires real changes in the environment; identification of barriers and facilitators; power for making changes; and usually intervention at a higher environmental level to facilitate conditions on a lower level	A program that targets improvement in drug users' self-efficacy for using clean needles must also facilitate accessibility of clean needles
Methods to change awareness and risk perception		
Consciousness-raising		
Providing information, feedback, or confrontation about the causes, consequences, and alternatives for a problem or a problem behavior (Prochaska et al., 2008)	Can use feedback and confrontation; however, raising awareness must be quickly followed by increase in problem-solving ability and (collective) self-efficacy	An HIV counselor reminds a person of recent episodes of failure to use condoms when having sex and the potential consequences of that behavior on significant others

Table 2.1 (continued)

Methods	Parameters for Use	Examples
Methods to change skills, capability, and self-efficacy and to overcome barriers		
Goal-setting		
Prompting planning what the person will do, including a definition of goal-directed behaviors that result in the target behavior (Latham and Locke, 2007)	Commitment to the goal; goals that are difficult but available within the individual's skill level	Dietician and patient discuss the weight loss goal for the next meeting, deciding on a goal that is acceptable to the patient and to the dietician
Basic methods at the environmental level		
Participatory problem-solving		
Diagnosing the problem, generating potential solutions, developing priorities, making an action plan, and obtaining feedback after implementing the plan (Cummings and Worley, 2009)	Requires willingness by the health promoter or convener to accept the participants as equals and as having a high level of influence; requires target group to possess appropriate motivation and skills	A health promotion consultant assists employees of a small company to identify the level and sources of stress and develop a plan with management to address and monitor work stress
Advocacy and lobbying		
Arguing and mobilizing resources on behalf of a particular change; giving aid to a cause; active support for a cause or position (Weible et al., 2009)	Form of advocacy must match style and tactics of the people, communities or organizations represented, and the nature of the issue; includes policy advocacy; often tailored to a specific environmental agent	Members of the American Public Health Association use the organization's action alert system to contact their legislators to urge them to vote for pending health care reform legislation
Technical assistance		
Providing technical means to achieve desired behavior (Flaspohler et al., 2008)	Nature of technical assistance will vary by environmental level but must fit needs, culture, and resources of recipient	A health department liaison helps a community health center design recruitment procedures, training, and

40

Methods to change organizations

Method		Example
Sense-making Leaders reinterpret and relabel processes in organization, create meaning through dialogue, and model and redirect change (Weick and Quinn, 1999)	Used for continuous change, including culture change	supervisory guidelines as they establish a new lay health worker program A supervisor in a hospital talks to his or her staff about the positive aspects of finding and correcting mistakes in documentation of medication administration
Organizational diagnosis and feedback Assessing of organizational structures and employees' beliefs and attitudes, desired outcomes and readiness to take action, using surveys and other methods (Cummings and Worley, 2009)	Methods appropriate to organizational characteristics, for example, size and information technology	An organizational consultant conducts a survey of employees' health behaviors and determinants and holds focus groups of employees to review the results and plan for health promotion programs
Increasing stakeholder influence Increase stakeholder power, legitimacy, and urgency, often by forming coalitions and using community development and social action to change an organization's policies (De Bakker and Den Hond, 2008)	The focal organization perceives that the external organization or group is one of its stakeholders	A community group uses media advocacy to highlight the groundwater pollution by gas storage tanks located in the community and to demand that the tanks be moved by the gas company that owns them
Structural redesign Change organizational elements such as formal statements of organizational philosophy, communication flow, reward systems, job descriptions, and lines of authority (Cummings and Worley, 2009)	Management authority and agreement. Participation of all stakeholders	A health promotion consultant works with an organization to renew the organizational vision statement to include the health of employees

Source: Adapted from Bartholomew et al. (2011, Chapter 6).

because environmental agents and organization and community members are also individuals and the determinants of their behaviors are similar to determinants of behavior at the individual level. The change target and the overall method, however, are specific to the environmental change level. For example, when the environmental-level method participatory problem-solving is used, the individual-level methods goal-setting, facilitation, and feedback will often be applied. Organizational diagnosis and feedback will include the individual methods of raising feedback and consciousness. These individual-level methods are bundled together to accomplish a change in an organizational-level problem. Organizational development, in fact, has been defined as the transfer of behavioral science knowledge to increase organizational effectiveness and the process resembles behavioral self-regulation applied to the organizational level for example (McLean, 2005).

Methods at the individual level can thus be directed toward agents at higher ecological levels. The theoretical process behind the method is the same; however, often the application of the method is somewhat different, depending on the target. In a study about interventions to change environmental conditions (Kok et al., 2008), persuasion was applied at various levels and originating from various levels. For example, in a project to decrease carbon dioxide transmission, the health promoter reported a persuasive communication approach that illustrated to businesses, corporations, and other companies the advantages of approaching and dealing with the issue of carbon dioxide emissions. The health promoter showed them how carbon dioxide reduction is profitable and made it clear to companies that being environmentally friendly is positive for the company image. The potential effect on the image of and profit for the company are typical organizational-level arguments.

There may be different methods targeting a level or being targeted from another level (Kok et al., 2012). On the one hand, organizations may apply methods for improving the health of their employees, for instance, to increase physical activity (Abraham and Graham-Rowe, 2009). Those methods might include feedback, modeling, goal-setting, and tailoring. The activities are initiated by the management and are directed at the employees. On the other hand, health promoters and health-promoting organizations may apply methods to get organizations to start health-promoting activities as in the earlier examples above, for instance reducing carbon dioxide transmissions. The Heart Foundation, a national organization of volunteers, may try to encourage companies to facilitate physical activity programs for their employees. Methods that will be used include persuasive communication, raising consciousness, and organizational diagnosis and feedback, in combination with facilitation and technical assistance. These activities are initiated outside the organization, usually by a health promoter, and are directed at the organization, often the management. An interesting parallel to this process can be found in the research tradition of corporate social responsibility or sustainable organizations (Maon et al., 2009). A recent application of sustainable organizations involves the concept of inclusive organizations, which is described in more detail below to illustrate health promotion at the organizational level (Zijlstra et al., 2012).

Intervention Mapping Step 4

Intervention Mapping Step 4 is the actual designing of the program, organizing the strategies into a deliverable program, and producing and pretesting the materials (Bartholomew et al., 2011; Schaalma and Kok, 2011). Intervention planners guide the production process, conduct small-scale pilots of program components, and continuously collaborate with target groups, decision-makers, and stakeholders to identify the optimal intervention for a particular problem, target population, and intervention context. For example, the worksite physical activity intervention of McEachan et al. (2008) consisted of ten components delivered over a 12-week period. The intervention pack contained copies of three different interactive leaflets encouraging workers to set targets, make plans and provide feedback, and a monitoring tool for recording activity levels. In addition there were eight A3 colored posters, electronic templates for newsletters, reminders, letters of management support, quizzes, instructions on how to run team challenges, and a practical and feasible timetable.

Intervention Mapping Step 5

A solid diffusion and implementation process is vital to ensure program success. Without implementation, the intervention will not have any impact on determinants, behaviors, or health. So, in Intervention Mapping Step 5, a plan is developed for systematic implementation of the program. The first thing to do, actually at the start of intervention development, is the development of a linkage system, linking program developers with program users. Then, an intervention is developed to promote adoption and implementation of the program by the intended program users. Intervention planners design a strategy to facilitate the implementation of the health promotion intervention. They design theory-based strategies to facilitate program adoption by key stakeholders, to support appropriate implementation by program users, and to encourage program institutionalization by considering opportunities for incorporating the program into organizational routines. Thus, interventions are required, not only to change individual behavior, but also to facilitate program implementation. Indeed, the same steps as for intervention development are repeated to anticipate program diffusion and target program implementers. Sustainable implementation almost always involves organizational change, for example in the school setting (Hendriks et al., 2013).

Intervention Mapping Step 6

Finally, Intervention Mapping Step 6 focuses on process and effect evaluation. Again, this process is relevant from the start, not only at the end. For instance, 'employees express their confidence in successfully asking support from their colleagues' is an objective, but is also a measure of that objective that can be asked in pre- and post-interviews with experimental and control group subjects. To evaluate the impact of the intervention on the objectives at the determinant level (proximal program objectives), and behavioral and environmental levels (performance objectives) an experimental study design is preferred (Whittingham et al., 2008). In addition, both qualitative and quantitative methods can be used to study the rate of program dissemination, adoption, and implementation, and program users' and participants' reactions to the program. The effect and process evaluations result in feedback and improvement of the program (Green and Kreuter, 2005) and relevant methodologies are well explained in the available literature on program evaluation (Rossi et al., 2004; Wholey et al., 2004).

Some Additional Notes

The six-step protocol of Intervention Mapping seems to suggest that program planners start with the assessment of quality of life and health problems, which is then followed by Steps 2–6 by formulating objectives, selecting methods of change, and planning the design, implementation, and evaluation of the health promotion intervention. In practice, that is a rare situation. Often health promotion practitioners start somewhere within the protocol, depending on their task description or the specific moment in the ongoing health promotion planning process. For example, a health educator may be hired to develop a program for healthy lifestyle as part of a 'sustainable employment' program for organizations. We then enter the protocol at the program development stage (Step 4). However, before planning the implementation and evaluation of the intervention, we might first want to go back to the diagnosis phase (needs assessment), and (re-)assess the quality of life and health problems as well as the personal and situational determinants of the behavior and environmental conditions that contribute to the problem, and check whether the program objectives relate to the targeted problem.

Furthermore, there is an increasing interest in systematic descriptions or taxonomies of health promotion interventions, the theoretical methods they contain, and the determinants that are targeted for change (Stavri and Michie, 2012). However, most of these taxonomies focus on individual behavior change and only a few also include behavior change of environmental agents (Khan et al., 2009; Bartholomew et al., 2011). Moreover, translating methods into applications demands a sufficient understanding of the theory behind the method, especially the theoretical parameters under which the theoretical process is effective or not (Schaalma and Kok, 2009; Peters et al., 2013). For example, modeling is a strong method but only when certain parameters are met, for instance, reinforcement of the modeled behavior (McAlister et al., 2008; see Table 2.1). People or environmental decision-makers do not just behave in the desired manner because a role model demonstrates that behavior; they behave comparable to the role model only when this role model is reinforced for that particular behavior and when they expect to be reinforced in a similar way. Translating the method modeling to a practical application includes taking care that in the actual program, from the perspective of the program participants, the model is reinforced. All theoretical methods have these parameters, which have to be taken into account when translating a method into a practical application.

SUSTAINABLE ORGANIZATIONS

Health promotion in organizations is mostly studied in worksite health promotion programs targeting changes in health behavior. Interestingly, the research tradition on corporate social responsibility is rarely involved with health issues (Maon et al., 2009). In the remainder of this chapter we will approach a work-related problem, inclusion and exclusion, with a health promotion approach and illustrate that approach first from an organizational perspective – inclusive organizations – and then with a specific case – inclusion or exclusion of employees with disabilities.

Inclusive Organizations

Numerous people are excluded from participating in the labor market because their levels of qualifications do not match the demands of the current labor market. The labor market has become too selective, in the

sense that organizations prefer young, healthy, strong, and highly educated people. However, the population that is trying to get access to the
labor market is highly diverse in terms of their qualifications and capacities, and this population does not always meet the criteria of organizations.
This is particularly true for people who have suffered from mental health
issues, which is still a taboo for many people. In order to accommodate the
future demand for labor and to make the social security system sustainable, new strategies to help people entering the labor market and to return
to work after illness should be high on the political agenda. From that
perspective it is worthwhile to examine the recently introduced concept of
'inclusive organizations' (Zijlstra et al., 2012; Zijlstra and Nijhuis, 2014).
It may be clear that this is a case with many stakeholders at various levels:
employees, colleagues, families, managers, unions, and politicians.

Inclusive organizations aim to enhance diversity in the organizations,
in particular, diversity in terms of capacities of employees. This means
that these organizations aim not to exclude those people that cannot meet
the current demands of work, but rather try to rearrange work in such a
way that there are jobs in the organization for people with a large range
of capacities, including people with (cognitive or mental) limitations. The
underlying principle here is 'task differentiation', that is, designing tasks
for people with different levels of capacities (Zijlstra et al., 2009, 2012).

The idea behind this concept is that work has become very complex
and demanding over the past decades as argued above, with the implica-
tion that an increasing group of people fail to meet the current requirements for the labor market. Or in other words: there are no 'simple jobs'
anymore, as a result of moving production to low-wage countries, and
introducing technology. And to help the group of people with a 'distance
to the labor market' to find a job, 'simple jobs' have to be created again –
jobs for which a high level of training and or skills are not required and for
which the demands are not as high as for 'regular' jobs. This would help
people with low levels of (or no) education, people with limited capacities (including those with psychological or social disorders, but still have
a capacity to work), and also to some extent people that try to return to
work from long-term absence (Zijlstra and Nijhuis, 2014). The underlying idea is that, although people may have limitations, they often have
some capacity to work. And this work capacity should be used, both for
personal (psychological) reasons as well as for societal reasons. However,
their working capacity cannot be used in the current arrangement of work
(work is too complex or too demanding). Therefore, this arrangement
should be adjusted by using the principle of task (or job) differentiation. A
job consists of a set of several tasks. The larger the variety, or complexity
of tasks, the more complex the job is. Task design is one of the traditional

topics in the discipline of work and organizational psychology, and is mostly used to design jobs that enhance effectiveness and efficiency of employees (without harming their well-being). However, task design (or job design) can also be used to facilitate optimal performance and well-being of workers with different levels of capacities. The reference point has always been: healthy, able, and fit people. The approach is seldom used to design jobs that match the capacities of people that might have limited capacities.

The dominant principle for organizing work nowadays is making teams responsible for the results. This is a consequence of the socio-technical systems approach that became very popular in the last decade of the previous century. Teams are very flexible elements in a production process, in particular when the teams function well. But one of the prerequisites of making teams flexible is that team members should be able to replace each other, and therefore need to be multi-skilled. As a consequence we notice that individual team members do all kinds of tasks, and some tentative estimates suggest that team members sometimes spend 30 or 40 percent of their time on tasks that do not match their level of training or skills, and for which they are thus actually overqualified. It is questionable whether this principle is nowadays still the most preferred way of organizing work processes. It might be time to reconsider and focus on the concept of 'task differentiation' (or job differentiation) in order to accommodate the needs of various groups, to allow them to participate in the labor market. This principle may also apply to elderly workers; currently all members of a team (no matter whether they are 35 or 55 years old) face the same demands, while they have different skills, experience, needs, motivation, and so on.

Evidently when differentiations are made according to level of jobs one also needs to reconsider the level of pay. For certain groups, in particular people 'with a distance to the labor market', it is impossible to be as productive as regular employees, and in order to give these people opportunities in the labor market there are ways to compensate employers for the gap between the level of productivity for these people and the minimum wage (a system of 'wage supplementation' or wage subsidies). It is evident that the problem here is to assess the level of productivity of people or to make an adequate assessment of work capacity of people with limitations. Thus far several 'systems' or 'approaches' have been developed for assessing work capacity. The systems that have been developed so far are roughly based on physical or energetic limitations of people to be productive. And although the various systems claim to be different from each other, the underlying principle of all these systems is largely based on time restrictions: the amount of time people can be active during a day, and or the physical limitation that rules our particular work. For most types of work nowadays this is not always adequate, as, as is argued earlier, for most types of work the social and cognitive skills are more relevant than the physical skills. None of the systems assessing work capacity are designed to take this into account. Therefore it is evident that this aspect of assessing the (remaining) work capacity needs further attention. Zijlstra and colleagues (2012) developed a 'protocol for inclusive assessment of work capacities'; see Box 2.1.

Important in this protocol is that through integrated analyses of the work processes in the organization, the basic tasks are identified, described, and translated to relevant task demands. For this organizational development project, the technique of process mapping may be helpful (Biazzo, 2002). As mentioned earlier, all change methods have parameters. Organizational development, in this case structural redesign (see Table 2.1), is only effective when all stakeholders actively participate and when the management supports the process (D'Amato and Zijlstra, 2010).

The Case of Employees with Disabilities

In recent years, the topic of 'social exclusion' has been very prominent on the political agenda of the European Commission (2011). From this perspective the employment of people with disabilities has become a central issue in Europe (ibid.). People with disabilities are to be helped to reach higher levels of acceptance, integration, and social inclusion in society (Scior, 2011; Coles and Scior, 2012). Sustainable employment is a way to achieve this goal. Work has a central place in people's lives and being employed will therefore lead to an integration in society (Jahoda, 1981), but also to an improvement of physical and mental health (Schuring et al., 2011). In this setting, corporate social responsibility and the rise of inclusive organizations, which aim to harbor a diverse work force, constitute a new mindset on employment issues. However, when entering the job market, one of the boundaries that people with disabilities face is the stereotypes and attitudes of employers and employees (Hunt and Hunt, 2004; Schur et al., 2005; Scior, 2011). This, often negative perception is one of the reasons why people with disabilities experience a bias in the way they are treated at work (Hunt and Hunt, 2004; Colella and Bruyère, 2011; Vornholt et al., 2013). Especially in inclusive organizations, the treatment and helping behavior by the co-workers is important for the sustainable integration and employment of people with disabilities.

Nelissen et al. (2014) studied effects of prosocial motivation and the effects of stereotypes on helping behavior towards co-workers with dis-

BOX 2.1   INCLUSIVE JOB REDESIGN IN NINE
            STEPS

1   Agreement of management and workers' representatives to
    integrate people with limitations in the organization.
2   Analysis of all work processes to find 'elementary tasks'
    (make a long list).
3   Agreement with management to explore the options in spe-
    cific departments of the organizations and make additional
    agreements under which conditions the process can proceed.
4   Participative redesign of jobs, discuss with focus groups
    of employees and supervisors of the departments that are
    involved, validate the tasks that have been found, and
    develop ideas for reallocation of tasks in order to create
    elementary (simple) jobs, and check relationship with other
    jobs in department (make shortlist).
5   Recruitment and selection of candidates with adequate com-
    petences and who are motivated to execute the available
    elementary tasks (shortlist).
6   Clustering of elementary tasks to make elementary jobs that
    are adjusted to the individual candidate's capacities, and the
    department's needs.
7   Introduction of candidates in their new work environment,
    manage mutual expectations, start initial training and super-
    vision with help (at first) of external job coach, and later on
    taken over by internal colleague/mentor/supervisor.
8   Frequent feedback by coach and supervisor and, if neces-
    sary new adjustments of tasks until a sustainable situation
    has been achieved: reintegration is successful. If not (reinte-
    gration was not successful): new candidate (go back to Step
    5).
9   Evaluation of the project by management and representatives
    of the departments that are involved to decide whether the
    project will be continued.

abilities. They showed that prosocial motivation is positively related to individual inclusive behavior (ibid.). From the perspective of the functional approach, people will try to satisfy their needs and goals by displaying inclusive behavior. Nelissen and colleagues (2014) also demonstrate that climate is an important contextual variable that has both direct and indirect effects on displayed helping behavior. In particular, when people with disabilities are concerned, colleagues showed more helping behavior when the group had an inclusive climate. More specifically, inclusive climate is not only directly related to individual inclusive behavior, but that it also moderates the relationship between prosocial motivation and individual inclusive behavior. This interaction reveals that a strong inclusive climate as a team-level variable seems to be strong enough to overrule an individual's (negative) prosocial motivation.

Vornholt et al. (2013) show that stereotypes towards people with disabilities are related to inclusive behavior. They also demonstrate that this relationship is mediated by attitudes towards the employment of people with disabilities. The cognitive appraisal that attitudes give to the beliefs employees have, gives rise to behavior that corresponds to these attitudes. Employees who have positive attitudes towards the employment of people with disabilities will be more likely to exhibit inclusive behavior and to allow people with disabilities to perform better, which will ultimately lead to sustainable employment. Furthermore, Vornholt and colleagues (2013) show that employees who do not experience work pressure will be more likely to display inclusive behavior, compared to those who are under high work pressure. They suggest that inclusive organizations that want their employees to display inclusive behavior should therefore be attentive to employees' perception of the workload, and maybe even lower the work demands of employees when trying to integrate people with disabilities in the work team. This should lead to more inclusive behavior, but eventually also to higher performance and well-being of employees with and without disabilities, which is most likely the best precursor of sustainable employment.

Inclusive organizations should keep in mind that the employment of people with disabilities will activate certain stereotypes and beliefs within their staff that have an impact on the treatment of people with disabilities at work. Attitudes toward the employment of people with disabilities and perceived work pressure play a role in determining the nature of this relationship. Both can be malleable by organizational-level interventions, therefore inclusive organizations need to adapt their strategy to their corporate social responsibility goals. Methods to increase inclusive behavior can be implemented on three levels: organizational, team, and individual level (Bartholomew et al., 2011). Interventions can be planned throughout entire organizations to focus on individual change. Stone and Colella (1996) have argued that organizations should develop training programs that focus on the correctness of stereotypes, on norms of day-to-day interaction, and on decreasing feelings of anxiety while working with people with disabilities. Hunt and Hunt (2004) state that attitudes can only be changed by challenging people's beliefs. They devised an educational intervention that increased knowledge on and yielded positive attitudes towards people with disabilities in the workplace. This indicates the importance of an active inclusive organization that needs to put organizational goals into practice. Also at team level there are many determinants of the amount of displayed inclusive behavior. As mentioned earlier, Nelissen et al. (2014) investigated cross-level effects of inclusive climate on inclusive behavior, and found that climate has an overarching effect on inclusive behavior, in such a way that individual features are suppressed. Team leaders can have major influence on the daily practices and procedures that constitute a climate and should therefore be made aware of the important role they play in the display of inclusive behavior. Lastly, inclusive organizations that wish to attain a diverse workforce are advised to incorporate corporate sustainable responsibility in their mission statements. An active implementation of the values that foster belonging is key to achieving sustainable employment for people with disabilities (Schur et al., 2009).

CONCLUSION

Health has increasingly become an issue in our society, and in this chapter we outlined that health promotion needs to take place, both at the individual and organizational level. We also argued that health promotion generally aims to change behavior of people, whether this is in organizations or elsewhere. These are difficult aims and in order to be successful it is necessary to use a systematic approach that has a clear theoretical basis regarding the object of change (be it human behavior, or organizations) and scientific evidence of successful interventions. In this chapter we have described and illustrated Intervention Mapping as such an approach. Intervention Mapping was originally developed for individual behavior changes; however, the principles of this systematic approach can also be applied at the organizational level.

We have tried to demonstrate an intervention at the organizational level with the example of 'inclusive organizations', which can be seen as an example of the ecological approach. In the example, all levels are affected: employees, teams, and managers, and also work processes were altered. It is clear that these steps can only follow when at the highest level of the organization (board level) this decision is made. Just as when an organization decides that 'sustainability' will be a key concept for organizational policy, 'inclusiveness of the organization' also requires a board decision that this will be the organizational policy, and that procedures will be adopted to facilitate this policy. Such a 'top-down approach' is necessary to facilitate the development of new values in the organization. This implies that evidently the support and focus of management is required: these changes require 'leadership'.

REFERENCES

Abraham, C. and E. Graham-Rowe (2009), 'Are worksite interventions effective in increasing physical activity? A systematic review and meta-analysis', *Health Psychology Review*, **3**, 108–44.
Bandura, A. (1986), *Social Foundations of Thought and Action: A Social Cognitive Theory*, Englewood Cliffs, NJ: Prentice-Hall.
Bartholomew, L.K., G.S. Parcel, G. Kok, N.H. Gottlieb and M.E. Fernández (2011), *Planning Health Promotion Programs: An Intervention Mapping Approach*, 3rd edition, San Francisco, CA: Jossey-Bass.
Biazzo, S. (2002), 'Process mapping techniques and organizational analysis: lessons from sociotechnical system theory', *Business Process Management Journal*, **8**(1), 42–52.
Butterfoss, F.D., M.C. Kegler and V.T. Francisco (2008), 'Mobilizing organizations for health promotion: theories of organizational changes', in K. Glanz, B.K. Rimer and K. Viswanath (eds), *Health Behavior and Health Education: Theory, Research and Practice*, 4th edition, San Francisco, CA: Jossey-Bass, pp. 335–62.
Buunk, A.P. and M. van Vugt (2013), *Applying Social Psychology: From Problems to Solutions*, London: Sage.
Champion, V.L. and C.S. Skinner (2008), 'The health belief model', in K. Glanz, B.K. Rimer and K. Viswanath (eds), *Health Behavior and Health Education: Theory, Research, and Practice*, 4th edition, San Francisco, CA: Jossey-Bass, pp. 45–65.
Chu, C., G. Breucker, N. Harris, A. Stitzel, X. Gan, X. Gu and S. Dwyer (2000), 'Health promoting workplaces – international settings development', *Health Promotion International*, **15**(2), 155–67.
Colella, A. and S. Bruyère (2011), 'Disability and employment: new directions for industrial and organizational psychology', in S. Zedeck (ed.), *APA Handbook of Industrial and Organizational Psychology*, pp. 473–503.
Coles, S. and K. Scior (2012), 'Public attitudes towards people with intellectual disabilities: a qualitative comparison of white British and South Asian people', *Journal of Applied Research in Intellectual Disabilities*, **25**(2), 177–88.
Cummings, T.G. and C.G. Worley (2009), *Organization Development and Change*, 9th edition, Mason, OH: South-Western Cengage Learning.
D'Amato, A. and F.R.H. Zijlstra (2010), 'Towards a climate for work resumption: the non-medical determinants of return to work', *Journal of Occupational and Environmental Medicine*, **52**(1), 67–80.
De Bakker, F.G.A. and F. Den Hond (2008), 'Introducing the politics of stakeholder influence: a review essay', *Business and Society*, **47**(2), 8–20.
Den Hond, F. and F.G.A. de Bakker (2007), 'Ideologically motivated activism:

how activist groups influence corporate social change', *Academy of Management Review*, **32**(3), 901–24.

DiClemente, R.J., R.A. Crosby and M. Kegler (eds) (2009), *Emerging Theories in Health Promotion Practice and Research*, 2nd edition, San Francisco, CA: Jossey-Bass.

European Commission (2011), *Communication from the Commission to the European Parliament, the Council, the European Economic and Social Committee and the Committee of the Regions: A Renewed EU Strategy 2011–14 for Corporate Social Responsibility*, Brussels, p. 15, accessed 27 June 2014 at http://eur-lex.europa.eu/LexUriServ/LexUriServ.do?uri=COM:2011:0681:FIN:EN:PDF.

Fishbein, M. and I. Ajzen (2010), *Predicting and Changing Behavior: The Reasoned Action Approach*, New York: Taylor and Francis.

Fishbein, M., H.C. Triandis, F.H. Kanfer, M.H. Becker, S.E. Middlestadt and A. Eichler (2001), 'Factors influencing behavior and behavior change', in A. Baum, T.R. Revenson and J.E. Singer (eds), *Handbook of Health Psychology*, Hillsdale, NJ: Lawrence Erlbaum, pp. 3–17.

Flaspohler, P., J. Duffy, A. Wandersman, L. Stillman and M.A. Maras (2008), 'Unpacking prevention capacity: an intersection of research-to-practice models and community-centered models', *American Journal of Community Psychology*, **41**(3–4), 182–96.

Foster-Fishman, P.G., B. Nowell and H. Yang (2007), 'Putting the system back into systems change: a framework for understanding and changing organizational and community systems', *American Journal of Community Psychology*, **39**(3–4), 197–215.

Glanz, K., B.K. Rimer and K. Viswanath (eds) (2008), *Health Behavior and Health Education: Theory, Research, and Practice*, 4th edition, San Francisco, CA: Jossey-Bass.

Gollwitzer, P.M. (1993), 'Goal achievement: the role of intentions', *European Review of Social Psychology*, **4**(1), 141–85.

Gollwitzer, P.M. (1999), 'Implementation intentions. Strong effects of simple plans', *American Psychologist*, **54**(7), 493–503.

Gollwitzer, P.M. and P. Sheeran (2006), 'Implementation intentions and goal achievement: a meta-analysis of effects and processes', *Advances in Experimental Social Psychology*, **38**, 69–119.

Green, L.W. and R.E. Glasgow (2006), 'Evaluating the relevance, generalization, and applicability of research: issues in external validation and translation methodology', *Evaluation and the Health Professions*, **29**(1), 126–53.

Green, L.W. and M.W. Kreuter (2005), *Health Program Planning: An Educational and Ecological Approach*, 4th edition, New York: McGraw Hill Professional.

Hassin, R.R., J.S. Uleman and J.A. Bargh (eds) (2005) *The New Unconscious*, New York: Oxford University Press.

Heaney, C.A. and B.A. Israel (2008), 'Social networks and social support', in K. Glanz, B.K. Rimer and K. Viswanath (eds), *Health Behavior and Health Education: Theory, Research, and Practice*, 4th edition, San Francisco, CA: Jossey-Bass, pp. 189–210.

Hendriks, A.M., M.W.J. Jansen, J.S. Gubbels, N.K. de Vries, T.G.W. Paulussen and S.P.J. Kremers (2013), 'Proposing a conceptual framework for integrated local public health policy, applied to childhood obesity – the behavior change ball', *Implementation Science*, **8**(1), 46–63.

Hofmann, W., M. Friese and R. Wiers (2008), 'Impulsive versus reflective influences on health behavior: a theoretical framework and empirical review', *Health Psychology Review*, **2**(2), 111–37.

Hofmann, W., M. Friese and F. Strack (2009), 'Impulse and self-control from a dual-systems perspective', *Perspectives on Psychological Sciences*, **4**(2), 162–76.

Hunt, C.S. and B. Hunt (2004), 'Changing attitudes toward people with disabilities: experimenting with an educational intervention', *Journal of Managerial Issues*, **16**(2), 266–80.

Jahoda, M. (1981), 'Work, employment, and unemployment: values, theories, and approaches in social research', *American Psychologist*, **36**(2), 184–91.

Kazdin, A.E. (2008), *Behavior Modification in Applied Settings*, 6th edition, Long Grove, IL: Waveland Press.

Khan, L.K., K. Sobush, D. Keener, K. Goodman, A. Lowry, J. Kakietek and S. Zaro (2009), 'Recommended community strategies and measurements to prevent obesity in the United States', *Morbidity and Mortality Weekly Report*, **58**(RR07), 1–26.

Kingdon, J.W. (2003), *Agendas, Alternatives, and Public Policies*, 2nd edition, New York: Longman.

Kok, G., N.H. Gottlieb, M. Commers and C. Smerecnik (2008), 'The ecological approach in health promotion programs: a decade later', *American Journal of Health Promotion*, **22**(6), 437–42.

Kok, G., N.H. Gottlieb, R. Panne and C. Smerecnik (2012), 'Methods for environmental change; an exploratory study', *BMC Public Health*, **12**, 1037–49.

Kuhl, J. and A. Fuhrmann (1998), 'Decomposing self-regulation and self-control: the volitional components checklist', in J. Heckhausen and C. Dweck (eds), *Lifespan Perspective on Motivation and Control*, Mahwah, NJ: Erlbaum, pp. 19–45.

Latham, G.P. and E.A. Locke (2007), 'New developments in and directions for goal-setting research', *European Psychologist*, **12**(4), 290–300.

Maon, F., A. Lindgreen and V. Swaen (2009), 'Designing and implementing corporate social responsibility: an integrative framework grounded in theory and practice', *Journal of Business Ethics*, **87**(1), 71–89.

Marlatt, G.A. and D.M. Donovan (eds) (2005), *Relapse Prevention: Maintenance Strategies in the Treatment of Addictive Behaviors*, 2nd edition, New York: Guilford.

McAlister, A.L., C.L. Perry and G.S. Parcel (2008), 'How individuals, environments, and health behaviors interact: social cognitive theory', in K. Glanz, B.K. Rimer and K. Viswanath (eds), *Health Behavior and Health Education*, 4th edition, San Francisco, CA: Jossey-Bass, pp. 169–88.

McEachan, R.R., R.J. Lawton, C. Jackson, M. Conner and J. Lunt (2008), 'Evidence, theory and context: using Intervention Mapping to develop a worksite physical activity intervention', *BMC Public Health*, **8**(1), 326.

McEachan, R.R.C., R.J. Lawton, C. Jackson, M. Conner, D.M. Meads and R.M. West (2011), 'Testing a workplace physical activity intervention: a cluster randomized controlled trial', *International Journal of Behavioral Nutrition and Physical Activity*, **8**(29), 1–12.

McLean, G.N. (2005), *Organization Development: Principles, Processes, Performance*, San Francisco, CA: Berrett-Koehler.

Milio, N. (1981), *Promoting Health Through Public Policy*, Philadelphia, PA: F.A.Davis.

Minkler, M. and N. Wallerstein (eds) (2008), *Community-based Participatory*

Research for Health: From Process to Outcomes, 2nd edition, San Francisco, CA: Jossey-Bass.

Minkler, M., N. Wallerstein and N. Wilson (2008), 'Improving health through community organization and community building', in K. Glanz, B.K. Rimer and K. Viswanath (eds), *Health Behavior and Health Education: Theory, Research, and Practice*, 4th edition, San Francisco, CA: Jossey-Bass, pp. 287–312.

Munir, F., K. Kalawsky, D.J. Wallis and E. Donaldson-Feilder (2013), 'Using Intervention Mapping to develop a work-related guidance tool for those affected by cancer', *BMC Public Health*, **13**(1), 6–16.

National Cancer Institute (2007), *Greater Than the Sum: System Thinking in Tobacco Control*, Publication No. 06–6085, Tobacco Control Monograph No. 18, Bethesda, MD: US Department of Health and Human Services, National Institute of Health, National Cancer Institute.

Nelissen, P.T.J.H., U.R. Hülsheger, G.M.C. van Ruitenbeek and F.R.H. Zijlstra (2014), 'Lending a helping hand: a multilevel investigation of prosocial motivation, inclusive climate and citizenship behavior' (under review).

Norman, P., H. Boer and E.R. Seydel (2005), 'Protection motivation theory', in M. Conner and P. Norman (eds), *Predicting Health Behaviour: Research and Practice with Social Cognition Models*, 2nd edition, Buckingham, UK and Philadelphia, PA, USA, pp. 170–222.

Oldenburg, B. and K. Glanz (2008), 'Diffusion of innovations', in K. Glanz, B.K. Rimer and F.M. Lewis (eds), *Health Behavior and Health Education: Theory, Research, and Practice*, 4th edition, San Francisco, CA: Jossey-Bass, pp. 313–33.

Oude Hengel, K.M., B.M. Blatter, C.I. Joling, A.J. van der Beek and P.M. Bongers (2012), 'Effectiveness of an intervention at construction worksites on work engagement, social support, physical workload, and need for recovery: results from a cluster randomized controlled trial', *BMC Public Health*, **12**(1), 1008.

Oude Hengel, K.M., C.I. Joling, K.I. Proper, H.F. van der Molen and P.M. Bongers (2010), 'Using Intervention Mapping to develop a worksite prevention program for construction workers', *American Journal of Health Promotion*, **26**, e1–e10.

Paton, K., S. Sengupta and L. Hassan (2005), 'Settings, systems and organization development: the Healthy Living and Working Model', *Health Promotion International*, **20**(1), 81–9.

Peters, G.-J.Y., M. de Bruin and R. Crutzen (2013), 'Everything should be as simple as possible, but no simpler: towards a protocol for accumulating evidence regarding the active content of health behavior change interventions', *Health Psychology Review* [online], DOI: 10.1080/17437199.2013.848409.

Petty, R.E., J. Barden and S.C. Wheeler (2009), 'The elaboration likelihood model of persuasion: developing health promotions for sustained behavioral change', in R.J. DiClemente, R.A. Crosby and M. Kegler (eds), *Emerging Theories in Health Promotion Practice and Research*, 2nd edition, San Francisco, CA: Jossey-Bass, pp. 185–214.

Prochaska, J.O., C.A. Redding and K.E. Evers (2008), 'The transtheoretical model and stages of change', in K. Glanz, B.K. Rimer and K. Viswanath (eds), *Health Behavior and Health Education: Theory, Research, and Practice*, 4th edition, San Francisco, CA: Jossey-Bass, pp. 97–121.

Rosen, R.H. (1992), *The Healthy Company: Eight Strategies to Develop People, Productivity, and Profits*, New York: Jeremy P. Tarcher/Putnam.

Rossi, P.H., M.W. Lipsey and H.E. Freeman (2004), *Evaluation: A Systematic Approach*, Newbury Park, CA: Sage.

Rothman, A.J., A.S. Baldwin and A.W. Hertel (2004), 'Self-regulation and behavior change', in R.F. Baumeister and K.D. Vohs (eds), *Handbook of Self-regulation: Research, Theory, and Applications*, New York: Guilford Press, pp. 97–121.

Ruiter, R.A.C., K. Massar, M. van Vugt and G. Kok (2013), 'Applying social psychology to understanding social problems', in A. Golec de Zavala and A. Cichocka (eds), *Social Psychology of Social Problems: The Intergroup Context*, New York: Palgrave MacMillan, pp. 337–62.

Schaalma, H. and G. Kok (2009), 'Decoding health education interventions: the times are a-changin', *Psychology and Health*, **24**(1), 5–9.

Schaalma, H.P. and G. Kok (2011), 'A school HIV-prevention program in the Netherlands. Case study 3', accessed 27 June 2014 at http://interventionmapping.com/sites/default/files/Case%20Study%203.pdf.

Schein, E.H. (2004), *Organizational Culture and Leadership*, 3rd edition, San Francisco, CA: Jossey-Bass.

Schur, L., D. Kruse and P. Blanck (2005), 'Corporate culture and the employment of persons with disabilities', *Behavioral Sciences and the Law*, **23**(1), 3–20.

Schur, L., D. Kruse, J. Blasi and P. Blanck (2009), 'Is disability disabling in all workplaces? Workplace disparities and corporate culture', *Industrial Relations: A Journal of Economy and Society*, **48**(3), 381–410.

Schuring, M., J. Mackenbach, T. Voorham and A. Burdorf (2011), 'The effect of re-employment on perceived health', *Journal of Epidemiology and Community Health*, **65**(7), 639–44.

Schwarzer, R. (1992), 'Self-efficacy in the adoption and maintenance of health behaviors: theoretical approaches and a new model', in R. Schwarzer (ed.), *Self-efficacy: Thought Control of Action*, Washington, DC: Hemisphere Publishing Co., pp. 217–43.

Scior, K. (2011), 'Public awareness, attitudes and beliefs regarding intellectual disability: a systematic review', *Research in Developmental Disabilities*, **32**(6), 2164–82.

Sheeran, P. (2002), 'Intention–behavior relations: a conceptual and empirical review', *European Review of Social Psychology*, **12**, 1–30.

Stavri, Z. and S. Michie (2012), 'Classification systems in behavioural science: current systems and lessons from the natural, medical and social sciences', *Health Psychology Review*, **6**(1), 112–39.

Strack, F. and R. Deutsch (2004), 'Reflective and impulsive determinants of social behavior', *Personality and Social Psychology Review*, **8**(3), 220–47.

Stone, D. and A. Colella (1996), 'A model of factors affecting the treatment of disabled individuals in organizations', *Academy of Management Review*, **21**(2), 352–401, accessed 27 June 2014 at http://amr.aom.org/content/21/2/352.short.

Strijk, J.E., K.I. Proper, A.J. van der Beek and W. van Mechelen (2009), 'The Vital@Work Study. The systematic development of a lifestyle intervention to improve older workers' vitality and the design of a randomised controlled trial evaluating this intervention', *BMC Public Health*, **9**(1), 408.

Strijk, J.E., K.I. Proper, A.J. van der Beek and W. van Mechelen (2011), 'A worksite vitality intervention to improve older workers' lifestyle and vitality-related outcomes: results of a randomised controlled trial', *Journal of Epidemiology and Community Health*, **66**(11), 1071–8.

Turner, J.C. (2005), 'Explaining the nature of power: a three-process theory', *European Journal of Social Psychology*, **35**(1), 1–22.

Van Oostrom, S., J. Anema, B. Terluin, A. Venema, H. de Vet and W. van Mechelen (2007), 'Development of a workplace intervention for sick-listed employees with stress-related mental disorders: Intervention Mapping as a useful tool', *BMC Health Services Research*, **7**(1), 127.

Van Oostrom, S.H., W. van Mechelen, B. Terluin, H.C.W. de Vet, D.L. Knol and J.R. Anema (2013), 'A workplace intervention for sick-listed employees with distress: results of a randomised controlled trial', *Occupational and Environmental Medicine*, **67**(9), 596–602.

Van Scheppingen, A.R., C.J.M. ten Have, G.I.J.M. Zwetsloot, G. Kok and W. van Mechelen (in press), 'Determining organization-specific factors for developing health interventions in companies by a Delphi procedure: "Organizational Mapping"', *Journal of Health Psychology*.

Vermeulen, S., J. Anema, A. Schellart, W. van Mechelen and A. van der Beek (2009), 'Intervention Mapping for development of a participatory return-to-work intervention for temporary agency workers and unemployed workers sick-listed due to musculoskeletal disorders', *BMC Public Health*, **9**(1), 216.

Vermeulen, S., J. Anema, A. Schellart, W. van Mechelen and A. van der Beek (2011), 'A participatory return-to-work intervention for temporary agency workers and unemployed workers sick-listed due to musculoskeletal disorders: results of a randomized controlled trial', *Journal of Occupational Rehabilitation*, **21**(3), 313–24.

Verweij, L.M., K.I. Proper, A.N.H. Weel, C.T.J. Hulshof and W. van Mechelen (2012), 'The application of an occupational health guideline reduces sedentary behaviour and increases fruit intake at work: results from an RCT', *Occupational and Environmental Medicine*, **69**(7), 500–507.

Vohs, K.D. and R.F. Baumeister (2011), *Handbook of Self-regulation: Research, Theory, and Applications*, 2nd edition, New York: Guilford Press.

Vornholt, K., S. Uitdewilligen and F.J. Nijhuis (2013), 'Factors affecting the acceptance of people with disabilities at work: a literature review', *Journal of Occupational Rehabilitation* [online], DOI 10.1007/s10926-013-9426-0.

Weible, C.M., P.A. Sabatier and K. McQueen (2009), 'Themes and variations: taking stock of the Advocacy Coalition Framework', *The Policy Studies Journal*, **37**(1), 121–40.

Weick, K.E. and R.E. Quinn (1999), 'Organizational change and development', *Annual Review of Psychology*, **50**(1), 361–86.

Whittingham, J.R., R.A.C. Ruiter, D. Castermans, A. Huiberts and G. Kok (2008), 'Designing effective health education materials: experimental pre-testing of a theory-based brochure to increase knowledge', *Health Education Research*, **23**(3), 414–26.

WHO (1948), 'Preamble to the Constitution of the World Health Organization as adopted by the International Health Conference', New York, 19–22 June.

Wholey, J.S., H.P. Hatry and K.E. Newcomer (2004), *Handbook of Practical Program Evaluation*, 2nd edition, San Francisco, CA: Jossey-Bass.

Wood, W. and D.T. Neal (2007), 'A new look at habits and the habit–goal interface', *Psychological Review*, **114**(4), 843–63.

Zijlstra, F.R.H. and F.J.N. Nijhuis (2014), 'Return to work for long-term absentees: an undervalued topic in (psychological) research', in M. Kröll (ed.),

Eüropäische Arbeitsmarktstrategien auf dem Prüfstand [European Labor Market Strategies Put to the Test], book series: Bildung und Arbeitswelt [Education and the Working World], Zurich: LIT-Verlag.

Zijlstra, F.R.H., H.P.G. Mulders and F.J.N. Nijhuis (2009), 'Speciale taken voor speciale groepen' [Special tasks for special groups], *Tijdschrift voor Bedrijfs- en Verzekeringsgeneeskunde*, **17**, 298–301.

Zijlstra, F.R.H., H.P.G. Mulders and F.J. Nijhuis (2012), 'Inclusieve Organisaties – Op weg naar duurzame arbeidsparticipatie' [Inclusive organizations – towards sustainable employment in the labor market], *Tijdschrift Voor Arbeidsvraagstukken*, **28**(1), 21–9.

3. Beyond wellness: broadening the discussion of well-being and performance

David W. Ballard

A healthy workplace is one that 'maximizes the integration of worker goals for well-being and company objectives for profitability and productivity' (Sauter et al., 1996, p. 250). While most organizations have performance metrics they look to for evidence of progress toward their operational goals, employee well-being is a more nebulous concept to grapple with. Perhaps that is why many organizations fall back on narrow measures of well-being, such as healthcare claims, biometric data from health screenings, the number of health risks identified in the company's health risk assessment (HRA), or even just participation rates in the wellness programs they offer. These sources of data can be valuable in identifying need areas, evaluating the impact of poor health, and demonstrating to senior leaders that healthy employees are critical to an organization's success, but fail to consider a multi-faceted view of well-being that captures the richness and complexity of the human experience.

This chapter will explore how work can contribute to a broader experience of well-being and use the American Psychological Association's 'Psychologically Healthy Workplace' model as a framework for considering the types of workplace practices that can enhance employee and organizational outcomes.

WORK AND WELL-BEING

Creating a healthy, high-performing organization requires more than simply offering wellness activities or desirable benefits. Done well, healthy workplace principles become ingrained in the very norms, values, and beliefs that are part of an organization's culture.

Core to this approach is a multi-dimensional view of employee well-being that includes good physical and mental health, strong interpersonal relationships, financial stability, and a meaningful life with positive experiences at work. This broad perspective has, unfortunately, not been the path historically explored by researchers, with most studies of workplace health emphasizing disease and dysfunction, rather than the pursuit of well-being, optimal functioning, and other positive outcomes (Warr, 1987). Some researchers (e.g., Hofmann and Tetrick, 2003) have begun to explore the characteristics of healthy work, with an emphasis on both the physical and psychological, but there is no generally agreed upon definition of employee well-being.

Although the health promotion industry has remained heavily focused on physical health outcomes, with some reference to mental health issues such as depression and anxiety disorders, psychology has broadened the discussion to include topics such as how job design, teamwork, and leadership practices can promote healthy work (e.g., Turner et al., 2002), individuals' cognitive and affective appraisals of their own lives (Diener, 1984), and how employees' day-to-day work experiences affect their well-being and performance (Amabile and Kramer, 2010). Gallup further broadens the concept of well-being by adding high-quality interpersonal relationships and financial security to the mix, along with connection to and pride in one's community (Rath and Harter, 2010).

Despite the lack of consensus about how to define employee well-being, the importance of a healthy workforce has come to be generally accepted. Many employers remain frustrated, however, that their health promotion and wellness efforts are falling short in terms of both employee and organizational outcomes. Too often, organizations apply a fragmented assortment of programs or rely on off-the-shelf solutions from vendors and fail to customize their practices to meet the unique needs of their workforce. This leaves employers facing skyrocketing healthcare costs and other business challenges and searching desperately for a silver bullet that will solve their problems. Employees are similarly struggling to manage the challenges they face and are feeling unheard and under-appreciated by their employers, as their broader needs go unmet.

According to a national survey by the American Psychological Association (APA, 2013a), more than one-third of American workers experience chronic work stress, with low salaries, lack of opportunity for advancement, and heavy workloads topping the list of contributing factors. Many employees appear to feel stuck, with only 39 percent citing sufficient opportunities for internal career advancement and just over half (51 percent) saying they feel valued at work.

Compounding the problem, less than half of working Americans reported that they receive adequate monetary compensation or non-monetary recognition for their contributions on the job (46 percent and

43 percent, respectively). Additionally, just 43 percent of employees said that recognition was based on fair and useful performance evaluations. In addition to feeling undervalued, employees also reported feeling unheard. Less than half (47 percent) said their employers regularly seek input from employees and even fewer (37 percent) said the organization makes changes based on that feedback.

Feeling valued at work is also critical to employee well-being and per-formance. In another survey of the US workforce, half of all employees who say that they do not feel valued at work reported that they intend to look for a new job in the next year (APA, 2012). Additionally, the survey found that employees who feel valued are more likely to report better physical and mental health, as well as higher levels of engagement, sat-isfaction, and motivation, compared to those who do not feel valued by their employers.

Almost all employees (93 percent) who reported feeling valued said that they are motivated to do their best at work and 88 percent reported feeling engaged. This compares to just 33 percent and 38 percent, respectively, of those who said they do not feel valued. Among employees who feel valued, just one in five (21 percent) said they intend to look for a new job in the next year (versus 50 percent of those who said that they do not feel valued). A variety of factors were linked to feeling undervalued at work, including having fewer opportunities for involvement in decision-making (24 percent vs 84 percent), being less satisfied with the potential for growth and advancement (9 percent vs 70 percent), having fewer opportunities to use flexible work arrangements (20 percent vs 59 percent) and being less likely to say they are receiving adequate monetary compensation (18 percent vs 69 percent) and non-monetary rewards (16 percent vs 65 percent). Overall, more than one in five working Americans (21 percent) said they do not feel valued by their employers.

Despite growing awareness of the importance of a healthy workplace, few employees said their organizations provide sufficient resources to help them manage stress (36 percent) and meet their mental health needs (44 percent; APA, 2013a). In fact, only 59 percent reported having adequate employer-provided health insurance. Just 42 percent of employ-ees said their organizations promote and support a healthy lifestyle and only 36 percent reported regularly participating in workplace health and wellness programs.

Work–life conflict and lack of flexibility is also an area of concern for the US workforce. Only 39 percent of American workers report that their employers provide options for flexible work and 30 percent say their employers provide benefits that help them more easily meet their non-work demands (APA, 2013a). One-third of working Americans

(33 percent) say that work interfering during personal or family time has a significant impact on their level of work stress, and one in four report that job demands interfere with their ability to fulfill family or home responsibilities. Despite the media attention given to work–life balance in recent years and the growing expectation of work flexibility in the US workforce, just over half of employees report that their supervisor supports their work–life balance (57 percent) and that their organization even values work–life balance (55 percent; APA, 2013b).

With more than two-thirds (69 percent) of US adults citing work as a significant source of stress (APA, 2013c) and 35 percent of working Americans reporting that they typically feel stressed during the workday (2013a), employers need to provide resources to help their employees face work-related challenges, so they can function at their best both on and off the job.

CHARACTERISTICS ASSOCIATED WITH SUCCESSFUL EFFORTS

A number of studies have examined best-practice programs in both workplace health promotion and organizational effectiveness in an effort to identify success factors (e.g., Fitz-enz, 1993; O'Donnell et al., 1997; Goetzel et al., 2001, 2007). Common characteristics that have emerged include: alignment with the organization's mission, values and goals; coordination of comprehensive efforts across the organization; customization to address issues and needs that are important to employees and the organization; involvement of employees through the design, implementation and evaluation of the program; leadership support; effective two-way communication mechanisms; ongoing evaluation; and continuous improvement.

For examples of employers with best-practice programs and documented evidence that their wellness programs have improved health and saved money, readers are directed to The Health Project website (www. thehealthproject.com), which includes a list of more than 50 organizations that have received the C. Everett Koop National Health Award.

Employers who understand that the well-being of their workforce and the performance and success of the organization are inextricably linked take comprehensive steps to create a positive work environment that supports and promotes good health and optimal functioning. In short, they create a psychologically healthy workplace. When an employer sees well-being as critical to the organization's success, workplace practices can be linked more closely to an organization's strategic goals, thereby supporting its mission and driving performance.

For example, the four organizations that received the American Psychological Association's 2014 Psychologically Healthy Workplace Award for their comprehensive efforts to promote well-being and performance reported an average turnover rate of just 7 percent in 2013 – significantly less than the national average of 38 percent, as estimated by the US Department of Labor (APA, 2014a). Additionally, only 15 percent of their employees say they intend to seek employment elsewhere within the next year, compared to almost double that number (27 percent) nationally in the United States. In surveys of the winning organizations, on average, more than six out of ten employees say their employer promotes and supports a healthy lifestyle (66 percent) and values work–life balance (67 percent) and employee recognition (61 percent; APA, 2014b).

Emotional well-being also plays a central role in these organizations, with around seven in ten employees reporting that the organization provides adequate resources to address their mental health needs (71 percent) and help them manage stress (69 percent), compared to just 45 percent and 36 percent, respectively, in the general US working population.

Employees notice when an employer is truly committed to their well-being and it can have a positive impact on their relationship with the organization. In APA's award-winning organizations, an average of 83 percent of employees say they are motivated to do their very best on the job, compared to just 70 percent nationally in the USA, and almost three-quarters (74 percent) say they would recommend their organization to others as a good place to work compared to just 57 percent in the US workforce (APA, 2014a). More information about APA's Psychologically Healthy Workplace Award winners and their efforts to promote well-being and performance are available at www.apaexcellence.org.

THE PSYCHOLOGICALLY HEALTHY WORKPLACE

A psychologically healthy workplace fosters employee well-being while enhancing organizational performance. In their work as research consultants for the American Psychological Association, Grawitch et al. (2006) reviewed previous research from a variety of disciplines that have contributed to the understanding of healthy workplace practices and created a framework for exploring the types of workplace practices that promote employee well-being and organizational improvements and the links between them.

Although there is no 'one-size-fits-all' approach to creating a psychologically healthy workplace, the practices that help create a healthy and productive work environment can be grouped into five categories:

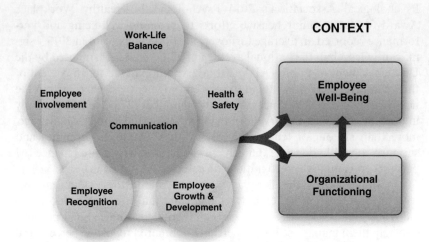

Figure 3.1 The psychologically healthy workplace

employee involvement; health and safety; employee growth and development; work–life balance; and employee recognition (Figure 3.1).

Employee Involvement

Efforts to increase employee involvement empower workers, involve them in decision-making, and give them increased job autonomy. Examples include participative decision-making, self-managed work groups, continuous improvement teams, and multi-rater performance evaluation systems. Employee involvement programs can increase job satisfaction, employee morale, and commitment to the organization as well as increase productivity, reduce turnover and absenteeism, and enhance the quality of products and services (Lawler, 1991; Freeman and Rogers, 1999; Vandenberg et al., 1999).

Case example: Coleman Professional Services (CPS)
When this behavioral healthcare organization decided to build a new facility for its senior day program, it looked to employees for guidance in creating an environment that would be functional, attractive, and safe for both staff and clients. When CPS acquired Portage Area Senior Services, a

community-based program that serves older adults with multiple physical and mental health needs, the program occupied a small, outdated building with inadequate work space and poor lighting. Staff safety was also compromised due to structural limitations that prevented the installation of assistive devices to help lift clients. Despite attempts to upgrade the facility, CPS continued to face low employee satisfaction and morale as well as high turnover. The organization realized that the program needed a new building and believed that staff held the keys to success.

Employees worked hand in hand with architects as the design evolved from concept to construction and regularly scheduled team meetings allowed for ongoing input throughout the construction stage. When employees suggested several additional improvements just one week before the scheduled move-in date, CPS was quick to make the changes, even though doing so delayed the opening.

The end result was a new 10 000 ft^2 facility with ample space for client activity areas, staff workspace and outdoor courtyards. In addition to being comfortable and safe, the new building provides the flexibility to accommodate clients who require different levels of care. Following completion of the new facility, turnover in the program dropped by more than 30 percent, employee morale and satisfaction improved and the number of clients served has grown by 60 percent.

Health and Safety

Health and safety initiatives improve the physical and mental health of employees through the prevention, assessment, and treatment of potential health risks and problems (Aldana, 2001), and by encouraging and supporting healthy lifestyle and behavior choices. Health and safety efforts include a wide variety of workplace practices that can help employees improve their physical and mental health, reduce health risks, and manage stress effectively. Examples of health and safety practices include the provision of high-quality health insurance that includes adequate mental health coverage, smoking cessation resources, healthy food options in vending machines and cafeterias, exercise classes, safety and ergonomic assessments, and on-site fitness facilities. By investing in the health and safety of their employees, organizations may benefit from greater productivity and reductions in healthcare costs, absenteeism, and accident/injury rates (Aldana, 2001; Munz et al., 2001; McFarlin and Fals-Stewart, 2002).

Case example: Beach Cities Health District (BCHD)

As a primary prevention agency dedicated to supporting healthy behaviors in the communities it serves, BCHD strives to promote the pursuit of

optimal health by employees and their families through its employee wellness program, Live Well: Healthy Working Families. Live Well: Healthy
Working Families began in 2007 as a pilot program called Wellness
Wednesdays, established in response to employee survey results. The
six-week program consisted of a series of nutrition education workshops
and fitness activities. About half of BCHD's workers participated in the
nutrition workshops and little more than a third in the fitness portion,
but nearly 70 percent expressed a desire for a comprehensive health risk
assessment. This feedback served as the genesis for consolidating all
employee-related programs and activities under the fully integrated Live
Well program, which BCHD launched in the fall of 2008.

By doing so, BCHD underscored its message to employees that it 'walks
its talk', offering them internally the same health and wellness mandate
that it promotes to residents in the Redondo Beach, Manhattan Beach,
and Hermosa Beach communities. In turn, BCHD employees serve as
wellness ambassadors, paying forward the support of optimal health
practices throughout the community. BCHD also supports local health
promotion and disease prevention actions through its partnerships with
city government, school districts, local businesses, non-profit organizations, and community groups.

Employee participation rates in the Live Well: Healthy Working
Families program have continued to grow, and workers show interest in
topics related to nutrition and stress management, two areas identified as
health risks. By assessing employee needs and applying custom-tailored,
evidence-based health promotion and disease prevention programs, Beach
Cities Health District takes workplace wellness out of the office and into
the community.

Employee Growth and Development

Opportunities for growth and development help employees build new
knowledge, skills, and abilities and apply them on the job (Grawitch et
al., 2006). The opportunity to gain new skills and experiences can increase
employee motivation and job satisfaction and help workers to more
effectively manage job stress (Pfeffer, 1994; Browne, 2000). Examples
include continuing education courses, skills training provided in house
and/or through external training centers, tuition reimbursement, coaching and mentoring, job enlargement and enrichment efforts, and career
counseling. This can translate into positive gains for the organization by
enhancing organizational effectiveness and improving work quality, as
well as by helping the organization attract and retain outstanding employees. By providing opportunities for growth and development, organiza-

tions can improve the quality of their employees' work experience and realize the benefits of developing workers to their full potential.

Case example: Toronto Police Service (TPS)
As the largest municipal police force in Canada, TPS knows that opportunities for career advancement can make the difference between a high-performing workforce and unhappy employees who search for work elsewhere. TPS has taken the initiative to ensure its employees can succeed within the ranks of the organization by developing a unique mentoring program that helps uniformed officers navigate the promotional interview process.

At TPS, the promotion process for uniformed officers can be stressful. Before a candidate is eligible for a promotional interview, he or she must complete a formal application, receive a positive assessment from the unit commander and pass a written exam. When it comes to the interview, the pressure is understandable – two candidates interview for every anticipated vacancy and the interview accounts for 60 percent of a candidate's total evaluation.

Because the process can be so stressful, the mentoring sessions arm candidates with the tools they need to go into their interviews prepared. Mentors provide candidates with detailed information about what will happen on the day of their interview and normalize the anxiety they may be experiencing. Candidates are also given sample questions to ease the stress of the unknown. The initiative also supports those on the opposite side of the interview desk. Each member of the promotion panel is required to undergo a mandatory training session that covers sources of interview bias, strategies for ensuring objectivity and consistency in interview ratings and other issues of fairness and ethics.

High participation rates and positive feedback demonstrate that the program is fulfilling a need. With less anxiety, interviewees can perform their best and interviewers can more accurately assess how well candidates meet job-related criteria. Being poised to recruit diverse staff to senior-level positions also helps TPS prevent discrimination and human rights problems and the police service anticipates long-term cost savings and reductions in turnover and absenteeism.

The police service's total separation rate for 2008 was a low 5 percent, with almost 60 percent of the turnover stemming from retirement. At TPS, more than 82 percent of employees report they are satisfied with their jobs and more than 86 percent feel their work is meaningful. By working for positive and constructive interactions internally and in the communities it serves, TPS is demonstrating its dedication to serving and protecting the members of its force and the people of Toronto.

Work–Life Balance

Programs and policies that facilitate work–life balance generally fall
into two categories: flexible work arrangements and resources to help
employees manage their non-work demands. Examples include telecom-
muting, flexible shifts, compressed work weeks, job sharing, adequate
time off, childcare and eldercare resources, flexible leave options beyond
the minimum that is required by law, and life management resources such
as on-site banking, concierge services, and dry cleaning. When employees
experience conflict between the demands they face on the job and in their
non-work lives, the quality of both their work and home life can suffer,
negatively affecting their functioning in both realms. Efforts to help
employees improve work–life balance can increase job satisfaction and
strengthen employees' commitment to the organization (Scandura and
Lankau, 1997). Additionally, the organization may reap benefits in terms
of increased productivity and reduction in absenteeism and employee
turnover (Higgins et al., 1992).

Case example: Northeast Delta Dental (NEDD)
This umbrella organization that provides dental benefits to individuals
and companies in Maine, New Hampshire and Vermont is responsive
to employee needs, including their non-work demands. NEDD's flexible
work policy is environmentally friendly, saves money, makes employees
happy, and improves customer service.

Flexible work schedules have been the norm at NEDD since 1995 and,
in 2008, rising gas prices led the organization to add a four-day work week
to the mix. Using a pilot program and feedback from participants, the
organization created a policy that works well for employees and managers
alike. To assure that NEDD remains responsive to customers, managers
in each department work with employees to determine adequate departmental coverage, set flex time parameters and staff their departments
accordingly.

Support for work flexibility at NEDD begins at the top. The CEO sets
the tone and models the leadership support that empowers employees to
make decisions about their work schedules, coordinate with team-mates
and be accountable for their performance.

NEDD's flex work policies are simple, easy to understand and admin-
ister, and take both employee and organizational needs into account. The
organization benefits by reduced absenteeism, better coordination of work
schedules, cross-training of staff members, and improved employee and
customer satisfaction. NEDD has also been able to retain high-quality
employees, with a turnover rate of just 3.26 percent in 2009.

Through the use of flexible work options, employees are better able to manage their caregiving responsibilities and other life demands and save money on commuting and childcare costs.

Employee Recognition

Employee recognition efforts reward employees both individually and collectively for their contributions to the organization. Recognition can take various forms: formal and informal, monetary and non-monetary. Examples include fair monetary compensation, performance-based bonuses, employee awards for exceptional performance, recognition events, verbal acknowledgement from managers and supervisors, celebration of accomplishments and major life events, and formalized peer recognition programs. By acknowledging employee efforts and making them feel valued and appreciated, organizations can increase employee satisfaction, morale, and self-esteem (Rosen and Berger, 1991). Additionally, the organization itself may benefit from greater employee engagement and productivity, lower turnover, and the ability to attract and retain top-quality employees.

Case example: Bethesda Hospital

As a long-term acute care hospital, Bethesda Hospital is dedicated to reinventing the lives of the people it serves and recognizes the effect employees have on patient experience. Bethesda's focus on employee recognition led to an incentive program called 'Bethesda Recognizes and Values Our Employees' or 'BRAVOe'. The program uses gift cards to recognize accomplishments such as providing exceptional service, supporting hospital programs, and fostering teamwork.

Through the BRAVOe program, introduced in 2006, employees receive gift certificates punctuating each year of service for their first nine years. Employees who work at least 104 hours per quarter earn a $25 gift certificate to the on-site Gallery Café. Bethesda staff are encouraged to acknowledge their co-workers' contributions by sending eye-catching 'Thank-You Grams'. The names of both sender and recipient are entered into weekly and monthly raffles for gift cards to retail and grocery store chains.

To promote teamwork, group recognition is integrated into the BRAVOe program. Nominated by peers, customers, supervisors, or even themselves, teams are rewarded for partnering with other departments and consistently demonstrating the hospital's core values. Winners are recognized in the employee newsletter, a team photo is displayed on an award board outside the cafeteria, the team is treated to a catered lunch and each team member is rewarded with a gift card. An average of 140 employees give or receive gift cards each month.

The anticipation and celebration surrounding the announcement of winners promotes camaraderie, and Bethesda notes high morale and motivation among its staff. In 2007, employee engagement levels increased, and turnover rates dropped below 9 percent. Beyond the financial incentives they receive, employees feel valued and know their contributions are appreciated.

The BRAVOe program has helped improve hospital outcomes as well, with healthcare consultancy Press Ganey patient satisfaction scores above 75 percent and net revenues for the hospital increasing 60 percent since 2001. The BRAVOe program has improved the experience for both patients and staff at Bethesda Hospital.

Additional Considerations

Communication plays a key role in the success of any workplace program or policy and serves as the foundation for all five types of healthy workplace practices (Pfeffer, 1998). Communication about workplace practices helps achieve the desired outcomes for the employee and the organization in a variety of ways (Fitz-enz, 2000). Bottom-up communication (from employees to management) provides information about employee needs, values, perceptions, and opinions. This helps organizations select and tailor their programs and policies to meet the specific needs of their employees. Top-down communication (from management to employees) can increase utilization of specific workplace programs by making employees aware of their availability, clearly explaining how to access and use the services, and demonstrating that management supports and values the programs.

In practice, the psychologically healthy workplace approach includes a population-based public health perspective that utilizes primary-, secondary-, and tertiary-level interventions to promote good health and prevent problems from occurring, reduce risks and improve health, and address disease and dysfunction, respectively. Tetrick and Quick (2011) integrate the psychologically healthy workplace model and the public health model and describe specific primary, secondary, and tertiary interventions for each of the five categories of healthy workplace practices (i.e., employee involvement, health and safety, growth and development, work–life balance, employee recognition).

It is important to note that the success of any workplace effort is based in part on addressing the challenges unique to the particular organization and tailoring programs and policies to meet its specific needs. Workplace practices do not exist in isolation and creating a healthy workplace culture goes well beyond a wellness program or health promotion initiative. Each workplace practice functions in relation to other programs and policies the organization has in place as well as internal and external environmental factors. The complex nature of these relationships highlights the importance of taking a comprehensive approach to creating a workplace in which both employees and the organization can thrive.

Case example: Tripler Army Medical Center
The attack on Pearl Harbor in 1941 led to the construction of Tripler Army Medical Center (TAMC), which today supports 264 000 local active-duty and retired military personnel, their families and veteran beneficiaries. As the only federal tertiary care hospital in the Pacific Basin, TAMC is home to the Pacific Regional Medical Command, one of six geographically based regional medical commands in the US Army, whose soldiers have been deployed to Iraq and Afghanistan as well as throughout the Pacific Theater.

Employee involvement   TAMC's structure promotes input from staff at all levels. Ten Functional Management Teams report to a Performance Improvement Council composed of staff from various departments. Self-managed work groups address specific standards of care within departments and generate improvement processes that address workload, efficiency, safety, and services. Physicians in training form a Resident Council, which inputs directly to the Director of Medical Education. In addition, two residents are also voting members of the Graduate Medical Education Committee. The Civilian Advisory Council addresses civilian workforce issues and the Partners in Trust of Team develop initiatives to educate and build a culture of trust within the organization.

Health and safety   Dedicated to a safe, healthful environment, TAMC boasts a team of Safety Officers with more than 50 years of collective experience. The Safety Officers represent all departments and are charged with orienting new employees to safe and effective practices. Annual safety education, semi-annual safety inspections, accident investigations, no-smoking policies, quarterly fire drills, a 'Take the Stairs' campaign and holiday safety messages all represent proactive efforts. With individual ergonomic assessments for employees, fitness rooms, on-site yoga, tai-chi, zumba, cardio kickboxing, and presentations from world-renowned speakers, TAMC takes a variety of steps to promote psychological, physical, social, and spiritual wellness in its workforce.

Employee growth and development   In addition to a comprehensive resiliency training, TAMC schedules physician continuing-education activities, nursing staff training events, and professional development offerings that range from basic life support to simulation training. All personnel have access to free Army-sponsored distance-learning courses that cover a broad spectrum of subjects from foreign language classes to computer applications. A locally developed, web-based training system hosts a searchable database of all available training courses, links to online training and completion reports, so department heads and individual employees can monitor attendance and plan their work and training schedules.

Work–life balance   Maintaining a healthy balance during and outside of work hours is paramount at TAMC. Benefits include flex schedules, telework options and 12 weeks or more of paid leave for family/elder-care/childcare. TAMC actively supports self-care and therapeutically trained counselors provide grief support and stress reduction for those who request it. Additionally, increased pay is offered for night shifts and employees have access to a co-op that provides childcare for less than a dollar per day.

Employee recognition   Each year, TAMC recognizes three levels of Employee of the Year, who advance to compete in the Army Medical Command Employee of the Year program. Military personnel test their professional excellence and military fitness in monthly, quarterly, and annual recognition programs. Departments are rewarded with bonuses based on how workload capacity, quality, and administrative processes are managed, which in turn enhance clinical outcomes and patient satisfaction and promote efficiency and data quality. Associated awards are approved at all levels from immediate supervisor up to the President of the United States. The Tripler Commander personally presents honorees with certificates, decorations, medals, and trophies at an official and public monthly awards recognition ceremony.

The bottom line   More than 4000 individuals have completed resiliency training and TAMC has experienced lower turnover rates along with increased clinical productivity, financial performance, and customer satisfaction. A robust collection of TAMC programs motivates both military and civilian personnel to high levels of performance and service, making Tripler the top-rated Army Medical Center in Army Medical Command for performance measures focused on cost, access, and quality of care.

CONCLUSION

From selecting job candidates whose goals and values are aligned with those of the organization and implementing training processes that ensure a match between available skills and the demands of the job, to designing healthy workspaces that are well suited to the nature of the work, the importance of fit is even more critical in unique and challenging work environments.

Whether addressing the isolation of a virtual workforce by training supervisors in the skills necessary to manage remote workers and building a technology infrastructure that helps employees feel connected regardless of their physical locations; managing the hazards of a high-risk industrial setting by fostering a safety culture where employees feel supported, rather than scrutinized; or providing flexible work arrangements that allow the increasing number of employees with caregiving demands to meet their work and non-work responsibilities, matching the employment experience to the needs and expectations of the workforce can help transform even the most challenging work environment into one that promotes high levels of well-being and performance.

REFERENCES

Aldana, S.G. (2001), 'Financial impact of health promotion programs: a comprehensive review of the literature', *American Journal of Health Promotion*, **15**(5), 296–320.

Amabile, T.M. and S.J. Kramer (2010), 'What really motivates workers (#1 in breakthrough ideas for 2010)', *Harvard Business Review*, **88**(1), 44–5.

American Psychological Association (APA) (2012), *Workforce Retention Survey*, accessed 27 June 2014 at http://www.apaexcellence.org/assets/general/2012-retention-survey-final.pdf.

American Psychological Association (APA) (2013a), *2013 Work and Well-Being Survey*, accessed 27 June 2014 at http://www.apaexcellence.org/assets/general/2013-work-and-wellbeing-survey-results.pdf.

American Psychological Association (APA) (2013b), *Communication Technology Implications for Work and Well-Being*, accessed 27 June 2014 at http://www.apaexcellence.org/assets/general/2013-work-and-communication-technology-survey-final.pdf.

American Psychological Association (APA) (2013c), *Stress in America: Are Teens Adopting Adults' Stress Habits?*, accessed 27 June 2014 at http://www.apa.org/news/press/releases/stress/2013/stress-report.pdf.

American Psychological Association (APA) (2014a), 'Psychologically healthy workplaces have lower turnover, embrace diversity and motivate employees to excel' [graph], accessed 27 June 2014 at http://www.apaexcellence.org/assets/general/phwa-2014-combined-charts-1–2.pdf.

American Psychological Association (APA) (2014b), 'Psychologically healthy workplaces support work–life balance, growth and development and employee well-being' [graph], accessed 27 June 2014 at http://www.apaexcellence.org/assets/general/phwa-2014-combined-charts-3–4.pdf.

Browne, J.H. (2000), 'Benchmarking HRM practices in healthy work organizations', *The American Business Review*, **18**(2), 54–61.

Diener, E. (1984), 'Subjective well-being', *Psychological Bulletin*, **95**(3), 542–75.

Fitz-enz, J. (1993), 'The truth about "best practice"', *Human Resource Planning*, **36**(1), 19–26.

Fitz-enz, J. (2000), *The ROI of Human Capital*, New York: AMACOM.

Freeman, R.B. and J. Rogers (1999), *What Workers Want*, Ithaca, NY: Russell Sage Foundation.

Goetzel, R.Z., A.M. Guindon, I.J. Turshen and R.J. Ozminkowski (2001), 'Health and productivity management: establishing key performance measures, benchmarks, and best practices', *Journal of Occupational and Environmental Medicine*, **43**(1), 10–17.

Goetzel, R.Z., D. Shechter, R.J. Ozminkowski, P.F. Marmet, M.J. Tabrizi and E.C. Roemer (2007), 'Promising practices in employer health and productivity management efforts: findings from a benchmarking study', *Journal of Occupational and Environmental Medicine*, **49**(2), 111–30.

Grawitch, M.J., M. Gottschalk and D.C. Munz (2006), 'The path to a healthy workplace: a critical review linking healthy workplace practices, employee well-being, and organizational improvements', *Consulting Psychology Journal: Practice and Research*, **58**(3), 129–47.

Higgins, C.A., L.E. Duxbury and R.H. Irving (1992), 'Work–family conflict and the dual career family', *Organizational Behavior and Human Decision Processes*, **51**(1), 51–75.

Hofmann, D.A. and L.E. Tetrick (2003), 'The etiology of the concept of health: implications for "organizing" individual and organizational health', in D.A. Hofmann and L.E. Tetrick (eds), *Health and Safety in Organizations: A Multilevel Perspective* San Francisco, CA: Jossey-Bass, pp. 1–6.

Lawler, E.E., III (1991), 'Participative management strategies', in J.W. Jones, B.D. Steffy and D.W. Bray (eds), *Applying Psychology in Business: The Handbook for Managers and Human Resource Professionals*, Lexington, KY: Lexington Books, pp. 578–86.

McFarlin, S.K. and W. Fals-Stewart (2002), 'Workplace absenteeism and alcohol use: a sequential analysis', *Psychology of Addictive Behaviors*, **16**(1), 17–21.

Munz, D.C., J.M. Kohler and C.I. Greenberg (2001), 'Effectiveness of a comprehensive worksite stress management program: combining organizational and individual interventions', *International Journal of Stress Management*, **8**(1), 49–62.

O'Donnell, M., C. Bishop and K. Kaplan (1997), 'Benchmarking best practices in workplace health promotion', *Art of Health Promotion*, **1**(1), 1–8.

Pfeffer, J. (1994), *Competitive Advantage Through People: Unleashing the Power of the Work Force*, Boston, MA: Harvard Business School Press.

Pfeffer, J. (1998), *The Human Equation*, Boston, MA: Harvard Business School Press.

Rath, T. and J. Harter (2010), *Wellbeing: The Five Essential Elements*, New York: Gallup Press.

Rosen, R.H. and L. Berger (1991), *The Healthy Company: Eight Strategies to Develop People, Productivity, and Profits*, Los Angeles, CA: Jeremy P. Tarcher, Inc.

Sauter, S., S. Lim and L. Murphy (1996), 'Organizational health: a new paradigm for occupational stress research at NIOSH', *Japanese Journal of Occupational Mental Health*, **4**(4), 248–54.

Scandura, T.A. and M.J. Lankau (1997), 'Relationships of gender, family responsibility, and flexible work hours to organizational commitment and job satisfaction', *Journal of Organizational Behavior*, **18**(4), 377–91.

Tetrick, L.E. and J.C. Quick (2011), 'Overview of occupational health psychology: public health in occupational settings', in J.C. Quick and L.E. Tetrick (eds), *Handbook of Occupational Health Psychology*, 2nd edition, Washington, DC: American Psychological Association, pp. 3–20.

Turner, N., J. Barling and A. Zacharatos (2002), 'Positive psychology at work', in C.R. Snyder and S.J. Lopez (eds), *Handbook of Positive Psychology*, Oxford: Oxford University Press, pp. 715–28.

Vandenberg, R.J., H.A. Richardson and L.J. Eastman (1999), 'The impact of high involvement work processes on organizational effectiveness: a second-order latent variable approach', *Group and Organization Management*, **24**, 300–39.

Warr, P.B. (1987), *Work, Unemployment, and Mental Health*, Oxford: Oxford University Press.

PART II

Improving workplace health and well-being

4. Enhancing the psychological capital of teams: adapting an individual-level intervention for multi-level delivery and evaluation

Sarah Dawkins and Angela Martin

Positive psychology interventions focused on the conditions and processes that contribute to the flourishing or optimal functioning of people, groups and institutions (Gable and Haidt, 2005) are increasingly used in organizations as a complement to those controlling risks to psychological health (LaMontagne et al., 2014). Team/group- and organizational-level positive approaches are being developed, and may prove to yield greater benefits than individual-level approaches or to enhance their effects (ibid.). However, given growing emphasis on multi-level conceptualization and measurement of the construct of employee well-being we note that assessing the impact of team interventions at the individual level is problematic (Martin et al., 2014).

This chapter outlines an example of a positive organizational behaviour intervention that has been reconceptualized for delivery and evaluation within a multi-level framework. First we describe the concept of psychological capital (a superordinate construct representing the psychological resources of hope, resilience, self-efficacy and optimism that positively impact work performance) and review the evidence on the effectiveness of interventions to develop these resources in employees. Next, we argue that teams could benefit from the development of psychological capital as a 'shared psychological resource', and develop a multi-level model showing how individual- and team-level psychological capital interact and how this could be harnessed in a team-level intervention. Finally, we discuss measurement and research design issues related to evaluating this form of intervention and provide recommendations to researchers and practitioners interested in implementing the model we have presented.

WHAT IS PSYCHOLOGICAL CAPITAL AND CAN IT BE DEVELOPED?

The paradigm of positive organizational behaviour (POB) encompasses research and practice specifically focused on positive human strengths applicable to the workplace (Luthans, 2002; West et al., 2009). It has tended to develop from the individual level (e.g., Luthans, Avolio et al., 2007), but more recently has started to include team/group (e.g., Clapp-Smith et al., 2009; Peterson and Zhang, 2011) and organizational (Avey, Wernsing and Luthans, 2008) levels of analysis. POB is differentiated from the general area of positive psychology and other positive organization research approaches (e.g., positive organizational scholarship; see Cameron et al., 2003) by its definitional inclusion criteria, which require a psychological capacity to be (1) measurable, (2) open to development and (3) impactful on work performance.

Since the inception of POB, several psychological capacities have been examined, both conceptually and empirically. To date, the four constructs deemed to best fit the POB inclusion criteria are 'self-efficacy', 'hope', 'optimism' and 'resilience' (Luthans, Youssef and Avolio, 2007). Research attention is now being devoted to a core construct representing an individual's positive psychological state of development known as psychological capital, or 'PsyCap', which is indicated by these four psychological resources (ibid.).

From a PsyCap perspective, 'hope' is defined as persevering towards goals, and when necessary, redirecting paths to goals (ibid.). Thus, it represents a positive motivational state that is based on successful agency and pathways to achieve goals (Snyder et al., 1991). Positive relationships between hope and job satisfaction and staff retention have been reported (Luthans and Youssef, 2004) and hope protects individuals against perceptions of stress (Snyder, 2000).

PsyCap 'self-efficacy' relates to having the confidence to take on and put in the necessary effort to succeed at challenging tasks (Luthans, Youssef and Avolio, 2007). Self-efficacy has been associated with desirable work-related outcomes such as performance and satisfaction (Stajkovic and Luthans, 1998) and is negatively related to job stress (Matsui and Onglatco, 1992) and turnover intentions (Harris and Cameron, 2005).

PsyCap 'resilience' refers to the capacity to 'bounce back' and even beyond to attain success when faced with problems and adversity (Luthans, Youssef and Avolio, 2007). Positive relationships between resilience and job satisfaction have been demonstrated (Youssef and Luthans, 2007). Additionally, resilience enables individuals to better cope with job-related tension (Tugade and Fredrickson, 2004) and enhances organizational commitment (Youssef and Luthans, 2007).

Finally, PsyCap 'optimism' refers to making positive attributions about succeeding now and in the future (Luthans, Youssef and Avolio, 2007). It has been theorized that positive expectations provide a motivational propensity that enhances the degree of effort expended by individuals (Scheier and Carver, 1985). This relationship has been empirically demonstrated; higher optimism is positively associated with increased job performance and satisfaction (Youssef and Luthans, 2007) and reduced turnover (Seligman, 1998; Luthans, Avolio et al., 2007). Moreover, optimism provides an important buffer against the effects of job tension (Totterdell et al., 2006).

PsyCap is positioned as a higher-order construct, ostensibly a manifest variable comprised of the four factors. It has been found that the second-order construct of PsyCap produces higher correlations with performance outcomes than any of its individual components alone (Luthans, Avolio et al., 2007). Thus, it is suggested that PsyCap appears to have a synergistic effect, whereby the whole (PsyCap) may be greater than the sum of its parts (Luthans, Youssef and Avolio, 2007). Avey et al. (2011) suggest that this effect occurs because PsyCap incorporates the coping mechanism(s) that the four factors have in common. This mechanism process is attributed to psychological resource theory (Hobfoll, 2002), whereby it is suggested that some constructs (i.e., hope, self-efficacy, resilience, optimism) are indicators of broader, multidimensional 'core' factors (i.e., PsyCap). Thus, while individual constructs may be psychometrically valid in their own right, they can also be considered as 'markers' of an overarching multidimensional core construct (Avey et al., 2011). To help illustrate this theoretical position, Avey et al. (2011) draw parallels with other organizational behaviour constructs including core self-evaluation traits (Judge and Bono, 2001), transformational leadership (Antonakis et al., 2003) and empowerment (Spreitzer, 1995) where each construct is considered a second-order factor consisting of shared variance between individual predictive components.

Consistent with POB criteria, PsyCap has been purported as a resource that can be leveraged for organizational competitive advantage (Luthans, Youssef and Avolio, 2007). As such, concerted research has been conducted to demonstrate the utility of PsyCap, particularly in relation to employee performance and functioning (see Avey, Reichard et al., 2011). This research has demonstrated manifold positive effects of PsyCap, even after controlling for demographic factors, personality traits (e.g., core self-evaluations) and employee/organization and employee/job fit analyses (Youssef and Luthans, 2011). Specifically, PsyCap is reported to be positively related to both employee-rated job performance (e.g., Luthans et al., 2005; Luthans, Avolio et al., 2007; Luthans, Avey et al., 2008; Luthans,

Norman et al., 2008; Rego et al., 2010; Avey, Avolio and Luthans, 2011) and objective or manager-rated employee job performance (Luthans et al., 2010; Peterson et al., 2011).

Additionally, PsyCap has been positively associated with other desirable employee attitudes and behaviours including job satisfaction (Larson and Luthans, 2006; Luthans, Avolio et al., 2007; Cheung et al., 2011), organizational commitment (Larson and Luthans, 2006; Avey et al., 2009), psychological well-being and work-related happiness (Avey, Luthans et al., 2010; Culbertson et al., 2010), and organizational citizenship behaviours (OCBs; Gooty et al., 2009; Avey, Luthans and Youssef, 2010).

Research has also demonstrated negative associations between PsyCap and undesirable employee attitudes and behaviours, including cynicism and intent to quit (Avey, Hughes et al., 2008; Avey, Wernsing et al., 2008; Avey et al., 2009; Avey, Luthans and Youssef, 2010), absenteeism (Avey et al., 2006) and workplace deviance (Avey, Wernsing et al., 2008; Norman et al., 2010).

The primary explanation for these relationships is that employees with higher PsyCap tend to expect good things to happen to them at work (optimism); believe they can create their own success (hope and efficacy); and are persistent in the face of challenges (resilience) when compared with employees with lower PsyCap (Avey, Reichard et al., 2011).

PsyCap and its individual components are also considered 'state-like' in nature (Avey, Luthans and Youssef, 2010). This state-like concept is supported by a theoretical distinction between PsyCap and other positive psychology constructs including Big Five traits and core self-evaluations (CSEs). This distinction is based on a continuum perspective dichotomized by 'pure' poles of state and trait, with PsyCap positioned as mid-range and therefore a 'state-like' construct that is relatively malleable and open to development (see Figure 4.1; Luthans, Youssef and Avolio, 2007). As such, PsyCap is differentiated from both stable, fixed traits (e.g., Big Five, CSEs) and pure, transient states (e.g., moods and emotions). Empirically,

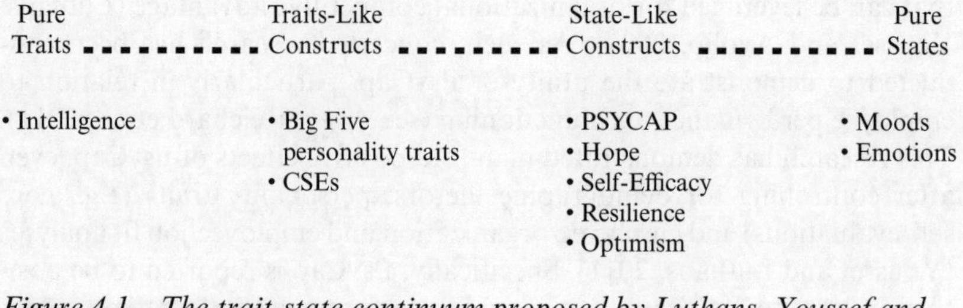

Pure Traits	Traits-Like Constructs	State-Like Constructs	Pure States
• Intelligence	• Big Five personality traits • CSEs	• PSYCAP • Hope • Self-Efficacy • Resilience • Optimism	• Moods • Emotions

Figure 4.1   The trait-state continuum proposed by Luthans, Youssef and Avolio (2007)

convergence and divergence evidence between PsyCap and other related positive constructs has been provided to further support the state-like nature of PsyCap and its overall construct validity (see Dawkins et al., 2013 for detailed psychometric review and critical analysis of the PsyCap construct).

As noted earlier, a definitional criterion for POB constructs is openness to development. Accordingly, a micro-intervention aimed at enhancing individuals' level of PsyCap has been developed. The PsyCap intervention (PCI: Luthans et al., 2006, 2010) has been empirically assessed, in both online (Luthans, Avey and Patera, 2008) and in-house delivery formats (Luthans et al., 2010). Initial evidence has demonstrated significant increases in PsyCap via these brief training interventions, with small- to medium-effect sizes reported ($d = 0.31–0.40$; ibid.). As controlled experimental methodologies were employed, this research suggests that PsyCap training has a causal impact on improving participants' performance (ibid.).

The PCI model (summarized in Figure 4.2) has been developed with three primary goals: (1) to be brief in duration and thus minimize

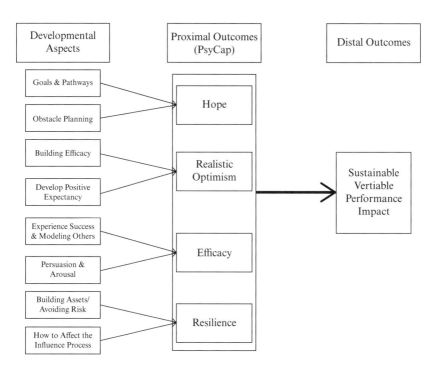

Source: Adapted from Luthans et al. (2006).

Figure 4.2   Overview of the PsyCap intervention

disruption to the workplace; (2) to enhance each of the four dimensions of PsyCap; and (3) to enhance overall PsyCap through integration of the underlying principles and developmental aspects of each of the four individual PsyCap resources (ibid.). Thus, the intervention focuses on the development of each individual state of PsyCap, as well as overall PsyCap.

The PCI involves a series of exercises specific to each individual component of PsyCap, along with more integrative reflective exercises that are aimed at incorporating the development of the individual component training into an understanding and operationalization of overall PsyCap (Luthans et al., 2010). For instance, employees are asked to consider a personally meaningful work goal. In identifying this goal, the employee is assisted by the facilitator to phrase the goal so as to enhance 'agentic capacity' (Bandura, 2008) and to 'step' goals into manageable units (Snyder, 2000). The employee is then guided to generate several pathways that could enable them to achieve this goal. Luthans et al. (2010) outline that a critical element of the PCI delivery is facilitated in small group discussions; thus employees are encouraged to share their goals and pathways with the group in order to generate additional pathways and model positive goal-setting behaviour to the group.

This bi-directional group process of vicarious learning and modelling is posited to further enhance participants' level of self-efficacy through the generation of additional pathways to achieve their stated goal, while also promoting positive expectations (optimism) to achieve it. In addition, it is theorized that the generation of multiple pathways for goal achievement increases participants' resilience as it enables them to 'bounce back' by selecting an alternative pathway, if an original pathway is blocked or met with challenge (ibid.).

The final element of the PCI is directed towards optimism development by increasing participants' self-awareness of negative cognitions they may possess when faced with a challenge or problem at work. The optimism development phase of the PCI is based upon cognitive-behavioural theory that posits that people tend to make automatic, unfounded, negative cognitions when confronted with problems or challenges, which in turn generates negative behaviours (e.g., 'This is hopeless, I can't possibly complete this report by the deadline. I give up!'). The PCI optimism development phase aims to counter negative cognitive distortions by encouraging participants to identify and challenge negative cognitions and replace these with more positively oriented and realistic expectations (e.g., 'This report is going to take a lot of work, but I have done similar reports before and can do this one if I keep working at it').

Building on research that has established the efficacy of the PCI in relation to enhanced PsyCap and improved job performance (ibid.), PsyCap proponents have also reported a quantifiable return on investment for the PCI. Preliminary utility analyses have estimated robust return of investment (ROI) in excess of 200 per cent (see Luthans, Youssef and Avolio, 2007, for detailed quantitative utility analysis based on varying corporate data).

PSYCHOLOGICAL CAPITAL: A TEAM-LEVEL RESOURCE

In addition to individual-level research, it has been assumed that PsyCap can also be experienced at team level (Clapp-Smith et al., 2009; Petersen and Zhang, 2011; Vanno et al., 2014). Although these studies have been divergent in the approach to the conceptualization and measurement of collective PsyCap (which will be discussed in more detail later in the chapter), they provide initial empirical support for the notion of collective PsyCap at the team level. In particular, these studies have demonstrated positive relationships between team-level PsyCap and team performance (ibid.). A comprehensive examination of the theoretical conceptualization of a collective, or team-level PsyCap construct has already been detailed (Dawkins et al., 2014a) and as such, an abridged synopsis of these theoretical foundations is provided here.

Drawing on the definition of collective efficacy ('a group's shared belief in its conjoint capabilities': Bandura, 1997, p. 477), collective (team-level) PsyCap has been defined as 'the team's shared positive appraisal of their circumstances and probability for success under those circumstances based on their combined motivated effort and perseverance' (Peterson and Zhang, 2011, p. 134).

Similar to other team-level constructs, such as collective efficacy, collective PsyCap refers to aggregation from the individual to the team level. Accordingly, Peterson and Zhang (2011) posited that like collective efficacy, collective PsyCap is 'the product of the interactive and coordinative dynamics of its members' (Bandura, 1997, pp. 477–8). Thus, by this reasoning, the social interaction and synergistic processes inherent to teams are critical for the emergence of team-level PsyCap.

Similarly, West et al. (2009) proposed that collective psychological resources (i.e., hope, efficacy and resilience) emerge through 'contagion' processes within a group. Accordingly, an individual's positive emotions and behaviours may elicit positive emotions and behaviours within other group members, creating a dynamic, spiralling process that may contribute to the formation of positive affective homogeneity (Fredrickson, 2003).

In our own research, we have further developed these early theories of collective PsyCap by positing the processes by which collective (i.e., team-level) PsyCap emerges (Dawkins et al., 2014a). As outlined above, a critical element of the current definition of collective PsyCap is a sense of 'sharedness' among members of a collective (i.e., team) regarding their perceptions of PsyCap. Specifically, we suggest that that social contagion processes play a role in the emergence of PsyCap at higher levels (i.e., team level). Social contagion refers to the process of communicating and exchanging information among members of a collective, which results in a shared perception regarding some aspect pertinent to the team (Degoey, 2000). Thus, individuals adopt the attitudes and beliefs of others who influence them.

PsyCap can become shared among team members via communications regarding the team's functions and operations. For instance, a central aspect for PsyCap hope development is a planning process for goals that involves goal design, pathway generation and planning for obstacles (Luthans et al., 2010). Thus, when team members are actively engaged in team goal-oriented discussions, they have the opportunity to exchange beliefs and generate multiple pathways towards team goals, establishing a greater sense of team agency. Similarly, team discussions related to obstacle planning may provide a foundation for shared optimism expectations and social exchange among team members regarding previous team failures or team goal attainment may also foster shared resilience and efficacy perceptions.

DESIGNING A MULTI-LEVEL PSYCHOLOGICAL CAPITAL INTERVENTION TO ENHANCE BOTH INDIVIDUAL AND TEAM CAPACITIES

We suggest that the primary components of the PCI, reviewed previously and summarized in Figure 4.2 are amenable to adaption to a team-focused training intervention. As such, a model for a proposed team-focused PCI (*t*PCI) is provided in Figure 4.3. This model demonstrates how the goals and training exercises of the current PCI could be adapted so to encompass a team focus and thereby aim to bolster team-level PsyCap. However, as shown in Figure 4.3, we suggest that the proposed *t*PCI retain elements of the individual-focused PsyCap development as they relate to identified team goals so as to potentially simultaneously enhance individual-level PsyCap, essentially creating a multi-level intervention. For example, the team efficacy component of the *t*PCI encourages the team to devise a specific plan for goal attainment, incorporating team reflection on past

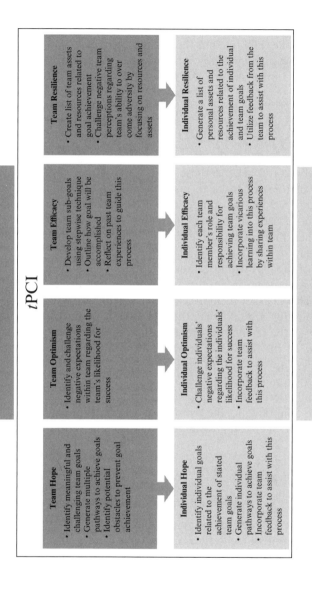

TEAM-LEVEL PSYCAP

Team Hope
• Identify meaningful and challenging team goals
• Generate multiple pathways to achieve goals
• Identify potential obstacles to prevent goal achievement

Team Optimism
• Identify and challenge negative expectations within team regarding the team's likelihood for success

Team Efficacy
• Develop team sub-goals using stepwise technique
• Outline how goal will be accomplished
• Reflect on past team experiences to guide this process

Team Resilience
• Create list of team assets and resources related to goal achievement
• Challenge negative team perceptions regarding team's ability to over come adversity by focusing on resources and assets

*t*PCI

Individual Hope
• Identify individual goals related to the achievement of stated team goals
• Generate individual pathways to achieve goals
• Incorporate team feedback to assist with this process

Individual Optimism
• Challenge individuals' negative expectations regarding the individuals' likelihood for success
• Incorporate team feedback to assist with this process

Individual Efficacy
• Identify each team member's role and responsibility for achieving team goals
• Incorporate vicarious learning into this process by sharing experiences within team

Individual Resilience
• Generate a list of personal assets and resources related to the achievement of individual and team goals
• Utilize feedback from the team to assist with this process

INDIVIDUAL-LEVEL PSYCAP

Figure 4.3   A model of the proposed team-focused PsyCap intervention (tPCI)

experiences to guide this process. However, as a sub-component of team efficacy development, team members would also be encouraged to identify their own related individual plans and responsibilities to ensure the successful achievement of stated team goals. Thus, while aspects of individual-level PsyCap development would be incorporated into the *t*PCI, the primary and overall focus of the *t*PCI remains the enhancement of *team-level* PsyCap.

The model also highlights how many aspects of the current PCI format (as described by Luthans et al., 2010) provide for a conceivable and logical extension to the team level. For instance, the current individual-level PCI delivery is provided in a small group format in order to enable vicarious learning and modelling between participants; thus, a *t*PCI would utilize a similar delivery format. However, as indicated in Figure 4.3, the *t*PCI would primarily focus on the generation of meaningful *team* goals and multiple pathways to achieve these goals (team hope), including specific designation of roles or tasks to team members. Likewise, the focus of the optimism development component of the PCI would be modified to become team-focused through examination of how the collective team responds when faced with challenges/problems and generating alternative, positively oriented team-based approaches. Finally, the resilience component of the PCI would be adapted so that team members focus on the identification of meaningful team resources and assets that the team possess, which will assist them in team goal attainment.

The reasons for arguing that the *t*PCI may be an effective training intervention at the team level are grounded in both theory and empirical research. At the individual level the PCI has been shown to bolster individual PsyCap and in turn have a positive effect on distal outcomes including performance (Luthans et al., 2010). Moreover, similar interventions originally developed to enhance individual-level efficacy have been shown to be adaptable to the team level – bolstering collective efficacy and subsequently increasing team performance (e.g., verbal self-guidance training; Brown, 2003).

Based on collective efficacy theory (Bandura, 1986, 1997), we suggest that the same mechanisms that bolster hope, optimism, resilience and efficacy and overall PsyCap at the individual level can also enhance these capacities at the team level. Chan (1998, p. 239) argued that collective efficacy is 'derived from the original construct [of] self-efficacy' and as such the basic content (self-efficacy) does not change as one moves to a new form (collective efficacy); rather, only the referent changes from self to team. Thus, similar to Chan's perspective regarding collective efficacy, we propose that the primary components of the PCI that serve to bolster individual-level PsyCap will also be effective in bolstering team-level PsyCap by adapting a team-referent focus.

KEY ISSUES IN EVALUATING A MULTI-LEVEL PSYCHOLOGICAL CAPITAL INTERVENTION

Measurement of Psychological Capital at the Team Level

Measurement of team-level PsyCap has been mainly operationalized in two ways: a direct-consensus approach, which aggregates individual PsyCap to the team level (Clapp-Smith et al., 2009; Peterson and Zhang, 2011), and a referent-shift approach (Vanno et al., 2014). The direct-consensus model implements within-group consensus of the lower-level units as the functional relationship to specify how the construct at the lower level is functionally isomorphic to another form of the construct at the higher level (Chan, 1998). Typically, a within-group agreement index (e.g., rWG: James et al., 1984) of the scores from the lower level with a certain cut-off value (i.e., 0.70) is employed to represent within-group consensus, and therefore justify aggregation of the construct to the higher level. When consensus within the unit does not reach the predetermined cut-off value, it is assumed that there is insufficient agreement in the unit to warrant aggregation to the higher level (Klein et al., 2001). Thus, team PsyCap measured using the direct-consensus model requires shared perceptions among team members with regard to their own individual-referent PsyCap (e.g., 'I feel confident helping to set targets/goals in my work area').

The referent-shift model shares some procedural similarities with the direct-consensus approach, in so far as justification for aggregation to the higher level is dependent upon sufficient within-group consensus. However, unlike direct consensus where the referent of interest is the individual's experience or perceptions (i.e., 'I feel confident. . .'), the referent-shift model focuses on the individual's perception of the unit as a whole (i.e., 'My team feels confident. . .'). This new referent is then combined to represent the higher-level construct providing sufficient within-group agreement (Rupp et al., 2007).

Although both the direct-consensus and referent-shift measurement approaches have demonstrated positive associations between team-level PsyCap and team-level outcomes, arguably two distinct constructs are being measured using these approaches. Mischel and Northcraft (1997) suggested that the cognition of 'Can *we* do this task?' (referent-shift consensus) is different from the cognition of 'Can *I* do this task?' (direct-consensus). Chan (1998) further suggested that referent-shift composition is important because it results in a new form of the construct that is conceptually distinct from the original construct. For example, it has been suggested that the aggregation of team members' individual self-efficacy scores as a representation of collective efficacy would be flawed, as mean scores would represent individual members' perceptions of themselves, and not their perceptions regarding the team as a whole (Guzzo et al., 1993).

Our own research has provided the first known empirical investigation of the viability of these two different compositional models for operationalizing team PsyCap (Dawkins et al., 2014b). Using hierarchical linear modelling (HLM), the study compared two compositional models of aggregation (direct-consensus and referent-shift; Chan, 1998) to represent the construct of team PsyCap. The findings revealed significant associations between team-level PsyCap and both individual-level (job satisfaction and turnover intentions) and team-level outcomes (performance, satisfaction and conflict). These relationships were significantly stronger when a referent-shift operationalization of team PsyCap was implemented. Thus, greater understanding regarding the influence of team PsyCap on outcome variables is achieved when team members are asked to reflect specifically on their team's shared capacities, rather than amalgamating team members' individual perceptions regarding their own individual psychological capacities.

These results also suggest that team-level PsyCap interventions could be more encompassing than those aimed at developing individual PsyCap (e.g., Luthans et al., 2010), as team-level PsyCap interventions may have the added benefit of enhancing both team-level and individual-level PsyCap, and subsequently, bolstering both team and employee performance and functioning. In providing the first known analysis of the cross-level influence of team PsyCap, our study also showed that in addition to having positive relationships with team-level outcomes (e.g., performance, satisfaction and conflict), team PsyCap was significantly related to individual-level outcomes (e.g., job satisfaction and turnover intentions). These results provide initial evidence to suggest that membership of a positively oriented work team can have multiple benefits in terms of both team functioning and individual employee functioning. Furthermore, the findings emphasize the importance of fostering team-level positivity in organizations, perhaps over and beyond that of individual employee positivity.

Intervention Assessment and Outcomes

A number of measures could be used to assess the utility and outcomes of the proposed *t*PCI. We recommend that direct effects of the intervention be assessed using both individual-level and team-level PsyCap. The 24-item version of the Psychological Capital Questionnaire (PCQ: Luthans, Youssef and Avolio, 2007) has also been adapted to reflect a team referent, rather than an individual referent. This adaption of the PCQ has been implemented in previous research (Dawkins et al., 2014b; Vanno et al., 2014). A 12-item brief measure is also available (PCQ-12; Luthans, Youssef and Avolio, 2007). At a minimum, we also recommend assessment of both individual- and team-level performance and functioning. Team performance and satisfaction assessed by both team members and team leaders (Hirst, 1999) and team organizational citizenship behaviours (Lee and Allen, 2002) may be useful measures. Similarly, both self-reported individual-level performance (Rego and Cunha, 2008) and team-leader rated performance could be assessed (Peterson et al., 2011). Employee mental health symptoms using the K-10 depression/anxiety scale (Kessler et al., 2002) or other more general measures of employee well-being (Goldberg, 1972; Goldberg and Hillier, 1979) and job satisfaction (Warr et al., 1979) are also recommended. Control variables that could be considered include employees' trait-like individual differences using the core self-evaluations measure (Judge et al., 2003) and the positive and negative affect schedule (PANAS-SF: Thompson, 2007) as these constructs have been positively associated with job performance and work success in previous research (e.g., Judge and Bono, 2001; Kluemper et al., 2009).

Data Analysis

There are various data analysis options available for assessing the efficacy of the *t*PCI for enhancing team- and individual-level PsyCap, performance and functioning (in comparison with a wait list or active control condition). We recommend multi-level growth modelling be used to simultaneously analyse intra- and inter-team as well as intra- and inter-individual differences in growth trajectory and post-intervention status across time (pre-intervention, post-intervention and follow up) (Raudenbush et al., 2004).

RECOMMENDATIONS FOR FUTURE RESEARCH AND PRACTICE

Testing the Propositions of the tPCI

Based on both individual- and team-level PsyCap research reviewed, we suggest that exploring the potential for a team-level PsyCap intervention (*t*PCI) would provide a logical and advantageous progression of enquiry. We have suggested that there is potential for developing training interventions aimed at bolstering team PsyCap using mechanisms similar to those aimed at developing individual PsyCap (Luthans et al., 2010). We have argued that the benefits of an intervention aimed at bolstering the collective PsyCap of a team could be more encompassing than interventions focused on individual employees, as both team and employee functioning may be enhanced (Dawkins et al., 2014b). Consequently, the proposed *t*PCI may be far more effective than interventions focusing solely on the individual. As such, it is also possible that a *t*PCI may provide an increased return on investment (ROI) than initial estimates based on the individual-level PCI (see Luthans, Youssef and Avolio, 2007). Future research is required that provides an empirical evidence base regarding these assertions.

Furthermore, team processes, including team communication and shared mental models may also be enhanced as a result of teams simply participating in *t*PCI training. For instance, it has been argued that shared mental models in terms of perceiving, encoding, storing and retrieving information in the same manner is critical for team effectiveness (Langan-Fox et al., 2000). To this end, the *t*PCI requires all team members to reflect and discuss past team experiences, and devise goals and pathways for achieving stated goals, which may also provide a method for generating shared mental models and enhancing communication within teams.

Based on the implications of *t*PCI, we provide a model of the potential benefits of the proposed *t*PCI and a series of testable propositions for future research. As illustrated in Figure 4.4, and based on individual-level research implementing the PCI (e.g., Luthans et al., 2010), the following propositions are made:

Proposition 1:   The tPCI will have a positive effect on team-level PsyCap.

Proposition 2:   The tPCI will a have positive effect on team-level outcomes including team performance and satisfaction and team conflict.

Furthermore, as shown in Figure 4.3, the proposed *t*PCI is an adaption of the PCI, and as such, it retains some individual-focused aspects for development, in addition to the core team-focused components. Thus, we suggest that it is conceivable that individual team member PsyCap may also be bolstered via participation in the *t*PCI:

Proposition 3:   The tPCI will have a positive cross-level effect on individual-level PsyCap.

Additionally, based on recent cross-level research (Dawkins et al., 2014b) we suggest that enhancement of team PsyCap via the *t*PCI may in

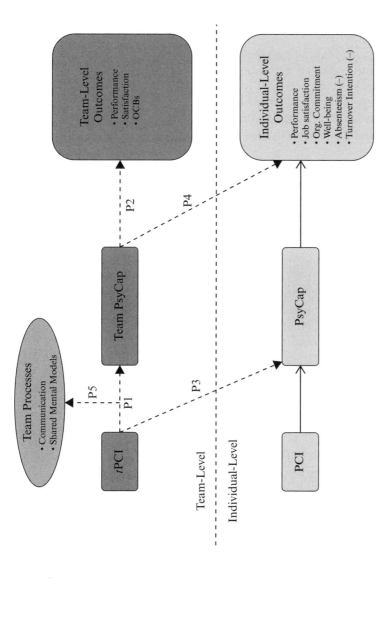

Note: P1–P5 indicate corresponding research propositions.

Figure 4.4 *Proposed team-level and cross-level benefits of the tPCI contrasted with empirically demonstrated effects of the current individual-level PCI*

93

turn have a positive effect on individual-level outcomes, such as job satisfaction and turnover intentions:

Proposition 4:   The tPCI will have a positive effect on individual-level outcomes including job satisfaction and turnover intentions.

Finally, given that the proposed *t*PCI requires team members to communicate and exchange perceptions regarding previous team performances and positive expectancies for future performance and functioning, we also suggest that engagement in the *t*PCI might provide opportunity for teams to enhance critical processes for team effectiveness including shared mental models and team communication:

Proposition 5:   Engagement in the tPCI will provide ancillary benefit by enhancing team processes including shared mental models and team communication.

Broader Research Opportunities

Future research that helps to create better understanding of the mechanisms of effect of PsyCap interventions may also help to inform further development and refinement of the both the *t*PCI described here and the original PCI (Luthans et al., 2010). Currently, it is assumed that individuals must engage in the development of all four components of PsyCap (hope, efficacy, resilience and optimism) in order to achieve the benefits of the PCI. However, research is yet to determine whether development of all four components is in fact necessary to produce the desired effects of PsyCap development (e.g., enhanced job performance). In other words, it may be possible that by focusing on the development of one or two PsyCap components, intervention effects similar to when overall PsyCap is developed could be observed (Luthans et al., 2010). This line of enquiry could result in the development of more cost- and time-effective PsyCap interventions.

Future research opportunities also remain to explore the application of the PCI and the *t*PCI proposed here to different work contexts. Research to date has been limited in exploring the efficacy of the PCI within mid- to large-sized companies and organizations (e.g., Luthans, Avey and Patera, 2008; Luthans et al., 2010). Given that the interaction between setting, intervention (training) and outcomes is complex, the question of transferability of the intervention to other contexts is crucial for evidence-based research (Cambon et al., 2012). Thus, further investigation is needed to determine the transferability of the PCI to other organizational contexts, including the SME sector (Martin et al., 2009) and to consider the potential influence of contextual predictors, moderators and outcomes in assessing the efficacy of the *t*PCI and PCI.

As multi-level PsyCap research continues to develop, avenues arise in which to investigate organizational-level PsyCap and the interplay between PsyCap at multiple levels (i.e., beyond individual/team level). Although it is generally acknowledged that positive organizational practices do not necessarily create positive individual employees or vice versa (Youssef and Luthans, 2012), there is untapped opportunity to investigate the mechanisms that facilitate or hinder the cross-level transfer of positivity. As outlined above, this line of enquiry would require sophisticated research methodologies (e.g., growth models) to consider the inter-relationships among constructs across various levels in a dynamic framework (e.g., changes across time). For instance, how does tenure moderate the relationship between organizational culture and employee PsyCap? Investigation of cross-level transfer of positivity will provide further understanding of the utility of PsyCap and PsyCap interventions for organizations, work teams and individual employees alike.

CONCLUSION

As organizations become increasingly reliant on team-based structures to function more effectively and efficiently, there have been calls from practitioners and researchers for methods of improving the functioning of teams. In response to such calls, this chapter leverages off emerging team-level PsyCap research, which has demonstrated positive associations between team PsyCap and team and individual employee functioning, to provide a rationale for the development of a team-focused PsyCap intervention aimed at bolstering team PsyCap. The chapter provides a proposed model for the team-focused intervention (*t*PCI), adapted from the current individual-level PCI, and highlights the potential benefits of such an intervention in terms of both team and individual employee performance and functioning. Finally, initial research propositions directed towards encouraging and guiding future team-level PsyCap development research have been provided. It is envisaged that adoption of these directives for future research will contribute to improving the effectiveness of teams and thereby enhance the utility of team PsyCap within HRD and management practices.

REFERENCES

Antonakis, J., B.J. Avolio and N. Sivasubramaniam (2003), 'Context and leadership: an examination of the nine-factor full-range leadership theory using the Multifactor Leadership Questionnaire', *The Leadership Quarterly*, **14**(3), 261–95.

Avey, J.B., B.J. Avolio and F. Luthans (2011), 'Experimentally analyzing the impact of leader positivity on follower positivity and performance', *The Leadership Quarterly*, **22**(2), 282–94.

Avey, J.B., F. Luthans and S.M. Jensen (2009), 'Psychological capital: a positive resource for combating employee stress and turnover', *Human Resource Management*, **48**(5), 677–93.

Avey, J.B., F. Luthans and C.M. Youssef (2010), 'The additive value of positive psychological capital in predicting work attitudes and behaviors', *Journal of Management*, **36**(2), 430–52.

Avey, J.B., J.L. Patera and B.J. West (2006), 'The implications of positive psychological capital on employee absenteeism', *Journal of Leadership and Organizational Studies*, **13**(2), 42–60.

Avey, J.B., T.S. Wernsing and F. Luthans (2008), 'Can positive employees help positive organizational change? Impact of psychological capital and emotions on relevant attitudes and behaviors', *The Journal of Applied Behavioral Science*, **44**(1), 48–70.

Avey, J.B., L.W. Hughes, S.M. Norman and K.W. Luthans (2008), 'Using positivity, transformational leadership and empowerment to combat employee negativity', *Leadership and Organizational Development Journal*, **29**(2), 110–26.

Avey, J.B., F. Luthans, R.M. Smith and N.F. Palmer (2010), 'Impact of positive psychological capital on employee well-being over time', *Journal of Occupational Health Psychology*, **15**(1), 17–28.

Avey, J.B., R.J. Reichard, F. Luthans and K.H. Mharte (2011), 'Meta-analysis of the impact of positive psychological capital on employee attitudes, behaviors, and performance', *Human Resource Development Quarterly*, **22**(2), 127–52.

Bandura, A. (1986), *Social Foundations of Thought and Actions: A Social Cognitive Theory*, Englewood Cliffs, NJ: Prentice Hall.

Bandura, A. (1997), *Self-efficacy: The Exercise of Control*, New York: Freeman.

Bandura, A. (2008), 'An agentic perspective on positive psychology', in S.J. Lopez (ed.), *Positive Psychology: Exploring the Best in People, Vol. 1*, Westport CT: Greenwood Publishing, pp. 167–96.

Brown, T.C. (2003), 'The effect of verbal self-guidance training on collective efficacy and team performance', *Personnel Psychology*, **56**(4), 935–64.

Cambon, L., L. Minary, V. Ridde and F. Alla (2012), 'Transferability of interventions in health education: a review', *BMC Public Health*, **12**(1), 497.

Cameron, K., J. Dutton and R. Quinn (eds) (2003), *Positive Organizational Scholarship: Foundations of a New Discipline*, San Francisco, CA: Berrett-Koehler.

Chan, D. (1998), 'Functional relations among constructs in the same content domain at different levels of analysis: a typology of composition models', *Journal of Applied Psychology*, **83**(2), 234–46.

Cheung, F., C.S. Tang and S. Tang (2010), 'Psychological capital as a moderator between emotional labor, burnout, and job satisfaction among school teachers in China', *International Journal of Stress Management*, **18**(4), 348–71.

Clapp-Smith, R., G.R. Vogelgesang and J.B. Avey (2009), 'Authentic leadership and positive psychological capital: the mediating role of trust at the group level of analysis', *Journal of Leadership and Organizational Studies*, **15**(3), 227–40.

Culbertson, S., C.J. Fullager and M.J. Mills (2010), 'Feeling good and doing great: the relationship between psychological capital and well-being', *Journal of Occupational Health Psychology*, **15**(4), 421–33.

Dawkins, S., A. Martin, J. Scott and K. Sanderson (2013), 'Building on the positives: a psychometric review and critical analysis of the construct of psychological capital', *Journal of Occupational and Organizational Psychology*, **86**(3), 348–70.

Dawkins, S., A. Martin, J. Scott and K. Sanderson (2014a), 'Advancing the conceptualization and measurement of psychological capital as a collective construct', provisionally accepted for publication in *Human Relations*, 6 June 2014.

Dawkins, S., A. Martin, J. Scott, K. Sanderson and B. Schüz (2014b), 'Comparing compositional approaches in a cross-level model of team psychological capital' (unpublished manuscript, PhD thesis, University of Tasmania).

Degoey, P. (2000), 'Contagious justice: exploring the social construction of justice in organizations', *Research in Organizational Behavior*, **22**, 51–102.

Fredrickson, B.L. (2003), 'Positive emotions and upward spirals in organizations', in K.S. Cameron, J.E. Dutton and R.E. Quinn (eds), *Positive Organizational Scholarship: Foundations of a New Discipline*, San Francisco, CA: Berrett-Koehler, pp. 163–75.

Gable, S.L. and J. Haidt (2005), 'What (and why) is positive psychology?', *Review of General Psychology*, **9**(2), 103–10.

Goldberg, D.P. (1972), *The Detection of Psychiatric Illness by Questionnaire*, Oxford: Oxford University Press.

Goldberg, D.P. and V.F. Hillier (1979), 'A scaled version of the General Health Questionnaire', *Psychological Medicine*, **9**(1), 139–45.

Gooty, J., M. Gavin, P.D. Johnson, L.M. Frazier and B.D. Snow (2009), 'In the eyes of the beholder: transformational leadership, positive psychological capital, and performance', *Journal of Leadership and Organizational Studies*, **15**(4), 353–67.

Guzzo, R.A., P.R. Yost, R.J. Campbell and G.P. Shea (1993), 'Potency in groups: articulating a construct', *British Journal of Social Psychology*, **32**(1), 87–106.

Harris, G.E. and J.E. Cameron (2005), 'Multiple dimensions of organizational identification and commitment as predictors of turnover intentions and psychological well-being', *Canadian Journal of Behavioural Science*, **37**(3), 159–69.

Hirst, G. (1999), 'The relationship between team communication and R&D project performance: a five factor model', PhD thesis, University of Melbourne.

Hobfoll, S. (2002), 'Social and psychological resources and adaptation', *Review of General Psychology*, **6**(4), 307–24.

James, L.R., R.G. Demaree and G. Wolf (1984), 'Estimating within-group inter-rater reliability with and without response bias', *Journal of Applied Psychology*, **69**(1), 85–98.

Judge, T.A. and J.E. Bono (2001), 'Relationship of core self-evaluation traits – self esteem, generalized self efficacy, locus of control, and emotional stability – with job satisfaction and performance. A meta-analysis', *Journal of Applied Psychology*, **86**(1), 80–92.

Judge, T.A., A. Erez, J.E. Bono and C.J. Thoresen (2003), 'The core self-evaluation scale: development of a measure', *Personnel Psychology*, **56**(2), 303–31.

Kessler, R.C., G. Andrews, L.J. Colpe, E. Hiripi, D.K. Mroczek, S.L.T. Normand,

E.E. Walters and A.M. Zaslavsky et al. (2002), 'Short screening scales to monitor population prevalences and trends in non-specific psychological distress', *Psychological Medicine*, **32**(6), 959–76.

Klein, K.J., A.B. Conn, B. Smith and J.S. Sorra (2001), 'Is everyone in agreement? An exploration of within group agreement in employee perceptions of the work environment', *Journal of Applied Psychology*, **86**(1), 3–16.

Kluemper, D.H., L.M. Little and T. DeGroot (2009), 'State or trait: effects of state optimism on job-related outcomes', *Journal of Organizational Behavior*, **30**(2), 209–31.

LaMontagne, A.D., A. Martin, K. Page, N.J. Reavley, A.J. Noblet, A.J. Milner, T. Keegel and P.M. Smith (2014), 'Workplace mental health: developing an integrated intervention approach', *BMC Psychiatry*, **14**(1), 131.

Langan-Fox, J., S. Code and K. Langfield-Smith (2000), 'Team mental models: techniques, methods and analytical approaches', *Human Factors*, **42**(2), 242–71.

Larson, M. and F. Luthans (2006), 'Potential added value of psychological capital in predicting work attitudes', *Journal of Leadership and Organizational Studies*, **13**(2), 75–92.

Lee, K. and N.J. Allen (2002), 'Organizational citizenship behavior and workplace deviance: the role of affect and cognitions', *Journal of Applied Psychology*, **87**(1), 131–42.

Luthans, F. (2002), 'The need for and meaning of positive organizational behavior', *Journal of Organizational Behavior*, **23**(6), 695–706.

Luthans, F. and C.M. Youssef (2004), 'Human, social and now positive psychological capital management: investing in people for competitive advantage', *Organizational Dynamics*, **33**(2), 143–60.

Luthans, F., J.B. Avey and J.L. Patera (2008), 'Experimental analysis of a web-training intervention to develop positive psychological capital', *Academy of Management Learning and Education*, **7**(2), 209–21.

Luthans, F., C.M. Youssef and B.J. Avolio (2007), *Psychological Capital: Developing the Human Competitive Edge*, Oxford: Oxford University Press.

Luthans, F., J.B. Avey, B.J. Avolio and S. Peterson (2010), 'The development and resulting performance impact of positive psychological capital', *Human Resource Development Quarterly*, **21**(1), 41–66.

Luthans, F., J.B. Avey, R. Clapp-Smith and W. Li (2008), 'More evidence on the value of Chinese workers' psychological capital: a potentially unlimited competitive resource?', *The International Journal of Human Resource Management*, **19**(5), 818–27.

Luthans, F., B.J. Avolio, J.B. Avey and S.M. Norman (2007), 'Positive psychological capital: measurement and relationship with performance and satisfaction', *Personnel Psychology*, **60**(3), 541–72.

Luthans, F., B.J. Avolio, F. Walumbwa and W. Li (2005), 'The psychological capital of Chinese workers: exploring the relationship with performance', *Management and Organizational Review*, **1**(2), 247–69.

Luthans, F., S.M. Norman, B.J. Avolio and J.B. Avey (2008), 'The mediating role of psychological capital in the supportive organizational climate–employee performance relationship', *Journal of Organizational Behavior*, **29**(2), 219–38.

Luthans, F., J.B. Avey, B.J. Avolio, S.M. Norman and G.M. Combs (2006), 'Psychological capital development: towards a micro-intervention', *Journal of Organizational Behavior*, **27**(3), 387–93.

Martin, A., M. Karanika-Murray, C. Biron and K. Sanderson (2014), 'A multi-level conceptualization of the relationship between the psychosocial work environment and employee psychological health: improving intervention design, implementation and evaluation' (under review).

Martin, A., K. Sanderson, J. Scott and P. Brough (2009), 'Promoting mental health in small-medium enterprises: an evaluation of the "Business in Mind" program', *BMC Public Health*, **9**, 239.

Matsui, T. and M.L. Onglatco (1992), 'Career self-efficacy of the relation between occupational stress and strain', *Journal of Vocational Behavior*, **41**(1), 79–88.

Mischel, L.J. and G.B. Northcraft (1997), 'I think we can, I think we can: the role of efficacy beliefs in group and team effectiveness', *Advances in Group Processes*, **14**, 177–97.

Norman, S.M., J.B. Avey, J.L. Nimnicht and N.G. Pigeon (2010), 'The interactive effects of psychological capital and organizational identity on employee organizational citizenship and deviance behaviors', *Journal of Leadership and Organizational Studies*, **17**(4), 380–91.

Peterson, S.J. and Z. Zhang (2011), 'Examining the relationships between top management team psychological characteristics, transformational leadership, and business unit performance', in M.A. Carpenter (ed.), *Handbook of Top Management Research*, Cheltenham, UK and Northampton, MA, USA: Edward Elgar Publishing, pp. 127–49.

Peterson, S.J., F. Luthans, B.J. Avolio, F.O. Walumbwa and Z. Zhang (2011), 'Psychological capital and employee performance: a latent growth modelling approach', *Personnel Psychology*, **64**(2), 427–50.

Raudenbush, S.W., A.S. Bryk, Y.F. Cheong and R. Congdon (2004), *HLM7: Hierarchical Linear and Nonlinear Modeling*, Lincolnwood, IL: Scientific Software International.

Rego, A. and M.P. Cunha (2008), 'Perceptions of authentizotic climates and employee happiness: pathways to individual performance?' *Journal of Business Research*, **61**(7), 739–52.

Rego, A., C. Marques, S. Leal, F. Sousa and M.P. Cunha (2010), 'Psychological capital and performance of Portuguese civil servants: exploring neutralizers in the context of an appraisal system', *The International Journal of Human Resource Management*, **21**(2), 1531–52.

Rupp, D.E., M.R. Bashshur and H. Liao (2007), 'Justice climate: consideration of source target, type, specificity and emergence', in F.J. Dansereau and F.J. Yamarino (eds), *Research in Multi-level Issues*, Oxford: Elsevier, pp. 439–59.

Scheier, M.F. and C.S. Carver (1985), 'Optimism, coping and health: assessments and implications of generalized outcome expectancies', *Health Psychology*, **4**(3), 219–47.

Seligman, M.E.P. (1998), *Learned Optimism*, New York: Pocket Books.

Snyder, C.R. (2000), *Handbook of Hope*, San Diego, CA: Academic Press.

Snyder, C.R., L.M. Irving and J.R. Anderson (1991), 'Hope and health', in C.R. Snyder (ed.), *Handbook of Social and Clinical Psychology*, Oxford: Oxford University Press, pp. 295–305.

Spreitzer, G.M. (1995), 'Psychological empowerment in the workplace: dimensions, measurement, and validation', *Academy of Management Journal*, **38**(5), 1442–65.

Stajkovic, A.D. and F. Luthans (1998), 'Self-efficacy and work-related performance: a meta-analysis', *Psychological Bulletin*, **124**(2), 240–61.

Thompson, E.R. (2007), 'Development and validation of an internationally reliable short-form of the positive and negative affect schedule (PANAS)', *Journal of Cross-cultural Psychology*, **38**(2), 227–42.

Totterdell, P., S. Wood and T. Wall (2006), 'An intra-individual test of the demands-control model: a weekly diary study of psychological strain in portfolio workers', *Journal of Occupational and Organizational Psychology*, **79**(1), 63–85.

Tugade, M.M. and B.L. Fredrickson (2004), 'Resilient individuals use positive emotions to bounce back from negative emotional experiences', *Journal of Personality and Social Psychology*, **86**(2), 320–33.

Vanno, V., W. Kaemkate and S. Wongwanich (2014), 'Relationships between academic performance, perceived group psychological capital, and positive psychological capital of Thai undergraduate students', *Procedia – Social and Behavioral Sciences*, **116**, 3226–30.

Warr, P., J. Cook and T. Wall (1979), 'Scales for the measurement of some work attitudes and aspects of psychological well-being', *Journal of Occupational Psychology*, **52**(2), 129–48.

West, B.J., J.L. Patera and M.K. Carsten (2009), 'Team-level positivity: investigating positive psychological capacities and team-level outcomes', *Journal of Organizational Behavior*, **30**(2), 249–67.

Youssef, C.M. and F. Luthans (2007), 'Positive organizational behavior in the workplace: the impact of hope, optimism and resilience', *Journal of Management*, **33**(5), 774–800.

Youssef, C.M. and F. Luthans (2011), 'Positive psychological capital in the workplace: where we are and where we need to go', in K.M. Sheldon, T.B. Kashdan and M.F. Steger (eds), *Designing Positive Psychology: Taking Stock and Moving Forward*, New York: Oxford University Press, pp. 351–64.

Youssef, C.M. and F. Luthans (2012), 'Psychological capital: meaning, findings and future directions', in K.S. Cameron and G.M. Spreitzer (eds), *The Oxford Handbook of Positive Organizational Scholarship*, Oxford: Oxford University Press, pp. 17–27.

5. Programmes and interventions for psychosocial risk and worker well-being; the psychosocial safety climate (PSC) framework

Tessa S. Bailey, Silvia Pignata and Maureen F. Dollard

INTRODUCTION

Psychosocial risk refers to the interaction between individuals and a range of workplace factors including job design, management practice, job demands, and resources that have the potential to cause harm to employees (International Labour Organization, 1986). These risk factors can become a hazard when one, or a combination of them, have a detrimental effect on employee health, engagement and/or productivity (Karasek and Theorell, 1990; Demerouti et al., 2001; Dollard and Bakker, 2010). Research shows that organizational initiatives to improve worker well-being benefit from having a holistic approach (LaMontagne et al., 2007) where strategies go beyond a focus on the individual worker. This is because those interventions address both the causes of stress and its consequences on the worker. The psychosocial safety climate (PSC) framework encourages interventions that encompass primary, secondary and tertiary aspects with a specific focus on the causes of work stress. PSC extends the well-known job demands-resources model (Demerouti et al., 2001) as a leading indicator of psychosocial risk factors and is therefore presented in this chapter as a primary focus point for work-related stress prevention and the promotion of employee well-being. This chapter will discuss different classes of organizational interventions and the importance of including PSC in programmes to effectively address psychosocial risks and hazards at work.

STRESS INTERVENTIONS

A stress management intervention is defined as 'any activity, programme, or opportunity initiated by an organization, which focuses on reducing the presence of work-related stressors or on assisting individuals to minimize the negative outcomes of exposure to these stressors' (Ivancevich et al., 1990, p. 252). The effective management of occupational stress is important, particularly to human resource (HR) and occupational health and safety (OHS) practitioners who are concerned with ensuring that HR practices promote worker well-being and positive work-related attitudes (Quick et al., 2007). Determining the relationship between psychosocial factors (organizational factors and interpersonal relationships in the work setting that may affect the health of workers) and specific organizational outcomes can assist management to determine where to focus an intervention and where to measure its effects (Carr et al., 2003).

Despite the wide variety of programmes to manage stress and improve workers' well-being and morale, few evaluative studies of stress interventions have been documented in the literature (Cooper, 2001; Caulfield et al., 2004). For example, a review of intervention studies conducted on Australian samples within the last decade found only six interventions (Caulfield et al., 2004), and a review of UK-based stress-intervention research examined 16 studies (Giga, Noblet et al. 2003). In particular, there is a lack of studies that assess organizational outcomes (Richardson and Rothstein, 2008). This is primarily due to the methodological (process) and the contextual difficulties inherent in stress-intervention research due to the unique and dynamic factors in workplaces such as the size of the organization, the duration of the intervention, and the level of engagement of employees and managers in the intervention process (McVicar et al., 2013). Accordingly, there have been calls for researchers to address the fundamental questions of what interventions work? When are they effective? And 'why should and how could organizational level stress interventions work?' (Briner and Reynolds, 1999, p. 648). Indeed, the literature on organizational interventions for stress remains underdeveloped in terms of the theoretical foundations that explain how changes occur due to these interventions (Biron and Karanika-Murray, 2013). To enhance the understanding of work stress mechanisms and the application of interventions in workplaces, the following section discusses the classes of interventions.

PRIMARY, SECONDARY AND TERTIARY INTERVENTIONS

There are three classes of interventions to reduce or manage work stress. 'Primary' interventions are concerned with stressor reduction; 'secondary' with stress management; and 'tertiary' approaches provide remedial support (Cartwright and Cooper, 1997).

According to Kompier and Cooper (1999), primary interventions are long-term approaches that aim to eliminate, reduce, or alter stressors at work (e.g. by reducing staff workloads, increasing workers' decision-making authority; increasing social support within the organization: Cooper and Quick, 1999; Richardson and Rothstein, 2008). Organizational-focused interventions are classified as primary approaches as they engage workers in the organization, and as a part of an intervention strategy have the potential to address the complexity of the workplace itself (McVicar et al., 2013). A review of primary organizational strategies found that they had positive effects in reducing occupational stressors (Burke, 1993).

Secondary interventions aim to reduce or eliminate the effects of stress in employees who are showing signs of stress before they lead to health problems. These approaches modify or change stress responses to inevitable or unchangeable demands, and intervention strategies include relaxation training, meditation, exercise, deep breathing exercises, stress management programmes, time management, programmes to increase employees' coping capacity, and health promotion activities (Giga, Cooper and Faragher, 2003; Richardson and Rothstein, 2008).

Finally, tertiary interventions treat employees with serious stress-related health issues by providing professional medical treatment or psychological counselling to heal specific problems (Cooper and Quick, 1999). Work stress interventions may also target the individual, the organization, or both the individual and the organization. Giga and colleagues found that the most common stress management interventions were secondary approaches that focused on the individual and comprised stress management and coping techniques.

Research has found that the success of a stress prevention programme depends on combining a bottom-up participative approach with a top-down approach that is supported by senior management (Kompier and Cooper, 1999). However, the difficulty in implementing successful organizational interventions is that they require cooperation and participation from employees, unions and management (Nytrø et al., 2000), who may be in conflict. Moreover, factors such as organizational structure, size, resources, culture and values determine the appropriateness of interventions (Marshall and Cooper, 1981), and both the strategy and process of implementing an intervention may be as important as its content in achieving an effective outcome (Giga, Noblet et al., 2003; Nielsen et al., 2007). Organizational stress-reduction interventions often have little or no effect, or may produce mixed effects, as their impact depends on various organizational characteristics that may be difficult to identify or control. As a result, Briner and Reynolds (1999, p. 659) urge researchers to examine a potential link 'between changes in objective job conditions, changes in subjective perceptions of those job conditions and changes in employee well-being'.

A study by Teo and Waters (2002) provides evidence of the effect of HR practices in creating a supportive HR environment to help to reduce workplace stressors. According to the authors, HR practices can follow two different pathways in stress intervention. They can aim to (1) remove occupational stressors from the work environment (a primary intervention approach), or (2) assist employees to reduce the strain that is associated with these stressors (a secondary intervention approach). In their cross-sectional study, Teo and Waters examined the role of eight HR practices (i.e., job training, employee communication, job redesign, promotional opportunities, employee involvement, family-friendly practices, pay equity, and stress management interventions) in reducing the stressors of role overload and responsibility, and in reducing vocational and interpersonal strain in a sample of 109 Singaporean employees. They found a direct negative relationship between several of these HR practices (i.e., family-friendly practices, job training, and stress management interventions) and interpersonal strain, although the interventions did not reduce the stressors of role overload and responsibility at work. The next section examines the literature to determine what factors make an intervention effective.

Primary prevention strategies that focus on causal factors using comprehensive interventions that focus on all levels of the organization is crucial and the most effective. A systematic review of the job stress-intervention evaluation literature by LaMontagne and colleagues (2007) found that intervention programmes that include primary, secondary and tertiary levels of interventions were effective in improving both individual (e.g., anxiety, depression) and organizational outcomes (e.g., absenteeism, job satisfaction). They conclude that prevention programmes integrating all classes of interventions are more effective because they address both the causes of stress and its consequences on workers and their well-being.

Richardson and Rothstein (2008) evaluated the effectiveness of various types of primary and secondary interventions in their meta-analytic review of 36 experimental studies, representing 55 interventions and a sample size of 2847. The authors analysed the effectiveness of cognitive-behavioural, relaxation, organizational, multimodal, and alternative types of interventions. Their findings showed that cognitive-behavioural programmes that involve teaching workers about the role of their thoughts and emotions in managing stressful events and educating them to change those thoughts in order to cope with stress in a more adaptive way, consistently produced larger effects than other types of interventions. Within the sample of studies, relaxation and meditation interventions were most frequently used. The effects of the interventions were mainly on self-reported psychological outcome variables and not on organizational outcomes such as performance or absenteeism.

In terms of the stress-intervention literature it seems intuitive to suggest that organizations employing predominantly organization-directed, primary prevention strategies will show greater levels of worker well-being and morale relative to organizations employing predominantly individual-directed interventions alone. The dominant view is that work stress and the resulting mental health outcomes are more strongly related to aspects of the work environment or job factors than to personal or biographical factors (Maslach and Schaufeli, 1993). Indeed, Burke (1993) pointed out that if the number and strength of occupational stressors were reduced, individuals at work would experience less stress. However, several reviews (Van der Klink et al., 2001; Richardson and Rothstein, 2008) have found a lack of empirical evidence to draw conclusions on the effectiveness of organizational-level interventions. The literature demonstrates clearly that work stress programmes are predominantly reactive (i.e., secondary or tertiary approaches) strategies directed at individuals (Kompier et al., 2000; Giga, Cooper and Faragher, 2003).

PSC FRAMEWORK AND PSYCHOSOCIAL INTERVENTIONS

Consistent with the research discussed above, the PSC theoretical framework (Figure 5.1) promotes a more holistic organizational approach to worker well-being as it encompasses a broad range of psychosocial factors and requires any interventions to consider primary, secondary and tertiary strategies including top-down and bottom-up approaches. PSC refers to organizational policies, practices and procedures for the protection of workers' psychological health and safety (Dollard and Bakker, 2010). It also reflects senior management commitment, participation, and consultation in relation to stress prevention and safety at work (ibid.). The PSC framework extends upon other well-known job stress theories such as the

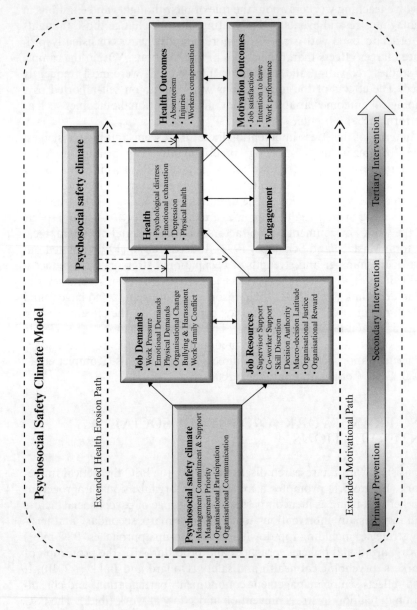

Figure 5.1   PSC theoretical framework

job demands-resources (JD-R) model (Demerouti et al., 2001) where psychosocial work factors can be classified in terms of job demands and job resources.

The JD-R theory considers job demands such as workload, emotional demands and bullying as significant predictors of employee psychological and physical well-being via a health erosion pathway (Figure 5.1). Coping with persistent job demands leads to depletion of a worker's energy reserve; in turn this leads to negative responses such as exhaustion, anxiety and depression. This depletion of personal resources can also contribute to health problems including cardiovascular disease or musculoskeletal disorders (Schaufeli and Bakker, 2004).

The motivational pathway (Figure 5.1) as proposed by the JD-R model describes how adequate resources (e.g., control, support, rewards, procedural justice) are motivating and lead to greater employee engagement, and in turn to positive organizational outcomes such as improved performance (Bakker and Demerouti, 2007). Cross-links between the health and motivation pathways are theoretically and practically important because they may explain, for example, how work performance can be impaired through the reduced health of workers (Schaufeli and Bakker, 2004; Hakanen et al., 2006). For instance, the relationship between lack of job control and psychological health is strongly supported in the literature (Karasek and Theorell, 1990).

Australian and international researchers have found that PSC acts as the 'cause of the causes' of work stress. In this regard PSC is viewed as a leading indicator or pre-eminent risk factor as it can predict levels of psychosocial risk such as workplace demands and resources as well as worker health and productivity outcomes (Dollard and Bakker, 2010; Dollard and Karasek, 2010; Hall et al., 2010; Idris et al., 2011). Previous research evidence shows lower levels of reported PSC is linked with more work pressure and emotional demands (Dollard and Bakker, 2010), workplace bullying and harassment (Law et al., 2011; Escartín et al., 2014), and workload (Dollard, Bailey et al., 2012).

High PSC has also been found to predict more resources including, skill discretion (Dollard and Bakker, 2010), work rewards (Law et al., 2011), job control and supervisor support (Dollard, Bailey et al., 2012). Studies have also found that PSC is a predictor for a range of employee health and productivity outcomes including psychological distress, emotional exhaustion (Idris et al., 2012), sickness absence (Dollard and Bakker, 2010), anger, depression (Idris and Dollard, 2011; Escartín et al., 2014), exhaustion and cynicism (Idris et al., 2011; Escartín et al., 2014), and worker performance and engagement (Idris et al., 2011; Law et al., 2011).

Another important aspect of PSC is that it moderates the relationship between psychosocial risk factors and well-being outcomes. For instance, in a study involving Australian police officers, in workplace environments with high PSC, where workers felt their psychological health was valued and supported, bullying behaviours were less likely to cause post-traumatic stress symptoms (Bond et al., 2010). Similarly, other studies show that PSC can reduce the effects of job demands on depression (Hall et al., 2010), emotional demands on workgroup distress (Dollard, Tuckey and Dormann, 2012) and bullying/harassment on employee engagement (Law et al., 2011). Collectively, these results demonstrate that PSC can reduce the impact of adverse workplace conditions on worker well-being by indicating whether there are adequate resources and support systems available for employees to appropriately manage their psychological health at work.

In addition, there is evidence that the levels of PSC in a workplace at the commencement of an intervention may determine the success of the process (Dollard, 2012). Researchers have found that current conditions in the working environment (PSC assessed at a group level) predicts how successful the implementation of the psychosocial intervention will be. An intervention-based study found that PSC was associated with the extent to which the intervention participants attended the capacity-building sessions, the quality of the intervention (e.g., whether trust was developed, whether they were being listened to), and the progress of the intervention (e.g., the extent of the implementation of risk prevention action plans). As such, PSC has been conceptualized as a primary focal point for the prevention of psychosocial risks and hazards.

ORGANIZATIONAL APPROACHES TO PSYCHOSOCIAL INTERVENTIONS

It is clear that a structural response is required to manage psychosocial risks within the workplace. Although researchers in the field have been keen to implement and evaluate interventions within organizations, many of these have involved 'add on' processes. We argue that interventions should be integrally linked to organizational frameworks and processes to ensure their sustainability. Here we outline the steps required for healthy workplace conditions in organizational environments (Figure 5.2).

Step 1: Generate management or political will
The first and foremost goal is to generate management or political will to build a strong PSC culture. Occupational health and safety (OHS), union and employee representatives need to be represented in decisions about

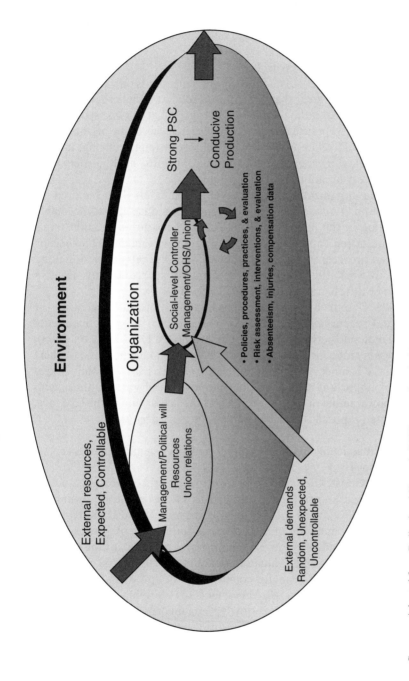

Source: Adapted from Dollard and Karasek (2010), reproduced with permission from Wiley Blackwell.

Figure 5.2   Healthy conducive production model

how frameworks and processes are built. Resources, both financial and social (e.g., trust) are required to facilitate change. These foundational aspects are the ingredients required to build a social level controller.

Step 2: Build a social-level controller

Dollard and Karasek (2010) maintain that the demands on workers within organizations are so great that control is needed at a higher level. Social-level control may be in the form of a committee that designs specific sets of well-coordinated policies across and between levels in the organization. The policies could relate to workplace behaviour (e.g., bullying, harassment, violence), work design (e.g., workload), profits, health, safety, and return to work programmes.

Within the organization, higher-level social control is required to coordinate and *resource* incoming demands to reduce threats to stable self-regulation at the individual level. Targeted resources at lower levels in the organization can create stable and safe environments. This means that workers are freer to use their resources, such as their decision-making authority to work effectively with the demands or reduce any negative impact on health (Karasek and Theorell, 1990).

Social-level control is via the social coordination and generation of policies and practices. Social-level control also provides an opportunity for social dialogue between competing interests (see Leka and Cox, 2008). Work stress is a reflection of the struggle between management and workers regarding the balance of demands and control over self-regulation. Social dialogue is important as it gives political power and voice to those with the least power in the organization, such as those working at the coal face, who are often exposed to the most stressful experiences.

Step 3: The functioning of the social-level controller should be evidence informed

First and foremost, the policies, practices, and procedures (e.g., action plans) developed and implemented need to be systematically evaluated and improved. Following international best practice and consistent with established OHS methods and continuous improvement processes, the controller needs to identify, assess and prioritize hazards, for the design of interventions and ongoing evaluation (Leka et al., 2011). Risk assessment provides a crucial mechanism for communication upwards about risks.

Conducting psychosocial risk assessments to determine the levels of risk is a relatively new concept that is slowly being incorporated into organizational policy and practice around the world (Leka and Jain, 2010; Leka et al., 2011). Many industrialized nations have systematic methods in place for collecting workforce data that includes some psychosocial risk aspects

(Dollard et al., 2007; Leka and Cox, 2008). A wide range of resources are also available to support employers seeking to address psychosocial risk factors in their organization. Many organizations use employee opinion surveys and we advocate modifying these to include psychosocial risks and psychological health measures, or running risk surveillance surveys in parallel (see Dollard and Gordon, 2014). Consider the use of tools with psychometric properties (e.g., PSC-12), and if possible, utilize wider industry, state or national prevalence data to assist with establishing priorities. The controller should also use workforce data such as incidents, injuries, absenteeism and turnover.

The best practice for psychosocial risk prevention and intervention, as stated by the Psychosocial Risk Management Excellence Framework (PRIMA-EF), is that organizational assessments be incorporated into industry standards (Leka and Cox, 2008). While workers within industries are likely to share similar risk factors, each organization will differ, and regular assessment at the organizational level can prompt a range of benefits such as identifying current hazards and providing an evidence base for focusing risk prevention strategies.

Risk assessment and interventions can be conducted at various levels within the organization as outlined earlier in the chapter (i.e., organizational level, team level, individual level). Every arrow presented in Figure 5.3 provides an intervention point (primary, secondary, tertiary) and the figure also gives additional details on psychosocial intervention development.

Follow up psychosocial risk assessment can be used to determine improvements by making comparisons with baseline data. This information can be used as part of a continuous improvement process where results from the evaluation can again be assessed for their level of risk and as a guide for further intervention (Noblet and LaMontagne, 2009).

PSYCHOSOCIAL SAFETY CLIMATE HIERARCHY OF CONTROL

Although we have been focusing on top-level management and the social controller, at each level of the organization there are roles and responsibilities that need to be socially coordinated in the organization's structural approach. In order to provide a practical means for employers and OHS practitioners to more effectively develop interventions and address specific psychosocial risks and hazards, the following PSC hierarchy of control (PSC HOC) was developed.

During the organizational assessment process, once level of risk has

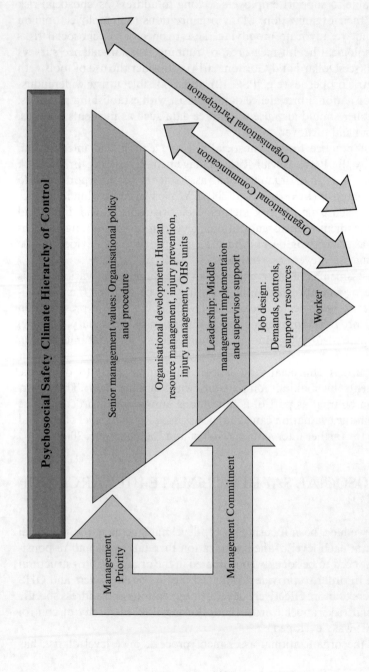

Psychosocial Safety Climate Hierarchy of Control

Senior management values: Organisational policy and procedure

Organisational development: Human resource management, injury prevention, injury management, OHS units

Leadership: Middle management implementaion and supervisor support

Job design: Demands, controls, support, resources

Worker

Organisational Participation

Organisational Communication

Management Priority

Management Commitment

Source: Bailey and Dollard (2014).

Figure 5.3 PSC hierarchy of control

been established and a hazard has been identified the PSC HOC can be used to guide the development of intervention strategies by addressing the psychosocial factor at each level of the hierarchy.

Level 1: Organizational workplace policy and procedure

Organizational workplace policy and procedure involves being specific in addressing the psychosocial risk factors and clearly incorporate best practice principles to promote worker physical and psychological well-being. This includes systems for prevention, risk assessment, and risk management for psychosocial factors. It would also include best practice principles for injury management and return to work processes.

Level 2: Implementation of procedures

Implementation of procedures by human resource management, injury prevention, injury management, organizational development, and OHS units stipulate that specific divisions or persons within an organization are responsible for enacting organizational policies and procedures to promote worker psychological safety and well-being. Further, representatives within these roles should be encouraged to act as change ambassadors and to include practices to prevent psychological harm and promote well-being such as psychosocial risk assessments, incident reports and actions, injury prevention interventions, health and well-being programmes, OHS committees, and OHS representatives. Communication about OHS practices such as seminars and training provided on psychosocial topics, support programmes for injured workers, and return to work processes should also be promoted throughout all levels of the organization.

Level 3: Manager, supervisor, team leader actions, and support

Manager, supervisor, team leader actions, and support relate to a leadership culture that values employee health and well-being equal to, or above, productivity. Leaders play a direct role in creating a psychologically safe and positive working environment. Action at this level would include promoting and role modelling appropriate workplace behaviour (e.g., no bullying/harassment), early identification of psychosocial risk, and addressing issues in an appropriate and timely manner. Leaders also need to provide a clear pathway for feedback from workers so that employees feel they can communicate their concerns regarding psychological health and well-being where their concerns are taken seriously and they are free from repercussions.

Level 4: Job design: demands, controls, resources, and support
Job design involves the promotion of worker psychological health and employee well-being when setting workloads by providing adequate resources including consideration of work pace, flexible working hours where possible, appropriate skill discretion, ability to be included in decision-making processes whenever practical, as well as opportunities for learning, training and career development. Forms of support can include team building, opportunities for debriefing, positive and constructive criticism, and supportive social interactions.

Level 5: Individual factors
Individual factors involve addressing the specific characteristics of each individual worker, such as personality factors, adverse emotional reactions to work (depression, anxiety), self-care, resilience, and coping strategies. Methods for addressing such factors may include career matching, strategies for self-care, resilience training, and increased accessibility to, and awareness of, Employee Assistance Programs.

To effectively use the organizational PSC hierarchy of control as part of a comprehensive prevention organizational intervention programme, it is important to address each risk or hazard at all levels of the hierarchy, starting at the top and working down. The arrows on Figure 5.3 represent PSC subscales and should also be considered when developing action plans. It is recommended that PSC measures be included in all psychosocial risk assessments. Box 5.1 provides a case study of an Australian public sector organization that implemented a work stress intervention.

CONCLUSION

Psychosocial approaches to programmes that promote worker well-being would benefit from adopting holistic methods that include primary, secondary and tertiary interventions. This is so that individuals feel supported by their management and organization to enact well-being policy as well as create a culture that reduces risk to worker psychological health and promotes well-being. International best practice advises organizations to conduct psychosocial risk assessments in order to identify risk factors unique to their organization that affect worker psychological health and thus provide an evidence base for interventions. Prior research supports PSC as a leading indicator of psychosocial risk factors including job-related demands and resources. In addition, higher levels of PSC can reduce the impact of these factors on worker health and productivity

BOX 5.1   EXAMPLE: AN AUSTRALIAN WORK
STRESS INTERVENTION

An intervention in an Australian public sector organization evaluated by Dollard and Gordon (2014) used a socially coordinated approach to implement a work stress intervention. The project was commissioned by the organization and had top management support, and was well resourced. It was coordinated by the OHS committee, which had representation from management, unions, and OHS personnel. The intervention was primary in focus as it intended to assess psychosocial risks and reduce them. Naturally occurring workgroups (managers and workers) attended capacity-building workshops convened by an external facilitator. They developed and implemented action plans to reduce work and organizational stress risk factors (e.g., job design, performance management, work quality, and organizational change) and address stress outcomes (e.g., work stress, morale, and sickness absence duration). An existing organizational development survey of work conditions and well-being was administered as a risk assessment and evaluation tool. There were five intervention and 17 control workgroups. Data were collected before the intervention (Time [$T1$], Intervention $n = 94$, Control $n = 511$) and 12 months after ($T2$, Intervention, $n = 123$, Control $n = 556$).

Results showed that there were significant improvements for the intervention workgroups in relation to work and organizational factors (i.e., job design, training and development, positive performance management, quality) and morale, but not for positive organizational change, and work stress. Organizational sickness absence duration data decreased consistent with an intervention effect. Top level management commitment and support, worker participation, and action plan implementation, appeared important for positive change. To improve sustainability, the project capitalized on existing systems (i.e., committees, organizational survey) but built new communication systems, for instance, between the work groups and the committee. Group action plans were sent to the committee and in this way the OHS committee learned what the issues were for the workgroup and what resources were required. There are always challenges associated with organizational stress interventions.

Although this project capitalized on organizational frameworks and processes, for practical and efficiency reasons, there were some drawbacks. For instance, in the project the organizational survey did not adequately assess some known psychosocial risk factors (e.g., bullying) and its assessment of psychological health was also very limited. In terms of evaluation, there were high response rates, and for good reasons the data collected by the organization was anonymous, and therefore could only be matched at the group level. This case study demonstrates the key components required for a socially coordinated approach to interventions to reduce psychosocial risks and increase productivity potential.

outcomes. Practical steps, as were outlined in this chapter, can be taken by organizations and employers to integrate PSC concepts into existing policy and procedure. Further, the PSC HOC was developed to provide a guide for OHS practitioners and employers to more effectively address identified hazards by developing intervention programmes that include all levels of the organization and thus promote a healthy working environment that reduces risks to worker well-being and supports employees to address hazards as they arise. Organizational approaches to psychosocial risk prevention and interventions that incorporate the PSC framework should be more effective in managing psychosocial hazards that affect their workers' psychological health and thus result in higher levels of productivity, worker engagement and well-being.

REFERENCES

Bailey, T.S. and M.F. Dollard (2014), 'Psychosocial hazard management and the Psychosocial Safety Climate Hierarchy of Control (PSC-HOC)', in M.F. Dollard and T.S. Bailey (eds), *Australian Workplace Barometer: Psychosocial Safety Climate and Working Conditions in Australia*, Samford Valley, QLD: Academic Press Australia.

Bakker, A.B. and E. Demerouti (2007), 'The job demands-resources model: state of the art', *Journal of Managerial Psychology*, **22**(3), 309–28.

Biron, C. and M. Karanika-Murray (2013), 'Process evaluation for organizational stress and well-being interventions: implications for theory, method, and practice', *International Journal of Stress Management* [online], DOI: 10.1037/a0033227.

Bond, S.A., M.R. Tuckey and M.F. Dollard (2010), 'Psychosocial safety climate, workplace bullying, and symptoms of posttraumatic stress', *Organization Development Journal*, **28**(1), 37–56.

Briner, R.B. and S. Reynolds (1999), 'The costs, benefits, and limitations of organizational-level stress interventions', *Journal of Organizational Behavior*, **20**(5), 647–64.

Burke, R.J. (1993), 'Organizational-level interventions to reduce occupational stressors', *Work and Stress*, **7**(1), 77–88.

Carr, J.Z., A.M. Schmidt, J.K. Ford and R.P. DeShon (2003), 'Climate perceptions matter: a meta-analytic path analysis relating molar climate, cognitive and affective states, and individual-level work outcomes', *Journal of Applied Psychology*, **88**(4), 605–19.

Cartwright, S. and C.L. Cooper (1997), *Managing Workplace Stress*, Thousand Oaks, CA: Sage Publications.

Caulfield, N., D. Chang, M.F. Dollard and C. Elshaug (2004), 'A review of occupational stress interventions in Australia', *International Journal of Stress Management*, **11**(2), 149–66.

Cooper, C.L. (2001), *Managerial, Occupational and Organizational Stress Research*, Hampshire, UK: Ashgate.

Cooper, C.L. and J.C. Quick (1999), *Stress and Strain*, Oxford: Health Press Limited.

Demerouti, E., F. Nachreiner, A.B. Bakker and W.B. Schaufeli (2001), 'The job demands-resources model of burnout', *Journal of Applied Psychology*, **86**(3), 499–512.

Dollard, M.F. (2012), 'Psychosocial safety climate: a lead indicator of work conditions, workplace psychological health and engagement and precursor to intervention success', in C. Biron, M. Karanika-Murray and C.L. Cooper (eds), *Managing Psychosocial Risks in the Workplace: The Role of Process Issues*, London: Routledge/Psychology Press.

Dollard, M.F. and A.B. Bakker (2010), 'Psychosocial safety climate as a precursor to conducive work environments, psychological health problems, and employee engagement', *Journal of Occupational and Organizational Psychology*, **83**(3), 579–99.

Dollard, M.F. and J. Gordon (2014), 'Evaluation of a participatory risk management stress intervention', *International Journal of Stress Management*, **21**(1), 27–42.

Dollard, M.F. and R. Karasek (2010), 'Building psychosocial safety climate: evaluation of a socially coordinated PAR risk management stress prevention study', in J. Houdmont and S. Leka (eds), *Contemporary Occupational Health Psychology: Global Perspectives on Research and Practice*, Chichester, UK: Wiley Blackwell, pp. 208–34.

Dollard, M.F., M.R. Tuckey and C. Dormann (2012), 'Psychosocial safety climate moderates the demand-resource interaction in predicting workgroup distress', *Accident Analysis and Prevention*, **45**, 694–704.

Dollard, M.F., N. Skinner, M.R. Tuckey and T. Bailey (2007), 'National surveillance of psychosocial risk factors in the workplace: an international overview', *Work and Stress*, **21**(1), 1–29.

Dollard, M.F., T.S. Bailey, S.S. McLinton, P. Richards, W.P. McTernan, A. Taylor and S. Bond (2012), *Australian Workplace Barometer (AWB) Results: Report on Psychosocial Safety Climate and Worker Health in Australia*, Canberra: Safe Work Australia.

Escartín, J., M.F. Dollard and D. Zapf (2014, in review), 'Workplace bullying as a mediator between psychosocial safety climate and psychological health and well-being: a multilevel mediation model'.

Giga, S.I., C.L. Cooper and B. Faragher (2003), 'The development of a framework for a comprehensive approach to stress management interventions at work', *International Journal of Stress Management*, **10**(4), 280–96.

Giga, S.I., A.J. Noblet, B. Faragher and C.L. Cooper (2003), 'The UK perspective: a review of research on organizational stress management interventions', *Australian Psychologist*, **38**(2), 158–64.

Hakanen, J.J., A.B. Bakker and W.B. Schaufeli (2006), 'Burnout and work engagement among teachers', *Journal of School Psychology*, **43**(6), 495–513.

Hall, G.B., M.F. Dollard and J. Coward (2010), 'Psychosocial safety climate: development of the PSC-12', *International Journal of Stress Management*, **17**(4), 353–83.

Idris, M.A. and M.F. Dollard (2011), 'Psychosocial safety climate, work conditions, and emotions in the workplace: a Malaysian population-based work stress study', *International Journal of Stress Management*, **18**(4), 324–47.

Idris, M.A., M.F. Dollard and A.H. Winefield (2011), 'Integrating psychosocial safety climate in the JD-R model: a study amongst Malaysian workers', *South African Journal of Industrial Psychology*, **37**, 1–11.

Idris, M.A., M.F. Dollard, J. Coward and C. Dormann (2012), 'Psychosocial safety climate: conceptual distinctiveness and effect on job demands and worker psychological health', *Safety Science*, **50**(1), 19–28.

International Labour Organization (1986), *Psychosocial Factors at Work: Recognition and Control*, Geneva: International Labour Office.

Ivancevich, J.M., M.T. Matteson, S.M. Freedman and J.S. Phillips (1990), 'Worksite stress management interventions', *American Psychologist*, **45**(2), 252–61.

Karasek, R. and T. Theorell (1990), *Healthy Work: Stress, Productivity, and the Reconstruction of Working Life*, New York: Basic Books.

Kompier, M. and C.L. Cooper (eds) (1999), *Preventing Stress, Improving Productivity: European Case Studies in the Workplace*, London: Routledge.

Kompier, M.A.J., C.L. Cooper and S.A.E. Geurts (2000), 'A multiple case study approach to work stress prevention in Europe', *European Journal of Work and Organizational Psychology*, **9**(3), 371–400.

LaMontagne, A.D., T. Keegel, A.M. Louie, A. Ostry and P.A. Landsbergis (2007), 'A systematic review of the job-stress intervention evaluation literature', *International Journal of Occupational and Environmental Health*, **13**(3), 268–80.

Law, R., M.F. Dollard, M.R. Tuckey and C. Dormann (2011), 'Psychosocial safety climate as a lead indicator of workplace bullying and harassment, job resources, psychological health and employee engagement', *Accident Analysis and Prevention*, **43**(5), 1782–93.

Leka, S. and T. Cox (2008), 'The future of psychosocial risk management and the promotion of well-being at work in the EU: A PRIMA time for action', in S. Leka and T. Cox (eds), *The European Framework for Psychosocial Risk Management: PRIMA-EF*, Nottingham, UK: I-WHO Publications.

Leka, S. and A. Jain (2010), *Health Impact of Psychosocial Hazards at Work: An Overview*, Nottingham, UK: I-WHO Publications.

Leka, S., A. Jain, M. Widerszal-Bazyl, D. Zolnierdzyk-Zreda and G. Zwetsloot (2011), 'Developing a standard for psychosocial risk management: PAS1010', *Special Issue on Occupational Health and Safety Management Systems, Safety Science*, **49**(7), 1047–57.

Marshall, J. and C.E. Cooper (eds) (1981), *Coping with Stress at Work: Case Studies From Industry*, Aldershot, UK: Gower.

Maslach, C. and W. Schaufeli (1993), 'Historical and conceptual development of burnout', in W. Schaufeli, C. Maslach and T. Marek (eds), *Professional Burnout: Recent Developments in Theory and Research*, London: Taylor and Francis, pp. 1–16.

McVicar, A., C. Munn-Giddings and P. Seebohm (2013), 'Workplace stress interventions using participatory action research designs', *International Journal of Workplace Health Management*, **6**(1), 18–37.

Nielsen, K., R. Randall and K. Albertsen (2007), 'The impact of implementation and participants' appraisal on the outcomes of stress management interventions', *Journal of Organizational Behavior*, **28**(6), 793–810.

Noblet, A. and A. LaMontagne (2009), 'The challenges of developing, implementing, and evaluating interventions', in S. Cartwright and C.L. Cooper (eds), *The Oxford Handbook of Organizational Well-being*, Oxford: Oxford University Press, pp. 467–96.

Nytrø, K., P.O. Saksvik, A. Mikkelsen, P. Bohle and M. Quinlan (2000), 'The role and effects of process in occupational stress interventions', *Work and Stress*, **14**(3), 213–25.

Quick, J.C., M. Macik-Frey and C. Cooper (2007), 'Managerial dimensions of organizational health: the healthy leader at work', *Journal of Management Studies*, **44**(2), 189–205.

Richardson, K.M. and H.R. Rothstein (2008), 'Effects of occupational stress management intervention programs: a meta-analysis', *Journal of Occupational Health Psychology*, **13**(1), 69–93.

Schaufeli, W.B. and A.B. Bakker (2004), 'Job demands, job resources, and their relationship with burnout and engagement: a multi-sample study', *Journal of Organizational Behavior*, **25**(3), 293–315.

Teo, C. and L. Waters (2002), 'The role of human resource practices in reducing occupational stress and strain', *International Journal of Stress Management*, **9**(3), 207–26.

Van der Klink, J.J.L., R.W.B. Blonk, A.H. Schene and J.H. van Dijk (2001), 'The benefits of interventions for work-related stress', *Journal of Public Health*, **91**(2), 270–76.

6. Implementing the Quebec 'Healthy Enterprise' standard: considering readiness for change and psychosocial safety climate

Marie-Eve Caouette, Marie-Esther Paradis and Caroline Biron

CONTEXT

In Canada in 2011, 85 percent of long-term disabilities and 83 percent of short-term disabilities were related to mental health or behavioral problems, representing the first cause of long-term and short-term disabilities (Towers Watson, 2012, p. 10). Regarding compensations for mental health problems ordered by the courts, there has been an increase of almost 700 percent from 2005 to 2010 (Shain and Nassar, 2009, p. 7). Several studies over the past two decades have highlighted that exposure to psychosocial constraints, such as poor decisional latitude, high job demands, effort–reward imbalance and poor social support at work, or the combination of these factors – increase the risks of physical and psychological ill-health (Siegrist et al., 1990; Marmot et al., 1997; Ferrie et al., 2005; Kivimäki et al., 2006; Aboa-Eboule et al., 2007; Vézina et al., 2011). About 20 percent of Canadian workers are exposed to these adverse psychosocial factors (Brisson et al., 2001). In the province of Quebec, a survey on working conditions, employment and health and safety (Vézina et al., 2011) conducted among a representative sample of 5071 workers, showed that 49 percent of workers reported low decision latitude, 48 percent reported low social support at work, 38 percent reported high psychological demands and nearly 25 percent were exposed to an imbalance between effort and rewards. In terms of psychological health, 33 percent of Quebec workers reported moderate or high levels of psychological distress, and 12 percent report depressive symptoms. Of these workers, more than 60 percent believed that these symptoms were partially or totally related to their employment. Among workers with depressive symptoms related to their jobs, more than 40 percent were absent from work because of this problem.

Overall, these statistics highlight the need to implement organizational interventions in order to reduce exposure to psychosocial risks, to improve workers' well-being, and to avoid direct and indirect costs related to health issues. Given that several studies show that exposure to these detrimental factors of psychosocial work environment can be diminished, they are relevant targets for prevention (Biron et al., 2012; Bourbonnais et al. 2005, 2006, 2011; Yarker et al., 2008; Egan, 2013; Nielsen et al., 2013; Jauvin et al., 2014). Moreover, the role of line managers is considered by many as an important determinant of the psychosocial work environment, so supporting managers to develop healthier management practices is also a relevant intervention target (Kelloway and Barling, 2010; Kraaijeveld et al., 2013).

However, this type of managerial training/intervention is more complex to implement than individual-level interventions. Indeed, organizational-level interventions addressing psychosocial risks often fail to get implemented properly, or to produce the intended results (see, for example, Biron et al., 2010). The lack of success may be due to the complexity of the interventions, because they have multiple targets, and the fact that they are rather demanding in terms of resources (Biron et al., 2012b). It has been suggested that by considering the processes by which interventions get implemented, and the context in which they are being developed and implemented, we may gain a better understanding of how interventions produce (or fail to produce) certain outcomes (Biron and Karanika-Murray, 2014; Nielsen and Abildgaard, 2013).

Various global and national initiatives have been implemented to decrease levels of occupational stress or promote mental health at work. At the global level, the WHO developed The Comprehensive Mental Health Action Plan 2013–2020 (World Health Organization, 2013), which recommends promoting good mental health and preventing disorders through the establishment of healthy work conditions, such as improvement in work organization and stress management. Some countries have adopted standards or are in development towards this option. For example, the United Kingdom established the Management Standards for Work-related Stress (MacKay et al., 2004, 2012). In Canada, in 2013, the National Standard on Psychological Safety and Health in the Workplace has been launched at the initiative of the Mental Health Commission of Canada; it was prepared by Groupe CSA (Canadian Standards Association) and the Bureau de Normalisation du Québec (BNQ: Standards Bureau of Quebec), and approved by the Standards Council of Canada. A few years before Canada, the Canadian province of Quebec developed a certification process for organizations wishing to be proactive in terms of overall health promotion, which is discussed in the next section.

QUEBEC'S 'HEALTHY ENTERPRISE' STANDARD

In 2004 in Quebec, a group, now called Groupe Enterprises en Santé (GES: Healthy Enterprises Group), was created at the initiative of business people concerned by the impact of the costs of health problems on public finances and economic development of the province. Starting from the basic assumption that healthy employees make healthy businesses, the group's goal was to educate the business community about the importance of good physical and mental health of its employees (Groupe Enterprises en Santé, n.d.). Four years later the GES, in collaboration with the BNQ, innovated by introducing a voluntary standard to encourage businesses to promote both physical and mental health of workers. The standard, better known as the 'Healthy Enterprise' standard, is officially titled 'Prevention, Promotion and Organizational Practices for Health in the Workplace' (BNQ 9700–800). Two types of certification were available: 'Standard' and 'Elite'. For 'Elite' certification, organizations must be active in four spheres of intervention: 'Lifestyle Habits', 'Work Environment', 'Work–Life Balance', and 'Management Practices' (e.g., management practices related to employees' decisional latitude, workload, social support, effort–reward imbalance). To be certified at the first level ('Standard'), actions in only two spheres are needed. To date, a total of 56 organizations in Quebec have already been certified as 'Healthy Enterprises' or 'Elite' (Bureau de Normalisation du Québec, n.d.).

Steps Towards Certification

To become certified as a 'Healthy Enterprise' the organization must go through five steps and meet the following requirements:

1. *Engage management.* The organization must have a policy approved by the direction of the standard that clearly states it engagement and its values in line with prevention promotion and organizational practices for health in the workplace.
2. *Form a health and well-being committee.* The committee must consist of representatives from the management team and diverse work categories.
3. *Collect data.* Data about the organization must be collected as well as employees' suggestions about health and wellness issues.

4. *Make an action plan and implement interventions.* An action plan must be developed and approved by the direction and communicated to the employees.
5. *Evaluate the interventions.* An evaluation must be made, for example, by assessing participation in the interventions or the achievement rate of the objectives (Bureau de Normalisation du Québec, 2008).

FOCUS OF THIS CHAPTER: PSYCHOSOCIAL SAFETY CLIMATE AND READINESS FOR CHANGE

Considering the popularity of national organizational health initiatives in various countries, and considering the notable difficulties in implementing and documenting organizational interventions (Karanika-Murray and Biron, 2014), this chapter describes the theoretical context of some of the process issues we are currently evaluating in certified Quebec 'Healthy Enterprises'. In this study, we focus on two particular process issues, namely, the psychosocial safety climate (PSC; Dollard and Bakker, 2010), which is thought to be an organizational context factor that influences the level of exposure to psychosocial risks, and readiness for change (RFC; Holt et al., 2007), which is conceptualized as an individual-level process variable likely to promote or undermine the adoption of the intervention's components.

The Importance of Management Practices as a Target for Interventions

The psychosocial risks factors that are quantified in this study are: psychological demands, poor decision latitude, lack of social support, and effort–reward imbalance. These are the dimensions of two internationally recognized models: the 'Demand-Control-Support' (DCS) model (Karasek and Theorell, 1990) and the 'Effort–Reward Imbalance' model (ERI: Siegrist, 1996). Given that these adverse factors are modifiable they represent highly relevant targets for preventive interventions. Line managers are an important determinant of employees' well-being (Dellve et al., 2007; Nyberg et al., 2008; Biggs et al., 2009; Mellor and Webster, 2013). The Standard evaluated in the current project has one area of intervention that is specific to management practices with a view to reduce exposure to these psychosocial risks. However, it remains unknown what influences managers' practices and what determines their level of ownership towards such initiatives. In an ongoing study, which will be briefly described later, it is expected that contextual factors such as PSC, and individual factors such as RFC, will influence the adoption of healthy management practices by line managers.

We first begin by explaining the theoretical context of our study and the pertinence of our key constructs. Then we will briefly present our study currently taking place in Quebec in order to evaluate the effects of RFC and PSC on the adoption of management practices.

THEORETICAL BACKGROUND FOR THIS STUDY

We begin by describing why RFC and PSC are specific determinants of success for the implementation of well-being programs, in this case the certification process for a voluntary health and well-being standard in Quebec. We first discuss the pertinence of the main components of the research: psychosocial safety climate, readiness for change and how these resources are theoretically likely to influence management practices and consequently, exposure to the interventions. Process evaluation is the background wallpaper on which our theoretical model is designed: we aim to understand process through PSC and RFC influence on management practices.

Considering process is important for several reasons. First, it provides insights into how and why interventions work, whereas evaluations strictly focusing on outcomes without considering implementation issues are often referred to as 'black box' interventions. Second, it is important to incorporate process issues in intervention evaluation in order to ensure that the intervention is adequately delivered (Dobson and Cook, 1980). This can lead to the conclusion that a program was ineffective, when, in fact, it was the implementation of the program that was flawed. To avoid this error, the research design must take into account the integrity (or fidelity) of the intervention, which is the degree to which the intervention is implemented as planned (Jackson and Waters, 2005). Third, process evaluation can help establish whether the changes in outcomes are related to the intervention per se, as opposed to an unspecified effect. As underlined by Semmer (2006), interventions are often complex and aim to change several aspects of the workplace simultaneously. Studies evaluating these complex changes have been criticized for not being sufficiently specific regarding the outcomes obtained.

There are also reasons to believe that organizational and work-oriented stress interventions could produce more consistent results if more attention was paid to the process and context within which they are developed, designed and implemented (Rossi et al., 2000; Goldenhar et al., 2001). Evidence of the effectiveness of organizational-level interventions is still scarce and often inconsistent (Biron et al., 2009). These inconsistencies are also found in other social programs and have led to reconsiderations about the appropriateness of outcome-focused evaluations that treat programs as 'black boxes' (Dobson and Cook, 1980). Black box is a metaphor that is used to describe evaluations with inadequate information about the contextual factors and processes that influence the relationship between the program and the effects (Nielsen et al., 2007).

Due to the lack of attention paid to process and context issues (Cox et al., 2007; Biron et al., 2012b), it is difficult to interpret the effects of occupational health interventions. Biron and Karanika-Murray (2014) suggest that process and context influence each stage of the intervention, namely the preparation, screening, action planning, and implementation. The process and context factors appear to be particularly important at the preparation stage to determine whether the intervention is likely to get beyond the screening phase (Biron et al. 2010). Table 6.1 is adapted from Biron and Karanika-Murray (2014) and highlights a range of factors affecting the preparation phase. At the individual level, stakeholders' levels of readiness to change, their commitment and interest to participate in interventions are likely to have an impact on the other stages of the

Table 6.1   Individual and organizational key markers for process evaluation during early preparatory stages of an intervention

Individual Key Markers	Organizational Key Markers
Readiness for change (stakeholders' beliefs and perceptions about the intervention; Holt et al., 2007): – Appropriateness of the change – Perceived efficacy in performing the change – Valence of the change (that it will be beneficial) – Perception of management commitment towards the change	*Psychosocial safety climate* Policies, procedures, and practices for psychological health and safety and: – Senior management support – Priority for health versus productivity – Communication – Organizational participation and involvement (Hall et al., 2010)
Level of commitment to the intervention from stakeholders	Strategy to identify employees' needs regarding psychosocial risks (e.g., quantitative risk assessment, focus groups, etc.)
Initial levels of exposure to psychosocial risks (i.e. ceiling effect)	Steering committee to overview the main phases of the project
Individuals' interest in the intervention (i.e. participating in training, committees, etc.)	Strategy and communication plan to diffuse information to participants throughout the project
	Resources are allocated to the change initiative (i.e. training, time, money)

intervention. Their initial levels of exposure to psychosocial risks also influence the magnitude of changes that can be expected. As Semmer (2011) indicates, delivering interventions to workgroups where exposure levels are low and functioning is already optimal is equivalent to delivering smoking cessation training to non-smokers. At the organizational level, the psychosocial safety climate, interventions' strategies and infrastructure are also important determinants of success.

Implementing this type of intervention in the context of a formal standard certification implies a strong commitment from senior management and from all organizational stakeholders. Although several authors have insisted on the importance of senior management commitment and engagement from stakeholders (Giga et al., 2003; Nielsen et al., 2007; Noblet and LaMontagne, 2009; Semmer, 2011) there is very little empirical evidence of how this influences the implementation of interventions. In the next section, we introduce the idea that organizational-level and individual-level factors such as PSC and readiness can influence the implementation of interventions, before we describe our methodology to study these hypotheses.

PSYCHOSOCIAL SAFETY CLIMATE

PSC is a facet-specific component of safety climate (Dollard and Karasek, 2010) that 'reflects a communicated management position about the value, and priority of worker psychological health and safety in the workplace' (Hall et al., 2010, p. 356). It is considered a macro-level resource for the psychological safety of employees. Dollard and Bakker (2010, p. 580) define it as the 'organizational policies, practices, and procedures for the protection of worker psychological health and safety'. According to Hall et al. (2010, p. 355) PSC has four dimensions:

> 1) senior management support and commitment for stress prevention through involvement and commitment; 2) management priority to psychological health and safety versus productivity goals; 3) organizational communication, that is, the organization listens to contributions from employees; and 4) organizational participation and involvement, for example, participation and consultation occurs with unions, and occupational health and safety representatives.

Many studies concerning PSC show that reported (Berridge et al., 1997) PSC level is related to less exposure to psychosocial risks factors, less psychological distress, more employee engagement and more organizational resources (Dollard and Bakker, 2010; Dollard and Karasek, 2010; Hall et al., 2010; Idris and Dollard, 2011; Law et al., 2011; Dollard et al.,

2012a; Idris et al., 2012). The PSC model was developed by extending the job demand-resources (JD-R) model (Demerouti et al., 2001; Dollard and Bakker, 2010). The JD-R model suggests two paths through which psychosocial work environment influences employees' health and motivation. These are (1) the motivational pathway and (2) the health erosion pathway, through which job demands and resources interaction play a role in predicting job strain, motivation and organizational outcomes (Bakker and Demerouti, 2007). The extension of the JD-R model suggests that the PSC is a determinant of work conditions (Law et al., 2011); for example, Idris et al. (2012) support that demands mediate the relationship between PSC and exhaustion. Moreover, PSC has been reported as a precursor of the JD-R model in Malaysian studies (Idris et al., 2011, 2012), in an Australian sample (Law et al., 2011) and with Australian education workers (Dollard and Bakker, 2010).

Several studies report that PSC acts as a buffer to the harmful consequences of psychosocial constraints on the individuals. Per se, PSC moderates the deleterious effects of bullying and harassment on emotional exhaustion, engagement and distress levels (Law et al., 2011). PSC also moderates the relationship between emotional demands and emotional exhaustion in a longitudinal study (Dollard and Bakker, 2010). In addition, Hall et al. (2013) have found that PSC moderates the effects of job demands on depression and that it also buffers the effects of depression on job satisfaction and engagement. Furthermore, authors have argued that PSC is a pertinent primary stress intervention target (Dollard and Karasek, 2010; Dollard, 2012; Dollard et al., 2012b). Since job demands and job resources can be considered causes of occupational stress (Cooper et al., 2001), it appears logical and more beneficial to act upon the causes of stress instead of the consequences on individuals (Semmer, 2011). PSC is conceptualized by Dollard and Karasek (2010) as a 'cause of causes', or in other words, as a determinant of exposure to psychosocial risks.

Knowing that PSC reflects an organization's priority for the psychological health of workers, it is a pertinent construct to use in the evaluation of a standard aiming at both the physical and mental health of employees. It is plausible to expect that organizations that are concerned by the health of their employees, voluntary certified 'Elite' organizations in this case, will report high PSC levels, whereas lower levels of PSC would be found in organizations that are focused on secondary prevention and individual interventions and are not involved in any psychosocial risk interventions. In this study, we aim to see how PSC is related to less exposure to psychosocial risk factors through better management practices and we will explain why we do so.

Psychosocial Safety Climate and Management Practices

Managing psychosocial risks can be a rather daunting task for line managers. Indeed, as the work by Yarker et al. (2008) shows, line managers have a strong influence on job demands, and job resources such as social support and job control. The literature on occupational health interventions insists on the importance of line managers for both employee well-being, and for the implementation of interventions aiming to improve psychosocial risks (Nyberg et al., 2008; Muller et al., 2009; Nielsen and Randall, 2009; Hasson et al., 2012; Mellor and Webster, 2013; Nielsen, 2013).

Despite the fact that the role of managers has been acknowledged explicitly as being a determinant of successful occupational health interventions (Dellve et al., 2007; Biron et al., 2010; Mellor and Webster, 2013), little is known about factors influencing their level of ownership and commitment to the implementation of such changes within their team. If line managers perceive that senior managers support and are committed to preventing psychosocial risks and are active in stress prevention, it is likely that line managers will be more inclined to participate in the various activities related to stress prevention. A high level of PSC reflects senior management commitment to stress prevention, and a participative culture where various stakeholders are involved in the decision-making process regarding psychological health and safety. In the context of the standard implementation, we thus expect that a high level of PSC is going to be associated with a higher rate of change regarding the fourth sphere of the standard ('Management Practices' of psychosocial risks). In a context where there is a high PSC level, it may be easier or facilitative for managers to adopt better management practices. High levels of PSC imply that policies, practices and procedures are in place in order to protect employees' psychological health. In such a context, a manager may be more aware and have more tools to deal with the organizational constraints faced by employees.

A manager who is aware of the procedures and practices already in place in his or her organization, may be more alert and acting upon organizational constraints that may cause stress to employees. For example, if an employee is overwhelmed with his or her workload, a manager in a high PSC context may be more inclined to talk about it, and see what could be done to rearrange or adapt the workload, knowing that procedures and practices are in place to protect employees from harm. The communication component of PSC implies that various stakeholders are aware of the organization's policies, practices and procedures regarding occupational stress (Dollard and Bakker, 2010). Awareness of an intervention is a crucial component that is generally measured in intervention studies, since an intervention is more likely to have an effect when participants have noticed it. Nielsen et al.'s study (2007) showed that participants who were aware of and who participated in designing interventions benefited more from them. Randall et al. (2005), in an adapted study design, report that supervisors who were aware of an intervention and exposed to it (taking control of fault reporting) showed decreased exhaustion (there was significant longitudinal within-subject improvement for the aware/exposed group and group post-intervention scores). If the same applies at the managerial level, it is possible that a high PSC has an effect on managers via two pathways: (1) managers are aware of existing resources in their organization and have access to senior managers' and colleagues' support in order to (a) deal with their own sources of stress, and (b) implement required changes in their unit; (2) managers benefit themselves from these resources (and from a high PSC), which makes them more inclined to implement changes in their team.

In a high-level PSC context, it is plausible to think that managers may have a higher level of 'mental health literacy', since it is in the priorities of their organization. For example, in 'Healthy Enterprise – Elite' certified organizations, prevention, promotion and organizational practices for health in the workplace (1) must be part of the organization strategic planning, and (2) must be the object of training for directors and managers. Moreover, managers' responsibilities towards employees' health must be clearly defined in their job description or in the policy for health in the workplace. These requirements for the 'Healthy Enterprise – Elite' level seem to promote the organization's commitment to employees' health.

As mentioned previously, PSC is an indicator of the success of an intervention (Dollard, 2012). Measuring PSC at every step of an intervention may be beneficial, for it would provide key indicators that would inform stakeholders about where employees and management stands in the process and if the organization is ready to undertake the next step. For example, if the PSC level is found to be low during the early stages of an intervention and stakeholders do not perceive senior management commitment, perhaps the organization should revise its involvement in the intervention before going further in the process. Intervening to improve basic 'musts' may foster the advancement to the next step and prevent failure (Biron et al. 2010).

Along those lines, Karanika-Murray and Biron (2013) suggest that one of the change mechanisms to consider in an intervention process evaluation (IPE) is 'shared meaning'. They support that shared meanings have not been much used in IPE aside from when considering PSC because it conveys management values, philosophy and priority for psychological health (Dollard, 2012; Biron and Karanika-Murray, 2014). In the case of a voluntary standard evaluation such as 'Healthy Enterprise', an evaluation process with PSC items would help inform the organization about the perceptions of stakeholders and about the actions that must be taken for the achievement of a certification process.

In summary, a high PSC context seems to facilitate the enactment of good management practices. Contextual elements were discussed in this section, but what about the personal experience of the manager? Is he or she willing and ready to change his or her behavior? In order to adopt management practices that are favorable to decreasing employee exposure to psychosocial risks, line managers have to: (1) feel supported (principal support), (2) perceive that tools are in place for them in their organization (self-efficacy), and (3) believe the change in their behavior is appropriate because it goes along with the organization's values. As seen here, the adoption of management practices may be related to PSC but also to beliefs about the change, which is discussed in the next section.

READINESS FOR CHANGE

The implementation of organizational interventions such as changes in the team's work demands, job control, or rewards is likely to involve the line manager's input and support (Yarker et al., 2008). Thus, the adoption of healthy management practices seems not only to be related to contextual aspects, but also to personal beliefs and perceptions. Adopting new behaviors entails a change, and changing requires some kind of a process, decision-making or 'unfreezing' stage, as Lewin (1947) would suggest. Readiness for change (RFC) concerns one's cognitive and emotional disposition towards the proposed change and it is defined as:

> a comprehensive attitude that is influenced simultaneously by the content (i.e., what is being changed), the process (i.e., how the change is being implemented), the context (i.e., circumstances under which the change is occurring), and the individuals (i.e., characteristics of those being asked to change) involved. (Holt et al., 2007, p. 235)

Holt et al. (2007) report that the four perspectives suggested in their definition were used in many of the instruments available to assess RFC. They propose a model including those items and, in relation to the latter, the authors have published an RFC scale, which contains four key beliefs: (1) the 'appropriateness' of the change, (2) the employees' perceived 'efficacy' in performing the change, (3) the belief that it will be beneficial for the enterprise ('valence'), and (4) the perception that senior management is committed to the change ('principal support'). Along similar lines,

Armenakis and Harris (2009) have described RFC as containing five key beliefs: discrepancy, appropriateness, efficacy, principal support and valence (personal).

Readiness for Change and Management Practices

In the current project, we suggest that RFC is related to the adoption of better management competencies, or, in other words, that managers who are more 'ready to change' may be more inclined to adopt healthy management practices to prevent exposure to psychosocial risks within their team. In general, referring to some of the key beliefs (Commission Européenne: Direction Générale de l'Emploi et des Affaires Sociales, 1999) suggested by Armenakis and Harris (2009), managers who report a high level of self-efficacy could be more inclined to adopt a new behavior. Along similar lines, managers who believe that such a change is appropriate and that senior management will support and provide resources required to implement the change, or who believe that the change will be beneficial for the organization or for the work unit might be more willing to take the risk try out a new practice for managing psychosocial risks.

When considering the link between RFC and healthy management practices, one cannot ignore the importance of the employees' perceptions of these practices. For example, Brun et al. (2007) report that during an 18-month quasi-experimental intervention study, although several organizational and work-related changes had been implemented in intervention units, focus groups with employees showed that some of these interventions caused conflicts among team members, while some were not salient enough to be perceived by participants. Similarly, Hasson et al. (2012) report that during a large-scale intervention, there were significant differences between managers and employees regarding the type and number of interventions that were implemented. Given these differences in what Nielsen and Randall (2012) call 'mental models', or perceptions, it is possible that if an employee does not believe in the appropriateness of change (for example, a manager adopting a new practice to adjust workload), the effect of this practice might not be what was expected. This implies that both managers' and employees' readiness for change is likely to have an effect on how interventions are perceived, and what effects can be expected as a result.

Readiness for change is also pertinent in the process evaluation of interventions. In fact, in the case of an organizational-level stress management intervention, Randall et al. (2009) have assessed RFC as a part of the intervention process measure. They refer to Egan et al.'s (2009) literature review and suggest that employee readiness and motivation influence the outcome of an intervention (Randall et al., 2009, p. 7). Also, a model presented by Nielsen and Randall (2012) suggests three levels of elements to consider while evaluating a given process: the context, the intervention and mental models, where readiness for change is included. Moreover, Biron and Karanika-Murray (2014) suggest that readiness for change should be documented at each phase of the intervention in an implementation process. In the case of implementation of a national standard, each organization has to start with a diagnosis in order to establish to what extent employees are exposed to psychosocial risks, and to what extent they report various health issues. Since readiness for change could be an early indicator of people's perceptions about the intervention, it appears logical to include a measure of readiness during the screening phase as a pre-diagnosis. Indeed, in some cases, it could be necessary to conduct an intervention for certain groups before implementing any substantial interventions affecting the work organization or work conditions. For example, Bond et al. (2008) showed that an organizational intervention aiming to increase job control had stronger effects on employees who had previously been attending a training session to become psychologically flexible. Another example of how readiness for change could affect interventions' implementation is reported by Randall et al. (2005), who report that some senior managers did not communicate an intervention to supervisors because of financial constraints. Almost a third of the supervisors were not made aware of the new process. Those who were uninformed shared the same communication pathway. Had the organization known about senior managers' perception and beliefs about the change, and supervisors' awareness of the change, perhaps adjustments could have been made to ensure proper communication and intervention. Moreover, readiness may be assessed and even be created in a readiness program that be used to prepare stakeholders for change (Armenakis et al., 1993).

Considering that RFC and PSC are key elements in the adoption of good management practices, we believe they should be included in an intervention process evaluation. It has been well documented that managers are key actors in an intervention process (Nielsen and Randall, 2009; Biron et al., 2010; Kelloway and Barling, 2010). If psychosocial safety climate and readiness for change really do influence their management practices, it is crucial to document their beliefs and behaviors to better understand an intervention process. The certification process leads to changes in the work organization and requires managers' and employees' involvement and commitment. In the following section, we describe the methods used to evaluate PSC and RFC with regard to the implementation of interventions related to management practices for a certified healthy organization.

RESEARCH PROJECT DESCRIPTION: IMPLEMENTING THE HEALTHY ENTERPRISE STANDARD

As previously mentioned, in order to be certified officially by the BNQ, organizations have to be audited externally, and demonstrate that they have been actively taking measures with regard to at least two of the following four spheres: (1) 'Lifestyle Habits' (compulsory); (2) the 'Work Environment'; (3) 'Work–Life Balance'; and (4) 'Management Practices' of psychosocial risks.

The main goal of the study is to document how PSC and RFC influence exposure to the interventions through management practices. The study aims to consider key concepts in an intervention process in order to understand what is mostly related to improvements in exposure to psychosocial risks factors and what are the key characteristics of organizations concerned with the psychological health of their employees.

It is hypothesized that RFC and PSC will be key determinants in the implementation of the standard by their influence on management practices. It is hypothesized that PSC and RFC levels will also be linked to employees' exposure to the interventions, to more engagement from employees and to less exposure to psychosocial risk factors (lack of autonomy, lack of social support, low recognition and high workload). A para-governmental institute has already collected data from some organizations that are in the process of being, or are already certified as a 'Healthy Enterprise'. The data is collected before and either two to three years after the baseline measure. So far, one organization has completed two waves of measurement, and others are planned over the next few months.

METHODOLOGY

The current study is based on a mixed-method design; qualitative and quantitative data were collected through interviews with managers and key actors, questionnaires and focus groups. The current research project is issued from two larger studies: one from which quantitative data will be used (with a para-governmental institute) and the other one from which the qualitative data will be obtained.

Participants

Questionnaires

Individual questionnaires assessing an organizational portrait of the four dimensions of the standard ('Lifestyle Habits', 'Managerial Practices', 'Work Environment' and 'Work–Life Balance') and employees' distress were administered at $T1$. At $T2$, three years after the baseline measure, measures of exposure to the interventions, RFC, and PSC were added to the original questionnaire. These questionnaires are currently being collected and will allow us to evaluate the relationship between exposure to interventions, RFC, PSC, and psychosocial risks.

Individual interviews with managers and key stakeholders

A total of 27 individual semi-structured interviews were performed in the larger project. The informants consist of 16 managers and 11 key stakeholders. A total of 13 informants were eligible for the current study as they are in the 'Healthy Enterprise' standard certification process. Interviews took place face to face, either at the participants' office, at the university or by phone. These interviews were conducted to document what drives managers to adopt healthy management practices, managers' RFC, their perception of employees' RFC, indicators of PSC and management practices. The material has been transcribed and is being coded by three separate researchers using template analysis (Crabtree and Miller, 1992).

Focus groups with managers

Focus groups with a total of 30 managers were performed. At $T1$ they aimed to present tools and explain associations between psychosocial risks and management practices, and verify feasibility. Participants were then asked to pick one concrete action to implement over a three-month period. At $T2$, managers were met with again in order to discuss obstacles and facilitators regarding the adoption of the practice they picked at $T1$. Information relevant to the current research project will be extracted from the focus groups. Information related to RFC, PSC, and management practices will be collected.

PRELIMINARY RESULTS (BASED ON QUALITATIVE DATA ONLY)

Different Priorities, Different Stakeholders

A diagnosis has to be made at baseline in order to measure improvements over time. The health and well-being committee (HWBC), or others responsible in an organization for the certification process, may decide to act upon dimensions of work that are not necessarily aligned with the needs of the employees. For example, in a current research project we have noticed that many organizations' diagnoses display a need for intervention in management practices, but since enterprises do not have the resources to do so, they end up choosing other areas for change. Evaluating RFC in the process of a voluntary certification may improve the process. For example, assessments of RFC may be made to see if there are any gaps between the committee's, senior management's and employees' beliefs about the change and to foster an appropriate intervention implementation.

Managers' Low Autonomy to Implement Practices

Policies, procedures and practices are not always compatible with the support that managers need in order to implement concrete actions within their team. For example, while managers are being told they should be adopting concrete actions regarding psychosocial risks such as workload, they are at the same time obliged to find suitable and inexpensive ways to replace staff who are on sick leave or retiring due to budget cuts. Managers report feeling this dichotomy between the health and safety discourse put forward by the proponents supporting the standard, and top management's priorities regarding public image, productivity, and financial issues. Organizational dimensions of work, such as PSC level, may support or obstruct managers in the adoption of these better practices. Also, we have noticed that employees' perceptions of the intervention (RFC) may restrain managers from giving more autonomy at work, for example. Some managers revealed not wanting to give more autonomy to their employees as it may be perceived as favoritism in their unit. Some contextual elements related to the organization's history revealed that favoritism has caused conflicts in the preceding years. We suppose that even with a high PSC level, employees' and managers' RFC is not to be neglected when aiming for better management practices.

Managers in organizations with strong staff unions and collective agreement are limited in their actions when wanting to implement practices.

In some cases, such conventions would limit the autonomy a manager could give to employees, and in other cases it would constraint inter-unit collaboration to deal with periodic workloads. A more crafty manager reported that she had to know the collective agreement very well and 'who to talk to' to work around some political measures in order to implement management practices that would diminish employee exposure to psychosocial risks.

Lack of Training/Psychosocial Risk Literacy

Focus groups with managers highlight that many are not showing high 'psychosocial risk literacy'. In other words, managers receive their diagnosis from the external consultant regarding exposure to psychosocial risks within their work unit. Based on this diagnosis, they are expected to implement appropriate interventions in order to reduce exposure. However, focus groups show that they are not cognizant about the relationships between their day-to-day management practices and their effects on employee well-being. They easily recognize that stress and mental health problems are indeed important issues that need to be addressed, but they seem to fall short of ideas when asked how they could personally address these issues. After receiving a catalogue of ideas of simple management practices and their relation with psychosocial risks, managers indicated that they had attempted adopting some of the practices suggested. By sharing this newly acquired set of behaviors and skills with their colleagues, it is possible that a process of social contagion (Karanika-Murray and Biron, 2013) will occur by increasing their colleagues' level of RFC. Improving literacy about the psychosocial risks and offering tools to managers may improve awareness and self-efficacy about those risks. Moreover, being in an organization where psychological health and safety of employees is a priority (high PSC) may foster such behaviors: for example, directors and managers in 'Healthy Enterprises – Elite' must receive training in prevention, promotion and organizational practices for health in the workplace.

Fear of Being Overloaded by the Standard (and by the Research Project)

Managers involved in the certification process report that it is demanding in terms of time. Even if they hold their committees and some activities during work time, their commitment to the certification process adds to their workload. Even if the standard is in line with the organization's values for physical and mental health, a contradictory message may be heard; managers are often already overloaded with their own tasks and more demands are piled up. This may negatively influence their RFC for they may perceive less self-efficacy and question the necessity of such an intervention.

DISCUSSION AND CONCLUSION

Considering RFC and PSC in the implementation of a voluntary standard will help to better understand some of the change mechanisms involved in the process at each stage of the implementation. In the case of a voluntary standard such as 'Healthy Enterprise', stakeholders may be more intrinsically motivated than when it is an obligation. Motivations to engage in a voluntary certification process such as 'Healthy Enterprise' may be diverse. They may be to improve employees' well-being, to reduce absenteeism problems or to increase employee retention (Murphy and Sauter, 2004). Motives may guide the process, from the original idea to the certification and adoption of behavior.

Readiness for change and employees' perceptions of the intervention may change as employees go through a changing process. As suggested by Nielsen and Abildgaard (2013), change mechanisms such as actors' beliefs and behaviors are 'drivers' of the implementation process. In line with Biron and Karanika-Murray (2014), it is likely that these beliefs change as the intervention progresses. Managers and employees are not just passive recipients of these interventions but are actively taking part in them. Managers' capacity and willingness to adopt behaviors and attitudes to reduce exposure to psychosocial risk are likely to either increase or decrease depending on several factors. Feeling support by employees and by top management, having access to adequate training and coaching, feeling competent and supported in the process are elements likely to increase levels of readiness for change, and subsequently influence the implementation of various interventions related to the standard. Armenakis et al. accentuate 'the importance of creating readiness as a precursor to organizational change' (1993, p. 699) and they stress the importance of assessing readiness to get a grasp of the stakeholders' beliefs. We suggest that RFC assessment could be relevant at each stage of an intervention process, as stakeholders' perceptions may evolve through time. This could help facilitate the dialogue so stakeholders are informed of the participants' position and beliefs about the intervention process.

Similarly, PSC is probably not a stable construct either, and its influence on the standard implementation is likely to fluctuate as new policies, practices and procedures are adopted. Moreover, active participation through involvement and consultation with employees is an important facilitating factor to consider in an intervention process (Jauvin et al., 2014) (the authors refer to three longitudinal studies that occurred over a ten-year period). Communication (listening to employees' contributions) is also one of the main four dimensions of PSC, as seen earlier in the chapter. Periodical measures of RFC and PSC through each stage of the process may foster a better understanding of both formal/organizational aspects of the intervention (PSC) and informal/individual (RFC) influences on the standard implementation. As suggested by Nielsen and Randall (2012) and Biron et al. (2012a), mixed methods should be used to tap into the complex dynamics of these processes.

In the context of the standard evaluation, for a regular certification, the organization does not *have to* intervene in the sphere of 'Management Practices'. Indeed, the organization must select 'Lifestyle Habits' and one other sphere, such as 'Work Environment' or 'Work–Life Balance'. An organization could *decide to act* on 'Lifestyle Habits' and 'Management Practices'. However, data and interviews conducted in the research projects tend to show that the latter area is often put aside, even when the diagnosis reveals this area as problematic. The 'Management Practices' area is seen as intangible and many participants do not know how to handle it. For the 'Elite' certification, the organization must act in all four spheres; therefore organizations must act on 'Management Practices'. LaMontagne et al. (2014) report that organizations approached in a project were more drawn towards the mental health literacy training than the stress intervention, which were both part of the project. Literacy training did improve the participants' mental health literacy but no change was observed concerning job stress. LaMontagne et al. (2014) suggest starting to intervene where the organization is receptive. Along those lines, concerning the 'Healthy Enterprise' standard, organizations who are not ready or willing to be 'Elite' and act upon 'Management Practices' may be just in the right place: they begin where they are disposed to and receptive.

Actions in spheres other than 'Management Practices' may still help diminish psychosocial risks. For example, lunchtime conferences or sports activities may foster friendships and/or support between stakeholders. Moreover, it may eventually diminish exposure to other psychosocial risks factors such as workload or lack of recognition, for stakeholders may become more supportive and helpful in their work activities (help/support to deal with workload or recognizing a colleague's work or efforts). Moreover, acting upon 'Lifestyle Habits' and 'Work Environment' could help to mobilize management and staff around common health and well-being values and objectives. Perhaps such a mobilization may help organizations to become more inclined towards eventual interventions on management practices and psychosocial risks. The organization's health may become a priority and communication (PSC) may be established to prepare the field for further interventions, therefore creating RFC even if actions are not taken directly to diminish psychosocial risks exposure through the 'Management Practices' sphere.

REFERENCES

Aboa-Eboule, C., C. Brisson, E. Maunsell, B. Masse, R. Bourbonnais, M. Vézina, A. Milot, P. Théroux and G.R. Dagenais (2007), 'Job strain and risk of acute recurrent coronary heart disease events', *Jama*, **298**(14), 1652–60.
Armenakis, A.A. and S.G. Harris (2009), 'Reflections: our journey in organizational change research and practice', *Journal of Change Management*, **9**(2), 127–42.
Armenakis, A.A., S.G. Harris and K.W. Mossholder (1993), 'Creating readiness for organizational change', *Human Relations*, **46**(6), 681–703.
Bakker, A.B. and E. Demerouti (2007), 'The job demands-resources model: state of the art', *Journal of Managerial Psychology*, **22**(3), 309–28.
Berridge, J., C.L. Cooper, C. Highley Marchington and V. Caroline (1997), *Employee Assistance Programmes and Workplace Counselling*, Chichester, UK: John Wiley and Sons.
Biggs, H.C., J. Muller, R. Maclean and H. Biggs (2009), 'The impact of a supportive leadership program in a policing organisation from the participants' perspective', *Work*, **32**(1), 69–79.
Biron, C. and M. Karanika-Murray (2014), 'Process evaluation for organizational stress and well-being interventions: Implications for theory, method, and practice', *International Journal of Stress Management*, **21**(1), 85–111. doi: 10.1037/a0033227
Biron, C., C.L. Cooper and F.W. Bond (2009), 'Mediators and moderators of organizational interventions to prevent occupational stress', in S. Cartwright and C.L. Cooper (eds), *Oxford Handbook of Organizational Well-being*, Oxford: Oxford University Press, pp. 441–65.
Biron, C., C. Gatrell and C.L. Cooper (2010), 'Autopsy of a failure: evaluating process and contextual issues in an organizational-level work stress intervention', *International Journal of Stress Management*, **17**(2), 135–58.
Biron, C., H. Ivers, J-P. Brun and C. L. Cooper (2011, May), *The more the merrier? A dose-response analysis of an observational study of organizational-level stress interventions*. Paper presented at the Work, Stress, & Health Orlando, Fl.
Biron, C., M. Karanika-Murray and C.L. Cooper (2012a), *Improving Organizational Interventions for Stress and Well-being: Addressing Process and Context*, London: Routledge.
Biron, C., M. Karanika-Murray and C.L. Cooper (2012b), 'Organizational stress and well-being interventions: an overview', in C. Biron, M. Karanika-Murray and C.L. Cooper (eds), *Improving Organizational Interventions for Stress and Well-being: Addressing Process and Context*, London: Routledge, pp. 1–17.
Biron, C., F. St-Hilaire and J.-P. Brun (2014), 'Implementing an occupational health intervention in a large public organization: methodological and theoretical issues', in C. Biron, R.J. Burke and C.L. Cooper (eds), *Creating*

Healthy Workplaces: Stress Reduction, Improved Well-being, and Organizational Effectiveness, Farnham, UK: Gower Publishing, pp. 261–80.

Bond, F.W., P.E. Flaxman and D. Bunce (2008), 'The influence of psychological flexibility on work redesign: mediated moderation of a work reorganization intervention', *Journal of Applied Psychology*, **93**(3), 645–54.

Bourbonnais, R., C. Brisson and M. Vézina (2011), 'Long-term effects of an intervention on psychosocial work factors among healthcare professionals in a hospital setting', *Occupational and Environmental Medicine*, **68**(7), 479–86.

Bourbonnais, R., C. Brisson, M. Vézina, B. Mâsse and C. Blanchette (2005), 'Psychosocial work environment and certified sick leaves among nurses during organizational changes and downsizing', *Relations Industrielles*, **60**(6), 483–508.

Bourbonnais, R., C. Brisson, A. Vinet, M. Vézina, B. Abdous and B. Gaudet (2006), 'Effectiveness of a participative intervention on psychosocial work factors to prevent mental health problems in a hospital setting', *Journal of Occupational and Environmental Medicine*, **63**(5), 335–42.

Brisson, C., B. Larocque and R. Bourbonnais (2001), 'Impact of occupational stress on health status in Canada', *Canadian Journal of Public Health*, **92**(6), 460–67.

Brun, J.-P., C. Biron and H. Ivers (2007), *Démarche Stratégique de Prévention des Problèmes de Santé Mentale au Travail* [Strategic Approach to Preventing Mental Health Problems at Work], Quebec: Institut de Recherche Robert-Sauvé en Santé et en Sécurité du Travail.

Bureau de Normalisation du Québec (2008), *Prévention, promotion et pratiques organisationnelles favorables à la santé en milieu de travail – Guide explicatif sur la norme BNQ 9700–800\2008* [Prevention, Promotion and Organizational Practices Contributing to Health in the Workplace – Handbook], Quebec: Bureau de Normalisation du Québec.

Bureau de Normalisation du Québec (n.d.), *Liste des certificats et des attestations* [List of certificates and credentials], accessed 30 June 2014 at http://www.bnq. qc.ca/fr/certification.html.

Commission Européenne: Direction Générale dc l'Emploi et des Affaires Sociales (1999), *Manuel d'orientation sur le stress lié au travail: 'Piment de la vie. . . ou coup fatal?'* [Guidance Manual on Work-related Stress], Brussels: Emploi and Affaires Sociales: Santé et Sécurité au Travail.

Cooper, C.L., P.J. Dewe and M.P. O'Driscoll (2001), *Organizational Stress: A Review and Critique of Theory, Research, and Applications*, Thousand Oaks, CA: Sage Publications.

Cox, T., M. Karanika-Murray, A. Griffiths and J. Houdmont (2007), 'Evaluating organizational-level work stress interventions: beyond traditional methods', *Work and Stress*, **21**(4), 348–62.

Crabtree, B.F. and W.L. Miller (1992), 'A template approach to text analysis: developing and using codebooks', in B.F. Crabtree and W.L. Miller, *Doing Qualitative Research: Multiple Strategies*, Thousand Oaks, CA: Sage, pp. 93–109.

Dellve, L., K. Skagert and R. Vilhelmsson (2007), 'Leadership in workplace health promotion projects: 1- and 2-year effects on long-term work attendance', *European Journal of Public Health*, **17**(5), 471–6.

Demerouti, E., A.B. Bakker, F. Nachreiner and W.B. Schaufeli (2001), 'The job demands-resources model of burnout', *Journal of Applied Psychology*, **86**(3), 499–512.

Dobson, D. and T.J. Cook (1980), 'Avoiding type 3 error in program evaluation: results from a field experiment', *Evaluation and Program Planning*, **3**(4), 269–76.

Dollard, M.F. (2012), 'Psychosocial safety climate: a lead indicator of workplace psychological health and engagement and a precursor to intervention success', in C. Biron, M. Karanika-Murray and C.L. Cooper (eds), *Improving Organizational Interventions for Stress and Well-being Interventions: Addressing Process and Context*, London: Routledge, pp. 77–101.

Dollard, M. and A.B. Bakker (2010), 'Psychosocial safety climate as a precursor to conducive work environments, psychological health problems, and employee engagement', *Journal of Occupational Health Psychology*, **83**(3), 579–99.

Dollard, M.F. and R. Karasek (2010), 'Building psychosocial safety climate: evaluation of a socially coordinated PAR risk management stress prevention study', in J. Houdmont and S. Leka (eds), *Contemporary Occupational Health Psychology – Global Perspectives on Research and Practice, Vol. 1*, Chichester: Wiley-Blackwell, pp. 208–33.

Dollard, M.F., M.R. Tuckey and C. Dormann (2012), 'Psychosocial safety climate moderates the demand–resource interaction in predicting workgroup distress', *Accident Analysis and Prevention*, **45**, 694–704.

Dollard, M.F., T. Opie, S. Lenthall, J. Wakerman, S. Knight and S. Dunn, G. Rickard and M. Macloed (2012b), 'Psychosocial safety climate as an antecedent of work characteristics and psychological strain: a multilevel model', *Work and Stress*, **26**(4), 385–404.

Egan, M. (2013), 'Psychosocial interventions and salutogenic organizations: systematic review evidence of theory, context, implementation and outcome', in G.F. Bauer and G.J. Jenny (eds), *Salutogenic Organizations and Change: The Concepts Behind Organizational Health Intervention Research*, Dordrecht: Springer, pp. 19–36.

Egan, M., C. Bambra, M. Petticrew and M. Whitehead (2009), 'Reviewing evidence on complex social interventions: appraising implementation in systematic reviews of the health effects of organisational-level workplace interventions', *Journal of Epidemiology and Community Health*, **63**(1), 4–11.

Ferrie, J.E., M. Kivimaki, J. Head, M.J. Shipley, J. Vahtera and M.G. Marmot (2005), 'A comparison of self-reported sickness absence with absences recorded in employers' registers: evidence from the Whitehall II study', *Occupational and Environmental Medicine*, **62**(2), 74–9.

Giga, S., B. Faragher and C.L. Cooper (2003), 'Identification of good practice in stress prevention/management', in J. Jordan, E. Gurr, G. Tinline, S. Giga, B. Faragher and C.L. Cooper (eds), *Beacons of Excellence in Stress Prevention*, HSE Research Report No. 133, Suffolk, UK: HSE Books, pp. 1–45.

Goldenhar, L.M., A.D. LaMontagne, C. Heaney and P. Landsbergis (2001), 'The intervention research process in occupational safety and health: an overview from NORA Intervention Effectiveness Research Team', *Journal of Occupational and Environmental Medicine*, **43**(7), 616–22.

Groupe Entreprise en Santé [Healthy Entreprises Group] (n.d.) [website], accessed 30 June 2014 at http://www.gp2s.net/fr/.

Hall, G.B., M.F. Dollard and J. Coward (2010), 'Psychosocial safety climate: development of the PSC-12', *International Journal of Stress Management*, **17**(4), 353–83.

Hall, G.B., M.F. Dollard, A.H. Winefield, C. Dormann and A.B. Bakker (2013), 'Psychosocial safety climate buffers effects of job demands on depression and positive organizational behaviors', *Anxiety, Stress and Coping: An International Journal*, **26**(4), 355–77.

Hasson, H., M. Gilbert-Ouimet, G. Baril-Gingras, C. Brisson, M. Vézina, R. Bourbonnais and S. Montreuil (2012), 'Implementation of an organizational-level intervention on the psychosocial environment of work: comparison of managers' and employees' views', *Journal of Occupational and Environmental Medicine*, **54**(1), 85–91.

Holt, D.T., A.A. Armenakis, H.S. Field and S.G. Harris (2007), 'Readiness for organizational change: the systematic development of a scale', *Journal of Applied Behavioral Science*, **43**(2), 232–55.

Idris, M.A. and M.F. Dollard (2011), 'Psychosocial safety climate, work conditions, and emotions in the workplace: a Malaysian population-based work stress study', *International Journal of Stress Management*, **18**(4), 324–47.

Idris, M.A., M.F. Dollard and A.H. Winefield (2011), 'Integrating psychosocial safety climate in the JD-R model: a study amongst Malaysian workers', *South African Journal of Industrial Psychology*, **37**, 1–11.

Idris, M.A., M.F. Dollard, J. Coward and C. Dormann (2012), 'Psychosocial safety climate: conceptual distinctiveness and effect on job demands and worker psychological health', *Safety Science*, **50**(1), 19–28.

Jackson, N. and W. Waters (2005), *Guidelines for Systematic Reviews in Health Promotion and Public Health Interventions*, Melbourne: Cochrane Health Promotion and Public Health Field.

Jauvin, N., R. Bourbonnais, M. Vézina, C. Brisson and S. Hegg-Deloye (2014), 'Interventions to prevent mental health problems at work: facilitating and hindering factors', in C. Biron, R.J. Burke and C.L. Cooper (eds), *Creating Healthy Workplaces: Reducing Stress, Improving Well-being and Organizational Effectiveness*, Farnham, UK: Gower Publishing.

Karanika-Murray, M. and C. Biron (2013), 'The nature of change in organizational health interventions: some observations and propositions', in G.F. Bauer and G.J. Jenny (eds), *Salutogenic Organizations and Change: The Concepts Behind Organizational Health Intervention Research*, Dordrecht: Springer, pp. 239–58.

Karanika-Murray, M. and C. Biron (2014), *Derailed Organizational Health and Well-being Interventions – Confessions of Failure, Solutions for Success*, New York: Springer (in press).

Karasek, R. and T. Theorell (1990), *Healthy Work: Stress, Productivity and the Reconstruction of Working Life*, New York: Basic Books.

Kelloway, E.K. and J. Barling (2010), 'Leadership development as an intervention in occupational health psychology', *Work and Stress*, **24**(3), 260–79.

Kivimäki, M., M. Virtanen, M. Elovainio, A. Kouvonen, A. Väänänen and J. Vahtera (2006), 'Work stress in the etiology of coronary heart disease – a meta-analysis', *Scandinavian Journal of Work and Environmental Health*, **32**(6) (Special Issue), 431–42.

Kraaijeveld, R.A., F.G. Schaafsma, C.R.L. Boot, W.S. Shaw, U. Bültmann and J.R. Anema (2013), 'Implementation of the participatory approach to increase supervisors' self-efficacy in supporting employees at risk for sick leave: design of a randomised controlled trial', *BMC Public Health*, **13**(1), 1–7.

LaMontagne, A.D., T. Keegel, C. Shann and A. Noblet (2014), 'Integrating job stress and workplace mental health literacy intervention: challenges and benefits', in M. Karanika-Murray and C. Biron (eds), *Derailed Organizational*

Health and Well-being Interventions – Confessions of Failure, Solutions for Success, New York: Springer.

Law, R., M.F. Dollard, M.R. Tuckey and C. Dormann (2011), 'Psychosocial safety climate as a lead indicator of workplace bullying and harassment, job resources, psychological health and employee engagement', *Accident Analysis and Prevention*, **43**(5), 1782–93.

Lewin, K. (1947), 'Frontiers in group dynamics: concept, method and reality in social science; social equilibria and social change', *Human Relations*, **1**(1), 13–31.

MacKay, C.J., R. Cousins, P.J. Kelly, S. Lees and R.H. McCaig (2004), '"Management standards" and work-related stress in the UK: policy background and science', *Work and Stress*, **18**(2), 91–112.

MacKay, C., D. Palferman, H. Saul, S. Webster and C. Packham (2012), 'Implementation of the management standards for work-related stress in Great Britain', in C. Biron, M. Karanika-Murray and C.L. Cooper (eds), *Improving Organizational Interventions on Stress and Well-being: Addressing Process and Context Issues*, London: Routledge.

Marmot, M., H. Bosma, H. Hemingway, E. Brunner and S. Stansfeld (1997), 'Contribution of job control and other risk factors to social variations in coronary heart disease incidence', *Lancet*, **350**(9088), 235–9.

Mellor, N. and J. Webster (2013), 'Enablers and challenges in implementing a comprehensive workplace health and well-being approach', *International Journal of Workplace Health Management*, **6**(2), 129–42.

Muller, J., R. Maclean and H. Biggs (2009), 'The impact of a supportive leadership program in a policing organisation from the participants' perspective', *Work*, **32**(1), 69–79.

Murphy, L.R. and S.L. Sauter (2004), 'Work organization interventions: state of knowledge and future directions', *Soz.-Präventivmed*, **49**(2), 79–86.

Nielsen, K. (2013), 'Review article: how can we make organizational interventions work? Employees and line managers as actively crafting interventions', *Human Relations*, **66**(8), 1029–50.

Nielsen, K. and J.S. Abildgaard (2013), 'Organizational interventions: a research-based framework for the evaluation of both process and effects', *Work and Stress*, **27**(3), 278–97.

Nielsen, K. and R. Randall (2009), 'Managers' active support when implementing teams: the impact on employee well-being', *Applied Psychology: Health and Well-Being*, **1**(3), 374–90.

Nielsen, K. and R. Randall (2012), 'Opening the black box: presenting a model for evaluating organizational-level interventions', *European Journal of Work and Organizational Psychology*, **25**(1), 1–17.

Nielsen, K., R. Randall and K. Albertsen (2007), 'Participants, appraisals of process issues and the effects of stress management interventions', *Journal of Organizational Behavior*, **28**(6), 793–810.

Nielsen, K.M., M. Stage, J. Simonsen Abildgaard and C.V. Brauer (2013), 'Participatory interventions from an organizational perspective: employees as active agents in creating a healthy work environment', in G.F. Bauer and G.J. Jenny (eds), *Salutogenic Organizations and Change: The Concepts Behind Organizational Health Intervention Research*, Dordrecht: Springer, pp. 327–50.

Noblet, A. and A.D. LaMontagne (2009), 'The challenges of developing, implementing, and evaluating intervention', in S. Cartwright and C.L. Cooper (eds),

Oxford Handbook of Organizational Well-being, Oxford: Oxford University Press, pp. 466–96.

Nyberg, A., H. Westerlund, L.L.M. Hanson and T. Theorell (2008), 'Managerial leadership is associated with self-reported sickness absence and sickness presenteeism among Swedish men and women', *Scandinavian Journal of Public Health*, **36**(8), 803–11.

Randall, R., A. Griffiths and T. Cox (2005), 'Evaluating organizational stress-management interventions using adapted study designs', *European Journal of Work and Organization Psychology*, **14**(1), 23–41.

Randall, R., K. Nielsen and S.D. Tvedt (2009), 'The development of five scales to measure employees' appraisals of organizational-level stress management interventions', *Work and Stress*, **23**(1), 1–23.

Rossi, P.H., M.W. Lipsey and H.E. Freeman (2000), *Evaluation – A Systematic Approach*, 7th edition, Thousand Oaks, CA: Sage Publications Inc.

Semmer, N.K. (2006), 'Job stress interventions and the organization of work', *Scandinavian Journal of Work and Environmental Health*, **32**(6) (Special Issue), 515–27.

Semmer, N. (2011), 'Job stress interventions and organization of work', in J.C. Quick and L.E. Tetrick (eds), *Handbook of Occupational Health Psychology*, 2nd edition, Washington, DC: APA, pp. 299–318.

Shain, M. and C. Nassar (2009), 'Stress at work, mental injury and the law in Canada: a discussion paper for the Mental Health Commission of Canada', Mental Health Commission of Canada via the Advisory Committee on Mental Health in the Workforce and the Advisory Committee on Mental Health and the Law.

Siegrist, J. (1996), 'Adverse health effects of high-effort/low-reward conditions', *Journal of Occupational Health Psychology*, **1**(1), 27–41.

Siegrist, J., R. Peter, A. Jung, P. Cremer and D. Seider (1990), 'Low status control, high effort at work and heart disease: prospective evidence from blue-collar men', *Social Science and Medicine*, **31**(10), 1127–34.

Towers Watson and National Business Group on Health (2012), *Pathway to Health and Productivity: 2011/2012 Staying@Work Survey Report*, New York: Towers Watson/NBGH.

Vézina, M., E. Cloutier, S. Stock, K. Lippel, E. Fortin and A. Delisle et al. (2011), *Enquête québécoise sur des conditions de travail, d'emploi et de santé et de sécurité (EQCOTESST)* [Quebec Study on Working, Employment and OHS Conditions (EQCOTESST)], Montreal: IRSST.

World Health Organization (2013), *Comprehensive Mental Heath Action Plan 2013–2010*, accessed 30 June 2014 at http://www.who.int/mental_health/action_plan_2013/bw_version.pdf?ua=1.

Yarker, J., E. Donaldson-Feilder, R. Lewis and P.E. Flaxman (2008), *Management Competencies for Preventing and Reducing Stress at Work: Identifying and Developing the Management Behaviours Necessary to Implement the HSE Management Standards: Phase 2*, London: HSE Books.

7. Value-based healthcare for employers

Jonathan Spero

American employers will be looking forward to another year of rising healthcare costs for their employees and dependents. Despite countless incremental solutions such as wellness programs, consumer-driven healthcare, and provider payment reform, there has been very little impact on both the quality and the price of healthcare for employers.

It is time for a fundamental new strategy. At its core is a need to maximize value for patients – 'value-based healthcare'. Value-based care delivers the best outcomes at the lowest cost. And every stakeholder has a role to play including employees, employers, benefit consultants, providers, health plans, and innovative healthcare vendors.

So what is the primary goal of value-based healthcare? To date, healthcare reform strategies have been hampered by lack of clarity in defining this goal. Limited goals such as discounted fee for service pricing or improving access to care have not delivered the proper results. Neither improving access to poor care nor reducing the cost at the expense of quality are desired objectives.

In healthcare, the primary goal must be improving the *health value to patients*, where the health value is defined as the patient outcomes achieved divided by the cost of achieving those outcomes. Furthermore, these outcomes must be defined by what matters most for patients. Improving value occurs by either improving outcomes or reducing costs or ideally both.

So, how do employers make the transition to value-based healthcare within their organization? To answer this question, we must first look at the existing healthcare system.

PROBLEMS WITH THE EXISTING HEALTHCARE SYSTEM

The US healthcare system is complex and it is easy to get overwhelmed by its sheer size. From a strategic perspective, however, the issues in healthcare can be divided into three broad areas. The first is cost. The second is access. The third is the structure of healthcare delivery itself.

While the vast majority of attention has been focused on cost and access, I believe that the model of healthcare competition and the way healthcare is delivered are the most fundamental issues. The structure of healthcare delivery drives the cost and quality of the entire system.

The fundamental problem in the US healthcare system is that the structure of healthcare delivery is broken. And the reason for this is found in the malfunctioning of healthcare competition. All of the well-intended reform solutions have failed because they do not address the underlying issue of competition. In a normal market, competition drives improvements in quality and cost. Excellent competitors prosper and grow, while weaker rivals are restructured or go out of business. Quality-adjusted prices fall and value improves. This is the story of all thriving industries.

Healthcare competition could not be more different. Costs are high and rising despite numerous efforts to control them. Quality problems are ubiquitous. There are wide differences in cost and quality for the same type of care across providers and across geographic areas. Higher cost is not correlated with higher quality. Regions with higher spending do not have better outcomes, higher satisfaction, reduced mortality, or improved access to care. Competition does not reward the best providers, nor do poor providers go out of business. Technological innovation is not associated with lower costs; instead, it is seen as part of the problem. The result: high costs, variable quality, costly lawsuits, restrictions on choice, and limited access.

VALUE-BASED COMPETITION

On the other hand, value-based competition improves both healthcare corporations and the patients they serve. The healthcare providers that find effective ways to deliver superior value are successful and rewarded by more business. And patients also win as quality increases and prices fall. Those providers that fail to deliver good value suffer and ultimately go out of business.

Value-based competition is the type of competition we see in almost every profitable industry. Unfortunately, this type of competition has not produced the same results in the healthcare industry. Below are three primary reasons why the healthcare industry has not been able to realize value-based competition and its rewards:

- cost shifting;
- price competition (not value);
- consolidation.

Cost Shifting

Current healthcare competition takes the form of cost shifting rather than cost reduction. All healthcare system participants seek to lower their own costs by shifting the financial burden to other parts of the system. Costs are shifted from payer to patient, from health plan to hospital, from hospital to physician, from the uninsured to government, from states to the federal government, and so on.

Passing costs from one participant to another creates no net value. Instead, the gains for one system participant come at the expense of others. Cost shifting does nothing to improve healthcare. Worse, it misaligns the attention from necessary action that would improve value and focuses this attention on administrative juggling maneuvers that actually erode value.

Competition Based on Price

Competition among hospitals and hospital systems for health plan network inclusions is not an effective means of controlling healthcare costs. Hospitals compete based on discounts to the carrier. On the surface this would seem to have the effect of lowering costs. However, to the contrary, it actually accelerates healthcare costs by not addressing value-based care.

The problem is that there are little or no economies of scale benefit or other cost-saving benefit for hospitals that participate in this competition. Healthcare delivery does not become more efficient when a hospital treats more patients with an unlimited number of diseases. Any meaningful economies of scale in healthcare delivery occur at the level of particular medical conditions and their treatment. Across-the-board discounts do not encourage value; rather, they simply lower the incomes of hospitals and doctors. This, in turn, creates intense pressure on practitioners to see more patients per day. Healthcare value is not improved; rather, it is weakened by cutting corners on time and resources.

Provider Consolidation

The pressure on providers triggered the formation of large, powerful, broad-lined provider groups. While this was a natural response to the increase in health plan bargaining power, it again failed to increase value in healthcare delivery. Providers sought to control a large share of capacity and form large delivery networks able to offer a complete array of services to gain advantages in contracting. Physicians joined into groups so they would not have to bargain as individual agents. But in both cases, cost efficiencies were not gained, except for modest reductions in overhead.

The primary economies of scale in healthcare delivery are in condition-based service lines, not for the hospital as a whole. But with few exceptions, hospital mergers have not resulted in integration at the service line level. Instead, duplicative services were left in place, even when the facilities were close to each other. Provider groups were not formed to create value. They were created to boost bargaining power.

The effect of such consolidation on prices is predictable. With little benefit in terms of value, the primary effect is that prices will rise due to less competition. Large hospital networks have won price increases far above the rate of inflation after threatening to cut off a region's largest health plans. These increases are unconnected to any quality improvements. Large provider groups severely limit competition because their referrals are heavily skewed toward affiliated physician groups and institutions, undermining competition on quality and price.

CREATING VALUE IN HEALTHCARE

Value in healthcare can only be realized at the medical condition level. A medical condition (e.g., back pain, diabetes, or cancer) is a set of patient health circumstances that benefit from dedicated, coordinated care. Only by focusing on a particular medical condition is patient value achieved. There are currently significant differences in cost and quality on the medical condition level. Lack of proper, value-based, competition allows providers with worse outcomes and higher charges to remain in business. It is only through competition at the condition level that there exists enormous opportunity to drive improvements in costs and effectiveness.

Unfortunately, competition at the level of medical conditions is almost absent in our current healthcare system. Competition at this level is hampered by lack of consumer outcomes and price information and network restrictions. Patients are referred to doctors and hospitals inside the network. Even if out-of-network care is allowed, it is severely restricted by higher copayments[1] and the requirement to pay list prices.

In healthcare the information most needed to support value-based competition has been largely unavailable. Physicians generally lack information on results, or their efficiency in achieving results, that is essential for critical evaluation of their practice methods. Today the knowledge, complexity, and specialization of care have grown exponentially, yet most physicians lack any objective evidence of how their results compare with other providers. If providers received feedback that their results are below average, this would create strong incentives to learn from those who are doing better and to improve. Without results information, referrals for specialty care are based not on measured excellence but on a doctor's personal network. Without objective information, the incentives to improve and learn from others are absent. Results information, in contrast, allows doctors to work continually to improve the patients' results and participate in value-based competition.

The same type of information on results is critical for patients. Patients have much better information available to them about homes, cars, appliances, airlines, and restaurants than they do about their healthcare. The information that is available – health plan overviews, subscriber-satisfaction surveys, and doctor and hospital reputation surveys – is of limited value. Much more relevant is information about providers' actual patient results and pricing is sorely lacking.

Access to provider quality information is essential for patients to be able to make an informed decision. Moreover, poor quality almost always raises costs through inefficiency, prolonging the need for care, and requiring further treatment secondary to complications or lack of improvement in a condition.

Many efforts, both public and private, are attempting to address poor quality, for example the National Quality Forum, the Institute for Healthcare Improvement, and the National Committee for Quality Assurance. Employers have also finally recognized the importance of quality, especially the dimension of safety. Employees' quality initiatives, such as the Pacific Business Group on Health and the Leapfrog Group, are making good headway. The Leapfrog Group, a consortium of employers with a membership of public and private companies, has been the most successful. Leapfrog members have used their combined influence to pressure and encourage hospitals to improve safety and quality. Leapfrog also advocates and encourages financial rewards by health plans to providers that improve the quality, safety, and affordability of healthcare. Such pay-for-performance initiatives are now widely endorsed as a way to reduce errors. There are many other pay-for-performance systems being designed and they hold promise for improving quality. However, these current efforts also carry some risks.

PAY FOR PERFORMANCE

Most current quality initiatives are not actually about quality (results), but processes. Most 'pay for performance' is really pay for compliance with medical flow charts. Providers are expected to conform to specific processes, but are not necessarily rewarded for better results. This approach has serious limitations.

First, the incentives have not historically been large enough to shift behavior, and do not compensate providers for lower reimbursement if quality means that less treatment is needed. Second, given the complexity of medical care, it is possible for providers to have wide variation in patient results even if process compliance is similar. Pay for compliance does not guarantee excellent quality. Even worse, if extra pay is tied to process conformance rather than to outcomes and results, the wrong incentives can be created. For example, many pay-for-performance incentives include compliance with specified processes in a few limited areas of medical care. Other pay-for-performance initiatives address a few hospital processes on which consensus has been achieved and data are available. These processes may not be the most important parameters related to outcomes. And if they are important, this may change over time. Yet the rewards are linked to these processes regardless of results. Compliance with too many process standards also runs the risk of inhibiting innovations. If providers are held to currently acceptable practices, this can deter innovation to find better ones.

Third, process compliance also ignores the importance of providers avoiding unnecessary care and educating patients on alternative options for treatment. Rewarding value, rather than process compliance, would enable physicians to benefit by helping patients to become better informed and choose the most appropriate care, even when that means less care.

Fourth, there is a danger with process compliance of not modifying the requirements as best practices change over time. Updating process measures and reflecting the latest learning is challenging. As a result, some patients are being treated with an out-of-date process.

Finally, pay for performance assumes that value only comes with increasing costs. In healthcare, better care often costs less. Better health is inherently less expensive. Better care reduces costs through prevention, less invasive treatment, and better management of chronic care. The bottom line is that healthcare delivery is simply too complex and rapidly evolving to be manageable by administrators.

COMPETITION BASED ON RESULTS PER CONDITION

The real proof of success is better patient results (quality versus cost), not compliance with processes specified by outside experts or administrators. Providers need to be compared on results, and excellent providers rewarded with more patients. Information about results, which is appropriately risk adjusted, must become the critical driver of behavior in the system – by referring physicians, by health plans, by patients, and by providers themselves. Results (outcomes divided by cost) also must be the ultimate basis of which drugs, medical devices, other technologies, and services are selected.

Results mean actual health value for patients. A hospital ranking per US News & World Report can be misleading. Unrestricted competition based on results is the best and only real solution for the problems of medical errors, under-treatment, and over-treatment. Practice guidelines have failed repeatedly to drive widespread process improvement. Outside review of treatments or investments has failed to control excess capacity and unnecessary care. Competition on results, not trying to control supply, is the only effective way to create accountability, motivate and inform process improvement, and drive up patient value. If, and only if, providers have to demonstrate excellent results in addressing specific medical conditions will errors decline, unnecessary tests not be performed, and unnecessary treatments stop.

In healthcare, as in all fields, identifying what constitutes the relevant business or market is critical to making good choices and ensuring that markets work. It is common to talk about healthcare as if it were one service. Instead, it is a myriad of distinct services. But each service is not the relevant business either. The relevant businesses in healthcare delivery are specific medical conditions seen over the cycle of care. A medical condition (e.g., chronic kidney disease, diabetes, pregnancy) is a set of patient health circumstances that benefit from dedicated, coordinated care. The term 'medical conditions' encompass specific diseases, illnesses, and injuries. A medical condition can also be defined as co-occurring conditions if care for them involves the need for tight coordination. As we have discussed, value in results can only be measured in a meaningful way at the medical condition level. Providers can offer services for a range of medical conditions, but the value they create is overwhelmingly determined by how well they deliver care for each one.

How to define the medical conditions around which to organize care delivery involves important judgments. A medical condition should be defined from the patient's perspective. It should encompass the set of illnesses or injuries that are best addressed with an integrated care delivery process.

Setting the start and the end of the care cycle for each medical condition is also an important judgment. For example, for chronic conditions like diabetes or kidney disease, the results are measured on an annual basis. For an acute condition like back pain, it includes everything from evaluation, to surgery, to the completion of rehabilitation.

Providers should organize themselves around medical conditions, not skills or discrete specialties or services necessary to address a medical condition. Integrated practice units should include all the services necessary to address a medical condition, usually in dedicated facilities. Providers will define integrated practice units somewhat differently based on their patient populations and their approaches to structuring and coordinating care. Competition in addressing medical conditions must take place over the full cycle of care, not on discrete interventions, treatments or services. Value can only be accurately measured over the cycle, not just a particular intervention.

There is merit in value improvement for each aspect of care delivery but the potential for value improvement is far greater by managing the full cycle of care. In today's fractured, procedure-centric system, tapping into this potential is still in its infancy. In the diagnosis the treatment of a medical condition, numerous specialties, departments, and even different organizations are typically involved. There are also important linkages or inter-dependencies across care delivery activities that must be optimized. Better preparation before treatment, for example, can make treatment more effective. More attention to rehabilitation and post-hospitalization follow up can raise the success rate of the surgery.

COST CONTAINMENT FOR EMPLOYERS

Rather than managing health, employers have attempted to manage costs. Instead of understanding the quality and value differences in healthcare offerings, employers have bought health plans based on price as if healthcare is seen as a commodity. Rather than working strategically with health plans to find ways to improve value and reduce the long-term costs of healthcare for the company and employees, employers have pushed for discounts in the lowest annual premium increases, thereby encouraging health plans to focus on short-term reduction and cost shifting. As employers shuffled healthcare offers almost every year in search of cost reductions, they triggered more cost shifting instead of encouraging longer time horizons that would align health plan, provider, and employer interests.

For all other services successful companies realize that suppliers are not equal. Few products or services are actually commodities, especially complex services like healthcare. Companies know that the relevant standard for choice is value, not just cost. Companies know that innovation is crucial to progress, not something to be minimized. They know that relevant information is essential to good decision-making, and that well-informed buyers get better value. Finally, companies know that the right kind of competition among their vendors is crucial. Unfortunately, when it comes to healthcare the common procurement concepts have been thrown out the window.

On the plus side, employer consortia are an important step in the right direction and Leapfrog has done much to counter the commodity mindset in employers' healthcare purchases while highlighting the importance of safety. However, medical errors and safety are only a part of the overall quality and value equation. Leapfrog has a focus on process compliance, rather than results, and is falling into the trap of trying to specify how hospitals should plan their operations. It is also attempting to certify hospitals as a whole, rather than at the medical condition level. Leapfrog's efforts to expand the amount and types of information are welcome initiatives. However, there is still much work to be done to focus on value-based competition.

Another relatively new strategy is 'pay for performance'. In this approach, higher reimbursement rates are set for providers that adhere to specific standards for care delivery. The goal is to improve the quality of care by encouraging the widespread use of evidence-based medicine and nationally recognized practice standards. These standards mostly involved hospital-wide practices or basic treatment standards for a few medical conditions, but they are beginning to include outcome measures. However, pay for performance has problems, as noted, because they primarily focus on performing discrete services rather than for achieving excellent results over the full cycle of care in particular medical conditions.

So how do employers move towards a value-based healthcare delivery system within their organization? The strategy involves four interdependent and fundamental components:

- population health management;
- directing care to maximize value;
- bundled case rates;
- measured outcomes and costs.

Of note, in an ideal world, employers, health plans, and providers would work in concert to deliver all four components effectively to employees and dependents. However, in our current healthcare environment, the most suitable solution to deliver this care is through what we call the 'next generation' of worksite health centers. We will discuss more details of this later in this chapter. Below is a description of each component of the employer value-based healthcare system.

Population Health Management (PHM)

Unfortunately a majority of patients in the USA are not getting the care they need. This gap between nationally recognized evidence-based medicine guidelines and the care patients are currently receiving is termed 'gaps in care'. These gaps lead to poor patient outcomes and much higher costs.

Physicians have traditionally acted in a reactionary fashion – managing acute problems with little focus on prevention. In addition, a RAND study in 2003 showed that 55 percent of medical care received by patients does not follow nationally recognized, evidence-based medicine recommendations. Worsening the issue is patient non-compliance with recommended care. With effective PHM strategy, high-risk patients, who usually have the most gaps in care and are predicted to cost the most in near-term future healthcare costs, are identified and targeted for clinical intervention. Telephonic engagement strategies have been widely ineffective to date and employers must look for worksite solutions or strategies that direct care to community providers who have demonstrated an ability to effectively execute PHM. Solutions that have demonstrated the most success utilize the following tools:

- predictive modeling software and electronic medical records with imbedded evidence-based medicine algorithms and alerts that identify high-risk patients;
- automated outreach systems that communicate with patients in a rule-based algorithm via multiple modalities to drive engagement;
- medical home model personnel that address healthy behavioral choices (health coaching) as well as psychosocial obstacles and issues with compliance;
- care coordination with all providers delivering care to the patient;
- continuous measuring and reporting to track performance.

In conjunction with population health management, employers must build in incentives for employees and their dependents to participate in managing and improving their own health. Incentive-based population health management programs should be part of every employer health plan. Employers should also include screening, risk assessment, and preventive services. Employers should expect their health plans to work with primary care physicians and others to identify member risk factors and provide systematic programs for disease prevention for high-risk members. Finally, a good plan should reward behavior for improved health.

Directing Care to Maximize Value

The second component of the strategy is to direct certain medical services to facilities and providers that have demonstrated the best outcomes at the lowest cost for those particular services. This component has several key features including partnering with centers of excellence, price and quality transparency, patient advocacy, and a value-based employee incentive plan.

Routine, low-complexity services should be moved out of academic centers and hospitals to lower-cost facilities with lower fees. An example of this is a knee arthroscopy, a simple procedure to diagnose a complaint of knee pain and swelling. Patients in need of this service should be shifted away from a tertiary hospital to an ambulatory surgery center where the price can be cut in half without jeopardizing quality. On the other hand, a patient requiring a complex surgery for a heart, spine, or cancer issue can be directed to an identified center of excellence that has the necessary resources and experience to maximize the patient outcome.

The features necessary to achieve this direction of care are described below:

Identifying centers of excellence
There exist in almost every region of the USA integrated medical systems that have demonstrated their ability to deliver superior patient outcomes at a lower cost for different groups of conditions such as heart, cancer, spine, and transplants. When surgery is required their patients recover faster, spend less time in the hospital, experience fewer complications, and have less days away from work.

These centers of excellence all share a common strategy, namely, the presence of an integrated practice unit (IPU) made up of a team of both clinical and non-clinical persons providing the full episode of care for the patient's condition. Take Virginia Mason's Spine Clinic approach to low back pain. The team works in an integrated way pairing a physician with a physical therapist. More serious cases are identified earlier and immediately placed into a process that can address these complex issues. The results are striking. Patients at the Spine Clinic miss fewer days of work as compared to regional averages, need fewer physical therapy visits, and utilize expensive MRI imaging considerably less.

Price and quality transparency

With the advent of consumer-driven healthcare the need for tools to empower employees in making informed healthcare decisions has never been greater. Provider price and quality transparency gives healthcare consumers the same type of information they have come to expect with other buying decisions (for example, when choosing to purchase an appliance utilizing consumer reports or when buying an automobile with the assistance of *Kelley Blue Book*).

Price transparency, offered as an employee benefit, leverages the wide range of negotiated carrier prices for a particular service in a geographic marketplace. A number of health plans offer watered down versions of this service and several vendors such as Healthcare Bluebook, Compass, and Castlight provide a much more granular picture including estimated out-of-pocket cost comparisons.

Layering quality rankings on top of price transparency allows consumers to calculate the value of the care (quality divided by the price) and make a sound healthcare decision that best meets their needs. Though meaningful, quality measures are much more difficult to assess and often require access to provider data, claims data, and sophisticated analytical tools.

Patient advocacy

Patient advocacy is not needed in a perfect world where the delivery of healthcare is organized into IPUs centered on the patient's needs. However, our current healthcare system is predominately delivering unorganized, fragmented care quite often in different locations with a multitude of providers who are not communicating with each other.

In such an environment patients need a patient advocate to assist them in navigating the healthcare system. The patient advocate can address a number of patient needs including directing care to value-based providers, answering questions about their medical condition and treatment plans, assisting with medical bills and insurance questions, scheduling appointments, and managing the transfer of medical records.

Value-based benefit design (VBBD)

VBBD is a way for employers to enable and encourage employees and dependents to make the best healthcare decisions for their medical condition. VBBD is focused on the manner in which a purchaser uses their buying power to maximize the value that they receive from its entire health benefit program.

An employer utilizing VBBD will integrate identified centers of excellence, price transparency tools, case rate negotiations, chronic disease evidence-based guidelines, and other relevant programs into their benefit design plan. The plan will modify employee contributions, employee deductibles and copays, and tiered pricing for different medical services and providers in order to direct care to value-based solutions.

Bundled Case Rates for Episodes of Care

Neither fee for service nor capitation,[2] the major payment models in healthcare, are aligned with incentives for value-based care. Fee for service rewards providers for how many services they provide. The more services, the greater the reward. Capitation rewards providers for spending less, but not necessarily for improving quality of care or outcomes.

The payment model best aligned with the goal of value-based care is bundled case rates. This bundled payment model covers all care delivered for an acute medical condition requiring medical care such as a surgery or hospitalization. It can also be tied to chronic conditions such as diabetes where the payment and outcomes are tied to a defined period, usually yearly, called a 'cycle of care'.

The payment for the acute or chronic condition is negotiated upfront and attached to performance guarantees. The performance guarantees are based on outcomes that can be controlled by the providers and measured. The performance guarantees are patient-centric, meaning they matter most to the patient. This approach is aligned with value-based care because providers are now given an incentive for cost-efficient care with the best outcomes. For example, with low back surgeries it turns out that the parameter most directly related to time away from work is not the facility, nor the surgeon, but actually how quickly a patient enters into a physical therapy program after surgery, how effective the program is, and the level of patient compliance with that program. Therefore, for spine surgery case rates, physical therapy parameters would be an important part of the performance guarantees.

Bundled payments for transplants have become very prevalent in the USA. And those medical facilities that have demonstrated the greatest value are now considered centers of excellence and have benefited greatly from higher revenue streams. Many employers have already adopted bundle payments. Companies like Walmart and Safeway have introduced programs to encourage employees to utilize centers of excellence that have demonstrated superior outcomes, not only for transplants, but also for surgeries such as cardiac, spine, and oncology. Such centers of excellence include facilities like Cleveland Clinic, Geisinger, Mayo Clinic, and Virginia Mason. The employers negotiate bundled case rates that cover all physician and hospital costs during the entire episode of care including post-operative care. The employer typically pays for all travel, lodging, and meals for the patient and caregiver.

Measured Outcomes and Cost

Systematic measurement of results is the key to improving results in healthcare. Therefore, it is critical that employers have a tracking system in place to measure both the cost of care and the associated patient outcomes. This is much like swimming against the tide because the healthcare industry is amazingly void of both quality and cost measurements. Few clinicians have any idea of the cost of care for each component of treatment they order. And when outcomes measurements are done, which is very rarely, they only track a few areas such as safety and mortality.

Outcomes should be measured in several different ways and all should be patient-centric. For acute conditions such as those that require surgery, the outcomes measured can be divided into three categories – namely, treatment experience, short-term improvement, and long-term improvement in health status:

- *Treatment experience* includes outcome measurements such as length of hospital stay, rate of complications, re-admission rate, need for second operation and patient satisfaction.
- *Short-term improvement* includes outcome measurements such as time to return to work, functional level of improvement, and pain improvement within the first year.
- *Long-term improvement* includes outcome measurements such as functional and pain levels at greater than a year, need for surgical revision, and long-term complications.

For chronic conditions such as asthma or diabetes or CHF, the outcome measurement parameters are different and include compliance with evidence-based guidelines, number of ER visits or hospitalizations, rate of complications, and quality of life scores.

When measuring cost of care it must be done on the condition level. That is tracking expenses involved in the treating of a condition over the full episode of care or, for chronic conditions, over the full cycle of care. This can be simplified if the employer enters into bundled case rate agreements with facilities for acute care. However, for chronic disease care such as diabetes it requires access to all claims data and the ability to track claims for a subgroup of patients based on a particular condition. Employers can then track the cost of care for patients with this chronic condition over time to determine if the costs are improving. Furthermore, employers can dissect the cost components to a more granular level and evaluate cost components individually such as hospitalizations, ER visits, pharmaceutical costs, and specialty costs.

WORKSITE HEALTH CLINICS AND VALUE-BASED CARE

A recent survey from Mercer (2012) found that worksite clinics are becoming an increasingly popular way to control healthcare spending and even enhance employee productivity. Until recently, worksite clinics were largely popular only in Fortune 500 companies; however, the trend is now spreading to local governments and mid-size companies of 250 or more employees who are self-insured.

Generally, the care received at the clinic is free to the member and there is an added convenience factor for employees. Worksite clinics to date have primarily experienced their return on investment for the employer by providing more efficient care at the worksite clinic rather than paying claims from community physicians. However, the next generation of worksite clinics offers the potential of a much more compelling value proposition and greater associated cost containment results. Worksite clinics can leverage the patient relationships they foster with employees and dependents to deliver all of the components of a value-based healthcare system as follows:

Population Health Management

Community physicians do not have access to the amount of comprehensive patient data that worksite health clinic vendors can possess. These vendors have access to member claims, PBM, biometric, EMR, and HSA data. The collection, integration, and analysis of this data allows employers and their health plan members to benefit from population risk stratification, evidence-based medical interventions, and continuous measuring of outcomes – all essential elements of an effective population health management program.

The patient engagement rates associated with this program at the clinic is considerably higher than what is currently achieved by similar programs through the carrier or remote disease management company. The clinic population health management program leverages the existing clinic's patient physician relationships to foster patient trust and participation in these programs.

Directing Care to Maximize Value

Clinic providers who are in alignment with value-based medicine are the perfect vehicles for directing care to value-based providers of costly diagnostic and specialty services in the community. Again, these providers can leverage their established patient–provider relationship in the worksite clinic to influence the care their patients are receiving outside of the clinic. The clinic provider can direct members to a patient advocate (either part of the clinic or through a separate vendor). The patient advocate can then offer patients price and quality transparency referrals to narrow networks of value-based providers. The providers in these narrow networks are those that have demonstrated an ability to deliver value-based medicine and/or are established centers of excellence. In addition, they can assist patients in navigating through the healthcare system.

One of the primary obstacles to directing patients to value-based providers is lack of support from the patient's primary care physician (PCP). PCPs tend to be biased based on established referral networks that are usually not value-based. The worksite clinic removes this obstacle and supports the patients' 'smart' healthcare decision-making and assists with an employers' consumer-driven health plan.

Bundled Case Rates

Since the next generation of worksite clinics are so influential in directing patient care outside of the clinic, it makes perfect sense for the clinic to drive the creation and implementation of bundled case rates with community providers. Worksite vendors can identify high cost drivers and associated healthcare services, reach out to community centers of excellence (COEs), and negotiated bundled case rates for full episodes of care. Cancer, orthopedics, cardiac, and other conditions can be directed by the clinic to these COEs or integrated practice units for specialty care. The clinic can monitor the care delivered by these providers and attach performance guarantees to the bundled case rates, further ensuring the delivery of value-based medicine.

Measured Outcomes and Cost

Worksite clinic vendors are ideally suited to measure tangible patient results and outcomes associated with care delivered to employees and their families. The clinic acts as a data repository by not only receiving all of the claims data from the health plan, but also receiving additional clinical data from the clinic's EMR and providers in the medical community caring for the employers' members. The clinical data from providers in the community is secured by way of data-sharing agreements between the worksite clinic and the value-based community providers.

Employers can finally collect the data necessary to systematically measure both the cost of care and the associated patient outcomes. The acute care results can be measured via treatment experience, short-term improvement, and long-term improvement. For chronic conditions the outcomes can be measured via compliance with evidence-based guidelines, number of ER visits or hospitalizations, rate of complications, and quality of life scores.

Employers' are empowered with the data necessary to select all health and wellness vendors and health plans based on the health results achieved for members per dollar of spending. Health results need to be measured over a two- to three-year period. This period is what it takes for the programs mentioned above to achieve the full benefits. Results need to be adjusted for the nature of the employee population. Employers also can then begin negotiating contracts with vendors and the health plan, which are tied to improvements in the health status of their covered population.

CONCLUSION

Building a value-based employee healthcare program requires an ongoing effort and commitment by the employer. By necessity, it requires strong leadership and vision. It cannot be accomplished with one monumental implementation effort. Rather, it requires a stepwise approach building upon the foundation of each prior accomplishment. All non-clinical stakeholders including benefits executives, financial executives, benefit consultants, health plans, third party vendors, and employees must all work together to realize their mutual goal.

Resistance will be inevitable and must be anticipated. However, maintaining a course towards a value-based system will lead to enormous financial rewards for any employer and improved health and productivity for the plan members.

NOTES

1. A payment defined in the insurance policy and paid by the insured person each time a medical service is accessed.
2. Capitation payments are a fixed pre-arranged monthly payment received by a physician, hospital, etc., per patient enrolled in a health plan with a capitated contract. It is calculated one year in advance, regardless of how often the patient needs services.

REFERENCE

Mercer Consulting (2012), 'Worksite Medical Clinics 2012 Survey Report'.

PART III

Developing, implementing and sustaining
corporate wellness programs

8. MD Anderson Cancer Center employee wellness program journey

William B. Baun

INTRODUCTION

There have been few publications that elucidate the evolution, the life journey, of an organizational wellness program from startup, through cross-promotion, maintenance and growth phases to program maturity. The Johnson & Johnson program is probably the longest wellness program followed in the peer review literature, but the studies have primarily focused on the financial aspects of the program, with few operational details (Goetzel et al., 2002, Carls et al., 2011; Henke et al., 2011). This chapter follows the life journey of the MD Anderson employee wellness program for the past 15 years, from program startup to its current newly transformed state. The author, William B. Baun, tells the story of developments during the 15 years he has served as the program startup manager and Wellness Officer. In preparation for writing this manuscript Baun interviewed two senior executives. Dr. Thomas Burke, MD was Chief Medical Officer at the time the organization initiated the employee wellness program. Dr. Burke recently became the Executive Vice President of the MD Anderson Cancer Network. Shibu Varghese, Vice President Human Resources/Chief Human Resource Officer currently 'owns' the employee wellness program, and has been in his position for the past six years. The author used the interviews to illuminate senior executives' thoughts and concerns along the way on the employee wellness program journey. The operational details provided along with senior management insights can help program managers and practitioners better understand the life journey challenges of organizational wellness programs.

WHO ARE THE PEOPLE OF MD ANDERSON CANCER CENTER?

In 1941 the Texas Legislature created MD Anderson Cancer Center (MDACC) as part of the University of Texas (UT) System. In 1943 Houston voters approved a special election that allowed the MD Anderson Foundation to buy land owned by the city south of Hermann Hospital. MD Anderson then donated the land back to the newly created legal entity Texas Medical Center, and the dream of creating a medical center in Houston was born. The donation served as the foundation for building what is now the largest medical center in the world, with 54 member institutions, 100 000+ employees, 17 500 faculty members, and over 7.2 million patient visits. MD Anderson and its 50 buildings represent the largest footprint in the Texas Medical Center, and the only system devoted exclusively to eliminating cancer. In 1971, MD Anderson became one of the original three organizations designated as comprehensive cancer centers by the National Cancer Act (Olson, 2008).

For ten of the past 12 years, MD Anderson was ranked number one in cancer care in the Best Hospitals Survey published by US News & World Report. MD Anderson's mission is to eliminate cancer in Texas, the nation, and the world through exceptional programs that integrate patient care, research and prevention. The mission hinges on education for undergraduates, graduate students, trainees, professionals, employees and the public. The mission is built upon three institutional core values: caring, integrity, and discovery. The vision states that MD Anderson will be the premier cancer center of the world, based on the excellence of its people, research-driven patient care and science.

In fiscal year 2013, more than 120 000 individuals sought cancer care at MD Anderson, and 40 000 of them were new patients. MD Anderson is also the largest cancer clinical trials program in the nation and included over 7600 patients in 2013. The list below underscores the large volume, scope of services and the clinical activities offered in 2013:

- hospital admissions: 27 905;
- inpatient beds: 656;
- outpatient clinical visits, treatments, procedures: 1 338 706;
- pathology, laboratory medicine procedures: 11 718 405;
- diagnostic imaging procedures: 501 887;
- surgery hours: 70 221;
- clinical research protocols: 1055.

Working at MD Anderson Cancer Center is like working in a small city, inside a city, and within the Texas Medical Center. The large volume of patients and complexity of cancer diagnosis, treatment and survivorship makes the work environment very demanding. Many individuals come to work at MD Anderson because of its excellence, but just as many are drawn by the power of the mission: to eliminate cancer. MD Anderson has nearly 20000 employees and over 1600 faculty members within 624 different departments. Over 1200 volunteers also contribute to the mission of eliminating cancer. The US military has listed MD Anderson as one of the 'Best Places to Work' and the American Association of Retired Persons selected it as a 'Best Employer for Workers over 50' (MD Anderson Communications Office, 2014).

If you work at MD Anderson in the clinical, research, or administrative divisions, it is all hard, complex, and demanding work. Dr. Tom Burke, a faculty member for 26 years and past Chief Medical Officer, said:

> It's not easy working with people who have cancer. There are long hours of patient-focused work and hours of preparation. Employees work too many hours where they can lose themselves and their own health through their dedication to the mission of eliminating cancer. Burnout for many can be right around the corner. We need employees and faculty for the long run, and must educate and support them in how to take care of themselves in order to come back each day energized to fight cancer another day.

It is easy to understand the need for an employee wellness program in such a work environment, but the program did not become a truly recognized organizational effort until 1999.

MD ANDERSON PROGRAM STARTUP

In Houston during the 1980s and 1990s, there was profound growth in worksite wellness in energy-related companies. Many of the large energy companies built corporate fitness centers in the 1980s, which eventually developed into wellness and then health management programs in the 1990s. The Association for Worksite Health Promotion during the 1980s and 1990s developed a regional strategy, and Houston was one of the largest and most active regions by number of company and individual members (Sparlings, 2010). During this time, several of the Houston hospital systems developed behavioral and disease screening programs to better serve the employers that were focusing on wellness and building health management efforts. MD Anderson developed a physician-led nurse team that provided comprehensive cancer screening for Houston companies, but offered little in the way of wellness services to their employees. Amazingly, most hospitals within the Texas Medical Center were doing almost no real organizational wellness work during this period of an upsurge in organizational wellness activities throughout the Houston business community and the USA.

William Baun had built and managed the internationally recognized Tenneco wellness program for 16 years, and in 1996 as Tenneco was selling off its assets around the world, Baun left the company to set up a global worksite wellness consulting practice. In 1998, Baun wrote the *Health Promotion Sourcebook for Small Businesses* with staff members from the Wellness Council of America (WELCOA) (Hunnicutt et al., 1998). In 1999, Hunnicutt and Baun hosted a presentation about the book in Houston. The Vice President of Human Resources and Director of Special Programs from MD Anderson Cancer Center attended the luncheon and arranged to meet with Baun the next week. It has been the author's experience that many worksites initiate organizational wellness efforts after their interest is peaked through attending presentations, reading case study articles or after peers or competitors begin wellness programs. For many companies, establishing a wellness program is not a strategic move, but more of an afterthought. This is one of the main reasons that sometimes these programs don't meet the senior executive's expectations, and quickly lose their support.

Baun's meeting led to a full-time job at MD Anderson, with the responsibility of managing the Special Programs department. The mission of the Programs department was to coordinate community program opportunities, internal rewards and recognition activities, and recreational and athletic teams and events. Baun added wellness to this mix, which at the time was almost non-existent. The wellness program startup was weak because of Baun's need to focus on other parts of the Programs department's operational mix.

At the end of the 1990s, several wellness operational articles were published that would significantly influence the wellness program's development at MD Anderson. In 1997, O'Donnell published his premier issue of *The Art of Health Promotion*, and the feature article was 'Benchmarking best practices in workplace health promotion' (O'Donnell et al., 1997). The article was built around interviews from survey data and from six US employers. Tenneco had been one of the six chosen companies, and Baun had been a study participant, which gave him full access to the study report. In 1999, two articles were published in the *The Art of Health Promotion* that also impacted the early conceptual program elements for the MD Anderson program. The first was an article about culture (Allen and Leutzinger, 1999) and the second about population health management (Chapman, 1999).

In his role as manager of the Programs department, Baun had access to the three Executive Vice Presidents (EVPs: senior leaders of MD Anderson) along with the President, through a monthly meeting he ran for them called 'Managers Forum'. The Managers Forum was a monthly meeting with a simple agenda held for all the managers within the institution. The meeting consisted of short information pieces about the growth of the institution, and time dedicated for a dialogue between the EVPs and the managers. It was during the preparation meetings for the Forum with the EVPs that Baun developed relationships that he was able to leverage as the wellness program grew. Chief Medical Officer Dr. Burke remembers this was a time when:

> treatment options were getting more complex as cancer research was exploding with new drugs, better diagnostic tests and more integrated protocols. We were looking for a way to try to balance things out for employees, show them we really cared! We knew we had to make this complex environment, that was growing at a rate of 1000 new employees a year, a good place to work, a place where people would want to work, create a career and stay.

By 2002, Baun realized that if the wellness program was to grow he had to focus his energy on wellness only, and with his EVP leverage he negotiated a move to the Employee Health department, which had just added an Employee Assistance component. The department then changed its name to Employee Health & Well-being. With his transfer to Employee Health & Well-being, Baun immediately went after reviewing the relevant data, but found MD Anderson's healthcare data was managed by UT Systems. MD Anderson had never had access to their claims data. He began working on a relationship with UT Systems to release the claims data, and without data translation capabilities this would take several years before the data was released. At this time, use of the provider Health Risk Assessment was less than 4 percent of the total population and no reports were being provided to the institution. The data to build a strong population health management strategy was missing, so Baun decided to maximize the 'walk-around' strategy he had described in the small business sourcebook published with Hunnicutt et al. and WELCOA (Hunnicutt et al., 1998).

By now the employee population had grown to 10 000 employees, all located in main and mid-campus locations. Wellness was still operating as a one-person team, so Baun spent much of his time forming relationships as he offered wellness classes through the Employee Development training catalogue. These classes grew into opportunities to attend and present at departmental staff meetings, but what was needed was a bigger and better organized social marketing effort. Several learnings moved the social marketing effort forward quickly. He started doing what he called

As-Soon-As-Possible (ASAP) wellness tip classes in the hallways after realizing the parking garages had 1000–3000 employee cars. Standing by the garage doors between the hours of 6am–9pm and 3pm–6pm led to 600+ individuals stopping to check out the ASAP wellness materials. He began calling the crash cart that he used to carry the materials 'Wellness on Wheels', and its notoriety went viral. In a domino effect, requests for Wellness on Wheels increased his access throughout the institution and built many new relationships.

By the end of his first year in Employee Health & Well-being, Baun had re-engineered a recreational room into a fitness room, had established two Weight Watchers locations and convinced one of the physicians in Employee Health to buy two automatic blood pressure stations. He ended his first year in Employee Health & Well-being by building a business case for hiring another employee and created a paid intern position. The wellness program began the year 2003 with a new employee and a paid intern, which gave the wellness program a staff of 2.5 FTEs.

EARLY PROGRAM MODEL DEVELOPMENT

In the early 2000s, the Johnson & Johnson wellness program's long-term results were published (Goetzel et al., 2002). The study indicated that participation was a significant factor in its success. Baun had learned through his experiences with ASAP, Wellness on Wheels, and departmental staff meeting presentations that there were three populations that were significant, and had to be reached if the program was to grow and become a value within the MD Anderson culture. The first population was individual employees with their health priorities, needs and interests. Second were groups of employees with similar interests or health priorities, who were easy-to-reach targets. One of the first targeted groups to rise up were the bikers and runners, both of whom were interested in training together and competing in local races or events. These individuals represented the early adopters and many became program champions. The third group were departments requesting presentations or special help with wellness or well-being related issues. The Employee Health & Well-being team quickly recognized the power of the third group. They represented the many mini-cultures that made up MD Anderson and were the level at which the value of the program would ultimately be decided. In a recent article in *Forbes* (Moore, 2011), Edward Schein, considered the father of corporate culture studies, suggests that it is within the micro-cultures or departmental cultures with different occupations and nationalities where teamwork and culture play out.

   This first program model emphasized the importance of departmental programming, where employees would learn to value wellness together, have opportunities to support each other, and begin building mini-cultures of health. Again, here is Dr. Burke's insight into the senior executive's leadership's thoughts about wellness at this time: 'We understood that if we were to influence the institutional wellness culture, we needed more participation, which meant we needed more wellness'. In a female-dominant workforce (68–70 percent women) the opening of two lactation or working mother rooms was also a viral event, even though these rooms touched only a very small percentage of the workforce. The opening of these rooms sent out a very strong message about how much senior management understood and cared. This simple win for senior management translated into real leverage for the program and increased senior management support and ownership. Recognizing that stress was a major factor at MD Anderson, a request from senior management sent the program team to an inpatient hospice unit. After listening to the high stress issues, the team left, with one physician flippantly suggesting that if they just had a treadmill in their unit, they could walk off their stress. The next week the team returned and suggested that they might be able to provide an elliptical trainer in the unit, a much safer alternative to a treadmill. It took several months for the elliptical 'stress buster station' concept to work its way through Employee Health, Legal and Purchasing, but after the concept was approved, the department paid for the elliptical and Precor StretchTrainer that had been negotiated with purchasing, a local vendor and the Wellness team.

   By the end of 2003, four more stress buster stations had been set up and paid for by various departments. The stress buster station innovation increased the confidence in the Wellness team, and participation began to grow significantly through multiple program opportunities created by the Wellness team. The success of the program caught the attention of the EVPs and they requested that a business plan be built for expanding the program. The program went into 2004 with three FTEs and a focus on building a business plan to leap the program forward.

   In 2004, Chapman published an article in *The Art of Health Promotion* about the best practices of worksite health promotion programs. The format of the study had an academic and practitioner group evaluate best practices. Baun had participated in the study as a practitioner thought leader, and through the process again gained valuable insight into program models and best practices. Baun and his supervisor, Dr. Georgia Thomas, Executive Director Employee Health & Well-being, began using the benchmark information and various return-on-investment (ROI) peer review articles to write a business case and develop a new program model. In the summer of 2004, Dr. John Mendelsohn, President of MD Anderson, attended a Cancer Roundtable meeting where participants discussed the newly developed CEO Cancer Gold Standard accreditation program. He came back from the meeting and immediately requested that Dr. Thomas and Baun prepare a report to be presented to the management committee in 30 days showing the current state of the program and a gap analysis of those things that must be added to achieve CEO Cancer Gold Standard accreditation. The report was completed in 30 days and presented to the management committee, where the Wellness team came away from the meeting with $563 000 in funding, two new positions, and a real operating budget.

In 2005, the first 'Leading by Example' materials from Partnership for Prevention would be released, providing examples of what successful programs were doing right. The MD Anderson Wellness team used this material to help build their program as they prepared their application for CEO Cancer Gold Standard accreditation. In 2006 the application was completed, and in 2007 MD Anderson was awarded accreditation and became the first healthcare institution and National Cancer Institute designated cancer center recognized as a Gold Standard program.

FOUNDATIONAL FACTORS IMPORTANT TO PROGRAM SUSTAINABILITY

The Gold Standard accreditation became the leap that built the business case, gained the President's support, gave the EVPs verification that the program was on the right track, and took the program viral to employees at all levels throughout MD Anderson. During the accreditation process, a clear program model was starting to emerge that would sustain the program and ensure its acceptance as a part of the MD Anderson culture. Again, Dr. Burke describes the senior executive's feelings at this time concerning the program: 'It was important to us that we receive outside verification that our program was built on a strong foundation that would ensure its sustainability'. The new VP of Human Resources, Shibu Varghese, arrived when the program was going through the accreditation process and he quickly realized that the wellness program he had inherited was, 'not simply nice to have, but a must have, and needed to be built to stay'. This was a program that he owned and that needed to be built for the long term, one that a culture could be built around. Varghese explained, 'It would be fitting for a healthcare institution fighting cancer to grow a wellness culture for employees, patients, and their families'. A culture of wellness or health became a foundational factor in the sustainability of the program.

A second foundational sustaining factor was the program's agility and flexibility. During this time, the employee population continued to grow at a rate of 1000 new employees per year, and the needs and interests of individual employees, employee teams and divisions were constantly changing. Missing the mark on this is a major failure of many worksite programs. Their inability to meet the changing needs of their employee populations significantly decreases their value to employees and senior management.

The third and final foundational sustaining factor, from which the program model was built, was engagement. Early in the program, high participation was recognized as a program must, but it was also recognized that participation and engagement were not the same. Shibu Varghese, VP of Human Resources, defined engagement as, 'Not just showing up, but making wellness a part of your life. When individuals become emotionally involved with wellness, it becomes an "I want", and not a "you want"... that's engagement'. Dr. Burke described engagement as when the lifestyle practices of individuals and teams reach a level that positively affects the financial and productivity outcomes of the institution.

THREE OPERATIONAL SEGMENTS

Over the years a program model was been built with nine core components supporting the three foundational sustaining factors (agility, culture of wellness, and engagement). From a program manager's view, the nine components are divided into three operational segments: (1) leadership ownership and support, (2) program design, planning and delivery, and last, (3) data (Table 8.1). The sections that follow will review each operational segment while elaborating on the nine core components over the life journey of the MD Anderson wellness program.

Table 8.1   MD Anderson wellness program model

Leadership Ownership and Support	Program Design, Planning and Delivery	Data
Multilevel leadership	Scope, relevance, comprehensiveness and quality	Integration
Alignment and compliance	Accessibility, availability and affordability	Program evaluation
Partnerships	Social marketing and communications	Stakeholder reports

All of the components can be found in the worksite wellness best practice literature that parallels the MD Anderson employee wellness program journey. Some arose from O'Donnell et al. (1997) and Chapman's (2004) early work on benchmarking best practices, followed by Goetzel et al.'s (2007) work on promising practices. This project took an interesting turn when Baun was invited to become involved in a qualitative study being planned to analyze the lessons learned from a group of successful worksite wellness programs. This work led to publication in *Harvard Business Review* (Berry, 2010) and helped to crystalize many of the core concepts the MD Anderson team had developed within its program model. That same year, a broader perspective was published in the Joint Consensus Statement on employer-sponsored wellness programs from five major health organizations (Loeppke and Dreger, 2010). More recently, Pronk (2013) published a best practice design principles paper in *ACSM's Health & Fitness Journal*, suggesting nine best practice dimensions. It solidified where the MD Anderson model is today.

Leadership Ownership and Support

Every best practice model has a core component focused on gaining and maintaining the ownership and support of leaders within the organization. The *Harvard Business Review* article (Berry, 2010) called this multilevel leadership. Readers should now have a good idea of how a mix of fate and proactive attention to senior leaders' needs and interests came together to build a relationship foothold for the MD Anderson wellness program. These 'relationship footholds' with senior executives and with a variety of other departments that had a stake in the health and wellness of MD Anderson (Facilities, Legal, Environmental Safety and Health, Communications, etc.) became increasingly important as the program grew in breadth and depth.

Leadership

The department's focus on meeting middle managers' needs and interests along with wellness solutions began to grow middle management support for the program. The Chief Human Resource Officer described the phenomenon: 'It's about senior leaders being responsible for the organizational wellness, and middle managers being responsible for employee wellness. It is middle management that controls employees' time, and they can make access to wellness resources easier for employees, ensuring their wellness needs get met'. In 2002, when the program moved to the Employee Health department, Baun continued to help manage the EVP Managers Forum meeting, which gave him access and recognition opportunity throughout the middle management level of the institution. Even when he turned over management of the Forum to the newly created Internal Communications department, he and his staff were actively involved in the meeting each month, updating managers and the EVPs on the wellness program opportunities, using novel brief communications techniques to gain attention and traction. The use of a wellness table outside the Managers Forum to promote special program offerings was very successful in engaging the hard to reach. A good example was the offer of a 'healthy back' class, which produced an immediate signup of 97 departments. The team managed to schedule 80 percent of the departments, and programs were delivered during the next six months, reaching over 1300 individuals with healthy back team training.

In 2007, the Wellness team began offering a wellness leaders class focused on providing managers with the knowledge and skills they could use to become wellness champions, and develop cultures of health/wellness within their departments. These classes were small and provided ample opportunity for discussion and problem solving. Early in these offerings it became apparent that many of the leaders who took these classes resided in the same building or neighborhoods. This prompted Baun to consider a neighborhood strategy that would better empower managers within a specific building or group of buildings linked together (neighborhoods) to meet and work on local wellness challenges together. The neighborhood concept is currently being piloted at MD Anderson.

Most program guidelines insist that programs gain employee ownership through the use of a wellness committee. It has been the experience of the author that wellness committees can help program managers create a sense of program ownership, but committees can also slow down the startup momentum necessary to ignite a wellness culture. A wellness committee was not initiated at MD Anderson until 2008 and 2009, but many wellness groups and task forces were used to gain employee input and feedback. The 'Be Well' Committee was initiated in 2009 with the help of the President to better align the internal departments and external food vendor involved with the five campus cafeterias and 110 vending machines. This committee had two senior executive sponsors: the VP of Clinical Support Services and the Chief Human Resource Officer. The committee became a powerfully positive force in developing a long-term strategy to increase healthy food availability, affordability, and accessibility throughout the institution. The Be Well Committee is currently being re-engineered to add committees to take responsibility for the physical and emotional wellness dimensions of the MD Anderson culture.

Another level of leadership is employee advocates or wellness champs and they reside at the department level. In 2003, 102 wellness champs were enlisted to become the voice of the wellness program. These employees represented all levels of job categories throughout the institution, and many departments had multiple champs. An internal and unpublished study of champs' effectiveness showed that where there were program champs the program had two to three times more participation. Champs were also used to orient new employees about the wellness programs, which gave new employees an immediate understanding of how wellness fits into the institution culture and the core value of caring. The program grew its champ program to a high of 534 champs, with an annual champ lunch where 'Super Champs' were recognized and champs shared what worked best in supporting and building wellness cultures in their departments.

A wellness mentor strategy was also initiated. Mentors were champs who had experienced a significant health behavior change, and were interested in helping others understand how the behavior change process works. The mentor program was piloted, but timing doomed its potential, as the institution, like many other companies, was feeling the effects of the 2008 economic downturn. Today, the champ program has challenged champs to become better liaisons between their departments and the program. Champs are being asked to step up and learn more about wellness by participating in wellness offerings and work their way through a champ certification process. Champs also received materials they can use to teach short wellness tip classes in departmental meetings, which many enjoy as they gain new wellness knowledge and skills, and become a more empowering wellness leader.

The various levels of leaders – senior executives, middle management, champs, and mentors – provide for full ownership of the program by major stakeholder groups. The most important leaders are the individual employees, who, through the cultural presence of wellness within their work environment, make wellness a part of their lives and become responsible and accountable for daily health and well-being choices. At MD Anderson, self-leadership and caring for oneself is core to its value of caring for others.

Alignment and compliance

Goetzel et al. (2007) emphasized program alignment, and early in the program journey the Wellness team recognized the importance of understanding and meeting senior management's expectations about the program. What makes this a challenge for wellness managers is that senior management have much higher priorities than wellness, so wellness managers must be proactive in educating senior managers about the possibilities of wellness solutions. The early connection with the management committee through the Managers Forum, followed by the President's interest in the CEO Cancer Gold Standard accreditation, kept the wellness effort in front of senior managers and helped the program align to their needs and interests. Goal Strategy 5.4 of institutional goals is: 'We will promote health and well-being through programs that help our people maintain wellness and balance their lives, at work and at home'. Today, the institution is working on a Strategic Framework process focused on its mission to eliminate cancer through enhancing the patient experience, enhancing the provider experience, assuring institutional sustainability, building an efficient, effective infrastructure and system support, and eliminating non-value-added work. Prevention and wellness are important components to the strategic framework that is being stretched to make cancer history, and many find the wellness alignment very exciting, and yet stabilizing, in times of big change.

When the program moved to the Employee Health & Well-being team, compliance became a hot issue. When the program resided in the Programs department, compliance concerns were non-existent, but under an Occupational Medicine department organization, compliance became a focus issue. The stress buster station approval process provided an opportunity for the Wellness team to build a relationship with the legal team. This relationship grew to the point where the Legal department was a regular client, with many classes taught for the legal team and the development of a legal office stress buster station. Understanding the compliance and risk management issues in a large organization is important, and compliance with institutional standards is just as important. Wellness programs can look very different from other departments in their companies and that can lead to being treated differently, and in many cases this results in a loss of value for the department's mission. The author recalls many instances when he was managing the Tenneco wellness program with a million-plus budget, yet was receiving comments from participants like, 'How can you understand, you wear gym clothes all day, and just work out in the fitness center'. Complying with standardized strategic plan formats, budget templates, and purchasing tools helped the author gain the trust and respect from other managers within the Human Resources department, and strengthened relationships, opening up many partnership opportunities.

Partnerships
Partnerships are the lifeblood of a wellness program. The initial partnership with Weight Watchers at Work (WWAW) grew from two sites to a high of five sites and MD Anderson became the Texas Medical Center Weight Watchers program coordinator. This made discounts possible for MD Anderson employees and gave the MD Anderson Wellness team an opportunity to improve the effectiveness and efficiencies of the newly initiated WWAW program. At one point the most successful WWAW program at MD Anderson was at 2am.

Partnerships with wellness vendors are also important, since vendors provide many of the educational materials that are used to increase the knowledge, skills, and commitments of participants. Successful vendor partnerships led to the co-development of team challenges that better fit the MD Anderson 24/7 work environment. It also led to the development of multiple stress and resilience materials, again focused on the special needs of healthcare providers in a high-stress environment. Ask anyone who works at MD Anderson what they would like more of relative to health and well-being, and the answer is always – more energy. Another successful vendor partnership led to the development of energy materials that could be used in a short course or individual/group coaching.

The most important partnerships are developed between the Wellness team and departments. These partnerships led to wellness segments in town hall meetings or divisional and departmental wellness mini-fairs focused on specific health and well-being issues. A good example is a resilience fair organized with a division where all the departments had a booth with a resilience theme. Thousands of employees participated in the fair, and the evaluation survey results suggested that not only did the fair provide employees with resilience knowledge and skills, but also energized employees to start taking the small steps leading to better resilience.

In 2010, MD Anderson opened a $20\,000^2$ ft employee fitness center in mid-campus. The planning, construction, and startup of this facility involved multiple internal and external partnerships. By opening day 5000 employees had been screened, orientated to the equipment and facility and became members ready to use the fitness center. This was one of the largest fitness center openings reported in a worksite in 2010. The power of successful partnerships is critical to program success. Partnership building is an art, and good mentors can help individuals with little partnership experience learn the lessons that only time and experience can grow.

Program Design, Planning and Delivery

Individuals who have made worksite wellness a career understand it's not about the money, but about their passion for the challenge of behavior change, culture change, and program sustainability. In the current worksite wellness program climate, management teams are not questioning the need for worksite wellness, but are focusing on how these programs will be delivered, and when can they expect results from specific program delivery techniques. Management teams today need results, but understand that in order to get results they must focus on the program delivery metrics that highlight program impact and ensure return on investment.

Scope, relevance, comprehensiveness and quality

The *Harvard Business Review* article (Berry, 2010) described scope as being programs that are relevant and meet the needs and interest of employees and expectations of middle and senior management. Without a Health Risk Assessment and health claims data, the program had to rely on departmental wellness surveys, wellness champ feedback, studies on other healthcare environments in the literature, and industry surveys/white papers published by provider and consultant groups. Using these sources, the program significantly grew its stress and resilience programs. In 2008, when the institution was feeling the challenges of economic downturn and was preparing to terminate groups of employees for the first time in its 70+ year history, the Executive Director of Employee Health & Well-being brought wellness to the HR Management Committee to discuss their potential to take a role in working with teams that had lost employees and now had overworked and stressed out survivors. The integrated Human Resource team developed a comprehensive strategy with tactics to meet the needs of employees being terminated and employee survivors who were now required to take on more work. Wellness developed several new courses that could be delivered, and helped teams understand the concept of individual and team resilience. One hundred and ten departments received this facilitated training, reaching thousands of employees and demonstrating a good example of the relevance of wellness.

Another good example that illustrates effective scope is the 'healthy back' class co-developed with Wellness and the Environmental Health & Safety department. In these classes, safety focused on ergonomics and correct lifting techniques and wellness focused on the importance of flexibility and strength training along with stress reduction throughout the day. The Healthy Kids Club, with over 800 members, is another example, but its success is not surprising in a work environment where 68–70 percent of the workforce consists of women, and 80 percent are married and 40 percent of childbearing age. In 2007, a menopause workshop was a real hit, along with a follow-up workshop called 'Healthy Aging'. Healthy Aging was so popular that it had to be developed into a two-hour course that was offered in the Employee Development training catalogue, allowing employees to get credit for taking the class. This supported many employees using classes in the training catalogue to meet their annual training requirements. It was a powerful lesson in relevance for the Wellness team, which led to the development of more catalogue courses.

In 2010, an integrated Human Resource team was looking into the Family and Medical Leave Act challenges in the Perioperative department and a worklife/wellness solution was considered, and with the support of the perioperative management team it was planned and implemented. The project involved different awareness tactics to ensure that perioperative employees understood their benefit and worklife options. It also involved resilience classes taught to groups that worked 24/7 in support of MD Anderson's 75 operating rooms. Again, program relevance and comprehensiveness were main aspects of the programming decision.

One of the larger challenges in worksite wellness programming today is the balance between high-tech and high-touch programming. When the program was initiated in 1999, there was no connection developed between the on-site program and the program portal offered by the healthcare benefit provider. In 2007–08, a partnership between the Benefits department and the Wellness team brought the opportunity of a Health Risk Assessment and health portal to all employees. Senior management agreed to provide a $50 incentive for completion of the health risk, and this resulted in 75 percent of the employee population completing the assessment. The Wellness team started to pilot programs that had components linked to the health portal and earlier success suggested that this would be a good strategy. But when the 2008 economic downturn hit, the Health Risk Assessment and health portal were lost due to a decrease in the Human Resource budget, and MD Anderson reverted back using the provider Health Risk Assessment and health portal. Another challenge at MD Anderson in use of high-tech options is that any employee who works on the clinical side is not allowed to surf on their MD Anderson computer while at work. If caught surfing at work they are fired on the spot, which of course prohibits clinical employees from taking a Health Risk Assessment at work or visiting a health portal.

In January 2015, MD Anderson will implement a no-tobacco hire policy. This has been a very interesting integrated project, but again very relevant to its mission. MD Anderson went smoke free in 1979, and was one of the first work environments in Houston to be completely smoke free. In 2006, with MD Anderson's support and gentle push, the Texas Medical Center went smoke free. Tobacco users pay a higher health care premium, and it is estimated that less than 4 percent of its employee population are tobacco users. Since the Gold Standard accreditation in 2007, wellness has partnered with MD Anderson's Behavioral Science department to offer comprehensive tobacco cessation program opportunities.

Accessibility, availability and affordability
Accessibility, availability and affordability are three key concepts that bring program scope, relevance and comprehensiveness to life. Remember the ASAP wellness lessons using the WOW (Wellness on Wheels) cart? A 24/7 work environment offers many challenges to wellness programmers who must move out of their normal programming box to create innova-

tive programming solutions to reach the hard to reach. In 2005, a water cooler communication program was quickly adopted by 75 departments that were not regular wellness department clients. The program was built with a 'wellness in your face' program goal, and surprisingly it increased departmental requests and wellness participation in hard-to-reach departments. Night shift employees can be impossible to reach with wellness program options. The fitness center is open from 5. 00am–8.30pm, so for many night shift employees, the benefit of a free fitness center is unavailable. In 2004, a project was initiated with the nursing division to expand evening wellness options to nurses. The project called for a partnership between Nursing and Wellness where the salary of an evening wellness coach would be shared by both departments. Unfortunately, budget constraints killed the concept, but the partnership was strong and over the years many different program options have been developed and implemented to reach not just night shift nurses, but also nurses working on the inpatient units. Inpatient units rarely have the luxury of staff meetings, and their shift changes can involve complicated handoffs. But wellness has become a part of their environment through short wellness presentations delivered in their units during work hours, and through leadership coaching for nurse unit supervisors, managers, and directors. Wellness has also partnered with the nurse training and counseling departments to deliver specific program requests.

Most individuals, when they hear the words accessibility, availability, and affordability immediately think about food and nutrition. When asked what his proudest moments were in his 15-year history as a senior executive involved in building and supporting the employee wellness program, Dr. Burke said:

> I'm very proud of what we've done on the food side, providing more healthy choices, and making healthy food affordable in our cafeterias. It's not perfect, but setting up our cafeterias so that the healthy choice is the easy choice is a big deal. Posting nutritional information on large LCD screens in the cafeteria, and having Be Well plates and Healthy Lite plates for individuals that can't make healthy choices without help has changed lives.

The Be Well Committee was formed in 2010, and its initial purpose was to defeat obesity. Unfortunately, the metrics chosen were BMI, waist circumference, and body weight, which were captured on the Health Risk Assessment. The UT System has changed Health Risk Assessment vendors several times, making tracking of the data unrealistic. But the Be Well Committee successfully developed multiple strategies that supported its slogan of 'Enabling, educating, encouraging, and engaging employees to daily make healthier choices around food and movement'.

One of the Be Well Committee's largest projects was waiting out the termination of the institutional vending machine contract, and coordinating the replacement of 110 vending machines with new machines that offer significantly healthier options. When the vending machines were replaced a surcharge was also placed on sugary drinks and calorie-free drinks prices were significantly reduced. This immediately led to a reduction of sugary drink sales by 15 percent. Dining services partnered with *Cooking Light Magazine* and a *My Café* employee web page was developed to help employees plan better for their meals at MD Anderson. The impact was immediate and prompted insights. Employees shared their stories about using the point-of-sale nutritional information to get their eating habits back on track. The dining service vendor initiated a 'Just 4U' awareness program that not only pointed employees toward healthy options, but also significantly decreased the time it took to make a selection and start eating.

The Wellness team supported the Be Well Committee efforts by developing several new program options. The 'Live It Lose It' weight management program using the Mayo Clinic Diet materials (Pellman, 2010) was very successful and was followed up with 'Live it – Rock Steady' support groups. These groups utilized social networking and small group process principles to support individuals who had lost weight or lost inches to kept it off. Wellness designed a departmental class called, 'It's Not a Diet, It's a Lifestyle', which also found traction in departments as the changes in MD Anderson's cafeterias became the talk at staff meetings and at water fountains.

Another successful food program that is still offered is the 'Beyond Salad' vegetarian club. Wellness started Beyond Salad as a pilot for a small group of vegetarians who wanted to eat together once a month and try some different recipes. The group grew and moved to a $5–7 plate charge, bringing in guest chefs from around Houston to show off their vegetarian dishes. The club meets in the prevention center demonstration kitchen, which can handle a group of 70 participants.

The Be Well Recipe contest has also been very successful and is a program where employees enter their recipes to be judged by internal and external dietetic experts. The recipes are first judged and then the winning recipes are prepared and cooked by the dining service department, and employees can try small samples or purchase a healthy portion for lunch.

Before the 20 000 ft^2 fitness center was opened in 2010, the Wellness team had already established a fitness room strategy that provided fitness options in five other buildings. These small, non-supervised fitness areas were financed through the sponsoring department budgets, and supervised by the Wellness team. By 2010 there were 12 stress buster stations and nine blood pressure units throughout the campus. Depending on the location of the stress buster stations, usage varied from 200 to 400 users per month, captured on a self-report system. The blood pressure stations were the real surprise and underlined the importance of accessibility. High blood pressure, diabetes, and obesity are MD Anderson's three top chronic diseases, and high blood pressure costs are almost three times higher than diabetes or obesity health claim expenditures. A well-placed blood pressure unit will experience 3000–4000 sessions each month. Total number of sessions for the nine blood pressure units ranged from 15 000 to 25 000 sessions. It was not uncommon when a blood pressure unit was moved to get a call from an employee asking, 'What did you do with my blood pressure unit?'

One more example of accessibility representing a key principle for effective wellness programs and making the healthy choice the easy choice is when the fitness center was being planned, and the Wellness team also considered an inside storage bike barn that would allow employees to store their bikes indoors and out of the Houston sun and rain. An indoor bike barn was designed and the initial bike barn had space for 47 bikes. When the fitness center opened, the Wellness team had worked for several years on a bike strategy that set up a building construction standard for bikers' showers to be placed in every new MD Anderson building. They regularly surveyed the 42 bike racks throughout the campus, and made recommendations to facilities concerning improvements to address safety and security issues. When the survey was first done it was apparent that neither Environment Health and Safety nor Facilities had ever taken a look at bike rack locations or the bike rack safety issue. When the fitness center opened, the new indoor bike storage site also opened, and since that opening two more indoor bike storage units or bike barns have been implemented with lockers, showers and restrooms. The bike strategy has increased the number of employees who ride their bikes to work, and in the annual survey, the number has been as high as 650 employees riding their bikes to work each day. We are currently working on a strategy within the Texas Medical Center to bring bike share B-Bike locations, which are credit card rental bike sites that are being used successfully in many Houston communities.

Social marketing and communications

The Chief Human Resource Officer describes our communication strategy as, 'in your face wellness communications'. His pride in the program, 'is the program sustainability and growth over my six years at MD Anderson, which is no doubt driven in part by our consistent message or program brand of Be Well, which simply says to employees that small steps to be well matter'. For several years the Internal Communications department filmed and produced a monthly 'Be Well with Bill' short video clip that was broadcast on the video monitors used as employee communication vehicles throughout the MD Anderson campus. The short clips were lightly scripted, and usually involved a key message about taking a step to be well. Many of the segments were of employees taking a wellness action step, or telling their wellness story. Again, a comment from the Chief Human Resource Officer about stories and program metrics: 'Don't get me wrong, metrics are important, but when success stories are tied to metrics, it connects the numbers to real people, and that changes the way we feel about and approach decisions'.

One of the most important lessons learned early in the MD Anderson program was communicating program results to individuals at different levels within the institution in different ways. Program results presented at Managers Forum helped develop program momentum, as managers shared stories about their employees' success or team success. Consistent communications with senior management was done through monthly reports, special reports and an annual review requiring the President's signature for CEO Cancer Gold Standard re-accreditation. Dr. Burke established a walk-n-talk strategy, which was adopted by the Wellness team to more successfully reach out and touch senior leaders. This increased relationship-building time, and kept many of the senior executives updated on the program without the pain of a meeting. The most important group to communicate program results is the program participants. Emails can get buried or lost, so creative and innovative ideas for communicating results are important. Passing trophies from department to department can be fun, and helps strengthen neighborhoods and add a sense of community. In the age of trying to balance the high-touch and high-tech programming with communication efforts, combined solutions may be the best solution. When the new mid-campus building was opened, Wellness added a demonstration kitchen, which was designed for small group classes to teach food selection, preparation and cooking, and took 'in your face wellness' to the max. The wellness dietitian added a 'Food for Thought' follow-up newsletter for those attending food demo classes.

Over the years, wellness newsletters have been used in a variety of ways. During program startup a vendor newsletter was sent home to all employees, and the back section was written by a staff member highlighting different aspects of the program. As stamp prices increased, an unwillingness to spend this much of the budget on a newsletter finally ended the strategy. At one point vendor wellness newsletters were emailed to the wellness champs, but through a quick evaluation project it was discovered that a staff-written champ newsletter was more effective. Surveys showed that champs found an every-other-week email newsletter from Wellness to be beneficial for it kept them connected to the program. On the first of the month, the champ newsletter would contain program information and updates, followed by the next issue providing champ stories and tips on how to be a more effective champ. Targeted newsletters were used in some clubs and support groups, but newsletters take time, and even with volunteer help they can become too much. It is important that newsletters be evaluated several times a year to ensure they are really helping to move a program forward and/or increasing its sustainability.

The communication specialists from Internal Communications supporting wellness have changed multiple times throughout the last 15 years. In an odd way this has been a blessing because new people bring in new ideas, but it also has challenged the wellness staff to ensure a consistent message that sustains the program's value within the culture. The Communications team has brought many wellness stories to life over the years, and it is apparent that stories get the attention of individuals thinking about a change, but the stories that are most helpful talk about the barriers and struggles, and not just about behavior change success.

Data

Eight years into the program, the first Health Risk Assessment was completed, with a participation rate of 75 percent. The data provided a good view of the health practices and health risks within the population. Unfortunately, at that time there was no way to tie the data collected to the MD Anderson healthcare claims data. The Health Risk Assessment was cut due to budgetary restraints, and now is managed by the UT System. MD Anderson consistently has the highest Health Risk Assessment completion rate, but this only represents between 30 and 35 percent of the total population. In 2013 the UT System began a 'New Year, New You' project that is working to link up the Health Risk Assessment data with health claims data. This project could result in UT System developing a wellness dashboard for each institution that could be used to better understand their integrated health risk stratification and health claims data. But this is probably several years away.

Data integration
Early on in the program development it was apparent that much of the health productivity management data that are considered 'a must' in the health management literature was not going to be realistic to capture. When the program was moved to Employee Health & Well-being in 2002, a monthly activity report was created to track participation and engagement. The activity report segmented the data into: awareness, behavior

change, and environmental support activities, following O'Donnell and Harris's (1994) original program intensity model. Awareness data were divided into two categories: participation in educational activities and events and the number of individuals receiving targeted or tailored communications pieces. Behavioral change data were defined as participation in behavioral change activities or events. Examples include participation in individual, buddy or team wellness challenges. At times they were further divided into registration and program completion numbers. Environmental support activities consisted of participation at the fitness centers, blood pressure stations, stress buster stations and other physical pieces that had been placed in the environment to make the healthy choice the easy choice. The activities report was not sophisticated, but it did give Human Resources and senior management a clear picture of monthly participation and program engagement.

In 2007, in preparation for the Health Risk Assessment to be rolled out in 2008, the decision was made to take program tracking a step further by using the employee badge, which has a computer chip that could be scanned, identifying individual employees' program participation. The basic concept was to link program participation to the Health Risk Assessment data and other data under the prevue of MD Anderson, such as short- and long-term disability, absenteeism, and workers' compensation data. Early data scanning units provided some challenges when in remote locations, but as scanning units became smaller and laptop computer databases more agile, it became exciting to watch this database grow. The worksite wellness dose–response literature is in its infancy, but building this kind of a participation tracking system expands possibilities. The program is still collecting dose–response data and is now segmenting it at the institutional division level, allowing for a look at wellness community involvement. In January of 2014, this data tracking reported that 12 513 individuals were involved in wellness activities, or 64 percent of the total population.

The 'New Year, New You' project currently coordinated by the UT System through the UT School of Public Health will hopefully link to fitness center participation data and the dose–response tracking database. The UT System effort will de-identify all the data, but allow for analysis at the department, division, building and neighborhood level. This will allow the Wellness team to use a better-targeted approach to their wellness programming.

Program evaluation
One of the strengths of the MD Anderson program has been its focus on ensuring that the 'little ps', or specific programs, are evaluated. Most worksite programs do very little evaluation and continue to offer programs that are not programmatically effective or not cost effective.

The MD Anderson Wellness team project manages wellness programs by assigning primary and secondary programmer roles. The primary programmer oversees the development, implementation and evaluation of specific programs with the help of the secondary programmer. They will discuss the evaluation of a program before program implementation to ensure evaluation tools and instruments are in place during program implementation and delivery. An example would be a pre-/post-resilience survey being used to test the effectiveness of a resilience program in a department. Or maybe a short three-question postcard or email at the end of a challenge program asking about the effectiveness of the registration process. This focus on short process evaluations in almost every program delivered helps keep programs working.

Another tool that has been used is cost-effective evaluations to determine the cost differences between two programs or different program components within a single program. An example reflecting this approach examined the cost to deliver a 'Go Red Heart Week' program consisting of Go Red door decorating team competition compared to a Go Red Fashion Show. The Go Red decoration contest had 450 individuals participate at a cost of $7.77 per participant, and the Go Red Fashion Show had 866 participants at a cost of $4.04 per participant. This kind of analysis has helped the Wellness team decide on how to get more 'bang' from the budget. Program evaluations also became a section on the monthly report that goes to the VP of Human Resources who uses the report to better describe program successes and learnings with senior management.

Stakeholder reports
A challenge for wellness programs is the diverse stakeholders to whom they must communicate program results. The wellness monthly report data rolls up from individual team members and are collectively reported in the manager's report to their supervisor. This report is then condensed and a portion is sent to the VP of Human Resources to be added to the Human Resources monthly dashboard. Portions of the wellness dashboard can be reported to the champs, and other portions might be communicated to specific managers whose departments are actively involved in specific programming. Internal and external vendor partners can also receive a full or portions of the report to strengthen the partnership and ensure they better serve our needs.

Special reports to stakeholders provide an opportunity for the Wellness team to focus on specific issues. A recent obesity report demonstrates a good example of special reports. Management had requested an updated obesity strategy that included an obesity strategy map (Figure 8.1) they could use to better explain the obesity programming efforts.

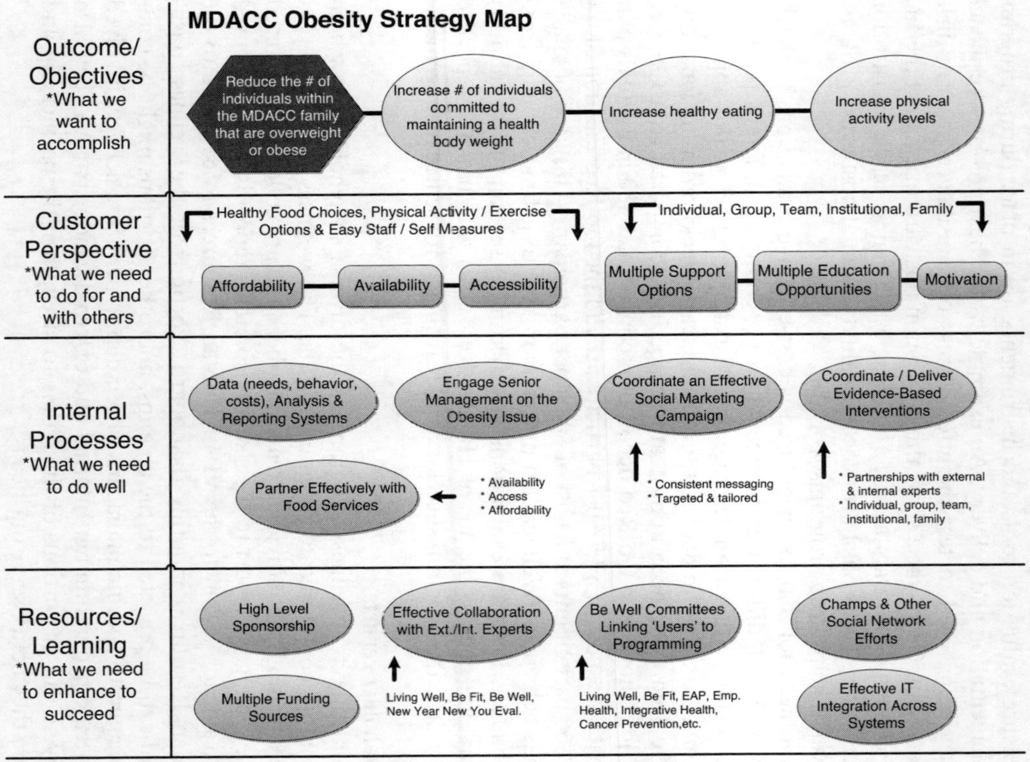
MDACC Obesity Strategy Map
Outcome/ Objectives
*What we want to accomplish
Reduce the # of individuals within the MDACC family that are overweight or obese
Increase # of individuals committed to maintaining a health body weight
Increase healthy eating
Increase physical activity levels
Customer Perspective
*What we need to do for and with others
Healthy Food Choices, Physical Activity / Exercise Options & Easy Staff / Self Measures
Affordability
Availability
Accessibility
Individual, Group, Team, Institutional, Family
Multiple Support Options
Multiple Education Opportunities
Motivation
Internal Processes
*What we need to do well
Data (needs, behavior, costs), Analysis & Reporting Systems
Engage Senior Management on the Obesity Issue
Coordinate an Effective Social Marketing Campaign
Coordinate / Deliver Evidence-Based Interventions
Partner Effectively with Food Services
* Availability
* Access
* Affordability
* Consistent messaging
* Targeted & tailored
* Partnerships with external & internal experts
* Individual, group, team, institutional, family
Resources/ Learning
*What we need to enhance to succeed
High Level Sponsorship
Multiple Funding Sources
Effective Collaboration with Ext./Int. Experts
Living Well, Be Fit, Be Well, New Year New You Eval.
Be Well Committees Linking 'Users' to Programming
Living Well, Be Fit, EAP, Emp. Health, Integrative Health, Cancer Prevention,etc.
Champs & Other Social Network Efforts
Effective IT Integration Across Systems

Figure 8.1 *MDACC obesity strategy map*

CHAPTER SUMMARY

As Dr. Burke and Shibu Varghese have both stated, the MD Anderson employee wellness program's major success is its sustainability while becoming a real value within the MD Anderson culture. Since the program inception, the department has moved from the Special Programs department to Employee Health & Well-being, and now resides in the Benefits department and reports through the Benefit Director. The wellness effort started out with one employee focused on wellness programs, grew to five under Employee Health & Well-being, and now under Benefits has six team members. The new team is an integration of the WorkLife program, with two employees, and the wellness program, with four employees. The WorkLife program manager now manages the day-to-day programming, integrating worklife and wellness. Baun, the former program manager, is now called Wellness Officer and oversees the strategic aspects of the program and is involved in the program research efforts with the School of Public Health. He also works in the cancer survivorship program and is involved in community projects related to wellness.

It is the author's hope that in his efforts to describe the journey of the MD Anderson program model the reader will get a glimpse into the operational side of worksite wellness rarely provided. It is this level of sharing that is necessary if the wellness practitioners are to begin delivering more effective programs, and meeting the expectations of senior management and the various wellness stakeholders. Be Well Bill.

REFERENCES

Allen, J. and J. Leutzinger (1999), 'The role of culture change in health promotion', *The Art of Health Promotion*, **3**(1), 1–12.

Berry, L., A. Marabito and W. Baun (2010), 'What's the hard return on employee wellness programs?', *Harvard Business Review*, December, 104–12.

Carls, G., R. Goetzel, R. Henke, J. Bruno, F. Isaac and J. McHugh (2011), 'The impact of weight gain or loss on health care costs for employees at the Johnson & Johnson family of companies', **53**(1), 8–16.

Chapman, L. (1999), 'Population health management', *The Art of Health Promotion*, **3**(2), 1–12.

Chapman, L. (2004), 'Expert opinions on "best practices" in worksite health promotion (WHP)', *The Art of Health Promotion*, **18**(6), 1–12.

Goetzel, R., R. Ozminkowski, J. Bruno. K. Rutter, F. Isaac and S. Wang (2002), 'The long-term impact of Johnson & Johnson's Health & Wellness program on employee health risks', *Journal of Occupational Environmental Medicine*, **44**(5) 417–24.

Goetzel, R., D. Shechter, R. Ozminkowski, P. Marmet, M. Tabrizi and E. Roemer

(2007), 'Promising practices in employer health and productivity management efforts: findings from a benchmark study', **49**(2), 111–29.

Henke, R., R. Goetzel, J. McHugh and F. Isaac (2011), 'Recent experience in health promotion at Johnson & Johnson: lower health spending, strong return on investment', **30**(3), 490–99.

Hunnicutt, D., A. Deming, W. Baun and E. Buffet (1998), *Health Promotion Sourcebook for Small Businesses*, Omaha, NB: Wellness Council of America.

Loeppke, R. and M. Dreger (2010), 'Joint consensus statement: guidance for a reasonably designed wellness program', **54**(7), 889–96.

MD Anderson Communications Office (2014), *Quick Facts 2014*, accessed 30 June 2014 at http://www.mdanderson.org/about-us/facts-and-history/quick-facts/qf2014-1.pdf.

Moore, K. (2011), 'MIT's Ed Schein on way corporate culture in no longer the relevant topic and what is', *Forbes*, accessed 19 April 2014 at http://www.forbes.com/sites/karlmoore/2011/11/29/mits-ed-schein-on-why-corporate-culture-in-no-longer-the-relevant-topic-and-what-is/print/.

O'Donnell, M. and J. Harris (eds) (1994), *Health Promotion in the Workplace*, Albany, NY, Delmar Publishers.

O'Donnell, M., C. Bishop and K. Kaplan (1997), 'Benchmarking best practices in workplace health promotion', *The Art of Health Promotion*, **1**(1), 1–8.

Olson, J.S. (2008), *Disease and Discovery at The University of Texas M.D. Anderson Cancer Center: Making Cancer History*, Baltimore, MD: The Johns Hopkins University Press.

Partnership for Prevention (2005), *Leading by Example: Improving the Bottom Line Through High Performance, Less Costly Workforce*, Washington, DC: Partnership for Prevention.

Pellman, P. (ed.) (2010), *The Mayo Clinic Diet: Eat Well, Enjoy Life. Lose Weight*, Intercourse, PA: Good Books.

Pronk, N. (2013), 'Best practice design principles of worksite health and wellness programs', *ACSM's Health & Fitness Journal*, **18**(1), 1–5.

Sparlings, P. (2010), 'Worksite health promotion: principles, resources, and challenges', *Preventing Chronic Disease*, **7**(1), 1–6.

9. Practical approaches to health improvement in corporate wellness programs

Rebecca K. Kelly and Melondie Carter

> The wealth of business depends on the health of workers.
> (Dr. Maria Neira, Director, Department of Public Health and Environment,
> World Health Organization)

Efforts to address poor health, rising healthcare costs, and chronic health conditions for today's workforce often involves expense management and cost shifting. Today more and more companies are addressing the poor health of their workers through efforts of prevention and wellness with the expectation that investments in a healthy workforce will drive behavior change for employees and family members. Workplace health and wellness programs can result in impactful change, improved quality of life and productivity, as well as create a healthy culture. This chapter provides a review of the business case for employee health, practical approaches to health improvement, key components of a corporate wellness program and a case study demonstrating best practices in employee health improvement.

THE BUSINESS CASE FOR WORKSITE HEALTH IMPROVEMENT PROGRAMS

A comprehensive employee health program is essential for improving the health, well-being and productivity of a workforce, while also allowing for competitiveness and sustainability of organizations, communities, national and regional economies. The health of the today's workforce is changing. Older workers make up a significant portion of the labor force. According to the World Health Organization (2012), more than 350 million people of all ages suffer from depression. Depression is the leading cause of disability worldwide and at the workplace. It is also a major contributor to the global burden of disease.

In the United States, over 18 million adults between the ages of 18 and

64, or 6 percent of the population were classified as disabled (Council for Disability Awareness, 2012). Of these, approximately 9 million were disabled wage earners also receiving disability benefits through the US government. According to the Council for Disability Awareness (2012), the leading causes for new disability claims in 2012 among US workers were: '(a) musculoskeletal/connective tissue disorders (28.5%), (b) cancer (14.6%), (c) injuries and poisoning (10.6%), (d) mental disorders (8.9%), and (e) cardiovascular/circulatory disorders (8.2%)'. Additionally, the most common causes of existing disability claims included musculoskeletal/connective tissues disorders, nervous system disorders, cardiovascular/circulatory disorders, cancer and mental disorders. Of importance is the fact that approximately 90 percent of disabilities are caused by illnesses and only 10 percent by accidents.

Corporate health programs continue to determine that poor health contributes to higher medical and workers' compensation costs, as well as increases in absenteeism, presenteeism (being at work while sick), disability claims and life insurance premiums (Pelletier, 2001; Loeppke et al., 2009; Baicker et al., 2010; Henke et al. 2010; Chapman, 2012). With increasing age comes increased risk and prevalence of chronic health conditions such as depression, diabetes, heart disease and anxiety (Anderko et al., 2012). As the prevalence rates of chronic conditions of employees rise, the result is an increase in the healthcare costs as well as productivity losses for an organization.

Many employers have recognized that employees with modifiable health risks have higher healthcare and productivity expenses when compared with lower-risk employees. Therefore, many employers have developed health improvement programs in an attempt to reduce risks and manage disease. Henke et al. (2010) performed multivariate analyses to estimate costs associated with having certain health risks in the Pepsi Bottling Company, the world's largest manufacturer, seller, and distributor of Pepsi-Cola beverages. They found high risk for weight, blood pressure, glucose and cholesterol had the highest impact on total costs. They concluded that targeted programs for health improvement and risk reduction would produce substantial cost reduction in multiple benefit categories.

Several meta-analysis reviews have determined that employee health programs demonstrate significant cost savings. Chapman (2012) conducted a meta-analysis, also resulting in findings that employee health programs demonstrate a 25 percent reduction in sick leave, health plan costs, workers' compensation and disability insurance costs. Baicker et al. (2010) conducted a meta-analysis of 32 publications addressing employee health improvement. This summary of literature indicated that for each dollar spent on employee health and wellness programs, medical costs dropped by approximately $3.27. Additionally, it was determined that costs related to absenteeism were reduced by approximately \$2.73. The review suggested that organizations could benefit from employee health and wellness programs through reductions in employee absenteeism, healthcare and workers' compensation costs, as well as enhanced productivity. Aldana et al. (2012) conducted a summary of literature of workplace health culture on Fortune 500 companies, resulting in the determination that a healthy culture was linked to both a highly supportive leadership and a positive work environment that included policies supporting a workplace health culture. More recently, Baxter et al. (2014) explored the relationship between return of investment and quality of study methodology in 51 health promotion programs delivered at the workplace between 1984 and 2012. Findings demonstrated a positive overall mean weighted return of investment, noting the higher the quality of the methodological design, the lower the financial return.

A workplace health program that combines both individual and organizational strategies may produce benefits both for individual employees and their families as well as the organization as a whole. Organizations can benefit from implementing a comprehensive set of strategies to address employee health and safety. These strategies include workplace policy, training and environmental tactics, thereby reaching the majority of employees at the worksite simultaneously (Centers for Disease Control and Prevention, 2012a, 2013a).

KEY CHARACTERISTICS OF A SUCCESSFUL HEALTH IMPROVEMENT PROGRAM

According to the World Health Organization (WHO, 2010):

> A healthy workplace is one in which workers and managers collaborate to use a continual improvement process to protect and promote the health, safety and well-being of all workers and the sustainability of the workplace by considering the following, based on identified needs: (a) health and safety concerns in the physical work environment, (b) health, safety and well-being concerns in the psychosocial work environment, including organization of work and workplace culture, (c) personal health resources in the workplace and (d) ways of participating in the community to improve the health of workers, their families and other members of the community.

This expanding definition of employee health now includes psychosocial and personal health issues, as well as the added focus on chronic disease management in the workplace.

On the basis of the WHO Global Plan of Action on Workers' Health 2008–17, WHO launched the Global Framework for Healthy Workplaces

(2010). Included in this model of employee health are five keys for the design of a healthy workplace: (1) leadership commitment and engagement, (2) involve workers and their representatives, (3) business ethics and legality, (4) use a systematic, comprehensive process to ensure effectiveness and continual improvement, and (5) sustainability and integration. These five keys provide an opportunity for organizations to further define their strategic plan for employee health. Following is an outline of this framework combined with practical approaches to employee health improvement.

Leadership Commitment and Engagement

The success of an employee health program begins with senior administrators who provide the strategic vision, overarching goals, and infrastructure for the employee health program. The support of the senior administration is critical to building a healthy environment and culture, while also helping to engage employees in their participation in programs.

A list of strategies to reach and sustain the support of senior administration includes the following (Kelly and Carter, in press; WHO, 2010):

- Mobilize and gain commitment from senior leadership and union leadership to integrate healthy workplaces into the organization's business goals and values.
- Get necessary support, funding and resources to support the employee health and wellness efforts.
- Share best practices to include policies and environmental changes that have been implemented with other organizations, demonstrating that healthy workplace initiatives are part of the organization's business strategy.
- Keep abreast of industry best practices and the programs that are demonstrating cost savings. Administrators can also benefit from the knowledge of their peers. The Partnership for Prevention's series of publications titled, *Leading by Example* (2007, 2011), provides organizations and their senior leaders (chief executive officers) with practical examples of how they can align employee health improvement programs with their core business strategies. These publications provide an assessment of health management initiatives, senior leader perspectives on employee health, and highlights from leading health improvement programs.
- Create a corporate health dashboard for administrators and managers to review employee participation, engagement, health risks, health improvements, testimonials, healthcare costs, claims data, and absenteeism reports.

Kelly and Carter (in press) also determined that an employee health program should include baseline organization and employee health and wellness assessments. To monitor progress and refine goals and priorities, these assessments should be repeated every two years. Key stakeholder interviews are an excellent tool to be used as part of leadership commitment and engagement. This assessment tool serves as one of five that are presented throughout the chapter in various sections. The other assessment tools include focus groups, employee demographics and surveys, environmental assessments, and benchmarking analysis.

Key stakeholder interviews
Key stakeholder interviews are usually conducted prior to launching – or expanding an employee health program. These interviews provide an opportunity to interview senior-level administrators (president and vice presidents) to gain a better understanding of the link between business operations and employee health, well-being, and productivity. The employee health program manager or consultant usually conducts the interview with senior administrators on an individual basis. Questions may include: (1) In the next five years, what do you believe will be the most critical health issues for your organization? (2) What barriers do you perceive to be the biggest challenges for your workforce? (3) What motivates your employees to modify their behaviors and do you believe this will translate to lifestyle changes? (4) What healthy workplace policies are in place? (5) What suggestions do you have to change the work environment?

Involve Workers and their Representatives

The second key to the WHO healthy workplace framework (2010) is 'Involve workers and their representatives'. Involvement should begin from the initial assessment through all phases of program planning, delivery, and evaluation. Selected employees should also be a part of an advisory committee.

Focus groups
Qualitative research connecting employees with a facilitator and small focus groups can help organizations capture ideas, feedback and suggestions for ways to improve their employee health programs, their communication strategies, as well as the overall strategic planning for the organization. Focus group questions may include: (1) What are the most common health issues among your co-workers and families? (2) How do you receive health information? (3) What are the barriers to participating in an employee health program? (4) What motivates you to modify your behavior?

Employee demographics and surveys

Employee involvement and an understanding of the employee and family population are essential to design an effective employee health program. To gain a better understanding of the opportunities for enhancing participation levels, organizations should capture data on employees and dependents to include gender, age, educational level, job role, absenteeism due to personal illness, healthcare costs, and workers' compensation costs. Furthermore, a health and wellness needs and interest survey is a valuable tool to use when developing a program. This tool can be modified to be used as an employee satisfaction and interest survey. Box 9.1 provides an example of a tool used at The University of Alabama.

BOX 9.1   SAMPLE NEEDS & INTEREST SURVEY

Thank you for agreeing to participate in this survey. The purpose of this survey is to find out how the Health and Wellness program can better serve you and other employees. There are no right or wrong answers. You can skip any questions you want. Your name will not be associated with the survey. This survey is completely voluntary and will in no way affect your relationship with [organization] or with your supervisor.

1. Which three (or more) health issues are high priorities to improve for you or your family in the coming year:

❏ Allergies
❏ Asthma
❏ Avoiding colds and flu
❏ Back care
❏ Blood pressure
❏ Care of elderly parent(s)
❏ Cholesterol

❏ Chronic pain management
❏ Dental care
❏ Diabetes
❏ Depression
❏ Exercise
❏ Financial management
❏ Injury prevention

❏ Nutrition/ weight loss
❏ Self-esteem
❏ Stress
❏ Tobacco
❏ Work/life balance
❏ Other

Other:_____

2. If programs on the following health topics or health services were available at work in the next 12 months which ones would you likely participate in? (Circle all that apply)

Avoiding injuries
Back care
Bicycle safety
Blood pressure check
Blood glucose (sugar) check
Cancer detection/prevention
Cholesterol check
Cold prevention & treatment
Flu shots
Eldercare
Exercise/personal training
Ergonomics for office
workers
Financial management

Headache prevention and
treatment
Healthy cooking/nutrition
Managing allergies and asthma
Managing depression
Managing diabetes
Managing heart disease
Pain management
Parenting
Stress management
Support groups for health and
wellness
Tobacco cessation
Vision exam
Yoga

3. If you began participating in a wellness improvement program then discontinued, why did you stop participating?

❐ I met my goals
❐ I was too busy
❐ I lack continued motivation/interest
❐ I did not have my supervisor's support

❐ I felt uncomfortable
❐ I was able to meet my needs in another way
❐ I was no longer interested
❐ I did not want to participate with my team

4. How important are the following choices in encouraging your participation in a university wellness program?

	Not Important	Somewhat Important	Very Important
Cash rewards			
Annual recognitions and awards			
Medical health care plan deductible waived			
Offered on university time			

Medical premium reduction			
Team programs			
Child care during program			

Other suggestions: _____

5. What ways do you get your health information? (Check all that apply)

❏ Asking health care professional
❏ Reading print materials (newspaper, newsletters)
❏ Reading information from the internet
❏ Talking to a co-worker
❏ Talking to a relative
❏ Talking to friends

6. What is the best way for you to receive information about health and wellness activities, news or tips? (Check all that apply)

❏ Announcements at staff meetings
❏ University online calendar
❏ Digital signs
❏ Employee newsletter/hard copy
❏ Employee orientation
❏ E-newsletter
❏ Facebook
❏ In person
❏ Newsletter sent to the home
❏ Postcards
❏ Posters
❏ Twitter
❏ Work website
❏ Work email address

Other suggestions: _____

Source: Kelly and Carter (in press).

Business Ethics and Legality

The third key in the WHO Healthy Workplaces framework (WHO, 2010) is 'Business ethics and legality'. This key focuses on the ethical principle to 'do no harm' to others and to ensure employees' health and safety. Organizations have a responsibility to adhere to workplace rules and regulations, and to avoid undue risks and suffering to workers, their families and the public.

Environmental assessment

In addition to the interview and surveys noted previously, an environmental assessment is a valuable tool to assess the work environment and culture to better support healthy behaviors, safety and well-being at both the organizational and individual level. An organization's health environment and culture can be crucial to the success of an employee health program. An assessment will help to better understand whether the workplace environment supports or hinders the efforts to promote employee health. Sample environmental audits are available online at the Centers for Disease Control and Prevention's Healthier Worksite Initiative website (CDC, 2010) and includes questions such as: (1) Does the on-site cafeteria have healthy food options? (2) Are healthy snacks available in vending machines? (3) Do supervisors support employees who wish to participate in a nutrition education session?

Use a Systematic, Comprehensive Process to Ensure Effectiveness and Continual Improvement

The fourth key of the WHO Healthy Workplace Model (WHO, 2010) is 'Use a systematic, comprehensive process to ensure effectiveness and continual improvement'. The steps in this process more fully define the key opportunities, ways to mobilize commitment, methods to build the infrastructure, consult with others, and benchmark with other organizations. This systematic approach allows for the development of a comprehensive strategic plan with accompanying action steps. These steps and accompanying practical approaches are more fully reviewed in the case study section of this chapter.

Benchmarking analysis

In the design and planning of a health improvement program, an organization can benefit from benchmarking assessment tools. These tools provide valuable content to assist an organization in establishing a strategic plan, engaging

Table 9.1   Employee health assessment and recognition tools

Resource	Website
CDC Worksite Health ScoreCard (2012b)	http://www.cdc.gov/dhdsp/pubs/docs/HSC_Manual.pdf
Health Enhancement Resource Organization (HERO) Employee Health Management Best Practice Scorecard (2012)	http://the-hero.org/scorecard_folder/HEROScorecardV3%201.pdf
The Health Project's C. Everett Koop National Health Award criteria (2012)	http://www.thehealthproject.com/
Partnership for Prevention's Leading by Example Health Publications (2007, 2011)	http://www.prevent.org/Initiatives/Leading-by-Example.aspx
US Department of Health and Human Services (2012) Healthy People 2020 Program Planning Tools	http://healthypeople.gov/2020/implementing/HP2020_MAPIT.pdf

Note: All websites last accessed 5 July 2014.

Source: Kelly and Carter (in press).

leadership support, building the organizational and staffing infrastructure, defining the program components, identifying the keys to employee engagement, and completing the methods for program measurement and evaluation. These tools are valuable for the early stages of program planning and for updating more advanced or mature programs. These assessment tools can help organizations identify the gaps and opportunities for improvement within their program and serve as instruments for recognition and awards. Individual health assessment tools and surveys are also valuable in helping to guide an organization's overall health improvement plan. These assessments are available through simple questionnaires or advanced online assessments with tailored messages and can be a part of the program's benchmarking for individual and organizational change. (Kelly and Carter, in press)

Table 9.1 provides resources for workplace health and assessment and recognition tools.

Mission and objectives
Vision and mission statements serve organizations and programs as they provide the purpose, direction, and shared visions of an organization or program. A mission statement defines the purpose and primary objectives of the employee health program. Its focus is internal – to define the key measure or measures of the program success – and its prime audience is the administration, employees, and family members. The vision state-

ments also addressed the organization's purpose, with a focus on values or guiding beliefs. This statement is usually shared with the broader community.

Sustainability and Integration

The final key of the WHO Healthy Workplace framework (2010) is 'Sustainability and integration'. This key focuses on the senior administration commitment to use health and well-being as a filter for all decisions. It also includes the focus on integrating healthy workplace initiatives into the organization's mission and strategic business plan. Support for cross-functional teams allow for greater integration, diversity, and teamwork. Evaluation is also a critical element and serves as a measure of the impact of the employee health program with business operations, employee engagement and overall outputs. In exploring and understanding sustainability and integration, there is a need to focus on the organization and its role in the community as an influencer in the overall health of the workplace.

CONNECTING KEY ELEMENTS OF AN EMPLOYEE HEALTH PROGRAM WITH PRACTICAL EXAMPLES

Building upon the assessment and business case for an employee health program, the next step is the development of a strategic operating plan. This plan should align the program with the vision, goals and objectives of the organization and include a marketing and communication plan, the infrastructure necessary to successfully deliver the program, implementation strategies, timeline, resources, budget details and an evaluation plan.

To provide additional insight as well as practical examples and approaches to health improvement, the authors have provided a case study of their own experience. This case study provides best practice examples and additional and detailed information to illustrate employee health program components, examples, impact and success in building a healthy culture.

Case Study: The University of Alabama

Founded in 1831, The University of Alabama (UA), the State of Alabama's oldest public university, is a senior comprehensive doctoral-level institution. Its mission is to advance the intellectual and social condition of the people of the state through quality programs of teaching, research, and service.

Infrastructure
Founded in 2007, the Office of Health Promotion and Wellness (OHPW, n.d.) was launched following the hiring of the first ever Director of Health Promotion and Wellness. The Director also serves as one of the over 1100 faculty members at UA. The Director is joined by an Assistant Director who serves in the office up to two days each week, while also serving as a faculty member in the Capstone College of Nursing. The organizational structure for promoting a healthy culture is guided by the Director and Assistant Director in collaboration with a variety of individuals and groups, including the Provost, the Wellness Advisory Board, Wellness Ambassadors and the OHPW staff. Multiple departments, colleges, and schools also support the office through collaborative research and the provision of students. Each entity plays a significant and positive role in creating the infrastructure of a healthy workplace.

The Director reports to the Provost, the senior academic leader who serves to provide the overarching vision, support and direction. Along with the President and other senior-level administrators, the Provost offers financial support and participates in ongoing updates with the Director.

The Director and Assistant Director work closely with key advisors to create the strategic vision, mission, goals and objectives to include the design of the overarching health and wellness programs. They are responsible for development and execution of the strategic operating plan, as well as integrating resources for maximum efficiency. OHPW staff members help in the design of the health promotion and wellness programs, and are responsible for the delivery and evaluation of the wellness programs and services.

The Wellness Advisory Board is a group of 15 UA faculty and staff members that provide guiding advice and support OHPW, while serving as champions for the faculty and staff wellness program. The Board represents diverse areas and identifies opportunities, resources, and tools for the wellness program, while also providing resources to include time, students and services. Wellness Ambassadors represent each of the colleges, schools and divisions at a ratio of approximately one to 100. They serve as program spokespersons and help to promote wellness programs and initiatives across campus year round. Ambassadors serve as an extension of the UA's commitment to advance the health and well-being of the UA faculty, staff and family members. Through the establishment of this network of individuals, UA is able to continue its efforts towards fostering a culture of health and wellness on campus.

Following the selection process, the teams of ambassadors participate in twice-annual planning retreats where they identify initiatives that they plan to implement in the short and long term in their designated areas.

Table 9.2   *Pillars of health and well-being at the University of Alabama*

Pillar	Description
Pillar 1	Create and sustain a culture of health and well-being that empowers UA and its families to maintain and improve health
Pillar 2	Communicate and coordinate the highest-quality health and wellness programs, resources, and opportunities in order to reduce health risks, prevent disease, and manage chronic conditions
Pillar 3	Build an environment that supports the health and safety of our employees
Pillar 4	Integrate health-related resources to include the coordination of incentives and benefits for optimal value-based health solutions
Pillar 5	Develop a research agenda and publish articles relating to the participation, impact and outcome measures of the program
Pillar 6	Provide education and training opportunities for undergraduate and graduate students in the area of community health, health and wellness program planning and delivery, and program evaluation and dissemination

Source: R. Kelly (2013), WellBAMA participation survey, 25 November, unpublished.

Ideas include the introduction of walking work stations and inviting group exercise instructors to a departmental meeting. Ambassadors are instrumental in identifying needs, sharing feedback and presenting ideas that will shape program offerings for the future.

At UA, the vision of the faculty and staff wellness program is 'To be a nationally recognized leader of university health & wellness programs, united in our commitment to enhancing the quality of life for all served'. The OHPW mission and objectives is 'To create and sustain a culture of health and wellbeing for UA faculty and staff and their families through a quality program of teaching, research and services'. This is accomplished through the identification of the six key priorities, also known as pillars of employee health. A list and description of the pillars is found in Table 9.2.

Strategic operating plan

A strategic operating plan is the blueprint to guide organizations on their path to improved health and well-being as identified through the mission and priorities. The strategic plan may include results of the baseline assessment measures with an overarching plan to deliver and evaluate the program. Sections within the operating plan should include the mission, goals and objectives, the signature brand, the implementation plan and timeline, the marketing and community strategy, and the evaluation plan.

Without a comprehensive and strategic guide, organizations are likely to fall short in the planning delivery and success. The implementation plan should include detailed information on key deliverables and assignments, responsible party and timeline, as well as locations of program services and events. The implementation timeline is a very effective tool in helping guide the overall direction and plan for the program and can be presented in multiple formats to include the use of Gantt charts.

Signature program: WellBAMA

Designed in 2007 to serve the UA faculty and staff, the director created the signature wellness program and brand called WellBAMA. WellBAMA serves the UA faculty, staff and family and as the gateway to other programs and resources. Through graphic elements, and the delivery of strategic messages, the WellBAMA program has gained visibility on campus, and become synonymous with a healthy lifestyle. Employee health programs that combine health screening and follow-up group or individual health coaching have guided employees to better understand their health status (Carter et al., 2011; Consensus Statement, 2012). The WellBAMA Health Check serves as a core element of UA's health and wellness programs. This program offers annual health screening and health coaching to all UA faculty and staff and was expanded in 2012 to include a financial reward. This program is currently referred to as the WellBAMA Rewards program.

Each year, over 200 Capstone College of Nursing students and their faculty join the OHPW team to provide the WellBAMA Rewards health screening and health coaching services to faculty and staff through its outreach efforts. During the health screening, baseline and follow-up measures are completed to include waist circumference, body weight, height, body mass index, blood pressure, blood work (glucose, lipids), tobacco and exercise status, as well as a health survey (Carter et al., 2013).

The right incentives to reach and engage the members

A Joint Consensus guidance document outlining a reasonably designed, employer-sponsored wellness program using outcomes-based incentives was developed in coordination with the Health Enhancement Research Organization, the American College of Occupational and Environmental Medicine, the American Cancer Society and the American Cancer Society Cancer Action Network, the American Diabetes Association, and American Heart Association (Consensus Statement, 2012). The purpose of this document was to provide employers with information and suggestions on ways to design employee health programs linked to outcome-based incentive programs in the United States. This document was also developed to improve health, lower cost, while protecting employees from discrimination and unaffordable coverage. This document serves as an excellent research for employers needing additional information and insight on incentive programs for employee health.

As outlined in the document, industry experts agree that incentive amounts ranging from $40 to $60 per month may be adequate to promote behavior change for many participants. However, they noted that incentives of greater cash value may actually decrease the participant's internal motivation. This intrinsic motivation is essential to help participants sustain their health improvements. The Consensus Statement (2012, p. 894) recommends considering the following questions when determining the incentive amount:

(a) Does the incentive amount fit with your culture? (b) Will the incentive amount drive behavior change? (c) If penalties are used, will they have disproportionate financial impact across different levels or racial/ethnic groups? (d) Is the incentive so large that it results in significant cost shifting to nonparticipating or non-attaining employees, jeopardizing their ability to afford coverage?

Employers should consider both participation-based (reimbursement of the partial or full cost for membership in a fitness or recreation center, waiving a deductible to increase preventive care, reimbursement for tobacco cessation programs, and recognizing achievements through token giveaways) as well as outcomes-based incentive programs. In 2014, the Affordable Care Act for citizens of the United States will allow the total amount of wellness program rewards to increase to 30 percent of health benefit costs.

To realize the potential benefits of a comprehensive wellness program, OHPW determined that employees were more likely to engage, participate, and sustain participation in programs with a well-designed and implemented incentive strategy. In 2012, the OHPW continued to promote the benefits and reach of WellBAMA health screening and health coaching, through the rollout of the WellBAMA Rewards program, the financial incentive wellness strategy. As the WellBAMA Rewards program was rolled out campuswide, the OHPW continues to solicit feedback from employees, and to shape communications in order to engage the population. Testimonials, success stories and photographs are used to further promote the success of employees who have embraced the healthy culture in order to inspire others to do the same. Data drawn from programs is used to promote the work of the OHPW and UA in the local, regional and national media.

Steps in the process
The WellBAMA Rewards program consists of four steps in the annual process. Step 1 is the opportunity for UA faculty and staff to get screened. The WellBAMA program begins with personal health screening.

Screenings can be completed by an employee's healthcare provider using the WellBAMA Medical Qualification Form or on campus at one of the WellBAMA Health Check events. During the WellBAMA health screening event, measurements are completed to include: height, weight, blood pressure, cholesterol, triglycerides, blood glucose, and other health factors. Once an employee completes the health screening, he or she meets with a health coach to review their WellBAMA score sheet and receive details on the club level achieved (Crimson, Gold, Silver). Crimson is the healthiest category for participants and Silver is the lowest category of health. Participants also receive additional follow-up during the year based on the results of their health screening.

Step 2 is the opportunity for participants to set goals. As participants strive towards living well, achieving their goals and reaching Crimson, their health coach is there to support and connect them to additional health and wellness resources. Group and individual health coaching sessions continue throughout the year with a minimum of one follow-up required for each participant.

Step 3 is the focus for participants to create a plan in order to achieve their goals with WellBAMA programs and services. The health coaching continues throughout the year with a minimum of one follow-up health coaching session, depending on club status. Group and individual follow-up health coaching sessions are available.

And finally, Step 4 is the opportunity for participants to receive their annual financial incentive in the form of a VISA reward card. The WellBAMA Rewards program pays employees to participate and improve their health. In the first year of participating, employees earn $25 just by participating. In their second year of participation, employees can earn $50–$200 based on club status and completion of health and wellness follow-up coaching and participation in programs. Rewards are distributed at the end of the calendar year. Information related to the promotion and marketing of WellBAMA are available on UA's website.

Additional interventions
Core components of the WellBAMA programs include interventions that address physical health, nutrition and weight management, tobacco control, stress management, preventive health. Additionally, OHPW partners with campus and community resources to deliver programs to address depression and anxiety (Employee Assistance Program), diabetes prevention and management (University Medical Center), parenting and child behavior services (Child Development Research Center), physical conditioning and recreation (University Recreation) as well as financial well-being (UA Benefits).

OHPW faculty and staff are trained in health behavior and use health behavior theories, models and framework to assist in the design and planning of their program interventions. One resource commonly used by the OHPW team is *Theories at a Glance* (National Cancer Institute, 2005). Leveraging many theories, the OHPW relies on the stages of change (transtheoretical) model (TTM) to be used most often with the WellBAMA Rewards health coaching (Prochaska and DiClemente, 1983). As noted in the stages of change model, change of behavior among individuals is a process and not an event. To modify a behavior, individuals must move through one of five stages: (1) precontemplation, (2) contemplation, (3) preparation, (4) action, and (5) maintenance. For OHPW team members, each stage is an opportunity to provide participants with different messages, educational information and interventions tailored to their needs.

OHPW also relies on the social ecological approach to create change within campus and greater community. Without the opportunity to create change within the organization and its community there are significant limits on the ability to create a healthy culture with sustained behavior change. The WellBAMA program takes into consideration the need to address individuals, families, campus environment, policies addressing health, health benefits, as well as the greater community in health-improving messages, activities, services, infrastructure, and leadership. Of significant importance are the two key concepts of the ecological perspective. These concepts help to identify intervention opportunities for promoting health: 'first, behavior both affects, and is affected by, multiple levels of influence; second, individual behavior both shapes, and is shaped by, the social environment (reciprocal causation)' (NCI, 2005).

The WellBAMA program focuses on an ecological approach to include supportive environment initiatives that increase access to healthy foods (in vending machines and cafeterias, at meetings or in break rooms) access to places for physical activity (walking paths, recreation centers, accessible stairwells). Healthy eating guidelines not only provide an opportunity for employees to eat well, but also make it easier to do so. Additionally, implementing smoke- or tobacco-free workplace policies and programs to assist employees in quitting their tobacco use will not only lead to a healthier work environment, but may also lower healthcare costs for employers.

In addition to the delivery of the annual WellBAMA Rewards program, a multitude of featured initiatives, events and services are offered through OHPW. As revealed by participant surveys and focus groups, employee health programs that include a team approach (clubs, support groups, team challenges and buddy system) benefit from group support and have been shown to boost morale, enhance motivation, engagement and self-esteem. One of the many signature health and wellness programs offered at UA is the 'Crimson Couch to 5K' program. Launched in 2009, this nine-week training program encourages participation by teams of three to five individuals who are interested in advancing their health and fitness levels. Participants are given one of three workouts to follow (walker, beginner runner, intermediate runner). The program includes monthly check-ins, free information, weekly group training sessions, incentives, and the support of health and wellness staff to help participants reach their goals. The nine-week training program culminates in a 'Crimson Couch to 5K Walk and Run' event held in the fall of each year. With approximately 25 percent of all faculty and staff participating each year, this health improvement program and event has been accepted as part of the healthy environment and culture at the university.

Marketing and communications plan
Another critical element of the strategic operating plan is the marketing and communications plan. The development of a strong communications plan can accomplish several needs for an employee health program (National Cancer Institute, 1989). The communication plan can provide: (1) increased awareness and brand recognition of the program, (2) increased awareness of employee health-related risks, (3) increased awareness of workplace health promotion opportunities for employees, (4) increased trust between management and employees, (5) increased program participation, and (6) improved health-related behaviors. The ultimate goal of the communication plan is to improve the health and well-being of the UA faculty and staff as coordinated with a comprehensive program design.

Many organizations are able to work closely with their own marketing, advertising, public relations or communications departments to assist to create a brand, crafting messages, developing a communications strategy, and measuring impact of the communication reach. However, not all organizations need or have multiple resources to accomplish this step. Informal techniques such as one-on-one conversations with co-workers, friends and family can also help the organization better understand its audience.

To help create a healthy culture at UA, the OHPW has implemented a strategic communications plan each year to reach an audience of faculty, staff and family members. Embracing a positive, energetic, competitive and inspiring tone, the plan delivers key messages: (1) WellBAMA provides valuable resources to help employees live a happier, healthier life, (2) WellBAMA is easily accessible on campus, (3) WellBAMA is easy to incorporate into any lifestyle, with a focus on nutrition, fitness, work–life balance, financial security and other areas of wellness.

A communication and marketing plan within the strategic plan focuses on the promotion of four key channels and includes an infographic

Source: R. Kelly (2007), WellBAMA infographic, The University of Alabama.

Figure 9.1   WellBAMA infographic used for program branding and recognition

(Figure 9.1): (1) Nourish: nutrition and weight loss program and services (2) Move: physical activity, opportunities, centers and events, (3) Balance: positive thinking and mindfulness training with the inclusion of the employee and family assistance program, and (4) Live: health screenings, chronic disease management, tobacco cessation and preventive exams.

Utilizing a variety of promotional vehicles, the communications plan is delivered in support of specific programs, and key themes throughout the year. These vehicles are listed in Box 9.2.

Itemized budget
A strategic operating plan will also include a budget that includes item-ized expenses for key elements needed to deliver a program. The OHPW budget includes the salaries for faculty and staff team members, graduate and undergraduate students, contract employees, overhead space, com-munication lines, equipment, supplies, educational and communication tools and materials, as well as incentives, and other health-related needs. Budget templates and guidelines specific to obesity control are available online at the Centers for Disease Control and Prevention obesity in the workplace LEAN *Works!* website (CDC, 2011).

Employee health promotion programs may not require enormous

BOX 9.2   MARKETING AND COMMUNICATION VEHICLES AT THE UNIVERSITY OF ALABAMA

Electronic (email/website/social media/TV/radio)
Partnerships (with other departments such as University Recreation)
Print (posters/postcards/fliers/program materials)
Speeches/seminars
Groundswell (activism towards health)
Articles in print (dialog, local media)
Calendars
Events (health fair, WellBAMA screenings/meetings/CC5K)
Networking (ambassadors/administrators/coordinators)
Around campus (signage)
Faculty/staff clinic
Word of mouth
Community events
Press releases to campus and local media
Advertising
Positive culture of health led by key leaders

---

resources; however, an investment in the health and well-being of the employees is essential. An investment of $200–500 per employee per year for a health improvement program is recommended to cover the costs for a comprehensive program design to allow for the best return on investment (Goetzel, 2012).

For UA, the institution carries the primary cost of the program, with employees sharing in a few expenses, such as paying for on-site weight loss programs, on-site recreation center membership, and entry fees for the 5K events. As noted earlier, rewards and prizes are used to increase the number of participants engaged in a workplace wellness program. In addition to financial incentives, OHPW provides an annual program T-shirt, free fruit at check-in and pedometers once a year. Incentives continue to be used extensively for engaging and sustaining employee participation in the WellBAMA health programs.

Removing barriers so more faculty and staff can participate
Identifying and eliminating the barriers that keep faculty and staff from participating is also an effective option when gaining participant involvement:

Suggestions for removing barriers include: (a) offering programs at convenient times, on company time, and with child-care options; (b) creating a supportive environment, which includes getting management involved in programs, giving employees an opportunity to establish ownership in the program, and establishing a highly-visible healthy organizational culture; and (c) removing financial burdens such as material or registration fees or other program costs. (Kelly and Carter, in press)

Evaluation plan

The final section of the operating plan should include details and information related to employee health program evaluation. The two basic types of program evaluations are process and outcome evaluations (CDC, 2013b). Process evaluations are used by OHPW to determine if the program design and delivery is working well. This method of evaluation is conducted during every initiative, event and service. The evaluation includes the review of program activities, staffing, schedule, budget, immediate impact of the intervention, and if the core elements of the program were delivered as planned. Process evaluations are conducted during the time of the program or event delivery and also include a review of participation rates, participant satisfaction, program improvements, and program budget. Participant testimonials, suggestions and ideas for future programs are also captured at this time.

Outcome evaluations are conducted to explore the greater impact of the program and determine if the goals and objectives were met. This type of evaluation is used by OHPW and includes a review of participant attitudes, knowledge, and behaviors, as well as clinical health indicators and risk factors (to include body weight, body mass index, blood pressure, tobacco status, exercise, status, lipid values). Outcome evaluations may also explore the cost benefit analysis and and/or the return of investment of the employee health program. Metrics evaluated include healthcare costs, medical utilization, change in health status, change in lost work time, and other factors as available (such as absenteeism, productivity). Table 9.3 provides a summary of the changes of behavior reported by a sample of WellBAMA participants.

SUMMARY

Companies looking for the edge on productivity and performance, while also addressing the impact of poor health, should consider the adoption of employee health programs. By improving the health and well-being of today's workforce, organizations can benefit from employees with

Table 9.3   Behavior changes as reported by participants in the WellBAMA Health Check

What have you done or plan to do as a result of participating in the 2013 WellBAMA health screening and health coaching program?

	Working Towards My Goal	Achieved My Goal	Number
Schedule an appointment with a dentist	7.8%	32.3%	359
Schedule an appointment with an eye doctor	9.2%	28.9%	349
Schedule appointment with a primary care provider	10.7%	26.3%	354
Increase water intake	41.1%	20.9%	387
Join a fitness/recreation center	11.5%	20.9%	330
Take my medication regularly	6.3%	16.7%	378
Exercise more	49.6%	16.5%	395
Increase fruits and vegetables	51.1%	12.2%	395
Decrease sugar intake	44.9%	10.2%	372
Decrease fat intake	45.4%	9.7%	372
Manage money	29.2%	9.3%	366
Make family time more active	36.5%	6.9%	362
Identify ways to reduce stress	40.1%	6.7%	357
Lose weight	47.8%	6.1%	393
Quit tobacco	2.2%	2.2%	372
Decrease tobacco	2.1%	1.3%	376

Source: Kelly (2013), 'WellBAMA participant survey', 25 November, unpublished.

lower risk, improved health, reduced healthcare costs and utilization, as well as improved performance. Since most adults spend a significant portion of their time at work, the workplace offers an excellent setting for providing health and wellness programs. Leadership commitment and engagement, worker involvement, business ethics, use of a systematic and comprehensive process, and sustainability and integration all play a critical role in improving the health of an organization and its workers and families.

REFERENCES

Aldana, S.G., D.R. Anderson, T.B. Adams, R.W. Whitmer, R.M. Merrill, V. George and J. Noyce (2012), 'A review of the knowledge base on health worksite culture', *Journal of Occupational and Environmental Medicine*, **54**(4), 414–19.

Anderko, L., J. Roffenbender, R. Goetzel, F. Millard, K. Wildenhaus, C. DeSantis and M. Novelli (2012), 'Promoting prevention through the Affordable Care Act: workplace wellness', *Preventing Chronic Disease*, **9**(120092).

Baicker, K., D. Cutler and Z. Song (2010), 'Workplace wellness programs can generate savings', *Health Affairs*, **29**(2), 304–11.

Baxter, S., K. Sanderson, A. Venn, L. Blizzard, and A.J. Palmer (2014), 'The relationship between return on investment and quality of study methodology in workplace health promotion programs.' *American Journal of Health Promotion*: **28**(6), 347–363.

Carter, M., R. Kelly, C. Alexander and L. Holmes (2011), 'A collaborative university model for employee health', *American Journal of College Health*, **59**(8), 761–3.

Carter, M., R. Kelly, M. Montgomery and M. Cheshire (2013), 'An innovative approach to health promotion experiences in community health nursing: a university collaborative partnership', *Journal of Nursing Education*, **52**(2), 108–11.

Centers for Disease Control and Prevention (CDC) (2010), *Healthier Worksite Initiative Environmental Audits*, accessed 20 November 2013 at www.cdc.gov/nccdphp/dnpao/hwi/programdesign/environmental_audits.htm.

Centers for Disease Control and Prevention (CDC) (2011), *CDC's Lean Works! Identify Program Budget*, accessed 20 November 2013 at www.cdc.gov/leanworks/plan/identifybudget.html.

Centers for Disease Control and Prevention (CDC) (2012a), *Healthier Worksite Initiative: Cost Calculators*, accessed 20 November 2013 at www.cdc.gov/nccdphp/dnpao/hwi/programdesign/costcalculators.htm.

Centers for Disease Control and Prevention (CDC) (2012b), *Worksite Health ScoreCard*, accessed 20 November 2013 at www.cdc.gov/dhdsp/pubs/docs/HSC_Manual.pdf.

Centers for Disease Control and Prevention (CDC) (2013a), *Worksite Health Promotion: Making a Business Case*, accessed 20 November 2013 at www.cdc.gov/workplacehealthpromotion/businesscase/index.html.

Centers for Disease Control and Prevention (CDC) (2013b), *Worksite Health Promotion: Evaluation*, accessed 20 November 2013 at http://www.cdc.gov/workplacehealthpromotion/evaluation/.

Chapman, L.S. (2012), 'Meta-evaluation of worksite health promotion economic return studies: 2012 update', *American Journal of Health Promotion*, **26**(4), TAHP1–TAHP2.

Consensus Statement of the Health Enhancement Research Organization; American College of Occupational and Environmental Medicine; American Cancer Society and American Cancer Society Cancer Action Network; American Diabetes Association; American Heart Association (2012), 'Guidance for a reasonably designed, employer-sponsored wellness program using outcomes-based incentives', *Journal of Occupational and Environmental Medicine*, **54**(7), 889–96.

Council for Disability Awareness (2012), *Disability Statistics*, accessed 20 November 2013 at http://www.disabilitycanhappen.org/chances_disability/disability_stats.asp.

Goetzel, R. (2012), *Demystifying ROI*, for the Wellness Council of America, accessed 20 November 2013 at www.welcoa.org/freeresources/pdf/rongoetzel011912.pdf.

Health Enhancement Research Organization (2012), *HERO Best Practice Scorecard in Collaboration with Mercer*, accessed 20 November 2013 at www.the-hero.org/scorecard_folder/HEROScorecardV3%201.pdf.

Health Project, The (2012), *C. Everett Koop National Health Awards Criteria*, accessed 20 November 2013 at www.sph.emory.edu/healthproject.

Henke, R., G. Carls, M. Short, P. Xiaofel, S. Wang, S. Moley, M. Sullivan and R. Goetzel (2010), 'The relationship between health risks and health productivity costs among employees at Pepsi Bottling Group', *JOEM*, **52**(5), 519–27.

Kelly, R. and M. Carter (in press), 'Health and safety: perspectives from the field', in M.J. Grawitch and D.W. Ballard (eds), *The Psychologically Healthy Workplace: Building a Win-Win Environment for Organizations and Employees*, Washington, DC: American Psychological Association.

Loeppke, R., M. Taitel, V. Haufle, T. Parry, R.C. Kessler and K. Jinnett (2009), 'Health and productivity as a business strategy: a multiemployer study', *Journal of Occupational and Environmental Medicine*, **51**(4), 411–28.

National Cancer Institute (1989), *Making Health Communication Programs Work*, Rockville, MD: US Department of Health and Human Services.

National Cancer Institute (2005), *Theory at a Glance: A Guide for Health Promotion Practice*, accessed 20 November 2013 at www.cancer.gov/cancertopics/cancerlibrary/theory.pdf.

Partnership for Prevention (2007, 2011), *Leading by Example*, accessed 20 November 2013 at www.prevent.org/Initiatives/Leading-by-Example.aspx.

Pelletier, K. (2001), 'A review and analysis of the clinical and cost-effectiveness studies of comprehensive health promotion and disease management programs at the worksite: 1998–2000 update', *American Journal of Health Promotion*, **16**(2), 107–16.

Prochaska, J. and C. DiClemente (1983), 'Stages and processes of self-change of smoking: toward an integrative model of change', *Journal of Consulting and Clinical Psychology*, **51**(3), 390–95.

University of Alabama Office of Health Promotion and Wellness (OHPW) (n.d.), accessed 20 November 2013 at www.wellness.ua.edu.

World Health Organization (2008–17), *World Health Organization Global Plan of Action on Workers' Health: Baseline for Implementation (2008/09)*, accessed 20 November 2013 at www.who.int/occupational_health/who_workers_health_web.pdf.

World Health Organization (2010), *Healthy Workplaces: A Model for Action. For Employers, Workers, Policymakers and Practitioners*, accessed 20 November 2013 at www.who.int/occupational_health/publications/healthy_workplaces_model_action.pdf.

World Health Organization (2012), *Depression Fact Sheet No. 369*, accessed 20 November 2013 at www.who.int/mediacentre/factsheets/fs369/en/index.html.

10. Increasing healthy habits and health behavior change in corporate wellness programs

Cindy W. Morris and Chad D. Morris

THE STATE OF CORPORATE WELLNESS PROGRAMS

Sedentary lifestyle, poor nutrition, tobacco and alcohol use, risky sexual activity and avoidable injuries are strongly linked to unnecessary death and disability (Mokdad et al., 2004, 2005; Schroeder, 2007; Centers for Disease Control and Prevention, 2010). Approximately 68 percent of US adults are overweight or obese (Flegal et al., 2010), and over 25 percent continue to use tobacco products (King et al., 2012). While in the past most US deaths were due to infectious disease, this is no longer the case. Most morbidity and mortality is now related to modifiable health behaviors. Because adults commonly spend the majority of their time on the job, worksites are often an ideal setting in which to encourage healthy living. Corporate wellness programs provide excellent opportunities to promote healthy habits and positive health behavior change to a population that is often less apt to initiate healthy living behaviors on its own (Goetzel and Ozminkowski, 2008). The popularity and investment in such programs is growing (Galinsky and Matos, 2012), with a large employer survey finding that 51 percent of US companies with 50 or more employees now offer some degree of wellness programming (Mattke et al., 2013). The larger the employer the more likely they are to provide a robust wellness program (KFF/HRET, 2012).

The growth observed in corporate wellness programs is, in large part, due to the evidence that such programming benefits both employees and organizations. Involvement in worksite wellness programs is clearly linked to improvements in participants' health habits and reduced health risks (Serxner et al., 2001, 2003; Aldana et al., 2005; Merrill et al., 2011). The return on investment (ROI) for worksite wellness programs includes decreased absenteeism and employee satisfaction (e.g., Aldana, 2001;

Parks and Steelman, 2008; Hyatt et al., 2010; Merrill et al., 2011). Meta-analyses have further demonstrated that wellness programs are associated with reductions in sick leave, health plan costs and workers' compensation and disability costs (Chapman, 2005, 2012; Baicker et al., 2010).

There are many potential avenues to wellness within worksite settings because organizations have multiple levels of influence over employee wellness. Organizations can support peer interactions, provide environmental cues and resources, set internal policy and be a point of linkage to greater community services (McLeroy et al., 1988; Glanz and Rimer, 1995; Stokols et al., 2003). Among employers offering wellness services, the majority provide interventions on nutrition, weight, fitness and smoking, but substance abuse and stress management options are also common (Mattke et al., 2013). The interventions themselves are diverse, from health risk screening (e.g., body mass index, cholesterol) to interventions addressing health risks (e.g., pedometers to increase number of steps per day, nutrition education), access to resources (e.g., gym membership), health benefits (e.g., Employee Assistance Programs), financial incentives (e.g., reduced insurance rates for reaching weight management goals) and supportive environmental change (e.g., no-smoking policies, aesthetically pleasing surroundings). Only a handful of employers (approximately 7 percent), typically large companies, have wellness initiatives that include all the above components (Linnan et al., 2008). Being relatively inexpensive and low burden, health risk screenings and policy changes are by far the most popular options (Trogdon et al., 2009; Mattke et al., 2013).

Potential facilitators of workplace wellness initiatives include existing access to large groups of adults in structured settings, established leadership and communication lines, peer networks, health promotion infrastructure, active recruitment techniques and organizational events and activities incorporating wellness (Katz et al., 2005; Fabius and Frazee, 2009; Merrill et al., 2011). But worksite wellness programs also face potential barriers such as unknown cost effectiveness, lack of resources and incentives, logistical barriers (e.g., time and location of wellness services) and potential low levels of employee interest (Lovato and Green, 1990; Person et al., 2010; Mattke et al., 2013). While the concept of corporate wellness is popular, overall engagement in worksite wellness programs remains low. Less than 20 percent of employees typically participate in lifestyle management programs (Mattke et al., 2013), with the lowest participation rates for smoking cessation services.

While the evidence base continues to grow in support of ROI and other positive outcomes for worksite wellness, much less is known regarding the specific behavior change strategies used in corporate settings. Typical programming such as weight loss competitions, tobacco cessation groups and education on nutritious diets may all be effective strategies. However, many of these programs are put into place with little attention to the existing evidence base for behavior change strategies that underlie such favored interventions. It is also often unclear how the behavioral components of these programs are vetted and justified. In limited cases, behavior change theory drives worksite wellness initiatives. But much more commonly, the existing literature describes programs that do not clearly operationalize behavior strategies or which mix multiple, widespread change strategies. Very few companies adequately address the guiding question 'What principles of behavior change guide your health promotion work?' (O'Donnell, 2005).

In this chapter, we explore specific behavior change theories and strategies on how corporate settings may capitalize on their influence to maximize employees' sustained behavior changes. We share the little evidence that exists for worksite wellness behavior change theories and describe behavior change strategies most often integrated into screening, prevention, promotion, incentives, policy and healthy lifestyle programming. In the next section, we structure our discussion on the four components that are essential to the development of effective corporate wellness programs, including increasing awareness and knowledge, enhancing motivation and encouraging action, building skills and providing opportunity (O'Donnell, 2005). The third section then provides pragmatic guidance to companies and worksite wellness champions for effectively implementing evidence-based behavior change strategies, including how companies might utilize facilitating factors and overcome historical barriers to change.

HOW PEOPLE CHANGE

Health behavior can be defined as 'those personal attributes such as beliefs, expectations, motives, values, perceptions, and other cognitive elements; personality characteristics, including affective and emotional states and traits; and overt behavior patterns, actions, and habits that relate to health maintenance, to health restoration, and to health improvement' (Gochman, 1997, p. 3). Over the last 100 years, there have been a growing number of theories and models of change regarding individual health behavior change, but only a subset of these has been applied to worksite wellness (Glanz et al., 2008). In this section, we review aspects of change theory and practice that are most prominent in worksites, including global concepts that target the organizational environment as well as aspects of individual employee health behavior change.

Increasing Awareness and Knowledge

Awareness is a necessary first step toward behavior change and an ongoing skill in sustaining desired behaviors. Providing wellness facts, health promotion materials and results from individual health risk assessments are helpful as employees weigh the pros and cons of their lifestyle choices. Employees are not a homogeneous group and have different tolerance for ambiguity, openness to change, motivation, confidence, skill sets and social values. Health promotion and educational resources are most effective when matched to individual differences and learning styles. Personalized feedback from health risk assessments or messages tailored to individual stage of change, in comparison to generic feedback, has been shown to have a positive effect on risk factors such as unhealthy diet or sedentary behavior (Kreuter and Strecher, 1996; Peterson and Aldana, 1999; Goetzel and Ozminkowski, 2008).

Employers must also consider the limitations of health promotion campaigns. Knowledge transfer is necessary but not sufficient for sustained behavior change (O'Donnell, 2005). As a compelling example, most smokers are fully aware of the potential dangers. If behavior change was as simple as reading the Surgeon General's warning on every pack of cigarettes, this unhealthy addiction would be a thing of the past. The same can be said of health risk assessment and biometric screenings. Both knowledge of risks and understanding of alternative and accessible healthy choices are prerequisites for action, but sustained change is dependent on interventions that build awareness, enhance motivation and assist employees' shift from external motivations to internalizing reasons for change.

Awareness is the cornerstone of conscious action. Mindfulness-based approaches to awareness move from knowledge and facts to 'paying attention in a particular way: on purpose, in the present moment, and nonjudgmentally' (Kabat-Zinn, 1994, p. 4). Langer and Moldoveanu (2000, p. 2) describe the subjective experience of mindfulness as being in a 'heightened state of involvement and wakefulness or being in the present'. Baer (2009) further describes components of mindfulness as observation, description, acting with awareness, non-judging of inner experience and non-reactivity of inner experience. Observation includes noticing and attending to internal and external experiences, such as thoughts, feelings, bodily sensation and other environmental stimuli. Description occurs when a person labels their experience with words. In order to act with awareness, an individual engages in behaviors with a focused attention. This stance can be contrasted with acting while on 'autopilot'. Non-judging inner experience occurs when a person is aware of their thoughts and feelings without evaluation or critique. It is a process of allowing thoughts and feelings to come and go without taking action to fix, change, or be distracted by the experience.

When a person can approach their daily routines and behaviors from a place of mindfulness, change is more likely to occur (Langer and Moldoveanu, 2000). There is an increased awareness of one's environment, openness to new information and observation from different perspectives. All of these facilitate a sense of empowerment and control, which can lead to decreased stress and increased creativity.

An offshoot of mindfulness, acceptance and commitment therapy (ACT), is thought to enhance psychological flexibility and decrease psychological distress through acceptance, defusion,[1] contact with the present moment, self-as-context, values and committed action (Hayes et al., 2006; Biglan et al., 2008; Flaxman and Bond, 2010). Similar to earlier mindfulness work, the fundamental goal in ACT is to strengthen the ability to be in the present and direct behaviors based on one's values (Hayes et al., 2004).

Enhancing Motivation and Encouraging Action

Financial incentives

As employers promote health and awareness, they can concurrently utilize corporate financial incentives for wellness. Incentives can accelerate employees' decisions to change, capturing the attention of those employees who may not be motivated to act independently (O'Donnell, 2005). But the evidence of effectiveness for incentives is mixed. Meta-analysis of over 100 randomized controlled studies found that if incentives are big enough, they will influence employees' behavior in the short run (Kane et al., 2004), and incentives can also be combined with financial penalties (Butler, 2010). As cases in point, corporate incentives have been demonstrated to increase attendance of weight management and smoking cessation programs (Follick et al., 1984; Curry et al., 1991). But if incentives are not large, the effect is small and unlikely to be clinically meaningful (Robroek et al., 2009; Volpp, 2009; Osilla et al., 2012; Mattke et al., 2013). There are many examples of how companies structure incentives. For instance, a medical center offers pre-tax wellness bonuses provided to employees over successive years, with employees who don't meet all target criteria still receiving smaller incentives. This program demonstrated 51 percent participation over ten years with a healthcare and sick leave saving of over $13 million (Seifert et al., 2012). Another large healthcare employer had 75 percent participation in a wellness program using a point system tied to financial incentives. In this program employees had to complete health risk assessments and web-based wellness tutorials to receive incentives.

Generally, the existing evidence taken together finds that financial incentives are an effective means by which to engage participants, but they may not lead to graduated or sustained change (Cahill and Perera, 2011).

Stage of change and motivational strategies

Once employers are able to catch the employees' attention through incentives, preventive screening and health promotions, they can then utilize strategies for developing intrinsic motivation, which is driven by an interest or enjoyment in the task itself outside of any external or environmental pressure. People can learn to identify their own internal values for new behaviors and be successfully weaned from external incentives. The end goal is for wellness practices to be their own reward.

To reach this ultimate goal, self-determination theory (SDT) has long suggested that individuals must believe that they are acting independently and with an internal sense of control for true behavior change to occur (e.g., Deci and Ryan, 1985; Williams et al., 1996). SDT argues that there are basic psychological needs that must be met to facilitate wellness:

- competence evidenced by being able to control outcomes and experience mastery;
- relatedness defined as the universal wish to interact, be connected to and experience caring for others; and
- autonomy or the universal urge to be causal agents of one's own life and act in harmony with one's integrated self.

It would follow that organizations might support the above factors and thus increase participation in workplace wellness programs. To the degree that the workplace can provide opportunities to act autonomously and increase options related to personal health and well-being, intrinsic motivation will increase. While to our knowledge SDT has not be been specifically tested in workplace settings, the core components of competence, relatedness and autonomy have been integrated in wellness initiatives in the form of the corporate culture and climate, skills building and social networking activities further detailed throughout the rest of this chapter.

A key to self-determined, healthy action is to meet employees where they are at in terms of their personal readiness for change. Organizational attitudes or norms will have little effect on behavior unless a person has intentions to change (Aizen, 1985; Glanz et al., 2008). Stage theories have a long-standing theoretical and research foundation for how to encourage desired behavior change, with the earliest of such theories appearing in the mid-twentieth century. Kurt Lewin (1951) looked at three stages of organizational and employee change: (1) unfreezing past behaviors and

Table 10.1   Stages of change

Stage	Behavior Process
Precontemplation	No intention to take action within the next six months
Contemplation	Intends to take action within the next six months
Preparation	Intends to take action within the next 30 days and has taken some behavioral steps in this direction
Action	Changed overt behavior for less than six months
Maintenance	Changed overt behavior for more than six months

Source: Prochaska and DiClemente (1983).

attitudes, (2) exposure to new information, attitudes and theories, and (3) refreezing new behaviors and attitudes through reinforcement and confirmation. Whether purposively or not, change theories continue to extend and refine these concepts.

The most widely disseminated and implemented model is the transtheoretical model (TTM). TTM has been extensively studied as a means to by which to both (1) assess individual and organizational readiness to change and (2) provide strategies for guiding change and maintenance of desirable behaviors. TTM has been effectively applied in many settings, including primary care (Goldstein et al., 1999; Hollis et al., 2005), home (Curry et al., 1995; Gold et al., 2000), churches (Voorhees et al., 1996), schools (Aveyard et al., 1999), campuses (J.M. Prochaska et al., 2004), communities (Fishbein et al., 1999) and worksites (J.O. Prochaska et al., 2008). The model grew from a comparative analysis of change among smokers. The study results suggested that successful quitters move through five stages of changes (Table 10.1) and utilize different behavior processes at each stage (Prochaska and DiClemente, 1983; Prochaska and Velicer, 1997).

In addition, Prochaska and Velicer conceptualized 'relapse' (or recycling), which is not a stage of change in itself but rather the return from action or maintenance to an earlier stage (Prochaska and Velicer, 1997).

Building on TTM, another widespread approach to change is motivational interviewing (MI). According to Miller (2004), MI can be applied in health promotion coaching offered through in-person, telephonic or email interventions. As motivation is key to activating health behavior change, the central challenge is the resolution of an individual's ambivalence to change (ibid.). Movement though the stages of change from precontemplation to contemplation involves an evaluation of personal pros and cons of making different lifestyle choices. When the disadvantages of changing a behavior appear more salient to the individual than the advantages, ambivalence is reflected through maintaining that status quo. In early stages of change, helpful strategies include personal cost–benefit analyses of possible behavior change as well as directing individuals to build awareness regarding the 'what, where and when' of specific behaviors. When perceived advantages mount, they tip the scale of outcome expectations toward behavior change. For MI, the goal of wellness counseling is to evoke change talk and commitment to change in a safe and accepting environment (Miller and Rollnick, 2002; Miller, 2009).

Throughout the TTM stages and MI interventions there are a number of processes that are key mediators for individual change (Prochaska and Velicer, 1997; Miller, 2004):

- collaboration;
- consciousness raising;
- dramatic relief;
- environmental reevaluation;
- self-reevaluation;
- self-liberation;
- social liberation;
- counterconditioning;
- helping relationships;
- contingency management;
- stimulus controls.

These general change factors are embedded in successful worksite wellness programming, and warrant further description. No matter how much assistance a person may receive from others or his or her environment, long-term change will only be sustained if the individual makes the choice to be an active participant. There is a tendency for healthcare providers and employers to advise individuals about what and how to change their health behaviors. This dynamic places the individual in a passive position, which can unintentionally decrease motivation. Employees may have the perception that they are being forced to change, which can quickly shut down the collaborative process. In order to increase motivation, individuals need to make decisions and seek health solutions in collaboration with healthcare providers and wellness personnel.

'Collaboration' can be increased through 'consciousness raising' or increasing an individual's awareness about current or potential health consequences they may face if they engage in unhealthy behaviors. Aligned with social cognitive theory, knowledge about health risks and behaviors that support good health is a core facilitator for adoption of healthy lifestyle habits (Bandura, 2004). Employees are unable to adjust behaviors if they are unaware of health risks and the range of behavioral choices open to them. They engage in their chosen lifestyle without knowing how it may affect their health. Individuals who are in the precontemplation stage of change often match this description. Consciousness-raising strategies teach employees how they can adapt behaviors to support healthy behavior change. Worksite interventions may consist of individual coaching, wellness groups, health education training and/or media campaigns. These strategies position employees to make informed health decisions.

'Dramatic relief' is a process in which an emotional reaction is triggered related to a specific health behavior, followed by some resolution that generates a feeling of relief. An example may be watching a media spot that focuses on an individual's struggle to maintain a healthy weight. The relief comes when the individual describes the transformational changes they have made. Through this process of feeling intense emotion and then reaching a resolution, an observer senses what it would feel like to make this change in their own life, potentially shifting them to contemplation of a range of health choices.

Being able to appreciate that making a health behavior change can have a positive or negative effect on the people around them is referred to as 'environmental reevaluation'. If someone is able to see themselves as a role model for others, they may be more open to change. For environmental reevaluation to occur, a person needs to be aware that their health behaviors do not just impact them. They affect all the people in their lives. It is the realization that being a positive or negative influence is a personal choice. Environmental reevaluation can occur at the worksite through peer and social networks and enhanced through group processes and assuming a leadership role.

'Self-reevaluation' occurs when a person is able to appreciate that making a change is important for their identity, happiness and success. With self-reevaluation, individuals are able to imagine or visualize themselves before and after they make a change. As people are able to visualize having made a positive change, those choices are easier to act upon. Wellness activities that clarify personal values, help identify role models and utilize guided imagery all encourage the process of self-reevaluation.

When people are ready to take action towards change, they engage in the process of 'self-liberation', during which a person is freed, or liberated, from any doubts that they can successfully change. Having experienced a discrepancy between current behaviors and broader beliefs and values, they exhibit an increase in change talk, make the commitment to change and then act accordingly (Apodaca and Longabaugh, 2009). In the workplace, self-liberation can be supported through opportunities for public testimonials, goal setting and engaging in behaviors that are consistent with personal wellness values.

'Social liberation' occurs when opportunities or alternatives that facilitate healthy behaviors are presented to people. Equipped with multiple healthy choices and resources, employees become empowered to take steps towards change. This is particularly salient for groups that have been historically deprived or oppressed. Social liberation may occur through advocacy or policy change, such as implementing a tobacco-free policy or providing healthy food options in the cafeteria or vending machines.

It is important to evoke action through education and skills building. In order to be successful in any health behavior change, people need to learn healthy behaviors and skills to replace undesired behaviors. This 'counterconditioning' occurs through skills-building classes, such as healthy eating and cooking, meditation, yoga and positive communication groups. As people learn new skills and coping strategies, it is important that they reinforce them through practice.

'Helping relationships' allow employees to practice and maintain behavior change. Supportive relationships are helpful whether a person is just considering change or looking to maintain a change they have already made. Defining characteristics include trust, openness, acceptance and care. These facilitating relationships include an expression of accurate empathy and positive regard. Helping relationships can be developed at a worksite through one-on-one health coaching, wellness groups and mentoring.

'Contingency management' enhances motivation for change. This includes identifying and providing intrinsic and extrinsic rewards for new behaviors. It also involves consequences that encourage movement in a particular direction. In contingency management, rewards work better than punishments, particularly for people who are self-motivated. Examples in the workplace include financial incentives, discounts on health insurance and employee recognition.

As individuals practice their new health behaviors, it is helpful to remove cues that may be triggers for the old undesirable behavior while adding cues to facilitate healthy change. There are many adjustments that employers can make in the worksite environment that can serve as these 'stimulus controls'. For instance, an employer may choose to provide signage that encourages taking the stairs or offer healthy eating options.

When Prochaska and Velicer (1997) further examined the above processes, they identified two factors most strongly affecting change and moving individuals toward committed action. The first is experiential processes that provide an internal experience, such as consciousness raising, dramatic relief and self-reevaluation. The second factor is behavioral processes that encourage external engagement. These include helping relationships, contingency management and stimulus control. As people have experiences that are personally meaningful and are able to practice new health behaviors, they develop a sense of mastery that sustains long-term change. These factors are integral to increasing wellness skills starting with the creations of realistic lifestyle goals.

Building Skills

Goal setting

Among multi-component workplace health promotion programs, the initiatives that included goal setting enjoyed success rates almost double those that did not (Heaney and Goetzel, 1997). Similarly, a review of self-management programs found that goal setting and action planning are critical to perceived health improvements (Lorig and Holman, 2003). Goal setting may be the most effective means by which to maintain participation in wellness programs, particularly when goals are challenging yet realistic, short-term, concrete, flexible and set autonomously by the employee (Bandura, 1988; Lovato and Green, 1990; Patalano and Seifert, 1997; Gollwitzer, 1999; Locke and Latham, 2002).

Clearly defined goals provide actionable direction and should be easily evaluated, allowing for regular feedback regarding individual progress. Effective wellness programs assist the change process by helping employees identify challenges to maintain interest but aren't so daunting that they appear unreachable. Delayed gratification in reaching ultimate health goals is difficult. To counter this, a long-term goal made up of many short-term steps strengthens motivation by providing regular feedback on the small wins that sustain effort. For example, setting a goal to lose 50lb may inadvertently lead employees to avoid wellness programming, whereas losing 1lb a month is much more realistic, motivating and sustainable. For this reason pre-packaged wellness programs are often ineffective because they do not encourage adequate collaboration with individuals to create personal goals that are both meaningful and motivating. As individual goals are achieved, self-efficacy and enthusiasm grow, engendering feelings of satisfaction and accomplishment and building momentum for overall long-term health (Bandura, 1988).

Self-efficacy

Beliefs play a powerful role in stress and health promotion. Whether a person believes they can successfully implement health behavior change predicts whether they will accomplish personal goals (Bandura, 2001). A person's belief in their ability to achieve their goal, referred to as self-efficacy, affects their motivation and the activities they choose (Bandura, 1988). Self-efficacy is defined as 'the conviction that one can successfully execute that behavior required to produce the outcomes' (Glanz et al., 2008, p. 49), and the 'situation-specific confidence that people can cope with high-risk situations without relapsing to their former behaviors' (ibid., p. 102). There are four primary means by which to develop self-efficacy: (1) mastery experience or experiencing success, (2) peer and social modeling, (3) improving physical and emotional states and (4) verbal persuasion (Bandura, 2004).

Self-efficacy is tied to physical, social, psychological and financial outcome expectations. Physically, employees may rapidly associate exercise, nutritious diets and other wellness activities to better health and a positive overall mood, particularly decreased anxiety and depression. As financial examples, general wellness decreases out-of-pocket health costs and no longer buying cigarettes has a huge impact on disposable income. Socially, a person's behavior is significantly shaped by how other people may perceive their actions. Peers have power, and acceptance by one's peer group has a major impact on the 'stickiness' of new behaviors. An individual will be hard pressed to stop drinking alcohol when their social outlet is the neighborhood bar, whereas positive social networking such as going to the gym with colleagues is a proven change strategy.

As people challenge themselves by successfully working towards their desired goals, they will gain a sense of mastery, which generates resilience and perseverance in the face of life's setbacks and difficulties. When individuals observe someone they perceive to be like them, such as work colleagues accomplishing the same goal they have set for themselves, their self-efficacy grows. Self-efficacy is also supported by realistic encouragement from other people. When people feel a physiological stress response when participating in certain behaviors, it generates doubt about their ability to be successful due to a sense of vulnerability. So another way to increase self-efficacy is to decrease stress when engaging in desired behaviors. This can be accomplished through one of many variants of stress inoculation therapy, which has been shown to have moderate effectiveness in improving employees' psychological health (Richardson and Rothstein, 2008). This typically involves a combination of cognitive restructuring, muscular relaxation and/or behavioral skills.

Providing Opportunity

Organizational culture and climate

Most employees need encouragement, and additional knowledge and skills to pursue personal wellness goals. Companies have a number of ways to provide opportunities for wellness, where 'opportunity is broadly defined as having access to the environment that makes choosing a healthy behavior a normative choice' (Aldana et al., 2012, p. 414).

A primary role corporate leadership can play is creating a culture and climate that fosters healthy lifestyle choices. Organizational climate is defined as the mood or unique 'personality' of an organization (Forehand and Gilmer, 1964; Tagiuri, 1968). It is the way people perceive their work environment (Verbeke et al., 1998). Climate factors such as leadership support, openness of communication, participative management, role clarity and conflict resolution are positively related to employee satisfaction, participation and implementation of action plans and negatively associated with stress (Schneider, 1985; Butterfoss et al., 1996; Kegler et al., 1998). Psychological climate refers to how the workplace impacts individual well-being (James and James, 1989), which may be measured across multiple dimensions such as emotional exhaustion, depersonalization and role conflict (Glisson, 2000).

Closely related to climate, organizational culture is broadly defined as the way things are done in an organization (Cooke and Szumal, 2000). Corporate culture involves the deep-seated assumptions, values, normative beliefs and behavioral expectations and patterns and corporate symbols such as mission statements and logos (ibid.). Often the principal elements of culture are unconscious. Collectively, the many factors taken together that promote health and wellness can be considered a 'culture' of health (Aldana et al., 2012). Such a culture might support opportunities to access wellness services or support healthy personal decision-making.

While corporate wellness programs are widespread, a review of 350 published reports describing health promotion programs revealed that few mention environmental or policy change, which might instill culture and climate change, much less operationalize, promote and sustain such efforts (Adams et al., 2004). The best models of worksite wellness programs incorporate more cultural elements into their strategies and yield more reduction in employee health risks compared to programs with fewer cultural elements. A mix of health assessments and didactic information, self-help materials, one-on-one, group, employee assistance programs and environmental supports facilitate increased participation in worksite wellness programs (e.g., Heaney and Goetzel, 1997; Terry et al., 2011). And senior leadership and middle management support is critical in the design and integrated communication of a culture and climate of wellness (Terry et al., 2011).

Comprehensive programming
When it comes to designing wellness programs, more robust programming is more effective. Well-conducted randomized trials suggest that individual

risk reduction counseling for high-risk employees in addition to comprehensive wellness programming leads to significantly better outcomes (Heaney and Goetzel, 1997). While increasing awareness and utilizing health screens might engage employees, a range of wellness programming is also necessary to effect employee change. Terry and colleagues (2011) suggest that comprehensive worksite wellness programs have a number of integral components including:

- comprehensive program design;
- management support;
- integrated incentives;
- comprehensive communication;
- dedicated on-site staff;
- variable program modalities;
- health awareness programs;
- biometric health screens;
- vendor integration.

As a programming base, organizations might encourage healthy choices by offering healthy food choices through cafeterias, vending machines and snacks, promoting tobacco-free policies, providing the time and space for physical fitness and offering health screenings and preventive care (Goetzel and Ozminkowski, 2008). Just as evidence suggests that wellness outcomes improve as the combination of modalities or approaches increase, there is also evidence that programs that target multiple risk factors (e.g., nutrition in combination with physical fitness) are more successful (Katz et al., 2005). While there is moderate evidence for interventions combining environmental and policy changes with individual-level strategies (Kahn-Marshall and Gallant, 2012), the evidence is the greatest for multicomponent interventions (Katz et al., 2005; Robroek et al., 2009; Kahn-Marshall and Gallant, 2012). Companies can also ensure vendor integration and direct subcontracting wellness entities to build integrated health management strategies.

Positive social networks
Social support and reinforcement is an important factor that can influence worksite wellness participation (Lovato and Green, 1990). This is consistent with Bandura's extension of perceived efficacy to collective efficacy, demonstrating its effects on how people work in organizations (Bandura, 1997; Fernández-Ballesteros et al., 2002). Aligned with the ecological model of change that theorizes that behaviors are influenced by different levels of factors, it is essential that worksite wellness programs include

social networks and community, colleagues, peers, wellness champions, and lay health advisors Campbell et al., 2002). Employees' peers often have an enhanced sense of the workplace health beliefs and barriers to health, and have a greater empathy for colleagues. Studies have found that interpersonal relationships, peer-driven programming or lay wellness educators can increase nutritious eating, weight management, physical exercise and tobacco cessation (e.g., Wing and Jeffery, 1999; Campbell et al., 2002). Taken together, results across studies suggest that social networks have causal links to greater health, less stress and the relationship between the two (House, 1987).

RECOMMENDATIONS FOR WORKSITE HEALTH BEHAVIOR CHANGE

Having examined the underlying processes and skills associated with health behavior change, we can provide integrated recommendations for how corporate wellness programs might best support employees' health and well-being. Given the diverse needs of employees, worksite health promotion programs should strive to be equally diverse in their offerings. Programs directed towards different stages of motivational readiness and change processes that focus on multiple behaviors rather than just on one wellness domain such as physical activity have the potential for broader reach and higher overall participation (Robroek et al., 2009).

Development of intrinsic motivation is more likely when the wellness activity matches the stage of change a person is in. It also enhances the retention rate. Worksite health promotion programs that offer many different types of interventions directed at these different stages of change create an opportunity for greater numbers of people to engage in their programs, even those who are not ready to take action. As people move through the various stages of change (precontemplation, contemplation, preparation, action and maintenance), it is useful to assess their progress based on the movement from one stage to another rather than based on a distal health goal. This approach decreases resistance and stress, while encouraging achievable action (Prochaska et al., 2001).

For people who are not yet prepared to make a change in their health behaviors, proactive recruitment into health promotion programs that match a 'precontemplation' stage of change will increase participation (Prochaska and Velicer, 1997). These would include educational campaigns that increase awareness about health risks, opportunities for improving health and available resources to support future change efforts. Momentum toward increasing healthy behaviors across an organization or community can be generated through this type of information exchange (O'Donnell, 2005). Communication about health risks should provide information about the causes and consequences of specific health problems rather than numerical probabilities (Rothman and Kiviniemi, 1999). Although the numbers and data may seem compelling, they often distance individuals from their own daily experience.

With increased awareness of their health risks and the related behaviors, each employee will benefit by personalized health screens and assessments. The information about potential health risks and opportunities assist individuals to weigh the pros and cons of often difficult daily changes. This individual feedback will assist with resolving ambivalence to change and increase overall motivation. Faghri et al. (2008) suggests keeping people engaged through such regular health risk appraisals.

Motivation to live a healthy lifestyle is the most important aspect of health behavior change programs. When an individual is motivated to change, they are able to use all of their resources to gain the knowledge and skills to achieve and maintain healthy behaviors (O'Donnell, 2005). It is easy to identify individuals who are motivated because they are typically already engaging in new behavior. For everyone else, increasing the motivation to change should be the primary focus.

Initially, businesses commonly use incentives to externally motivate employees to participate in worksite health promotion programs. Although evidence shows that incentives do work to attract people to participating in programs, they do not increase sustained health behavior change (e.g., Kane et al., 2004). This may be due to the fact that incentive programs attract people from all stages of readiness to change, including a large pool of people who may have minimal investment in achieving or maintaining health behavior change goals. However, incentives also provide an opportunity to expose these employees to salient wellness information and opportunities to practice new behaviors. As they experience the positive benefits of these activities, employees may develop intrinsic (or internal) motivation for action and find the new activities inherently rewarding (Seifert et al., 2012).

Other motivational interventions include the application of MI in health promotion (Miller, 2004). A motivational consultation or coaching session following a health risk assessment or routine screening can begin to shift employees' perspective towards changing their health behaviors. It can also act as a cost-effective catalyst for other interventions. MI is particularly suited for worksite health promotion programs with MI-based health coaching addressing multiple behaviors, health risks and disease management (Butterworth et al., 2006). It has been found to be an effective way to improve both physical and mental health functioning among high-risk employees. Even short, infrequent exposures to MI can be effective with ambivalent individuals across diverse employee demographics. MI interventions can create a sense of organizational belonging that increases personal satisfaction, improved mood and encourages a culture of worksite wellness (Seifert et al., 2012). And MI interventions can easily be used in conjunction with other health promotion programs. For example, corporate health fairs are an excellent opportunity to offer brief MI interviews following biometric tests.

Learning new skills is necessary to support long-term adoption of healthy habits. For many people, the idea of making changes in their health behaviors can be daunting when they have little existing knowledge or self-efficacy. Individuals may be interested in healthy eating but have little nutritional knowledge or cooking skills. The provision of classes that teach basic skills in the worksite or access to these resources in the community will foster intrinsic motivation and self-efficacy.

The content of these courses should address several key components. To start, it is essential that the classes have an experiential format that builds knowledge on the subject while also allowing individuals to learn through practice (O'Donnell, 2005). To develop a sense of empowerment and expertise, active engagement in the process is key. As people practice skills in a supportive environment, they begin to learn they are capable of behaving differently, and self-efficacy grows. For many people, the barriers they face when making a major behavior change can seem insurmountable. Successful skills-building programs need to address barriers that unnecessarily decrease participation such as realistic scheduling, transportation, peer support and general access to resources.

Another integral ingredient of wellness programming is goal setting. The best goals are a series of individually determined, short-term milestones towards ultimate healthy living goals. Short-term steps need to be challenging yet attainable. In this way, the wellness program will set up the employee for success. An employer can support programming that shapes behaviors through successive approximations toward long-term health goals. Instead of making incentives contingent on a target BMI, employees might be rewarded for reaching realistic goals such as losing 5lb. A helpful strategy is to use first-person narratives that describe successful achievement of health goals by people to whom employees can relate, such as fellow employees or people with similar characteristics. This can be shared in video format, small or large group settings or in one-on-one conversations. When a person achieves their long-term goal, a good strategy for maintenance is to set another long-term health goal, which supports the continual interest in maintaining health over the course of their life.

Organizations can boost the effectiveness of their health promotion programs by creating policies and environments that support health behavior change (Aldana et al., 2012). Although organizational policies and environments alone cannot change health behaviors, there is evidence that multi-component interventions are effective (Kahn-Marshall and Gallant, 2012). Some examples of environmental support for health behavior change include a safe environment to work and be physically active, supportive employees and leadership, convenient access to affordable and nutritious food that tastes good, a workplace culture that values and supports employee wellness, flexible schedule to help employees incorporate healthy habits and a tobacco-free environment (O'Donnell, 2005). Social support is also critical. Not only does social support encourage the practice of healthy behaviors, but positive relationships are also in themselves health inducing. Social support reduces work stress overall as well as the negative effect of work stress (Viswesvaran et al., 1999).

Utilizing the Limited Evidence Base to Move Forward

There is a wide range of quality and rigor among worksite wellness programs, and most companies have no organizing or theoretical framework for their wellness programs (Chapman, 2005; O'Donnell, 2005). Studies to date have generally examined successful companies and their programs and made post-hoc assessments of quality components (Terry et al., 2008). Moreover, investigation of theory-driven programming, primary prevention and single component behavioral interventions are lacking (Katz et al., 2005). It is therefore unclear whether environmental workplace policies (e.g., greater access to healthy foods or physical activity programs) are effective independent of each other.

Worksites often have dramatically different characteristics, employee demographics and cultures. In response, to maximize effectiveness, wellness strategies must be flexibly tailored to this variability. Large corporate entities usually have the most well-developed combination of wellness offerings, but wellness must be also individualized to the needs of the approximate 30 million US businesses, almost all of which are small businesses (Small Business Association Office, 2012). If we are to have real impact in the workplace, wellness strategies must be geared toward the resources small businesses typically possess.

Worksites provide excellent opportunities for reducing health risks and shifting long-term health trajectories, but we know that some demographics, particularly younger employees, do not engage in wellness services nearly as often as middle-aged employees. For example, Merrill and colleagues (2011) found that participation was the highest among employee ages 40–49 and lowest in the 18–29-year-old range. Many companies are also geographically dispersed or have virtual networks of employees, and it is unclear what wellness strategies work best within these contexts. We also know very little about the preferred interventions across gender, race and ethnicity. All of which are important considerations given rapidly shifting US demographics.

Further work is warranted in elucidating the environmental supports and behavioral strategies that are effective for this diversity of employees. For example, will extant and emerging technology platforms be of high utility in engaging expanded demographics and maintaining healthy life-styles? For example, one modality that holds great promise is telephonic counseling (Terry et al., 2011). Also, might greater flexibility of serv-ices increase participation among lower-income and less educated shift workers (Adler and Newman, 2002)?

Wellness research and practices are still in their infancy, and program evaluation of wellness initiatives is often lacking. Worksites often fail to track outcomes for their worksite wellness programs (Nyce, 2010), making it very difficult to determine what practices are the most success-ful. Insufficient evidence exists to determine the effectiveness of health promotion strategies like health assessments and educational outreach (Task Force on Community Preventive Services, 2010; Kahn-Marshall and Gallant, 2012). Well-designed, large-scale, multi-site studies are needed to examine practice-based interventions, both in terms of employee outcomes and ROI for companies.

We do know that a coordinated, multi-pronged wellness approach that addresses multiple risk factors and health conditions is the most effective corporate direction. And leadership can support the most advantageous strategies covered throughout this chapter to influence multiple organi-zational levels from individual employee behavior change to transformed organizational cultures and climates. Ubiquitous health risk assessments can be used as a vehicle to assess participants' readiness to change, status of behavioral skills and other psychosocial factors affecting sustained engagement, and then provide a spectrum of wellness offerings that meet individualized stages of change and learning styles (Goetzel and Ozminkowski, 2008). In this way, workplaces move toward distal goals of greater staff satisfaction and productivity, lower risk factors, less medical cost and dramatically decreased chronic conditions and death.

Providing access to multiple avenues toward personal health goals increases the impact of wellness programming. Even if the initial behavior change is not related to the greatest risk factors, a whole health approach will enable participants to build upon initial success to eventually move with greater confidence toward more difficult lifestyle changes (ibid.). Most employees are ready to walk through at least one door toward personal health. Organizations that offer a menu of options fare the best in building skills by matching individuals' motivations, skill sets and learning styles. For instance, among smokers, we have found that if individuals autonomously choose any actionable step toward whole health, smoking will eventually no longer meet their self-image as a healthy person, and they will more effectively tackle this addiction. This type of incentive design may encourage individuals to improve their health status rather than initially attempt goals that seem unattainable (Schmidt, 2012). When it comes to corporate wellness, new practices are consistently touted as effective. While encouraging innovation, we hope that the practical guidance in this chapter will help wellness practitioners utilize proven strategies for assisting employees to lead meaningful, healthy lives.

NOTE

1. Defusion involves distancing or seeing thoughts and feelings for what they are (e.g., streams of words, passing sensations), not what they say they are (e.g., facts).

REFERENCES

Adams T.B., S.M. Keup, D.R. Anderson and A.M. Brockmann (2004), 'Review of the studies cited in the database section of the *American Journal of Health Promotion*', *American Journal of Health Promotion*, **18**(4), 328–32.

Adler, N.E. and K. Newman (2002), 'Socioeconomic disparities in health: pathways and policies', *Health Affairs*, **21**(2), 60–76.

Aizen, L. (1985), 'From intentions to action: a theory of planned action', in J. Kiehl and J. Bechman (eds), *Action–Control: From Cognition to Behavior*, New York: Springer, pp. 11–39.

Aldana, S.G. (2001), 'Financial impact of health promotion programs: a comprehensive review of the literature', *American Journal of Health Promotion*, **15**(5), 296–320.

Aldana, S.G., R.M. Merrill, K. Price, A. Hardy and R. Hager (2005), 'Financial impact of a comprehensive multisite workplace health promotion program', *Preventive Medicine*, **40**(2), 131–7.

Aldana, S.G., D.R. Anderson, T.B. Adams, R.W. Whitmer, R.M. Merrill, V. George and J. Noyce (2012), 'A review of the knowledge base on healthy worksite culture', *Journal of Occupational and Environmental Medicine*, **54**(4), 414–19.

Apodaca, T.R. and R. Longabaugh (2009), 'Mechanisms of change in motivational interviewing: a review and preliminary evaluation of the evidence', *Addiction*, **104**(5), 705–15.

Aveyard, P., K.K. Cheng, J. Almond, E. Sherratt, R. Lancashire, T. Lawrence, C. Griffin and O. Evans (1999), 'Cluster randomized controlled trial of expert system based on the transtheoretical ("stages of change") model for smoking prevention and cessation in schools', *British Medical Journal*, **319**(7215), 948–53.

Baer, R.A. (2009), 'Self-focused attention and mechanisms of change in mindfulness-based treatment', *Cognitive Behaviour Therapy*, **38**(S1), 15–20.

Baicker, K., D. Cutler and Z. Song (2010), 'Workplace wellness programs can generate savings', *Health Affairs*, **29**(2), 304–11.

Bandura, A. (1982), 'Self-efficacy mechanism in human agency', *American Psychologist*, **37**(2), 122–47.

Bandura, A. (1988), 'Organisational applications of social cognitive theory', *Australian Journal of Management*, **13**(2), 275–302.

Bandura, A. (1997), *Self-efficacy: The Exercise of Control*, New York: W.H. Freeman.

Bandura, A. (2001), 'Social cognitive theory: an agentic perspective', *Annual Review of Psychology*, **52**(1), 1–26.

Bandura, A. (2004), 'Health promotion by social cognitive means', *Health Education and Behavior*, **31**(2), 143–64.

Biglan, A., S.C. Hayes and J. Pistorello (2008), 'Acceptance and commitment: implications for prevention science', *Prevention Science*, **9**(3), 139–52.

Butler, K.M. (2010), 'Instead of cash wellness incentives/penalties, try piano stairs', *Employee Benefit News*, 24 May, 3–4.

Butterfoss, F.D., R. Goodman and A. Wandersman (1996), 'Community coalitions for prevention and health promotion: factors predicting satisfaction, participation and planning', *Health Education Quarterly*, **23**(1), 65–79.

Butterworth, S., A. Linden, W. McClay and M.C. Leo (2006), 'Effect of motivational interviewing-based health coaching on employees' physical and mental health status', *Journal of Occupational Health Psychology*, **11**(4), 358–65.

Cahill, K. and R. Perera (2011), 'Competitions and incentives for smoking cessation', *Cochrane Database of Systematic Reviews*, **4**(CD004307).

Campbell, M.K., I. Tessaro, B. DeVellis, S. Benedict, K. Kelsey, L. Belton and A. Sanhueza (2002), 'Effects of a tailored health promotion program for female blue-collar workers: health works for women', *Preventive Medicine*, **34**(3), 313–23.

Centers for Disease Control and Prevention (2010), *Chronic Diseases and Health Promotion*, accessed 11 March 2013 at http://www.cdc.gov/chronicdisease/overview/index.htm, accessed 11 March 2013.

Chapman, L.S. (2005), 'Meta-evaluation of worksite health promotion economic return studies: 2005 update', *American Journal of Health Promotion*, **19**(6), 1–10.

Chapman, L.S. (2012), 'Meta-evaluation of worksite health promotion economic return studies: 2012 update', *American Journal of Health Promotion*, **26**(4), 1–12.

Cooke, R.A. and J.L. Szumal (2000), 'Using the organizational culture inventory to understand the operating cultures of organizations', in N.M. Ashkanasy, C.P.M. Wilderom and M.F. Peterson (eds), *Handbook of Organizational Culture and Climate*, Thousand Oaks, CA: Sage, 147–62.

Curry, S.J., E.H. Wagner and L.C. Grothaus (1991), 'Evaluation of intrinsic and extrinsic motivation interventions with a self-help smoking cessation program', *Journal of Consulting and Clinical Psychology*, **59**(2), 318–24.

Curry, S.J., C. McBride, L.C. Grothaus, D. Louie and E.H. Wagner (1995), 'A randomized trial of self-help materials, personalized feedback, and telephone counseling with nonvolunteer smokers', *Journal of Consulting and Clinical Psychology*, **63**(6), 1005–14.

Deci, E.L. and R.M. Ryan (1985), *Intrinsic Motivation and Self-determination in Human Behavior*, New York: Plenum.

Fabius, R.J. and S.G. Frazee (2009), 'Workplace-based health and wellness services', in N.P. Pronk (ed.), *ACSM's Worksite Health Handbook: A Guide to Building Healthy and Productive Companies*, Champaign, IL: Human Kinetics.

Faghri, P.D., E. Blozie, S. Gustavesen and R. Kotejoshyer (2008), 'The role of tailored consultation following health-risk appraisals in employees' health behavior', *Journal of Occupational and Environmental Medicine*, **50**(12), 1378–5.

Fernández-Ballesteros, R., J. Díez-Nicolás, G.V. Caprara, C. Barbaranelli and A. Bandura (2002), 'Determinants and structural relation of personal efficacy to collective efficacy', *Applied Psychology*, **51**(1), 107–25.

Fishbein, M., D.L. Higgins, C. Rietmeijer and R.J. Wolitski (1999), 'Community-level HIV intervention in 5 cities: final outcome data from the CDC AIDS Community Demonstration Projects', *American Journal of Public Health*, **89**(3), 336–45.

Flaxman, P.E. and F.W. Bond (2010), 'A randomized worksite comparison of acceptance and commitment therapy and stress inoculation training', *Behaviour Research and Therapy*, **48**(8), 816–20.

Flegal, K.M., M.D. Carroll, C.L. Ogden and L.R. Curtin (2010), 'Prevalence and trends in obesity among US adults, 1999–2008', *Journal of the American Medical Association*, **303**(3), 235–41.

Follick, M.J., J.L. Fowler and R.A. Brown (1984), 'Attrition in worksite weight-loss interventions: the effects of an incentive procedure', *Journal of Consulting and Clinical Psychology*, **52**(1), 139–40.

Forehand, G.A. and B. Gilmer (1964), 'Environmental variation in studies of organizational behavior', *Psychological Bulletin*, **62**(6), 361–81.

Galinsky, E. and K. Matos (2012), *2012 National Study of Employers*, Families and Work Institute, accessed November 2013 at http://familiesandwork.org/site/research/reports/NSE_2012.pdf.

Glanz, K. and B.K. Rimer (1995), *Theory at a Glance: A Guide to Health Promotion Practice*, Bethesda, MD: National Cancer Institute.

Glanz, K., B.K. Rimer and K. Viswanath (eds) (2008), *Health Behavior and Health Education: Theory, Research, and Practice*, San Francisco, CA: John Wiley and Sons.

Glisson, C. (2000), 'Organizational culture and climate', in R. Patti (ed.), *The Handbook of Social Welfare Management*, Thousand Oaks, CA: Sage.

Gochman, D.S. (1997), 'Health behavior research: definitions and diversity', in D.S. Gochman (ed.), *Handbook of Health Behavior Research, Vol. I: Personal and Social Determinants*, New York: Plenum Press.

Goetzel, R.Z. and R.J. Ozminkowski (2008), 'The health and cost benefits of work site health-promotion programs', *Annual Review of Public Health*, **29**, 303–23.

Gold, D.B., D.R. Anderson and S.A. Serxner (2000), 'Impact of a telephone-based intervention on the reduction of health risks', *American Journal of Health Promotion*, **15**(2), 97–106.

Goldstein, M.G., B.M. Pinto, B.H. Marcus, H. Lynn, A.M. Jette, W. Rakowski, S. McDermott, J.D. DePue, F.B. Milan, C. Dubé and S. Tennstedt (1999), 'Physician-based physical activity counseling for middle-aged and older adults: a randomized trial', *Annals of Behavioral Medicine*, **21**(1), 40–47.

Gollwitzer, P.M. (1999), 'Implementation intentions: strong effects of simple plans', *American Psychologist*, **54**(7), 493–503.

Hayes, S.C., J.B. Luoma, F.W. Bond, A. Masuda and J. Lillis (2006), 'Acceptance and commitment theory: model, processes and outcomes', *Behaviour Research and Therapy*, **44**(1), 1–25.

Hayes, S.C., K.D. Strosahl, K. Bunting, M. Twohig and K. Wilson (2004), 'What is acceptance and commitment therapy?', in S.C. Hayes and K.D. Strosahl (eds), *A Practical Guide to Acceptance and Commitment Therapy*, New York: Springer.

Heaney, C.A. and R.Z. Goetzel (1997), 'A review of health-related outcomes of multi-component worksite health promotion programs', *American Journal of Health Promotion*, **11**(4), 290–307.

Hollis, J.F., M.R. Polen, E.P. Whitlock, E. Lichtenstein, J.P. Mullooly, W.F. Velicer and C.A. Redding (2005), 'Teen reach: outcomes from a randomized, controlled trial of a tobacco reduction program for teens seen in primary medical care', *Pediatrics*, **115**(4), 981–9.

House, J.S. (1987), 'Social support and social structure', *Sociological Forum*, **2**(1), 135–46.

Hyatt, N.B., R.M. Merrill and K.L. Kumpfer (2010), 'Longitudinal outcomes of a comprehensive, incentivized worksite wellness program', *Evaluation and the Health Professions*, **34**(1), 103–23.

James, L.A. and L.R. James (1989), 'Integrating work environment perceptions: explorations into the measurement of meaning', *Journal of Applied Psychology*, **74**(5), 739–51.

Kabat-Zinn, J. (1994), *Wherever You Go There You Are: Mindfulness Meditation in Everyday Life*, New York: Hyperion.

Kahn-Marshall, J.L. and M.P. Gallant (2012), 'Making healthy behaviors the easy choice for employees: a review of the literature on environmental and policy changes in worksite health promotion', *Health Education and Behavior*, **39**(6), 752–76.

Kaiser Family Foundation and Health Research and Educational Trust (KFF/ HRET) (2012), *Employer Health Benefits: 2012 Annual Survey*, Menlo Park and Chicago: KFF/HRET.

Kane, R.L., P.E. Johnson, R.J. Town and M. Butler (2004), 'A structured review of the effect of economic incentives on consumers' preventive behavior', *American Journal of Preventative Medicine*, **27**(4), 327–52.

Katz, D.L., M. O'Connell, M.C. Yeh, H. Nawaz, V. Njike, L.M. Anderson, S. Cory and W. Dietz (2005), 'Public health strategies for preventing and controlling overweight and obesity in school and worksite settings: a report on recommendations of the Task Force on Community Preventive Services', *MMWR Recommendations and Reports*, **54**(RR10), 1–12.

Kegler, M., A. Steckler, S. Malek and K. McLeroy (1998), 'A multiple case study of implementation in 10 local project assist coalitions in North Carolina', *Health Education Research*, **13**(2), 225–38.

King, B.A., S.R. Dubé and M.A. Tynan (2012), 'Current tobacco use among adults in the United States: findings from the National Adult Tobacco Survey', *American Journal of Public Health*, **102**(11), 93–100.

Kreuter, M.W. and V.J. Strecher (1996), 'Do tailored behavior change messages enhance the effectiveness of health risk appraisal? Results from a randomized trial', *Health Education Research*, **11**(1), 97–105.

Langer, E.J. and M. Moldoveanu (2000), 'The construct of mindfulness', *Journal of Social Issues*, **56**(1), 1–9.

Lewin, K. (1951), *Field Theory in Social Science*, New York: Harper and Row.

Linnan, L., M. Bowling, G. Lindsay, J. Childress, C. Blakey, S. Pronk, S. Weiker and P. Royall (2008), 'Results of the 2004 National Worksite Health Promotion Survey', *American Journal of Public Health*, **98**(8), 1503–9.

Locke, E.A. and G.P. Latham (2002), 'Building a practically useful theory of goal setting and task motivation', *American Psychologist*, **57**(9), 705–17.

Lorig, K.R. and H. Holman (2003), 'Self-management education: history, definition, outcomes, and mechanisms', *Annals of Behavioral Medicine*, **26**(1), 1–7.

Lovato, C.Y. and L.W. Green (1990), 'Maintaining employee participation in workplace health promotion programs', *Health Education and Behavior*, **17**(1), 73–88.

Mattke, S., H. Liu, J.P. Caloyeras, C.Y. Huang, K.R. van Busum, D. Khodyakov and V. Shier (2013), *Workplace Wellness Programs Study: Final Report*, Santa Monica, CA: RAND Corporation.

McLeroy, K.R., D. Bibeau, A. Steckler and K. Glanz (1988), 'An ecological perspective on health promotion programs', *Health Education and Behavior*, **15**(4), 351–77.

Merrill, R.M., S.G. Aldana, T.P. Vyhlidal, G. Howe, D.R. Anderson and R.W. Whitmer (2011), 'The impact of worksite wellness in a small business setting', *Journal of Occupational and Environmental Medicine*, **53**(2), 127–31.

Miller, W.R. (2004), 'Motivational interviewing in service to health promotion', *American Journal of Health Promotion*, **18**(3), A1–A10.

Miller, W.R. (2009), 'Toward a theory of motivational interviewing', *American Psychologist*, **64**(6), 527–37.

Miller, W.R. and S. Rollnick (2002), *Motivational Interviewing: Preparing People for Change*, New York: Guilford Press.

Mokdad, A.H., J.S. Marks, D.F. Stroup and J.L. Gerberding (2004), 'Actual causes of death in the United States, 2000', *Journal of the American Medical Association*, **291**(19), 1238–45.

Mokdad, A.H., J.S. Marks, D.F. Stroup and J.L. Gerberding (2005), 'Correction: actual causes of death in the United States, 2000', *Journal of the American Medical Association*, **293**(3), 293–4.

Nyce, S. (2010), 'Boosting wellness participation without breaking the bank', Towers Watson newsletter, July, accessed November 2013 at http://www.tower-swatson.com/assets/pdf/2395/2395.pdf.

O'Donnell, M.P. (2005), 'A simple framework to describe what works best: improving awareness, enhancing motivation, building skills and providing opportunity', *American Journal of Health Promotion*, **20**(1), 1–7.

Osilla, K.C., K. van Busum, C. Schnyer, J.W. Larkin, C. Eibner and S. Mattke (2012), 'Systematic review of the impact of worksite wellness programs', *American Journal of Managed Care*, **18**(2), 68–81.

Parks, K.M. and L.A. Steelman (2008), 'Organizational wellness programs: a meta-analysis', *Journal of Occupational Health Psychology*, **13**(1), 58–68.

Patalano, A.L. and C.M. Seifert (1997), 'Opportunistic planning: being reminded of pending goals', *Cognitive Psychology*, **34**(1), 1–36.

Person, A.L., S.E. Colby, J.A. Bulova and J.W. Eubanks (2010), 'Barriers to participation in a worksite wellness program', *Nutrition Research and Practice*, **4**(2), 149–54.

Peterson, T.R. and S.G. Aldana (1999), 'Improving exercise behavior: an application of the stages of change model in a worksite setting', *American Journal of Health Promotion*, **13**(4), 229–32.

Prochaska, J.M., J.O. Prochaska and D.A. Levesque (2001), 'A transtheoretical approach to changing organizations', *Administration and Policy in Mental Health and Mental Health Services Research*, **28**(4), 247–61.

Prochaska, J.M., J.O. Prochaska, F.C. Cohen, S.O. Gomes, R.G. Laforge and A.L. Eastwood (2004), 'The transtheoretical model of change for multi-level interventions for alcohol abuse on campus', *Journal of Alcohol and Drug Education*, **47**(3), 34–50.

Prochaska, J.O. and C.C. DiClemente (1983), 'Stages and processes of self-change of smoking: toward an integrative model of change', *Journal of Consulting and Clinical Psychology*, **56**, 520–528.

Prochaska, J.O. and W.F. Velicer (1997), 'The transtheoretical model of health behavior change', *American Journal of Health Promotion*, **12**(1), 38–48.

Prochaska, J.O., S. Butterworth, C.A. Redding, V. Burden, N. Perrin, M. Leo, M. Flaherty-Robb and J.M. Prochaska (2008), 'Initial efficacy of MI, TTM tailoring and HRI's with multiple behaviors for employee health promotion', *Preventive Medicine*, **46**(3), 226–31.

Richardson, K.M. and H.R. Rothstein (2008), 'Effects of occupational stress management intervention programs: a meta-analysis', *Journal of Occupational Health Psychology*, **13**(1), 69–93.

Robroek, S.J.W., F. Lenthe, P. van Empelen and A. Burdorf (2009), 'Determinants of participation in worksite health promotion programmes: a systematic review', *International Journal of Behavioral Nutrition and Physical Activity*, **6**(26), 1–12.

Rothman, A.J. and M.T. Kiviniemi (1999), 'Treating people with information: an analysis and review of approaches to communicating health risk information', *JNCI Monographs*, **25**, 44–51.

Schmidt, H. (2012), 'Wellness incentives, equity, and the 5 groups problem', *American Journal of Public Health*, **102**(1), 49–54.

Schneider, B. (1985), 'Organizational behavior', *Annual Review of Psychology*, **36**, 573–611.

Schroeder, S.A. (2007), 'We can do better – improving the health of the American people', *New England Journal of Medicine*, **357**(12), 1221–8.

Seifert, C.M., L.S. Chapman, J.K. Hart and P. Perez (2012), 'Enhancing intrinsic motivation in health promotion and wellness', *American Journal of Health Promotion*, **26**(3), TAHP-1–TAHP-12.

Serxner, S., D. Gold, D. Anderson and D. Williams (2001), 'The impact of a worksite health promotion program on short-term disability usage', *Journal of Occupational and Environmental Medicine*, **43**(1), 25–9.

Serxner, S.A., D.B. Gold, J.J. Grossmeier and D.R. Anderson (2003), 'The relationship between health promotion program participation and medical costs: a dose response', *Journal of Occupational and Environmental Medicine*, **45**(4), 1196–200.

Small Business Association Office of Advocacy (2012), *Frequently Asked Questions*, accessed 5 July 2014 at http://www.sba.gov/sites/default/files/FAQ_Sept_2012.pdf.

Stokols, D., J.G. Grzywacz, S. McMahan and K. Phillips (2003), 'Increasing the health promotive capacity of human environments', *American Journal of Health Promotion*, **18**(1), 4–13.

Tagiuri, R. (1968), 'The concept of organizational climate', in R. Tagiuri and G.W. Litwin (eds), *Educator's Handbook: A Research Perspective*, New York: Longman.

Task Force on Community Preventive Services (2010), 'Recommendations for worksite-based interventions to improve workers' health', *American Journal of Preventive Medicine*, **38**(2 Suppl.), 232–6.

Terry, P.E., J.B. Fowles, M. Xi and L. Harvey (2011), 'The ACTIVATE study: results from a group randomized controlled trial comparing a traditional work-site health promotion program with an activated consumer program', *American Journal of Health Promotion*, **26**(2), e64–e73.

Terry, P.E., E. Seaverson, J. Grossmeier and D.R. Anderson (2008), 'Association between nine quality components and superior worksite health management program results', *Journal of Occupational and Environmental Medicine*, **50**(6), 633–41.

Trogdon, J., E.A. Finkelstein, M. Reyes and W.H. Dietz (2009), 'A return-on-investment simulation model of workplace obesity interventions', *Journal of Occupational and Environmental Medicine*, **51**(7), 751–8.

Verbeke, W., M. Volgering and M. Hessels (1998), 'Exploring the conceptual expansion within the field of organizational behaviour: organizational climate and organizational culture', *Journal of Management Studies*, **35**(3), 303–29.

Viswesvaran, C., J.I. Sanchez and J. Fisher (1999), 'The role of social support in the process of work stress: a meta-analysis', *Journal of Vocational Behavior*, **54**(2), 314–34.

Volpp, K.G. (2009), 'Paying people to lose weight and stop smoking', *LDI Issue Brief*, **14**(3), 1–4.

Voorhees, C.C., F.A. Stillman, R.T. Swank, P.J. Heagerty, D.M. Levine and D.M. Becker (1996), 'Heart, body, and soul: impact of church-based smoking cessation interventions on readiness to quit', *Preventive Medicine*, **25**(3), 277–85.

Williams, G.C., V.M. Grow, Z.R. Freedman, R.M. Ryan and E.L. Deci (1996), 'Motivational predictors of weight loss and weight-loss maintenance', *Journal of Personality and Social Psychology*, **70**(1), 115–26.

Wing, R.R. and R.W. Jeffery (1999), 'Benefits of recruiting participants with friends and increasing social support for weight loss and maintenance', *Journal of Consulting and Clinical Psychology*, **67**(1), 132–8.

11. Wellness program outreach, recruitment and engagement: case studies in new approaches

Adam Kaufman

CHAPTER OUTLINE

This chapter presents two case studies on the topic of wellness program participation and, in particular, new approaches to wellness program recruitment and engagement. In this chapter, experiences at dLife and DPS Health will be shared as these two companies evolved their outreach approaches, and the positive impact these evolutions had on program participation. Participation and engagement are both critical for wellness program success for two (probably obvious) reasons. First, if any wellness program is to achieve its desired population-level outcomes, a significant level of participation is required. This is just mathematics, as the wellness program's population impact is simply the average impact on the participants times the percentage participating from the population. Second, wellness programs generally attempt to change individual behaviors and, in these cases, participation and engagement are often directly related as a prerequisite to success in behavior change and thus program success at the individual level.

Connecting with users prior to them being actively engaged with the program, through to sustained behavior change, is a key objective and a necessary condition of success for all wellness programs. Generally this process is divided into two major stages, with 'participation' referring to the act of signing up for or enrolling in the program, and 'engagement' used to define a user's ongoing interactions with the program. For purposes of this chapter I'll use the following definitions: (1) *Wellness program participation*: the act of enrolling in or beginning to interact with the wellness program. The term 'participation' can be used to refer to both the individual level (i.e., John Smith is *participating* in the program), and also to the population level (i.e., what percentage of the population is *participating* in the program). (2) *Wellness program engagement*: defined as a participant's ongoing interactions and level of continuous use of the wellness program. We'd use 'engagement' thus defined in a statement such as: 'The program has poor *engagement*, as less than 5 percent of participants return to a subsequent meeting after their first session'.

Note that sometimes participation and engagement are used interchangeably, both referring to what is defined here as participation. However, the distinction is helpful and it is suggested that participation and engagement refer to different points of a user's interaction with the solution. Additionally, in this chapter, the act of driving members to participate in a wellness program is described as 'outreach and/or recruiting' into that program, and the chapter will refer interchangeably to strategies to drive participation and outreach and/or recruitment strategies. This chapter will focus on participation as well as recruiting users into these programs; it will not focus on subsequent program engagement. If needed, 'engagement' will refer to post-sign-up interactions. This is not to imply that participation is more important than engagement; engagement is equally if not more important to wellness program success as participation, but in this chapter we'll focus on participation.

The heart of this chapter is the presentation of two case studies in program recruiting, and the two companies' approaches to driving program participation. The second section of this chapter justifies the importance of the topic and presents general definitions, background and a summary of current best practices. The third section extends these basic concepts to present DPS Health's case study, and the fourth presents dLife's case study. Together these case studies are presented as examples of broader approaches to program recruitment that extend the best practices presented in the second section. The fifth section of the chapter presents three implications in terms of organizational capabilities to implement the models described in the case studies. The final section concludes.

BACKGROUND – MAINSTREAM APPROACHES TO PROGRAM RECRUITMENT

As discussed elsewhere (Kaufman, in press), the best practices in recruiting participants for wellness programs rigorously consider the activity while mapping out and executing a defined strategy. There are different ways to structure and define a recruitment strategy. Below, the best practice that considers the activity is summarized in five distinct steps:

1. *Situation assessment*. The first step in defining a recruitment and outreach strategy is to understand the situation of the program; in

other words, to understand and document the goals of the program, the target population, and any past learnings and lessons from similar programs or outreaches to similar populations. Ideally, profiles of desired enrollees are defined through public information and interviews. The situation assessment step provides the background information that the team will take into the tactical definitions phase.

2. *Point-of-contact exploratory*. The second step in defining the outreach tactics is to explore and define the points of contact the program operators will have with the desired participants. Program operators are often confined by their relationship with the target population, which places natural limits on tactics. For example, if the points of contact are employees through their employer(s), this often places constraints on the form and specificity of future messages. In particular, employers are generally reticent to outreach to employees with messages around specific disease states. As another example, while program outreach through healthcare providers usually doesn't face the same limitations in engaging individuals with condition-specific messages, healthcare providers often don't have email or telephone numbers readily available to engage a population. Thus, program outreach strategy development should start with understanding the available points of contact with the target population, as well as a clear understanding of the benefits and limitations of those points of contact. This activity typically concludes with a list of the practical outlets for reaching potential participants, including available 'direct channels' such as email, print and 'indirect strategies' such as HR departments or healthcare providers. Modern recruitment programs also consider points of contact such as online advertising, town meetings, and social media channels like Twitter and Facebook.

3. *Outreach strategy*. After a complete understanding of the potential points of contact and channels has been developed, the next step is to define an outreach strategy. The outreach strategy broadly defines the approaches and frequency of communications. It is a high-level plan that is designed to generate interest, attention and awareness among the target population and, ultimately, move the target participants to action to become participants in the wellness program. In this stage of the strategy development, the broad message themes, as well as the frequency of outreach and expected costs, are defined. Essentially, the outreach strategy should project enrollment rates by outreach and ensure that, at least in expectation, the strategy will yield the desired participation rates. The outreach strategy step of this process concludes with a plan for the recruitment communication, including general messaging, channels and frequency.

4. *Communications tailoring*. Before launching the recruitment campaign, communication elements are adjusted to reflect prospective enrollees' attitudes, beliefs, values and perceptions. If the target population can be divided into sub-populations, then messaging is tweaked and tailored to each relevant sub-population. Some channels such as email lend to easier tailoring than others, so care should be paid to the appropriate tailoring of each channel. In this phase, the profiles of prospective enrollees developed during the initial situation assessment can be used to model the tailored messaging. In addition, if indirect channels such as HR departments or healthcare providers are going to be used in the outreach, messages should be adjusted to reflect the role and relationship.

5. *Delivery and measurement*. Step 5 represents the fun work of actually deploying the strategy. The effectiveness of Steps 1–4 will not be known until the program is deployed and the messages are delivered. It's critical to ensure a process is defined to measure effectiveness as ongoing metrics are collected. If the program allows, tactics should be reviewed and altered based on success.

In practice, modern wellness program recruiting that is implemented after effective strategy definition through a process like the one above can generally be classified into two distinct paradigmatic ways. Wellness programs are often considered clinical services, and participation is planned similarly to health services referrals. In this first model of promoting wellness program participation, the program could be 'referred' from biometric screening activities, visits to clinics (either on-site or in network) or through other interactions with the healthcare delivery system where participants are recruited through other services. Recruitment therefore occurs as a normal part of delivering other services. When organizations conduct their strategic assessment of recruitment approaches and realize that, for example, the target population can only be identified after a clinician visit or lab test, often this leads to a natural decision to recruit participants through these same clinicians or in a manner integrated with the lab test. Programs deployed through clinicians, or programs targeting more disease-specific conditions, often fall into this approach.

The clinical referral approach to recruiting has the benefits of integrating the wellness program directly with other services and viewing it as part of the continuum of care. Additionally, it has the added benefit of ensuring that identification of the eligible population (i.e., the population that would benefit from the wellness program) is determined in a process that is integrated with the program recruiting. Considering this approach through the five-step process, and assuming each program has a unique situation assessment:

- Points-of-contact are through a clinical process and often one to one with a clinician. This is a powerful point of contact as it generally leverages a relationship of trust and helps position the program as important and impactful. It is a difficult point of contact as it is often infrequent and may not have broad population coverage if members of the target population do not engage with the clinician frequently.
- The outreach strategy is generally through indirect channels and leverages the conversation the clinician has with the potential participant. The opportunity is there to include posters, flyers and other broader messages accessed in the setting as well. There may be limited access to direct outreach approaches between the program and the participants. In this case, ideal strategies accept that the messaging frequency will be low but intense. Ideally there is a mechanism to enroll the participant directly in the interaction and/or provide for follow-up information after the interaction. Essentially, the messaging can be very personal and related directly to the clinical conditions.
- While the person-to-person form of the communication allows for infinite degrees of tailoring and the opportunity to incorporate unique personal messages, in practice it is often difficult to provide tailored content and it often becomes about tone and delivery. This is because it is very hard to train many clinicians on the entire breadth of potential and personalized messaging and, in practice, the clinicians conducting the recruiting generally receive common language about the wellness program itself. They are able to tailor the context of the program and relate it to the individual's other clinical services.

The second model of promoting program participation and recruiting users is to consider that participation-generating activity is similar to a direct marketing campaign against a targeted list of potential 'consumers'. This approach generates marketing-style outreaches through direct channels such as email, direct mail or telephone. In this approach the identification of eligible members for the wellness program is conducted separately and prior to the recruiting. This generates a list of eligible members to which the outreach and recruiting marketing activities are applied. This model considers the wellness program as similar to other services that individuals sign up for as consumers, and leverages similar outreach approaches.

As wellness programs have become more sophisticated in understanding the demographics of the target user population, and as healthcare population analytics have similarly become more sophisticated, modern direct marketing approaches are increasingly applied to wellness program recruiting. Wellness program recruiting has begun to leverage (1) sophisticated population segmentation, (2) digital outreach through email and online, and (3) ongoing analytics and campaign optimization. The 'direct marketing' approach to drive program participation along the key tactical steps is presented below:

- The potential points of contact depend on the information possessed by the program operators. Wellness program operators generally have basic demographic information either from the employee, provider or health plan records. Depending on the source of the information, different data such as telephone, address, mobile number or email may or may not be available. The program will generally be limited to outreach among the available points of contact. However, it is also possible to purchase additional contact information from list vendors. Each program will have to determine if this is a viable option. Programs generally leverage more than one point of contact but often do not leverage all the potential points of contact. For example, programs may leverage digital means such as email and direct mail but not simultaneously consider telephonic or text message outreach. These opportunities will be addressed for broad multi-channel outreach in a subsequent section of this chapter.
- The outreach strategy generally begins with one large and broad outreach to the entire list. Wellness programs usually aim for maximum and early enrollment and thus leverage a mail or email piece to the entire eligible list. This first communication introduces the program and invites participation. Sophisticated programs consider a campaign of multiple touch points and recognize the learnings of marketing so that multiple impressions are often needed to connect with the target audience to drive action. The messaging styles after direct marketing campaigns present the value of the program and leverage the idea of an 'offer' or 'hook' to entice engagement. For example, employer-sponsored wellness programs are either free or heavily discounted for employees; this style of direct outreach may leverage that sort of messaging. Wellness program operators generally leverage this type of messaging for two reasons: they parallel the best practices in consumer direct marketing, and through these mediums wellness program promotions are restricted from using condition-specific information for privacy and/or regulatory concerns.
- Tailoring of messages relates to consumer demographics. For example, through digital outreach it is quite easy to adjust messag-

ing by gender or age or other general information usually available along with the point-of-contact information. Effective ways to tailor may include presenting user testimonials of past participants who are more similar to the particular individual being targeted. It is often possible to test messaging on a subset of the target population through what is known as 'A/B testing', and refine messaging based on actual response and sign-up rates. In this context A/B testing refers to the practice of simultaneously presenting two different messages (an A and a B) to two segments of the population and then measuring the different response rates. Thus, message tailoring can occur both prior to the launch of the outreach campaign but also on an ongoing basis based on learnings throughout the process.

In summary, modern and sophisticated wellness program marketing for recruitment leverages many of the same tools as modern marketing. It recognizes that the outreach campaign must connect with the potential participants and present the value of the program in a manner that drives action. The five-step structure presented in this chapter is but one approach to rigorously considering and defining the outreach and recruitment approach. Whether they use this approach or another, program operators should take the time to strategically plan and ensure that they are measuring and refining their approach. In practice, program recruitment strategies fall broadly into two distinct approaches that carry with them best practices: to leverage clinical or 'indirect relationships' and conduct the recruitment through other clinical providers, and to consider the outreach as a 'direct marketing' campaign and utilize tools of modern marketing. Both approaches carry intrinsic benefits and challenges, and both can be successful if properly planned.

Two companies going beyond the current best practices as outlined in the previous section are rethinking wellness program outreach and recruiting. They will be presented in the next two sections. The next section presents DPS Health's case study and the work to recruit potential participants through an ongoing multi-channel strategy. The subsequent section presents the work done at dLife to implement the outreach campaign as an integral element of the behavior change program.

DPS HEALTH CASE STUDY

In 2013, DPS Health's primary solution was an obesity and lifestyle intervention called Virtual Lifestyle Management (VLM) Service. VLM aims to engage a moderate-risk/moderate-severity population and support improved diet and physical activity behaviors as well as sustained weight loss. Two of DPS Health's clients help exemplify the opportunity to extend the recruiting strategy to multiple channels over the course of the relevant time period.

One DPS Health customer first determined that its ideal outreach was through a clinical interaction. Clinicians, and in this particular case, nurses, would see members of the broader population, and through their interaction determine if an individual was in the VLM target population. It was estimated that about 25 percent of individuals would fall into the eligible category of being obese, with at least one additional weight-related co-morbidity. Thus, the client determined that with regular frequency, the clinicians would encounter individuals from the eligible population, and that it was the best approach to leverage the clinical interaction and clinician relationship to recruit into the VLM program. Nurses were trained to promote the VLM program and support, and to provide materials and outreach. However, while nurses successfully recruited some participants, the pace of enrollment did not meet the client's objectives. DPS Health worked with the client to identify possible opportunities for improvement and realized two important things. First, the nurses' promotion was a single event for most patients and, while impactful, if it did not drive immediate sign-up the individuals did not encounter subsequent VLM recruitment messages. Second, not all target members were necessarily ready to engage around their lifestyle behaviors at the time they met with the nurses. Together DPS Health and the client implemented an additional recruiting approach through targeted email outreach. The email was designed to complement the strong clinical positioning of the previous recruitment activities and was deployed several months after the initial clinician-based recruiting. The approach was very successful at driving program enrollment, illustrating the importance of engaging in recruitment activities over time to the same population and leveraging multiple channels of communication.

A second DPS Health case study further exemplifies the opportunities to drive improved program participation by extending the recruiting campaign across time and utilizing various media channels. DPS Health's customer had actively promoted the VLM program to a defined population of approximately 20 000 targeted individuals through direct email outreach as well as newsletter and social media mentions. The results from these direct email outreaches were quite strong and produced a 1.9–2.4 percent conversion rate per single outreach, conversion defined here as the percentage of individuals targeted with each communication who opted to enroll in the VLM program. However, despite the strong response to each individual outreach, the population-level participation was still not as strong as the customer wanted. In order to increase the overall enrollment in VLM from this targeted group, DPS Health and the customer collaborated to supplement the direct email outreach with two automated interactive voice response (IVR) phone-calling campaigns. The phone calls followed a common script starting with a general health/wellness message and a brief overview of the VLM program. The calls were delivered to all members in the targeted 20 000 population who had not already enrolled in VLM. These individuals had already received at least three targeted emails as well as newsletter and social media impressions of VLM. And importantly, the IVR calls were deployed during months when other outreaches were not scheduled. Thus, DPS Health and the client were able to (1) extend the number of interactions over time and (2) engage targeted individuals. The IVR proved successful even as it was deployed to individuals who had received the previous outreaches, as an additionally almost 2 percent of people enrolled in the program across the two calls, thus demonstrating that despite receiving multiple prior outreaches members responded to the new medium.

The DPS Health case studies illustrate the importance of using multiple channels to reach program participants. Although each individual in the target population had received messages via email and direct mail, a significant percentage had not responded to these messages to enroll in the program. Upon receiving the automated telephony outreach a significant additional portion did opt to enroll. It is unclear whether these individuals simply respond better to telephonic outreach or whether the layering of communications across channels helps reinforce the message and drive the program brand awareness. Most likely both effects are working in that there are individuals with clear preferences for channels of outreach and those who may have never responded to email or direct mail but prefer the phone. Additionally, the layering of the channels serves to edify the program and build brand recognition so that individuals are more likely to opt in. Through this example we see the importance of ongoing outreach over time that builds on previous approaches. If the entire effect was simply channel related we would not have observed the continued and actually increased opt-in in the second telephonic outreach two months after the first.

dLIFE CASE STUDY

dLife, a respected leader in information, education and marketing for people with diabetes, entered the wellness programming space in 2010. The programs successfully engaged individuals with diabetes and showed measurable improvement in diabetes-related quality metrics and outcomes. For example, a number of dLife's programs targeted health plans looking to improve the HEDIS and STAR scores for diabetes. These scores contain measurements such as the percentage of members with diabetes who have had certain examinations within a defined time period. The population-based success of dLife's programs were deeply connected to the population participation levels, as improving quality metrics is about moving the entire population sufficiently to move the quality scores, and not only about impacting those engaged with the program.

dLife's clients were spending significant resources marketing to prospective program enrollees using the best tactics of direct outreach including email, mail and automated IVR telephony. dLife collaborated with its clients to help define outreach strategy in a method similar to the process presented in the previous section, and included dLife providing the best practice messaging from its years of experience engaging diabetic consumers. The rigorous and intensive recruiting approach had yielded impressive participation rates, but dLife clients demanded still higher levels. A wellness program's one-year success became the base expectation for the following year, thus success demanded even more success. Or said another way, the challenge became that past recruitment success generated even higher expectation for each subsequent year, and this required not just incremental improvements but rethinking the outreach campaign.

In 2013, dLife re-imagined the approach to recruiting program participants. Two goals were set for this reconceptualization. First, that the recruiting budgets its clients were already spending were efficiently used and, second, that recruiting activities promoted healthy behavior change and the program's broader objectives, even if individuals did not enroll in the core program. Its model was to re-imagine the recruitment process as an integral element of the program itself. In other words, the company conceptualized all the messages as part of a continuum of health promotion that drove towards behavior change and simultaneously recruited individuals to engage deeper in the program with more intensive elements. Redefining what was meant by participation and recruitment was necessary as every member approached was considered eligible for the program as a participant at different levels. Thinking in terms of 'opting in' for more intense engagement and setting the goal to progressively move individuals to engage even further was also accomplished.

Thus, dLife removed the distinction between the marketing messages and the program elements and instead positioned the various program elements along a continuum of individual commitment and intensity of engagement. This shift required more than just new terms. It required a multi-tiered approach to the program. In dLife's case, it designed a two-tier solution that leveraged multiple channels and media in each tier.

Low-intensity Outreach

The low-intensity tier presented an ongoing communication stream to the targeted individuals. Essentially the communication stream leveraged opt-out only mediums such as automated telephony and other channels where dLife clients had received prior approval to message. All targeted members received communication and all who did not 'opt out' were considered participants in the program – a nice way to increase participation by definition. The low-intensity outreach program presented messages that were health promoting and drove towards the broader program goals even as they were 'marketed' to individuals to engage more intensely. In dLife's case, the original wellness program was deployed as the second-tier 'high-intensity' program and the low-intensity outreach tier replaced the original program recruiting efforts.

These efforts were structured around a calendar of messaging and health promotion so that topics were themed and relevant to individuals' lives. This also kept the messaging fresh and helped ensure ongoing engagement with the outreach activities.

dLife defined monthly topics that were used to structure all the communications and engage the user around a health promotion topic. February, for example, was healthy heart messaging, playing on Valentine's Day and providing a framework for the healthy tip and call for greater action. Each month an individual would receive an outbound call and in February, the script of the automated call referenced tips for healthy heart living. The call also promoted additional elements of the more intense tier and 'marketed' these features to the individuals. In some months, the automated calls would be complemented by email campaigns and/or direct mail pieces. When possible the messaging was carried into client outreach such as newsletters.

High-intensity Behavior Change Program

As briefly described above, dLife's original wellness program formed the core high-intensity behavior change program. This program presented a co-branding between dLife and its client, a website that contained a series of consumer-style media content such as newsletters, articles and videos. The structure of the program presented a tunneled path of education and behavior change experience in the form of a regular topical weekly newsletter and deeper content and engagement through a web portal.

The flow between the weeks was based on clinical input and designed to cover the key topics in diabetes self-care. dLife leveraged the vast library of dLife content to ensure it was engaging and that every individual would find something. The program's desired outcomes were improved self-management leading to better diabetes disease control and improved adherence to therapy guidelines. Prior to launching the service in 2010, dLife had studied the approach in a clinical trial and showed that the over-time curriculum with structured digital experiences could drive sustained and impactful behavior change.

When dLife first launched its wellness service, this curriculum-based program was the entire offering. Individuals enrolled in the program and participation was measured based on those signing up; engagement and outcomes were measured only in the enrolled group. The conceptual evolution of the program was to embed this more intensive behavior change intervention in the two-tiered solution and wrap the messaging campaign of the low-intensity outreach around the broader experience with the original program. The intensive behavior change element portal experience was integrated with the low-intensity messaging for a seamless user experience. The low-intensity messaging tier replaced the standard recruitment strategies of dLife clients, providing for a richer ongoing interaction, one that continuously promoted both engagement with the intensive program and behavior change – even of those who did not opt in to the deeper program. If an individual had already opted into the portal experience, for example, the automated phone call would reference elements of the portal that complemented the monthly topic. For example, in February, the call referred users to videos and recipes in the program about heart-healthy eating. In this manner the entire concept of program recruiting was replaced by choice of how deep to engage at the individual level.

dLife first launched the new program in late 2013. The approach has shown tremendous promise. First, virtually all individuals in the target population have received health-promoting messages as the 'opt-out' rate has been very low. Second, the overall outreach budgets have been roughly the same as the previous model, where all program outreach was spent as recruitment. And most importantly, dLife is seeing 'opt-in' rates to the intensive program approximately twice as high as the enrollment rates to the curriculum-driven portal when it was the only element of the program. At this time, the new approach has only been deployed for several months, therefore dLife has no data about long-term engagement and outcomes. However, the initial results seem positive along all three of the key dimensions.

In constructing this new approach to wellness program design, dLife hypothesized several factors that would make incorporating the recruitment strategy into the program more effective. The very early evidence, at least, does not contradict any of these initial hypotheses. Defining an over-time, regular outreach campaign that promotes both general health behavior change and deeper program engagement may do the following:

- More efficiently using the program 'marketing' budget. First, it may allow the organization to leverage existing internal communications (i.e., already budgeted) channels. For example, a particular month's messaging could be sent in regular newsletters, or combined into other outreaches. Second, it may allow the organization to leverage less expensive outreach methods as costs of marketing usually increase with urgency and as more needs to be accomplished in terms of enrollment in shorter periods. The majority of this budgetary savings comes from the longer and more efficient planning horizon, and also from the fact that the messaging contains positive outreach in addition to the 'recruitment' message.
- Build a relationship with potential users and program brand affinity over time. The regular, less aggressive communications help position the program more positively for potential users. Simply put, more impressions relate to more positive perception and more positive action.
- Recognize that individuals' readiness to engage with the wellness program varies over time. Motivation to address the target behaviors of the wellness program grows and wanes in each individual at different points over time. The ongoing low-intensity outreach campaign maximizes the likelihood that the individual receives a program message when he or she is ready to engage. This is in contrast to recruiting programs that often aim to maximize exposure in a relatively short window of time.
- Provide choice for individuals on the intensity of their engagement. The fact that all members are engaged, and some are engaging more deeply into specific elements of the program, is an active choice and can promote more overall engagement. Providing choice leads to supporting an individual's own decision-making and is correlated with behavior change.
- Promote change among individuals who previously would have only received marketing messages. This represents a huge potential benefit of this approach. In the previous model, only a small fraction of the target population – say 20 percent – who enrolled received any programmatic messaging, and now 100 percent of the target population receives wellness messages. Thus, population level impact is increased by the small impact on the additional 80 percent.

IMPLICATIONS

Extending standard wellness outreach and recruiting activities along the approaches described in the DPS Health and dLife case studies implies three organizational capabilities not always found in wellness providers:

Expertise and/or Partnerships

Expertise and/or partnerships in a broad array of communications channels and approaches to obtaining consumer contact information: while these capacities are those generally found in direct marketing organizations there is one key distinction for wellness programs. Typical direct marketing aims to find and market to a set of target prospects that match a target demographic. This means defining an ideal customer and then identifying these targets from among a general population and then finding channels to reach individuals of these types. A key distinction for wellness programs is that recruiting is generally against a list of targeted individuals defined by clinical conditions or healthcare utilization not by consumer demographics. So the goal is to connect with as many of these individuals as possible. Thus, the wellness provider's capacities cannot be only in those channels or data information acquisition methods associated with a particular demographic and must be broader. dLife and DPS Health partnered with companies and individual consultants who were experts in various channels and methods for securely acquiring email addresses or telephone numbers. For example, both companies leveraged partners to help deploy the automated telephony components of their campaigns. Not only do vendors have significant technology infrastructures, they also have deep experience in practical issues such as the best time of day to call for certain target audiences.

Content Experience and Staff

As described in the case studies a key element of these re-conceptualized recruiting activities is structuring the outreach as a positive, health-promoting message that engages the individual and invites further interactions. The approach found most effective at DPS Health and dLife to constructing this messaging stream is to leverage best practices from publishing, and to define an editorial calendar that integrates the various important themes of the program with date-specific references such as dLife using February to highlight heart health in the context of diabetes self-care. This approach requires a wellness program provider to involve editors and writers and ensure the requisite skills in building editorial calendars and weaving topics together. Additionally, a company will either need to employ writers directly or develop licensing partnerships with content producers across various media. Lastly, the program provider will need to understand how different content works when delivered via different channels and ensure the ability to tailor messages to delivery in print, online, through email, telephonically and potentially in person. Generally, wellness companies have a stronger core capacity around interventional content and curriculums that drive change but not necessarily in the tools, approaches and practices of consumer-media-style content generation and delivery.

Sophisticated Technology Infrastructure

Sophisticated technology infrastructure is necessary to manage the coordinated multi-channel campaigns. It can provide a unified view of each individual's interactions while aggregating for population reporting. In particular, the system needs to integrate with various different channels of outreach and often with multiple vendors who provide the management of these services. The system will ideally have a central single view of each member's interactions across these different channels (although in practice this is actually pretty hard to accomplish completely). Depending on the clients and populations the solutions may also need to integrate with claims or medical records systems and pass information between them. Thus, the system requirements for these types of integrated multi-tier programs are more complex than general wellness solutions. And the organizational capacities to manage interfaces and compliance issues with vendors and clients often require additional skill sets and expenses.

CONCLUSION

Successfully recruiting individuals to participate in wellness programs requires significant planning, outreach strategy and unique capabilities. Customers of wellness programs are not wrong to demand greater and greater participation levels, knowing that the true program success at the population level requires broad participation and engagement. Wellness program outreach and recruiting should follow the best practices of other marketing campaigns and rigorously consider the population, the outreach channels, and the messages. The programs should be measured and refined as they progress. And in my experience, innovative companies are going beyond leveraging the best practices of modern marketing to conceptualize year-long, multi-channel outreach that re-imagines the recruiting as an actual part of the wellness program. While these approaches are just evolving, early evidence shows that they more cost-effectively drive participation and program engagement. After all, driving program participation is the same form of behavior change as the core target objectives of all wellness programs.

REFERENCE

Kaufman, A. (in press), 'Participation key for wellness programs: lessons learned from improved outreach efforts', *Managed Healthcare Executive*, forthcoming.

12. Developing and implementing corporate wellness programs: lessons from the firing line

Quan Campbell

> The scenario – most people know that a diet high in fruits and vegetables is healthier than one high in hamburgers and French fries. The problem – most people don't think that eating broccoli is sexy.

Today, corporate wellness is certainly the hot topic. There's an overwhelming amount of data that supports a solid wellness program, it's impact to the bottom line of the company and healthy changes made by employees. Smart companies are quickly adding these programs not only to boost their bottom line, but also to identify themselves as the employer of choice and to enhance culture. Yet despite lush budgets, well-meaning committees and the most solid research on behavior change, there is a chasm between theory and practice. . .and sometimes it can be a very big chasm.

There are many reasons for this huge gap. First, wellness is poorly defined. Second, due to the poor definition of wellness in the workplace, expectations of a successful program can be unclear. Additionally, the success or failure of a program can rest in the individual employee's most private behavior change. Finally, what may work wonderfully for one company may not work for another.

This chapter will explore the implementation of corporate wellness programs and give specific guidance on focusing programs for their greatest success. It is intended that the reader will understand the need for creativity while applying a behavior change model and appreciate the emotional IQ that is needed when implementing complex programs.

For clarification, this chapter refers to both wellness programs and wellness events. Wellness programs are defined as multi-disciplined and layered services that promote health and wellness to a group of individuals or employees. Wellness events are defined as a singular happening that is part of the overall wellness program. Wellness programs can go on for years, and while they morph and change with the companies' needs, the wellness events are elements of the wellness program activities that are designed to make the overall wellness program appeal to a broad range of people.

LESSONS FROM THE FIRING LINE

As a corporate wellness consultant for over 12 years and leader of a multi-disciplinary team, I have seen tremendous growth in the industry. My team consists of physicians, behavior change experts, registered dietitians, exercise physiologists, nurses, ergonomic specialists and health and wellness coaches. We've acted as consultants to start and advise programs as well as been implementers of multi-year wellness programs to companies in the United States, Canada and the United Kingdom, with shorter specialty programs conducted in Latin America and Asia. My resource team is much deeper than most consultants' out there, and this is why there are many lessons to be learned from our collective experience in starting and managing corporate wellness programs.

I find that there are essentially two types of companies that want to implement wellness programs. The most common is the one that wants to implement a program with facets that are expected and common: health risk assessments, lunch-and-learn lectures, walking programs and the like. The second less common client is one that wants to have some of the tried and true elements but also wants to create programs that no one has ever heard of in order to keep their employees engaged and excited about wellness.

Regardless of the client type, there are elements to any program that when addressed properly will help ensure success. Looking beyond the day-to-day aspects of limited resources and privacy laws, it's important to know the reasons why a wellness program may fail and how to manage expectations. There's a certain amount of emphasis placed on knowing your target audience, in size and structure. It is of great importance to know how to manage and refresh an existing wellness program. Being creative with both your resources and communications is of utmost significance in reaching your target audience as well as the level of emotional awareness of this audience. Finally, knowing your wellness medicine is crucial to mitigating risk and upholding the reputation of both the program and your company.

THE CHALLENGES

There comes a place and time where you sometimes have to fire your clients. I was two years into providing services for a medium-sized software engineering firm. Our focus, from the beginning, was general nutrition education with a very healthy dose of education that focused on how to avoid getting sick. The CEO wanted her employees to be able to recognize when they were feeling under the weather and to know when to seek medical attention. Prevention and early detection, as any good clinician knows, often helps reduce the duration of illness and its associated expenditures. We did flyers and lectures on personal hygiene, hand-washing, how colds are spread and the importance of keeping your immune system in tip-top shape.

Then came the day when she told me that I needed to tell her employees that they couldn't come into work if they were sick. I explained to her that I would be happy to work with her HR department to draft protocols, but that the ultimate responsibility to send home employees would fall on her managers. As an outside vendor and a non-medical provider in this instance, I could not decide when someone was sick enough to be sent home, nor did I have the authority.

She insisted that I find a way. And it was at that moment that I realized that she really had unrealistic expectations of what a wellness program could accomplish. After much thought, I realized that she was the client and should be 'right' – but that I couldn't provide what she was ultimately looking for. I decided to conclude and terminate the contract, giving her resources that I thought would be appropriate in our place. The lesson: Recognize the challenges and expectations of the wellness program early on. Additionally, set reasonableness of success and the method of achieving each.

Any wellness program has the odds stacked against its success, even though wellness is supported with research as having a positive impact both on individual lives and the corporate bottom line. In the last ten years alone, the cases, studies and publications on the effectiveness of wellness programs has exploded. As compared to this sudden increase of positive research, there are fewer, yet significant, publications on why a company should *not* implement a wellness program. From not actually impacting the bottom line in a positive manner, to companies over-testing employees, to only addressing those employees that are open for change – a good wellness implementer needs to know how to tackle these hurdles and still build a successful program.

Looking at the impact of wellness programs on a large scale, at the heart of most wellness programs is an element of informing the employees of their potential or real health risks. In addition to healthy behavior change, wellness programs often promote seeing a physician early to not only establish care but to identify risk factors before they become disease. The problem with this model is that suddenly an otherwise blissfully unaware population has become aware of their risks and rush off to the doctor. Not only does this mean higher use of medical dollars for visits that were previously not occurring, but it also means more time off work to attend these appointments. For companies that are looking at their bottom line, especially on a quarterly basis, having employees at the doctor's office is not making the company money.

Let's now add that the typical employee stays with their company between three and four years. If most wellness programs take two to three years to show impact, one can see why there is a lot of push back from CFOs to invest in a wellness program. Taking into account decreased attendance, increased medical costs and questionable loyalty of employees, one can easily see reasons why not to invest in a wellness program.

Looking at wellness programs on an individual scale, health and wellness are very personalized concepts; the locus of control is in the employee. Clinicians and behavior modification experts can often disillusion themselves with the idea that their programs make people change behaviors. Accepting that a wellness program will never *make* someone change their behaviors is key to setting realistic goals and expectations for a program. Great programs educate and entice people to make changes. Put simply, a program cannot make someone change a health behavior; instead it gives them choices. In the end, if the person is not willing to make a change, it's not going to happen.

Adding to the complexity, wellness programs often need to affect the person's behavior during all 24 hours of the day. Even great business managers will report that it's hard enough to influence their teams to produce the desired results during eight work hours of the day. Wellness programs need to follow the employee home and impact choices that they make with their families. The core message of a successful wellness program needs to inspire the person on such a level that they are aware of the message during work, during their commute, at home, and even while they sleep.

Here's more bad news. The whole concept of wellness is defined differently from one person to the next, making your success target ever changing. The CEO of a company may think that wellness is fitness and nutrition excellence, while the Managing Director thinks that it means work–life balance, and the office custodian defines wellness as spiritual harmony. Who's right? They all are – then you have to remember who's funding the program.

The list of hurdles and arguments again wellness programs could go on and on. Ready for some good news? Knowing which arguments need to be answered can help anyone build a stronger, more sustainable program. It can help create metrics of success, clarify the values of the corporation and can guide the style in which the program is implemented.

MANAGING EXPECTATIONS

Six months into a program, I almost had a contract taken away because the CEO of the company said that the fat people were still fat. I'm 100 percent confident that I'm not the only wellness provider to have this battle. It didn't matter to him that all the 'fat' people lowered their health risks by walking more, eating more fruits and veggies or lower their blood pressure. He was more concerned with what he saw, day in and day out, and what he saw was still waddling down the hallway in their baggy clothes.

I've never faulted him for his stance. I faulted myself for not recognizing that to him, health and wellness equaled skinny. Instead, I should have set expectations that healthy behavior change takes time and that the change is not always outwardly apparent. Setting this expectation from the onset would have saved me a lot of time defending the success of the program after the fact. Simply put: don't set yourself up to fail.

Wellness in the marketplace is poorly defined and it often leaves a lot of room for interpretation when it comes to what defines a success program. Knowing this is crucial when the person that controls the wellness budget has a different interpretation than the program designer. As discussed elsewhere in this book – establishing program metrics and goals is elemental to demonstrating success and can help bridge the gap between differences in wellness definition.

Like any new service, starting a wellness program with simple goals can be the key to success. As the first set of expectations are met, then the program can add more components and complexities to meet the needs of the second set of expectations, and so on. Conversely, when expectations are not set and defined, the wellness program can appear to have no structure, fall short of assumed goals and does not display a program backed by science and research.

One can liken a wellness program to the introduction of cellular phones. Novel in its own right, the initial expectation was that the cell phone was used for voice calls. At the beginning there was no expectation of email management, web surfing or listening to music. We all had to get used to the idea that we could make calls on the go. After we were all successful in making those calls then users started to think 'Wouldn't it be nice if. . .?' As the needs and expectations of the user changed over the years, so did the service. Successful wellness programs need to meet the basic defined expectations from the beginning, then add layers and complexities.

If you've ever seen a technologically inept grandparent gifted with a smartphone, then you've seen the confusion and frustration of just getting the device to make a phone call. As educators and wellness professionals, our excitement often urges us to deliver a smartphone when a basic cell phone with call features only would be more appropriate.

Starting with a small, manageable program is key not only to meeting expectations and defining success but also to building the foundation for growth in years to come. At the same time, the program gains credibility because it has met the most basic needs. As wellness is better defined and basic expectations are met, then the program can expand the services and grow the reach.

Just as meeting expectations and key metrics is critical, it is also highly beneficial to stay keenly aware of management's true expectations and to educate them on their reasonableness (or lack thereof). As the wellness programs educate the masses, there needs to be a certain amount of education to management about what a wellness program can and cannot do. Sometimes, tactful conversations need to be had about how not all skinny people are healthy or fat ones unhealthy.

BE CREATIVE AND ASSESS EXISTING RESOURCES

One of the first things I do with any new client is assess the resources available to me. This is beyond the budget numbers and who's going to hang up posters. These are things that already exist in the company's environment and culture that can help make the wellness program successful.

Launching a new program or event not only takes a lot of work on the implementer's side, but it also takes a lot of concentration and focus on the employee's side. It takes effort to understand what the program is offering,

I'm currently working with a non-profit that has zero money for a wellness program. Literally, there are no funds that can be allotted for the program. The Human Resource director believes strongly in the power of a wellness program, has seen wellness programs work at previous companies and knows that a strong program can decrease the benefits costs – and yet, he is still given no budget for it. The beauty of wellness programs is that resources don't have to be expensive to be impactful. After assembling thought leaders in the company and delivering our message through established channels, we're making progress on reducing worker compensation injuries and decreasing health risk. No expensive health assessments and no specialty programs – just sound education, leaders exciting employees about the virtues of health and giving practical tools for employees to make small and meaningful changes.

And to answer the question that I know you're thinking of, I'm getting paid a percentage of the amount that I save the company in their benefits costs.

how and if it will benefit them personally and, ultimately, how to use it. If the employees get confused or overwhelmed and don't understand the program, then eventually they don't participate.

Looking for existing platforms to increase your wellness reach is key. Consider it subliminal messaging, and embed wellness events in existing communication mediums. Can you get 15 minutes at the next executive meeting? Is there a summer picnic that you can make healthy and place the wellness stamp on? Is there a walking group already established or a group of friends that go to evening Weight Watchers meetings?

The idea is not to have to come up with new concepts and ideas that you'll need to 'sell' to the employees. Instead, start with a concept that they already understand – like a company picnic made a little healthier – and increase your traction and reach through this 'understood' platform. Whether or not your budget is lush, piggybacking wellness programs and events onto existing communication mediums makes resources and impact go further.

In my experience, the worst thing that a wellness program can do is act in its own little silo – it must be integrated into other aspects of the current environment. To my clients, I recommend that the wellness program does not have executive sponsorship from the HR department, but instead from another department. This sends the message that health and wellness is important on a global level, not just through the eyes of HR. This is why multi-department wellness committees are so valuable; they're the eyes and ears of resources. I like to pull from a variety of departments, yet have certain skills for each member.

The most successful wellness committees have the following people and talents:

- *The planner*. This project manager keeps the team on task and makes sure that they meet deadlines. They also are a major component of making sure that on the day of events, little things like tables, chairs or whatever else is ready to go. I often look for someone from the Facilities department.
- *The end-user*. This person represents the employees and by appearance should not 'look' like they should be on the wellness committee. This person is expressive and comfortable in their own skin. They want to have more wellness in their life – they're just not sure how to achieve it.
- *The gate keeper*. This person knows when the big sales meeting is and when those important clients are coming to visit. They understand the general ebbs and flows of scheduling for the entire company. This person is integral to making sure that you don't spend three months planning an event that will happen on the same day as the company's all-hands meeting.
- *The salesperson*. This person has a lot of social clout and can spread the program's wellness ideas. They don't need to 'sell' anything as much as get people to listen and pay attention to the message. They are sometimes also the 'gate keeper' and I recommend that they are not the 'clinician' to keep the science impartial.
- *The designer*. At one point or another, the program will need graphics. Like any marketing campaign, the wellness program needs to evoke emotions to entice employees to use the service. Saying 'eat an apple a day' evokes much more emotion when the words are associated with a great photo of a happy woman biting into a fresh, ripe apple.
- *The clinician*. In the end, you want to make sure that your wellness program is promoting sound health and wellness advice. Health fads need to be avoided and all the wellness program's recommendations should be backed up with evidence-based medicine. The program will lose credibility and the participation levels will diminish the instant that someone finds out that a health statement is not true.

ESTABLISH THE CURRENT CLIMATE

A company that I work with regularly just acquired a new location and was very excited to integrate the employees with the rest of the company. I was told that as soon as possible the wellness program should be delivered to them to assist with the culture of caring, health and wellness. Seeing this great opportunity to positively affect more lives, I conducted a little research on the current climate of that particular location. What I found is that 90 percent of the office population smoked, that there was a much-loved and frequented restaurant next door that served local American southern deep-fried foods and (to top it off) the current employees were a bit wary of the acquisition. The wellness expert in me cried out that this new acquired team was in dire need of education and support to become healthier individuals. Their baseline was so low that any positive habit change was good change. Despite that, I begged to NOT start a wellness program at this location until more time had passed. Between the acquisition and the parent company's global non-smoking employment requirement, the last thing I wanted to do was to come in as the 'health police' or 'that skinny Asian girl from California that doesn't understand how we do things around here'. There is only so much that individuals can change at one time before the change itself becomes detrimental.

Six months later, with a lot less animosity in the way, we were able to integrate the group into the wellness program and even got them to visit the restaurant next door a little less often. It took a lot of timing and trust development, but they eventually welcomed 'that little skinny girl from California' into helping them be healthier.

Culture and climate are ever-changing non-tangible aspects of any company. Both ebb and flow can be dependent on day-to-day business matters like CEO attitude, budget changes, growth rate and employee demographics. As highlighted elsewhere in this book, the culture of wellness can have a significant impact on the style and success of a program.

Culture and climate are two different things. Think of culture as an ocean. The Atlantic and Pacific are both oceans, and, just like different companies, each has their own drifts, currents and species of fish. Just like you can sail a ship in different waters, generally you can run the same programs and events in different companies. What can really throw a ship off course is a major climate change. Like a good captain, implementers of wellness programs and events need to be able to read the horizon for thunderstorms and decide if they want to sail around it or head right in through the middle.

Wellness programs and events need to be timed on the business climate. If the business just cut back 20 percent of its workforce, asking everyone to go out and take an hour walk makes perfect sense from a stress-relief perspective but a horrible idea from a logistical sense of getting work done. It would be like sailing a ship right into a storm. One could argue that if supervisors are on board and see the big picture, that it's a risk worth taking. On the other hand, if the walking initiative is only going to foster bitterness from supervisors and employees collectively, it would be better to wait.

Programming events should be timed when the employees will be most receptive to new ideas; when the climate is calm and the program doesn't have to compete with tsunamis of layoffs, budgets that drop sails or gale-force winds that finish that company-wide project. This is where a solid wellness committee and an open communicative relationship with top management is key. They can help navigate the wellness program to safety.

Implementing wellness programs usually involves long lead times and it's extremely helpful to be 'in the know' when it comes to climate change. Like a good radar system, open communication about the climate allows the implementation team to change course, put into queue appropriate events and stall or speed up others – all for the sake of avoiding crashing on the rocks.

MARKETING AND COMMUNICATIONS PLANS

I'll never forget the time that our dietitian forwarded me an email from her husband. Paraphrasing, the email said something to the effect of 'At my new job, I think they have a wellness program. I'm not sure. Check out their version of the wellness program – some webinar that I can listen to. How boring. I think you guys should bid for the business, you could do better'.

To my shock and horror – I recognized the topic for the webinar. It was one of ours. We often act as content resource for other vendors, and the webinar in question was going to be given by one of my physicians on Skin Health.

The lesson: The employees need to fully understand what the wellness program is before they can appreciate the content.

Part of my job includes going into companies and evaluating why past wellness programs didn't have the high participation rates that were expected. What I typically see is a good amount of effort to promote the program or event – but not the care that is needed. Wellness programs are most successful when an innovation adoption marketing strategy is applied.

Promoting a wellness program is like promoting the latest high-tech gadget. There's a lot of misconception on what this gadget can do, why you might need it and whether it's worth the resources. A good model to consider is Geoffrey Moore's (2002) variation of the diffusion of innovation theory. His model depicts a normal distribution towards adoption with few people at the extremes (few innovators and early adopters, few very late adopters) and most in the middle (early majorities and late majorities). Hopefully, you'll have the 'innovators' – the people who have little understanding about the service but are willing to try anything and see how it goes. When the innovators walk away from a program with a smile on their face, talking about how much fun it was or how much they learned, then you can catch the 'early adopters'.

As program designers, it's easy to forget that the masses don't always know how to process, understand and use the wellness services – much like a new gadget. In every culture the innovators and early adopters will help you define your message for the 'early majority' and, with the right communication early in the program, the chasm that existed between commencement and putting the wellness program into daily practice can be overcome.

After designing the wellness program, a plan needs to be created to effectively market the message to the employees. Wellness programs and events don't gain participants just because they exist. Remember, eating broccoli isn't perceived as sexy – but that's what being sold.

I encourage all program implementers to conduct a SWOT analysis when it comes to their wellness programs. Yes, it's time to break out the basic marketing textbooks. Ascertaining the programs 'Strengths, Weaknesses, Opportunities and Threats' will not only help define the customer's (or employee's) needs, but it will also help define what the competition looks like.

Usually, your toughest competition in a wellness program is a contest of time and attention. Does the employee participate in an educational lecture or get that report done? What are the costs and benefits to both? On one hand, she could learn how to control stress, eat healthier or better recognize signs of disease by attending the lecture. She will have potentially done her life some good. On the other hand, getting that report done may please her boss and could lead to a big raise.

As with any product or service, branding the wellness program is a key element to employees understanding the wellness program and its events.

Employees need to instantly understand what the wellness program stands for and needs to be graphically identifiable. As mentioned before, the word 'wellness' means a lot of different things for a lot of different people. It's important to help define what the wellness program will be providing by proper naming.

Graphically, branding a wellness program can be a lot of fun. The consistent use of logos can help employees quickly identify the associated message. Additional use of graphically designed mascots or spokespersons can't hurt as well. Consider the very successful use of a mascot and tagline in the US Forest Service campaign to prevent forest fires. Smokey the Bear is a mascot is easily identifiable with his ranger hat and he speaks directly to the public about what their part in the campaign is. Since behavior change is an individualized and private matter, having a mascot that can serve as the voice of the wellness team can help individualize the message and make it resonate on a private level. The brilliance in the Smokey the Bear campaign is that the message spurs behavior change.

Smokey is currently supported with his own website (www.smokeybear. com), which hosts videos, educational information and entices users to get involved. He even has a Facebook page, YouTube and Twitter page. In essence, the campaign is being treated like a sellable product or service. It's also exactly how marketing and communications should be treated for a wellness program; it needs to be 'sold'.

ONE MESSAGE, MANY VOICES

In one of our most creative companies, our wellness program has the tagline: 'Fitness. Health. Wellness'. This really helps define what the program is trying to accomplish and communicate. Despite the clear messaging – it was a real hurdle to reach the variety of employees. The company had multiple national and international locations, some employees that worked solely from their computers, a variety of shifts, not to mention a wide range of super fit employees and employees that were occasionally getting 'stuck' in the security portals due to their size.

The solution was to make the program multi-faceted and to use as many mediums of communication as possible to promote the program. The lesson learned was that with a clear message of what the program represented, the ability to market and communicate to the variety of employees was key in the success of the program.

In today's business environment, we're all about economies of scale. Particularly in the corporate wellness arena the aim is to design a program or program structure that you can take into multiple companies and have the same positive impact on lives. At the end of the day, you want your end-users, the employees, to learn the material and make habit changes.

We'll get into the medical core of program design later in this chapter – but for a few moments, let's explore the importance of having a great marketing campaign. In my opinion, this is where a lot of great programs go wrong in implementation. Countless hours of time and energy go in to developing the perfect wellness program, making sure that the incentives meet budget and that logistically you can deliver the services. Once the program is decided on, you can't just sit back and assume that employees are going to rush in and sign up for this program. . .you have to sell it.

And guess what – there's a ton of competition. For example, the email to get up and go for a 20-minute walk is likely right next to the email from the boss asking why a report is late. Guess which one is going to win?

Let's take a cheap, self-monitored walking program as an example. Simple and effective in getting people moving, it's an easy concept to grasp (10 000 steps per day) and fairly cheap to implement (pedometers and self-recording). This type of program is great in fostering internal competitiveness ('I'd like to get 500 more steps tomorrow'), external competitiveness ('I bet I can beat Joe by 500 steps') and it is easy to monitor incremental improvement – to name a few.

So why do I hear over and over again that the HR department tried to implement a walking program and it fell dead on its feet? It goes back to the original example: spending time eating broccoli is rarely more inciting than getting that report done. Convincing the market, or the employees, that eating broccoli is worth their time – that's the true challenge.

Part of implementing any successful wellness program is the marketing and communications of the service. Incentives, communication methods and mediums are just a few of the aspects of marketing the program that needs to happen. The smart programmer also needs to consider localization of words and graphics when devising a strategy.

As a corporate wellness consultant, it's time efficient to implement programs that are already designed and instead take time to customize it for the client. Taking the approach of 'One Message, Many Voices' helps immensely. A great, recognizable example is Coke's international marketing campaign. The core message is 'Happiness' – while the graphics, incentives and style are changed from country to country.

Take a real life example of an software engineering firm: employees consist of corporate administration, a sales force, engineers, and 24/7 call operators in domestic and international locations. To add to the mix, a high level of perfection is insisted upon in this company. What's drilled into the employees: 'mistakes costs lives'.

The first year the program was launched, all messaging was centered on being active and eating better. This is the 'one message' that everyone could grasp. Every employee, despite department or region, understood that the wellness program equaled information and programming around fitness and nutrition.

Just like any other global marketing campaign, you need to convey your core message and then adapt it to appeal to each audience. This is the 'multiple voices' part. For a wellness program, this is easily achieved by customizing the events, educational pieces, and other elements that have been approved for that year's program.

Events were announced through posters, intranet sites and through social media. If you worked in the building, you saw posters. If you worked from email, you received notices. Just like any other great marketing campaign, you would receive the same message, multiple times in a variety of formats.

What is nice about companies that are willing to be more creative is that the message can be communicated when the potential user is least expecting it. Social media and bathroom flyers are a great example. One designer that I've worked with stated, 'If they're offended at the poster, then at least they're reading and looking at it'. Granted, not all companies will allow you to be that liberal, and there are certain parameters that you need to adhere to within the corporate setting, but the point is well taken.

Not only is the variety of the outbound communication scheme important, but the event programming itself needs to be in 'One Message, Multiple Voices'. Events need to appeal to a variety of users, not just the healthy people that will show up to every wellness event because it's already a priority in their lives.

We designed events to appeal to all segments. A photo contest where people submitted photos of themselves doing something 'active' allowed the sales force and 24/7 employees to participate in the program. A 5K training program allowed both domestic and international employees to train for the same 'event'. And 'Office Olympics', complete with parade of teams and their flags and events such as Frisbee golf captured athletically shy graphic designers, engineers and number crunchers.

Put simply, 'One Message, Many Voices' in this example was that wellness for that year's programming met fitness and nutrition in many different mediums and events. Note that there was no mention of work–life balance seminars, stress reduction training or the like. It's not that those factors aren't globally important to a wellness program – it's that it was not the appropriate single message to send at that time.

There are several elements that have to be understood before One Message can speak with Many Voices. The first, as with any marketing campaign, know your target audience. In particular, what appeals to them, how they consume information, and whatever other activities or interests the wellness program would be competing with.

Exploring the example above in detail, Table 12.1 helps illustrate the target audiences:

Table 12.1   *An example of event planning using the 'One Message, Multiple Voices' framework*

Group	General Description	Communication Mediums	Attention Competitor
Administration	Work as teams at various company sites, mainly desk and computer bound, generally predictable hours	Intranet site, email, posters, social media	Every other program being put on by the company, other educational opportunities, department meetings, deadlines
Computer engineers	Work as teams at various company sites, mainly desk and computer bound, predictable to unpredictable hours depending on function	Intranet site, email, posters, social media	Every other program being put on by the company, department meetings, deadlines, perfectionist work is required
24/7 call operators	Work in very small teams, extremely tied to their workstation, company and client sites, variable hours, many night shifts	Email, social media	They need to be at their workstation to receive a distress call, perfectionist work is required
Remote sales force	Work as individuals, rarely in front of a computer for long periods of time, variety of hours	Intranet site, email, social media	Always engaged either with the client or traveling from place to place, not a lot of 'consecutiveness' with the rest of the company

KNOW YOUR MEDICINE

I'll never forget the professional frustration that I felt when a friend called me after getting her body fat assessed during a company-wide health assessment screening via bioelectrical impedance. The reason for her concern – she was 7 months pregnant. With her very visually pregnant belly the assessment went along as it had any other year, yet when she questioned whether or not there was concern for her unborn child there was no resource for her to obtain an answer. This, of course, spiraled into panic and ultimate loss in faith in the wellness program.

  This is a great lesson in solid protocols; it is critical to have knowledgeable professionals to act as resources and be current with the latest research.

In the quest to further the reach and impact of wellness programs, the focus is often on the implementation and application of the wellness program and events. Not to say that isn't important, but all programs should be based on sound medical reasoning. Every wellness event should be able to answer two questions: (1) What health or wellness benefit is this event trying to achieve? (2) What research can support that this activity will achieve that benefit? If these two questions can't be answered, think hard and long about the costs and benefits of that particular event. The costs can be devastating: as a program, as a professional, and both legally and financially.

  From the example above, there is the question of whether actual harm had been inflicted on the fetus. To explore the magnitude of this factor, just look at malpractice rates of obstetricians. In the United States, obstetricians can be sued for perceived or real harm inflicted during pregnancy, the birthing process and any residual effect up to the child's 18th birthday when they become an adult. Having protocols in place about assessment conducted on pregnant women and an individual on the team that could speak to the subject would have prevented mother from panicking and the worst-case scenario that her unborn child had been put at risk.

  Another result the above example illustrates is the sudden lack of confidence in the wellness program and its implementers. Keep in mind that health and wellness is a very personal and intimate relationship; any time that there is a conflict, mistake or even a lack of response from the wellness team it can be perceived as an attack on the individual. This can lead to the assumed stance on the individual's part that the wellness program and individuals that supply the service aren't professionals and are therefore not credible. All it takes is one influential person to question the credibility of the service. In the void of a proper response, participation can plummet. When no one is participating in the wellness program, programs get cut.

Medicine is constantly changing, often disproving the validity of old notions and proposing new ones. Keeping up with the research can be a full-time task and is part of the reason why medicine has become focused with its experts. As providers of wellness services, it's incredibly important to at least have access to peer-reviewed research; and if not, someone that can interpret the conflicting data between research projects.

A short word about alternative medicine. What was once alternative medicine sometimes become mainstream medicine. That being said, there are still a lot of alternative medicine schools of thought that never withstand the rigors of research and never make it to the mainstream. As an element of style, it's my belief that alternative medicine can be a part of wellness programs as long as there is an educational component that fully discloses the pros, cons and unknowns of the theory. The program should provide unbiased education on the subject matter – with no intent to sell or promote.

GETTING CREATIVE AND MANAGING ONGOING PROGRAMS

Managing ongoing wellness programs comes with its own set of hurdles. It can sometime be difficult to keep the content fresh and appealing. Again, cognitively most people know that fruit and vegetables are better for them than hamburgers and French fries. As a wellness provider, there can be times that you are at a loss to reiterate the message that you feel you've spoken a million times over. Yet, in order to keep participation up and continue to spark positive behavior change, the programming needs to evolve and mature to stay alive.

There are two important concepts to focus on when implementing mature programs. The first, is that not everyone is hearing your message for the hundredth time. The second goes back to using your resources and figuring out what's already preoccupying the participant's time.

Prochaska's stage model of change (Prochaska et al., 1994) tells us the target audience (the company's employees) are in a continual state of change. As programs and events try to incentivize individuals to move from the 'pre-contemplation' stage (in which employees have no intention

5K training as part of a program is pretty common. Usually, as part of a walking program you encourage people to train to complete this race, everyone shows up on race day and there's a celebration. Participation isn't typically great for this event – because the super fit want nothing to do with a 5K and the distance intimidates the couch potatoes.

So how do you turn this staple of wellness programs into something new? Change the distance to a short obstacle course, add upper management zombies, revamp the training program, communication mediums and event set-up.

Suddenly, you have a shorter distance to train for the couch potatoes and an element of technical difficulty for the super fit. Participation goes through the roof because no one is going to pass up the opportunity to be chased by their boss while he's dressed up as a dead guy. The program is suddenly 'hip' with current culture and the most interesting thing found while running this event was the amount of laughter. Being chased by someone (even a slow dead guy) harks back to our days on the playground: laughing, screaming and having fun.

Make a wellness program fun and you'll move more minds and bodies; broccoli just got a little séxier.

of changing behavior); through the stages of 'contemplation', becoming aware of the problem, and 'preparation', becoming intent on taking action; to the 'action' stage, when employees engage in active modification of behaviour, and the 'maintenance' stage, characterized by sustained change, we as implementers often forget that 'relapse', falling back into old patterns of behaviour, is also a part of this model. Therefore, repeating the same behavior change messages is just as important for the new employee who has never participated in a wellness program as for the person who has relapsed and needs to be inspired once again.

Running successful events yearly can help reiterate the message and cut down implementation time for the wellness team. Annual events also give participants something to look forward to and rally around. These events, as long as they're fun and exciting, can also capture a wider breadth of participants over the years. As in providing great customer service, happy customers breed good word of mouth about your event, which drives more participation at your next event.

The other key to maintaining existing programs and keeping events 'fresh and exciting' is to add subtle changes. Running the same program year on year with no changes and you're likely to lose interest and participation over time. Instead, leverage what works one year and add more of the same the next year. If participants like recognition more than t-shirts, add new and inventive ways to recognize participation.

Getting creative is essential to keeping existing programs noteworthy. Like the above example, turning old events into new ones is pretty easy in implementation. The hard part is to gauge what's 'hot & trending' in the eyes of the end user.

The wellness committee is key in this element to assess untapped resources, as they are the eyes and ears of what the participants are paying attention to. Whether it's a play on words with the latest sales goals, TV shows that everyone is watching or the new first-person shooter game that the entire engineering team is caught up in – it's worth taking a second to figure out if the concept can help promote the wellness program or events.

Finally, never underestimate the power of being creative for pure silliness. In today's hard economy, people are yearning to laugh and have fun. If the wellness program can help provide that and promote behavior change all the better.

One event that's been super successful is 'The Calories Are Right' – a complete knockoff of the American game show 'The Price is Right'. The event isn't booked far in advance because the participants know that they might win a good prize or that they'll get to test their knowledge of the number of calories in a variety of foods. The event sells out because participants get to run down the theater aisle to theme music, their friends get to yell support from the stands and they get to share the excitement on bidding for items. Implementing caloric knowledge test under the cloak of pure silliness. Creativity in wellness is not only in program design, but also in recognizing what will appeal and entice people to participate in activities and create healthy behavior change.

The best corporate wellness consultants take what they learn from the most innovative clients, blend it with their medical knowledge and apply it to their other clients to meet predetermined goals. Hurdles to successful design and programming will always be there; from unrealistic expectations to defining what wellness is. The goal is to overcome these hurdles and impact lives in a positive function through creative programming and events.

At the heart of each successful wellness program is a well thought out marketing and communications plan that reaches a variety of people in a way that creates a positive impact toward the program's goals.

REFERENCES

Moore, G.A. (2002), *Crossing the Chasm: Marketing and Selling Disruptive Products to Mainstream Customers*, New York: Harper Collins.
Prochaska, J.O., J.C. Norcross and C.C. DiClemente (1994), *Changing for Good: The Revolutionary Program that Explains the Six Stages of Change and Teaches You How to Free Yourself from Bad Habits*, New York: W. Morrow.

13. The use of health risk assessments in corporate wellness programs – an alternative view

Lisa M. Holland

The economic challenges over the past five years coupled with escalating healthcare cost and the potential negative impact of the Affordable Care Act (ACA) continues to force employers to seek employee health and benefit solutions that will effectively address the health and overall well-being of their workforce in order to improve productivity, mitigate healthcare costs and improve their bottom line.

In the USA alone, people with chronic disease account for more than 75 percent of the nation's $2 trillion in medical spending. Whether healthcare is financed by employers, individuals or social programs, the impact of chronic disease is placing a significant burden on our health systems, taxes and costs of coverage.[1]

According to the Centers for Disease Control and Prevention (CDC, 1994), 75 percent of chronic disease is preventable.[2] High employee health risks lead to higher implications of increased healthcare costs and subsequently, the lower an employee health risks, the greater is the likelihood of achieving lower healthcare costs. Therefore, it makes sense that over 85 percent of large companies and 81 percent of small companies have a wellness program in place. The primary objective of 77 percent of employers is to use wellness programs to address rising healthcare costs.[3] Secondary objectives include improving the overall health of their workforce, improve employee productivity and improve employee satisfaction.

Numerous employers have found that offering employee health management (EHM) programs to their employees leads to a long list of benefits such as:

- retaining hardworking employees;
- recruiting healthy, productive workers;
- reducing absenteeism;
- decreasing turnover;

- reducing healthcare benefit claims expenditures;
- decreasing workers' compensation claims expenses;
- reducing presenteesim;
- enhancing job satisfaction.

Employer sponsored returns on investment (ROI) range from a low of $1.87 to a high of over $6 for every dollar spent on wellness.[4]

A comprehensive wellness strategy includes many components that should intersect to build a balanced program that will address the diverse needs of an organization's workforce. A variety of wellness models have been introduced over the years and most include similar fundamental elements such as senior-level support, assessment, communication, program interventions and evaluation.

APPLICATION OF THE HEALTH RISK ASSESSMENT

The one foundational element that is consistently used in corporate wellness programs is the health risk assessment (HRA). The HRA has become the hallmark methodology for organizations that want a valid and reliable tool to measure population health risk and is generally implemented as the first step by employers in their wellness programs.

The concept of the HRA dates back to the 1970s and was a tool used to support patient assessment by physicians.[5] The main objective of an HRA is to:

- assess individual health status;
- estimate the level of individual health risk;
- inform and provide feedback to participants about identified risk;
- motivate individuals to change their behavior to reduce identified risks;
- provide employers with aggregate population health data.

The HRA is typically administered annually to employees and includes a series of self-reported lifestyle and behavior questions, including 'readiness to change' questions. The number of questions may range anywhere from 30 questions up to as many as 52. In most instances, individuals who complete the HRA receive a custom, personal health report that will provide them with their health risks and recommendations to improve their health. Aside from the employer data value, the premise behind the value of the HRA to an employee is that their participation will motivate them to make behavioral changes that will reduce their personal health risks, because their self-reported information has been reported back to them and therefore increases risk awareness.

There are a wide range of HRAs being utilized in the marketplace. Some HRAs are simple calculators, health education tools or tools that calculate risk for disease and morbidity, or a comprehensive HRA can be a combination of all of these functions. Ideally, the employer is ultimately responsible for selecting the HRA tool that will yield optimal outcome data in order to assist them with targeting the high-risk individuals of their population.[6]

Employers who wish to continue to implement the HRA as part of their wellness program should ensure that the following elements are included in an effort to ensure optimal value:

- *Questionnaire*. This should include a robust set of questions relating to general health status, health habits such as physical activity, nutrition, stress, safety, family history (must be Genetic Information Nondiscrimination Act [GINA] compliant), substance use/abuse, mental health, chronic health conditions, biometric measures and the ability to add custom questions.
- *Risk computation*. The use of a reliable and valid tool to ensure that the self-reported data is processed through an algorithm that has the ability to produce high-quality predictive data based on evidence-based principles.
- *Reporting*. This includes risk reports for the individual including lifestyle and behavior change recommendations. Aggregate reporting for the organization with culturally specific program recommendations and intervention will reduce the population health risks, improve productivity and address return on investment and the company's bottom line.

Due to the fact that most HRA results and outcomes are based on the self-reported information, the reliability and validity of the data have been consistently challenged over the years and continue to be an area of debate for those who are for and against the value of the assessment tool. However, there are strong proponents of the HRA who argue that instances of employees providing false data on their health assessments are isolated incidents and blame a flawed implementation process, rather than the tool for its reliability and validity outcome and assessment gaps.

The ability of an organization to obtain valid and reliable results is important if the organization is relying solely on the outcome data of the HRA to measure its population health. As mentioned, the reliability and validity of the HRA has been challenged because the questionnaire is self-reported. There are HRAs that allow organizations to upload personal health information into the tool that has been measured by non-bias means, such as biometric screening, and many organizations have adopted this tactic to help improve the reliability of results.

According to HRA proponents, there is enough evidence and research that demonstrate a high degree of agreement between self-reported HRA and objective measures. A 2011 HealthPartners research study reported on the validity of self-reported body weight as compared to directly measured body weight. The results revealed a small discrepancy between self-reported body weight and measured body weight. Another study in 2010 demonstrated a strong relationship between self-reported data and measured values for cholesterol levels, including high density lipoprotein (HDL) also known as the 'good cholesterol'.[7] StayWell, a leading provider and reseller of online and paper health assessment tools, reported that health assessment data is nearly as accurate as medical or pharmacy claims data in predicting healthcare claims costs.[8] If this research is correct, then the information from an HRA is highly useful to fully insured companies who cannot obtain medical trend reports about their population due to risk pool sharing and the inability of the healthcare administrator to provide client specific data to a fully insured company.

Since the inception and recognition of formal worksite wellness programs, the health assessment has become a recognized best practice with 83 percent of employers (500 people or more) implementing the HRA as part of their overall strategy.[9] However, many of these same organizations have reported over the last two years that they are uncertain if their worksite wellness efforts have made any significant impact on the health of their population or healthcare costs.[10] The main failure of health risk assessment is that the tool does not necessarily change behavior. Employers are paying their employees to take an HRA, but it doesn't have a measurable impact on the health outcome on an individual. In a 2011 employer wellness survey implemented by Shape Up, Inc.,[11] employers were asked if they believed the HRA provided any significant value as part of their company-sponsored wellness program. Forty-three percent of employers survey felt that the HRA was 'pretty useless' and are considering eliminating the HRA altogether (Figure 13.1).

Additionally, the promoted purpose of the HRA is to improve health outcomes by targeting the 'at risk' population and provide proactive outreach and behavior change programs. Yet, based on the continued rise in chronic health conditions, the rising rate of obesity in the United States workforce and escalating healthcare costs, it would appear that these 'targeted' behavior change programs are not always empowering the change in behavior needed to improve the health of the population and mitigate healthcare costs.

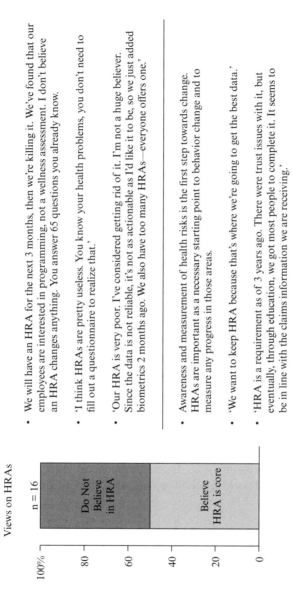

Views on HRAs

n = 16

Do Not
Believe
in HRA

Believe
HRA is core

100%

80

60

40

20

0

• We will have an HRA for the next 3 months, then we're killing it. We've found that our employees are interested in programming, not a wellness assessment. I don't believe an HRA changes anything. You answer 65 questions you already know.

• 'I think HRAs are pretty useless. You know your health problems, you don't need to fill out a questionnaire to realize that.'

• 'Our HRA is very poor. I've considered getting rid of it. I'm not a huge believer. Since the data is not reliable, it's not as actionable as I'd like it to be, so we just added biometrics 2 months ago. We also have too many HRAs—everyone offers one.'

• Awareness and measurement of health risks is the first step towards change. HRAs are important as a necessary starting point to behavior change and to measure any progress in those areas.

• 'We want to keep HRA because that's where we're going to get the best data.'

• 'HRA is a requirement as of 3 years ago. There were trust issues with it, but eventually, through education, we got most people to complete it. It seems to be in line with the claims information we are receiving.'

Source: ShapeUp/Parthenon employer interviews.

Figure 13.1 Health risk assessments: some are believers, others question their value

The adoption and use of employer-sponsored incentive strategies to increase participation in wellness programs has increased over the past five years, with employer incentives reaching as high at $430 per employee by 2010[12] for employee participation. While this strategy has seen some improvements in overall participation rates, the evidence of behavior change and improvement in population health is still lacking. In fact, what appears to be happening among these employer groups and incentive-based design is an apathetic population that participates in these programs for the overall monetary purpose of 'checking a box' to receive a reward rather than using any of the information from the HRA to address personal health risk or engage in healthier lifestyles or behaviors. In 2012, the National Business Group on Health implemented an employee survey that measured the overall satisfaction of employer-sponsored benefit plans. One of the interesting findings is that employees opposed linking the cost of their health plan to wellness program participation or improved health.[13] In a self-funded arrangement, this finding should be disconcerting to employers since the health and wellness of the workforce has a significant impact on the success of any business.

Employers are committing tremendous resources via benefit and human resource professionals in terms of implementation campaigns and monetary resources for incentives to attract participation, but in most instances, even with a linked incentive, employee participation is limited and the aggregate results provide the employer with no real value.

While the HRA is touted as a foundation of company wellness efforts, given recent findings and surveys from both employers and employers, it may be time to re-think the use and value of the HRA and explore 'New Practices' that will assist employers with achieving their wellness objectives and will actually motivate individual health behavior change.

Considering the evidence, it is apparent that the HRA may be a needless investment that consumes employer resources, costs employers an enormous amount of money (i.e., incentives) and provides no meaningful data that would drastically change the workforce health issues facing employers today.

HEALTH RISK ASSESSMENT VALUE CONSIDERATIONS

The following factors substantiate the notion that HRAs provide little value and offer employers significant rationale for contemplating the elimination of the HRA from their wellness program strategy:

- The 2008 implementation of the GINA legislation prohibited employers from asking pertinent family history questions in an HRA when the employer links incentives to the participation and/or completion of the HRA. As many fully insured and self-funded employers understand, family health history information can be an important piece of information that may assist with forecasting future medical trend of the population. These health predictors could be used by employers to support preventive program intervention, benefit plan design and even the selection of ancillary benefits could assist employees with appropriate and timely adoption of preventive health practices. The elimination of these types of questions significantly reduces the value of the outcome aggregate data employers receive.
- One of the benefits of self-funding is access to all non-identifiable employees (and covered dependents) medical, pharmacy, workers' compensation and other related data points. Since this data is readily available to the employer and can easily be compiled and analyzed, employers may want to consider using this data set as a primary snapshot of population medical trend in lieu of HRA data. These data can be extrapolated to target, design and implement an appropriate wellness strategy that will offer the same preventive impact on the health of the employee population. However, it should be noted that while these data are robust, they do omit certain data elements such as health needs and interest as well as financial wellness/risk and other relevant risks that require measurement.
- As discussed, the HRA are self-reported tools. Reliability and validity of the outcome data are questionable unless they can be validated by another dataset, such as medical trend reporting or biometric screening. Biometric screening has become one of the most popular worksite wellness measurements tools over the last five years. According to the 2013 BSwift Wellness & Benefits Administration Benchmarking Study,[14] biometric testing has emerged as the new foundational measurement method with 77 percent of large employers (greater than 500 employees) indicating that they have biometric testing in place for employees and in some instances for covered spouses and dependents. This data can be used with other company-specific health data to determine HRA validity. However, this combination of the HRA and biometric screening leads to cost inefficiencies and administrative burden, especially when the outcome results of biometric screening can be used with medical trend reporting to assess the population health. Biometric screening is emerging as the measurement of choice for worksite wellness. When

considering biometric screening, employers should consider the most cost-effective and most relevant health risks to screen for the population. Selection of appropriate screening is easy and should focus on the health risk factors that drive 75 percent of today's chronic disease, such as type 2 diabetes, hypertension, heart disease and stress.[15] The conditions can be prevented or delayed through the adoption of certain lifestyles and health behaviors. When employees are provided with an opportunity to learn about potential key risk indicators (in real time), they are more likely to be motivated to take action to address the identified risk. In most cases, worksite biometric screenings are performed by qualified health professionals who may be able to offer individual counseling at the time of the screening and increase personal awareness, value, and ignite immediate behavior change.

ALTERNATIVE POPULATION RISK MEASURES

When considering alternative measures to eliminate the HRA, as the foundational population measurement tool, it is highly recommended that employers focus screening activities on the following four categories:

- *Blood pressure*. Blood pressure refers to the force exerted by circulating blood on the walls of blood vessels. According to recent estimates, nearly one in three US adults has high blood pressure but, because there are commonly no symptoms, nearly one-third of these people don't know they have elevated blood pressure. Uncontrolled high blood pressure can lead to stroke, heart attack, heart failure or kidney failure.[16] These annual, low-cost screenings are essential for early detection to help participants prevent or delay the ill effects of hypertension (high blood pressure) through lifestyle change. This intervention is well worth the investment.
- *Body mass index (BMI)*. BMI is a number calculated from a person's weight and height. BMI is a reliable measure of a person's weight in relation to height, not body composition. BMI does not measure body fat directly, but research has shown that BMI correlates to direct measures of body fat. BMI is an inexpensive and easy-to-perform method of screening for overweight and obesity categories.[17] According to the CDC, 63 percent of the US adult working population is either overweight or obese – negatively impacting individual chronic disease, workplace safety and individual quality of life. Annual review of these statistics can assist an employer with

determining appropriate ancillary benefits, health plan benefits and environmental policies that may be helpful to address proper nutrition, which leads to healthy weight management.

- *Cholesterol panel.* A cholesterol and triglyceride blood screening measures the total amount of fatty substances (cholesterol and triglycerides) in the blood. A lipid panel measures total cholesterol, LDL cholesterol, HDL cholesterol and triglycerides. The United States Preventive Service Task Force found good evidence that lipid measurement can identify increased risk for coronary heart disease, and concludes that benefits of screening for and treating high-risk adults outweigh harms.
- *Tobacco screening/policies.* Employers have begun implementing tobacco-free workplace policies and/or nicotine screening as part of their worksite wellness strategies in an aggressive attempt to keep costs under control. The costs of smoking to the overall economy as a whole are enormous. The Centers for Disease Control and Prevention (CDC) reports that cigarette smoking and tobacco use is the leading cause of preventable death in the United States, resulting in 438000 premature deaths each year and an average of 12.6 years of potential life lost per smoker. In addition, tobacco use in the workforce costs employers on average $3500 per tobacco user per year in excess medical costs and about $1700 per user per year in lost productivity.[18] The economic impact of tobacco use in the workplace makes smoke-free workplace policies and preventive programs directed at tobacco cessation an obvious intervention with or without the use of an HRA. In fact, the optimal intervention is to create a workplace policy that prohibits the hiring of tobacco users.

Each of the measures listed contribute directly to the total health of an individual. When these measures are maintained within established clinical ranges, optimal health can be achieved and chronic disease and illness can be prevented or delayed, ultimately equating to improved population health and healthcare affordability. In addition, the use of these screenings offers participants the opportunity to establish actual baseline health data (as opposed to self-reported data), re-check the status of existing health issues or discover health issues previously undetected. An HRA is unable to discover undetected health risks and therefore the value of the output for both the individual and the employer is reduced. Objective data collection and continuous objective measurement of these critical indicators will assist employers with easily measured outcomes, year after year; early identification of health risk mitigation, targeting core drivers of healthcare costs. Biometric screening alone can easily replace the use of an HRA.

BEHAVIOR CHANGE USING BENEFIT PLAN DESIGN

Wellness programs, including the administration of an HRA, are designed to address and change individual behavior. Employers may be able to achieve a sustainable healthy population with an appropriate benefit design that supports actual long-term change. While most wellness experts agree that monetary incentives motivate, the evidence today is clear: most company wellness programs that are linked to a monetary incentive are not achieving the sustained behavior change needed to improve population health. As companies continue to struggle with stressed economy, continuing to increase their wellness budgets and pay more for limited results is fruitless. A preponderance of literature and research has demonstrated that the health of any organization can only be achieved through the concept of self-responsibility and accountability for health. While wellness programs have shown some promise, the best way for employers to empower their employees to embrace accountability and responsibility for their health is through the implementation of a benefit plan design that has proven to change health behavior patterns: a high deductible health plan (HDHP), also called CDHPs – consumer directed health plans.

The inclusion of a 'consumerism' benefit plan model may be the 'silver bullet' that provides employers with the ideal intervention that activates sustainable and improved employee health. Consumerism by design is *wellness* because it fosters the self-responsibility and accountability for health that most of the healthcare literature cites as the panacea of success. Recent research reveals that employees benefit from HDHP because these plans encourage members to become more responsible users of healthcare services, thus more responsible and accountable. The study tracked participation and utilization of plan members who adopted an HDHP and found that plan participants changed their health behaviors resulting in reduced medical and pharmacy spend by as much as 11 percent, reduce healthcare utilization by more than 12 percent and were 4 percent more likely to engage in preventive services.[19] These results represent just a portion of the behavior change that employers were able to achieve through benefit plan design alone. These changes came about by elevating the self-responsibility and accountability for health to the individuals and not through any raised awareness of health risk through the administration of an HRA. In this example, it is clear that money motivates, and when the incentive is aligned to promote personal economics, behavior change will likely follow. The recent healthcare changes and impact from the Affordable Care Act may ultimately have a powerful impact on employees and their health behaviors since most of the private and public exchanges are comprised of HDHPs. In addition, more and more employers are turning to self-funded plan options and using an HDHP as their primary offering. This shift in benefit design may drive further reduction in use of an HRA as well as its value, since immediate behavior change occurs with this type of plan design.

A move to an HDHP is probably the best "wellness program" an employer could implement to support a healthier workforce and a healthier bottom line. An HDHP fosters the highest level of self-responsibility because the value is seen by the individual in terms of their own dollars and cents and not the employer's. Additionally, the value of the behavior change can be further increased if employers use creative incentive designs that directly impact personal economics (financial wellness) by offering health savings account deposits for participation in interventional aspects of their wellness programs. HDHPs help to diminish employee entitlement, and as individuals become more knowledgeable about the cost of healthcare they learn to spend their money wisely and appropriately. As individuals engage, they begin to re-examine how they perceive personal health and begin to link how good health translates in wealth, in hard dollars, ultimately achieving financial well-being. HDHPs offer a more efficient and effective 'wellness plan' that will maximize an employer's healthcare investment and create a health and wealthy workforce. Wellness programs are still a key component of an HDHP benefit plan, but given how the design itself positively impacts behavior change, employers could eliminate unnecessary wellness participation hurdles like the HRA and use financial resources to purchase more robust interventions that will support better healthcare choice within their benefit plan design.

INCLUDING, ASSESSING AND MEASURING FINANCIAL RISK

In 1992, a large consulting firm surveyed a group of employees to determine what they wanted most from life. The survey revealed that employees had two major goals: (1) retire with wealth; (2) retire with health. The consulting firm explored the connection between these two goals and noticed that if individuals (employees) were to achieve these goals, it would require taking self-responsibility and accountability for their own actions at the earliest age possible.[20] These findings have always been relevant among the workforce but have never been as important as they are today given a multi-generational workforce, our economic climate, and healthcare reform. The importance of the health to wealth connection cannot be measured by an HRA. An HRA does not offer a personal economic motivator that will show participants how to achieve wealth through behavior change. Current corporate wellness initiatives and those leading up to 2013 have concentrated on tactical tools like the HRA to promote individual awareness and behavioral change, but, after 40 years of programming, it is clear the results have been disappointing and the overall outcomes are stuck in a less than optimal position within nearly every organization. If employer wellness programs are truly going to have an impact on the health and wealth of their populations, then employers must re-examine the current tools and strategies, and make adjustments in wellness programming, including measurement tools, interventions and plan design. Understanding that the individual's ultimate goals are optimal health and wealth, employers should redesign and reconfigure their wellness programs, which will help employees achieve these goals rapidly. This paradigm shift in delivery and implementation may positively impact employee perception of an employer-sponsored wellness program in a favorable way since the participation would be perceived as a long-term personal economic gain rather than an employer economic gain. The implementation and incentive structure currently tied to an HRA (and other wellness programs) does not offer participants any ability to achieve long-term financial wealth, which may translate into apathy, reduced participation and reduced outcomes.

As the economy changes, so do the needs of organizations and their employees. Therefore, it is incumbent upon organizations to re-examine their workforce and their overall health management strategies to ensure they are effective, and if they are not effective do something different that will change the outcome. Large organizations are spending millions of dollars on employee health management programs, including robust incentives linked to participation in an HRA and only 45 percent of those employers know if their wellness program has impacted their healthcare cost trend. These same employers continue to implement the same programs year after year with no results. Albert Einstein would define this as insanity: doing the same thing over and over again and expecting different results. While the HRA may be deemed the 'die hard' element of an employer-sponsored wellness plan design, the fact is this measurement tool does not measure other risk factors that impact health such as financial risk and may focus on other areas that are just not that important – making the tool tedious. Employers must understand that the simple administration of an HRA can't make their employees healthy. The true value of wellness is to help employees achieve their primary objectives: health and wealth. Employers who are able to provide useful tools and resources that result in a higher awareness of the health to wealth connection, reduce economic strain by value-based incentive designs (such as rewards deposited directly into defined contribution plans or 401k plans) and empower individuals to engage in healthier behaviors, will realize their wellness investment and return. The evidence is clear that the application of behavioral economics in health benefit selection and wellness programs positively impacts participation, but over the past few years, regardless of the amount of the incentive, employee participation is reaching a plateau. Embracing the idea of personal economics may finally lead to employee satisfaction and higher levels of participation because of the perceived notion of the long-term personal economic gain.

A value-based wellness program does not have to be overwhelming or complicated to achieve its objectives. Measurement is still a fundamental component, but finding innovative and low-risk maintenance strategies that will obtain more meaningful population measurements is critical. Companies must move toward progressive approaches (outside the box thinking) to help their workforce and business thrive in a sustainable way. The recent economic downturn and the changes brought on by healthcare reform are creating personal economic hardships, stress and adding to unhealthy habits. Individuals are complex and are motivated by many factors but primarily health and wealth. The good news; employers are recognizing the need to include financial wellness as part of their over-arching wellness programs and are seeking non-traditional ways to engage employees in both their physical health and financial well-being as traditional models have not been successful. With the renewed understanding that health and wealth are primary employee goals, employers must explore assessment options that will help individuals assess their financial risks and money management skills as well as their physical health. This includes helping individuals understand how maintaining a balance that consists of being comfortable with where money comes from and where it is going. The 'rub' is that many individuals neglect to understand the relationship of money and health, which is why financial wellness risk assessment is becoming so important.

Early data is showing that the average adults age 24–64 are spending $630 dollars a month on unhealthy habits; behaviors that are completely preventable by the adoption of a healthy lifestyle.[21] The tricky part is getting employees to understand how much of their disposable income is 'locked up' in poor health habits in order to ignite actionable and immediate behavior change that will result in long-term personal economics. The HRAs that exist today do not offer this kind of capability. Employers who are not considering ways to boost financial wellness alongside their physical wellness programs may be missing a critical opportunity to realize their wellness objectives.[22] Over the last ten years, more than 200 studies and surveys have tracked, measured, and documented the link between financial stress and illness. The American Psychological Association recognizes financial stress as the leading cause of unhealthy behaviors like smoking, weight gain, and alcohol and drug abuse. Other behaviors linked to financial stress are gambling and overextending credit balances. Each time employees turn to these temporary stress relievers, the possibility of personal financial stability is further impacted as well as jeopardizing the overall health and wellness objectives of an employer-sponsored plan. Financial illness negatively impacts employers through reduced productivity and increased absenteeism. When you combine financial illness with poor health the results contribute to an even higher medical spend. Between 58 and 78 percent of employers state that financial 'illness' impacts employee absenteeism and productivity and indirectly costs employers up to $2000 per employee per year.[23] Employers should strongly consider incorporating a measurement solution that can capture the physical health and financial health of their population. Emerging technology is being introduced into the marketplace that will assist employers with this kind of holistic measurement, and employers should make it a point to start to investigate these new solutions with an open mind. Similar to traditional wellness program benefits, these new financial assessment tools assess the primary health and wealth goals of an individual, and have been proven to:

- improve accountability and self-responsibility for health;
- improve health and wealth;
- reduce physical and financial stress;
- increase productivity;
- reduce healthcare costs;
- increase engagement and participation;
- replace the HRA.

THE FAILURE OF THE HRA

One of the biggest failures of the HRA is that employers, small and large, believe that including an annual survey is their wellness program. An HRA is exactly what its name suggests: it is a comprehensive assessment tool used to estimate population health and health risk, but as a stand-alone solution it does not constitute a wellness program. While many employers continue to implement and provide incentives to employees for participating in an HRA, it is becoming clear based on employee perceptions, economic needs and waning participation rates that an HRA may not be a necessary component of a wellness program. The true value of an HRA is to provide demonstrable data to employers that will assist them with appropriate interventions to address the population risk in an effort to prevent or delay future risk. However, if the measurement tool is unable to assess the most important factors of the population (i.e., health and wealth) is the administration and outcome data providing meaningful information that will support improvement? Health risk assessments are failing employee wellness programs because they offer limited information to employees; the output to the individual is information they already know. Employers provide HRAs and feel that they are doing something to better employee health, but without any pertinent information that will lead to reason for action, the HRA is a useless tool and does nothing more than increase dissatisfaction among employee populations. True value and behavior change will start when the data collected captures population health and wealth risk and individuals are able to correlate personal benefit from their participation. The use of appropriate and meaningful measurement tools will motivate employees to take the next step, by placing a larger emphasis on personal economics as the ultimate incentive toward better health.

The bottom line is that there are pros and cons to implementing an HRA. Every employer needs to consider both sides of the value equation in order to determine if an HRA is the right choice for their company. There is little evidence to support that the use of the HRA is positively impacting the health or productivity of employees. What has emerged, however, is a growing awareness of the potential of a healthy workforce! Corporate and political leaders have never been so interested in how good health can impact costs and productivity, so now is an opportune time for organizations to re-evaluate current wellness program strategies and tactics in an effort to improve the value of their programs and achieve the desired outcomes. It is time for new practices, new innovations and new thinking if employers are going to achieve their worksite wellness objectives and healthcare affordability.

NOTES

1. PricewaterhouseCoopers (2008), *Working Towards Wellness: The Business Rationale*, Geneva: World Economic Forum and PWC.
2. Centers for Disease Control and Prevention (CDC) (1994), *Healthy People, 2000*,

accessed 14 July 2014 at http://www.cdc.gov/nchs/data/hp2000/hp2k93acc.pdfhttp://
www.cdc.gov/nchs/data/hp2000/hp2k93acc.pdf.
3. bswift (September, 2013), *Wellness and Benefits Administration Benchmarking Study.
    An Analysis of How Companies Are Leveraging Employee Wellness Initiatives and
    Benefit Technology to Control Healthcare Costs*, Arlington, VT: Employee Benefit
    News.
4. See http://www.dol.gov/ebsa/pdf/workplacewellnessmarketreview2012.pdf, accessed 14
    July 2014.
5. Schoenbach, V.J. (1987), 'Appraising health risk appraisal', *American Journal of Public
    Health*, **77**(4), 409–11.
6. Edington, D.W., PhD (2009), *Zero Trends: Health as a Serious Economic Strategy*, Ann
    Arbor, MI: Health Management Research Center, University of Michigan.
7. The Prudential Group (2010), *Study of Employee Benefits: Today & Beyond*, accessed 14
    July 2014 at http://www.prudential.com/media/managed/StudyofEmployeeBenefits_
    TodayandBeyond6th.pdf.
8. Terry, P. and D. Anderson (2011), *The Role of Incentives in Improving Engagement and
    Outcomes in Population Health Management. An Evidence-base Perspective*, St Paul's,
    MN: StayWell Health Management Research Department.
9. bswift: see note 3.
10. Dunning, M. (2013) Business Insurance Wellness Study, accessed 14 July
    2014 at http://www.businessinsurance.com/article/20120403/NEWS03/120409977?
    tags=|63|307|74|305|257#.
11. ShapeUp (2011), *2011 Employer Wellness Survey: Understanding How Large, Self-
    Insured Employers Approach Employee Wellness*, Providence, RI: ShapeUp Inc.
12. Employee Benefit Adviser (28 February 2011), 'Financial incentives driving wellness
    participation', *By The Numbers, EBN*, accessed 8 July 2014 at http://eba.benefitnews.
    com/blog/bythenumbers/-2710127–1.html.
13. Darling, H. and K. Marlo (26 July 2012), *Perceptions of Health Benefits in a
    Recovering Economy: A Survey of Employees*, National Business Group on Health,
    accessed 8 July 2014 at http://www.businessgrouphealth.org/pub/f314a3d7–2354-
    d714–51ed-4a1cf9fc4990.
14. See note 3.
15. US Department of Health and Human Services, CDC (1994), *Healthy People 2000
    National Health Promotion and Disease Prevention*, Hyattsville, MD: Public Health
    Service
16. Joint National Committee on Prevention, Detection, Evaluation and Treatment
    of High Blood Pressure (2004), *Seventh Report of the Joint National Committee on
    Prevention, Detection, Evaluation, and Treatment of High Blood Pressure*, Bethesda,
    MD: US Department of Health and Human Services.
17. Centers for Disease Control and Prevention (CDC) (2011), accessed 8 July 2014 at
    www.cdc.gov/nccdphp/dnpa/bmi/adult_BMI/about_adult_BMI.htm.
18. Center for Disease Control and Prevention (CDC) (2005), 'Annual smoking- attrib-
    utable mortality, years of potential life lost, and productivity losses – United States,
    1997–2001', *Morbidity an Mortality Weekly Report*, **54**(25), 625–8, accessed 14 July
    2014 at http://www.cdc.gov/mmwr/preview/mmwrhtml/mm5425a1.htm.
19. Change Healthcare (2012), *The Case for CDHPs: Why Your Business and Your
    Employees Should Consider Abandoning The Traditional PPO*, accessed 8 July 2014 at
    http://www.changehealthcare.com/Change-Healthcare-The-Case-for-CDHPs.pdf.
20. Mahoney, J. and D. Hom (2006), *Total Value, Total Return. Seven Rules for
    Optimizing Employee Health Benefits for a Healthier and More Productive Workforce*,
    GlaxoSmithKline.
21. *2013 Health Index Calculator Post Survey: Behavioral Change Assessment Outcomes.
    Simplicity Health Plans*, accessed 14 July at http://websites.networksolutions.com/
    share/scrapbook/71/716088/HIC_Post_Survey_BehavioralChangeResults__Simplicity
    Health_Plans2013.pdf.

22. MetLife (2012), *Financial Education: An Essential Component of Your Wellness Strategy*, accessed 14 July 2014 at https://www.metlife.com/assets/mlr/403b-resource-center/Financial-Education-whitepaper.pdf.
23. Prawitz, A.D. and E.T. Garman (2006), 'Employee financial distress, emotional health risk and absenteeism', Northern Illinois University School of Family, Consumer, and Nutrition Sciences.

PART IV

Evaluating corporate wellness programs

14. Broadening the metrics used to evaluate corporate wellness programs – the case for understanding the total value of the investment

Jessica Grossmeier, Paul E. Terry and David R. Anderson

INTRODUCTION

Including a comprehensive evaluation strategy as part of employee health management (EHM) or wellness programs has been identified as an important driver of program performance. It stands to reason, and has been well documented, that when organizations do not have clearly stated goals and objectives with regular measurement against those objectives, their wellness program is less likely to achieve its full potential (O'Donnell et al., 1997; Goetzel et al., 2001, 2007; Serxner et al., 2006). A 2007 study assessed organizations with wellness programs that had demonstrated health and healthcare cost outcomes in an effort to understand variables associated with their success (Goetzel et al., 2007). Researchers used an inductive approach to identify a list of common practices across these organizations and found strong program evaluation to be one of seven recommended 'promising practices'. A more recent study used a deductive approach to identify practices associated with wellness program outcomes and found that organizations including data management and evaluation practices as part of a comprehensive approach to wellness were more likely to report a positive impact on healthcare cost trends than organizations not including strong evaluation practices to support their wellness program (Gold and Umland, 2012). Despite this evidence for the importance of program evaluation, only a third of US-based employers build strong program evaluations into their wellness programs (Health Enhancement Research Organization, 2013).

Strong wellness program evaluations are comprehensive in nature and include process, impact, and outcome measurement methods (Chenoweth, 2002; Grossmeier et al., 2010). Process evaluation involves the use of data collection instruments and methods that help practitioners understand if the program is operating as intended. Impact evaluation methods are those that assess the extent to which a program achieves the goals and objectives the program was designed to produce, including measures such as increased awareness about health risks, changes in relevant knowledge or skills, and improvements in targeted behaviors such as increased physical activity and reduced fat, sugar or sodium consumption, as well as reductions in risk factors such as overweight/obesity, blood pressure, and cholesterol. Outcome evaluation methods are those that quantify downstream effects driven by the impacts the program produced. When it comes to corporate wellness programs, one of the key outcomes of interest for US employers has been reduced healthcare costs and whether these 'direct' cost reductions yield a positive return on investment (ROI). ROI is typically calculated as a ratio of dollars saved per dollar invested or, alternatively, net dollars saved, with amounts adjusted as needed to account for multi-year timeframes (Chenoweth, 2002). The savings side of the equation is typically limited to healthcare cost savings but sometimes also includes savings associated with reduced absenteeism or presenteeism (being less productive while at work due to illness).

In response to what the authors and others consider to be an inordinate focus on ROI based solely on healthcare cost containment, this chapter presents a case for the advantages both to providers and purchasers of wellness programs of moving to a broader value proposition (Loeppke and Hymel, 2006; Loeppke, 2008; Lynch and Terry, 2014; Sherman and Lynch, 2014).

WHY BROADEN THE VALUE PROPOSITION FOR WELLNESS FROM ROI TO THE VALUE OF INVESTMENT (VOI)?

Existing ROI Evidence is Substantial but Imperfect

The wellness industry has invested significant effort in demonstrating that well-designed, comprehensive wellness programs increase appropriate utilization and decrease unnecessary and inappropriate utilization of health services. A substantial number of studies have demonstrated that participation in risk reduction and health improvement programs is associated with less frequent and less costly use of the healthcare system (Baicker et al., 2010; Soler et al., 2010). A 2010 review of peer-reviewed ROI studies reported that the average medical cost savings per dollar of invested in wellness programs was $3.27 (Baicker et al., 2010). This review appeared in the highly respected journal, *Health Affairs*, was conducted by Harvard health economists, and based its conclusions on a thorough analysis of more than 20 peer-reviewed ROI studies. Despite this favorable review, it is noteworthy that the studies varied widely in methods and rigor. A more recent published review suggests ROI methods have improved over time and that when more rigorous study methods are used, wellness program ROI results may be lower (Baxter et al, 2014). A common limitation for research that links wellness programs to reduced healthcare costs is that these findings are typically based on comparing cost trends of voluntary program participants to non-participants, typically beginning in a pre-program baseline period and extending over one or more years of program implementation. While the most rigorous of these pre-/post-, participant versus non-participant studies used multivariate statistical adjustment to control for the baseline differences between the participants and non-participants in wellness programs, they were still limited in their ability to overcome possible 'selection bias'. Selection bias may occur when employees choose whether or not to participate in the voluntary wellness program rather than being randomly assigned into a wellness treatment group or control group as would be the case in a randomized controlled trial (RCT) of the effectiveness of a wellness program. For example, it is reasonable to hypothesize that motivational differences between the groups may lead those who choose to participate in wellness programs to make more life-style changes and realize concomitant healthcare cost reductions, and that these changes would have occurred even without exposure to the wellness program. Accordingly, those skeptical about the effectiveness of wellness programs will argue that when significantly improved healthcare cost trends are found among participants in wellness programs, these changes may be partly or even primarily due to selection bias rather than to the wellness program.

Due to the potential for self-selection bias arising from motivational differences between wellness program participants and non-participants, as well as other uncontrolled drivers of healthcare utilization and costs in some existing studies, it is challenging to definitively isolate the influence of wellness program exposure relative to other contributors to healthcare costs (Oscilla et al., 2012; Lynch and Sherman, 2014). Moreover, considerable evidence suggests that it may take several years for most wellness programs to produce a meaningful, statistically significant impact on healthcare costs (Grossmeier et al., 2012; Heinen, 2012; Goetzel, 2013; Mattke et al., 2013). While researchers and program evaluators have designed increasingly more sophisticated approaches to demonstrate the link between wellness program exposure and healthcare cost impact (Baxter et al, 2014), and in spite of expert consensus panels endorsing the effectiveness of wellness programs (Soler et al., 2010), there will continue to be skeptics about the effectiveness and ROI of wellness programs (O'Donnell, 2013) because of inherent limitations in data and research designs available to program evaluators in the workplace setting and the lack of definitive RCT-level evidence provided by third-party researchers.

The Perfect Should Not be Made the Enemy of the Good

Even if robust RCT studies demonstrated that changes in the healthcare costs of employees exposed to the wellness program were *caused by* the program and that these cost changes were large enough to yield a positive ROI, the time needed to produce these results may not satisfy those who expect a quick financial return (i.e., one- to two-year timeframe). Indeed, a wellness program evaluation that reports a short-term cost impact at a level needed to pay for the program must be accompanied by substantial evidence supporting this finding, since most experts believe – and research has demonstrated – that healthcare cost savings are likely to accrue over a longer time period of three or more years (Goetzel, 2013; Mattke et al., 2013; Caloyeras et al., 2014). That relatively few organizations embark on a formal ROI evaluation (HERO, 2013; NBGH and Fidelity Investments, 2013) suggests that most decision-makers are willing to rely on health risk reduction as 'good enough' support for their investment in wellness, with the belief that health risk reduction will eventually contribute to their goal of healthcare cost containment. Because wellness is, by its very nature, a prevention-focused endeavor, this leap of faith in the merits of worksite wellness is not much different than investments in air bags for cars or guard rails in parks that are justified not by their ROI but, rather, by their well-documented contribution to reducing serious injury or death when accidents occur.

The population health tenet 'to do the greatest good for the greatest number' brings with it an implicit bias toward working on the root causes of problems instead of focusing on amelioration of symptoms or intervening late in the etiology of disease. Rose's famous 'prevention paradox' holds that more societal benefit accrues from affecting very small changes in large segments of the population than from reducing the risks of the much smaller segment already afflicted (Rose, 1990). To truly capture all of the benefits a wellness program could have, one would need to demonstrate that preventable use of the healthcare system was avoided as a result of program exposure. This prevention paradox presents a challenge for demonstrating the value of prevention because the success measure is avoidance of a potential problem that did not actually occur. In the case of ROI calculations for wellness, the problem averted is inappropriate or excessive healthcare utilization. A well-conducted RCT would help better understand how an intervention group's health risks and costs change in comparison to control group outcomes, but employers are neither willing nor, often, able to withhold programs from a portion of their population (Goetzel et al., 2011). It may not even be feasible to isolate a comparison group that is truly unexposed to wellness in a worksite setting because population-level cultural practices such as leadership support and health-promoting policies are an essential component of program success (Goetzel et al., 2007). One large multi-employer study measured the healthcare cost impact associated with health risk change and found that health risk reduction was associated with less healthcare utilization and cost. Just as important relative to the case for prevention, the opposite pattern was also observed where health risk increases resulted in substantial increases in utilization and cost (Nyce et al., 2012).

Rather than a reliance on the ROI of risk reduction as the prime justification for wellness, the business case for wellness should include the merits of prevention and the recognition that, if health were maintained for the population that would otherwise become less healthy, the costs associated with increased risk would be prevented. Proving avoidance of a predicted event will always require a leap of faith. A 2009 commentary commissioned by the Partnership for Prevention posits the futility of trying to prove the cost impact of prevention, suggesting that health is a good that is more appropriately viewed as something investments aim to optimize (Woolf et al., 2009). This kind of thinking would argue for a shift from cost–benefit analysis (CBA) to cost-effectiveness analysis (CEA), which changes the question to be answered from, 'Do the financial benefits produced by the program exceed the costs associated with the program?' to 'Does this wellness program deliver population-level health benefits more cost-effectively than investing the same dollars in another program or approach?' (Cellini and Kee, 2010).

Non-financial Benefits of Wellness Enriches the Value Proposition of Investment

While healthcare costs are a significant concern for employers, healthcare cost containment and ROI provides an overly limited value proposition for wellness programs. Indeed, Rose was prescient in his critique of American health screening practices when he argued that ascribing a disease label for those screened and moving more people into medication management may have the inadvertent effect of diminishing a focus on disease preven-tion (Rose, 1990). As an increasing number of American employers offer biometric screening, those without a concomitant investment in lifestyle change or healthy lifestyle maintenance may find that over-medication, rather than medication avoidance, becomes a costly consequence of investing more in detection and referral than in prevention and supports for a healthy lifestyle. A primary focus on ROI as the key marker for wellness program success reinforces the flawed assumption that the sole value of wellness lies in quickly offsetting program costs with reductions in healthcare costs, which would most likely be possible by focusing only on the most costly health risks or the most prevalent chronic conditions.

In summary, the current state of the evidence on the financial impact of wellness programs is imperfect. Even well-designed studies have limita-tions, so evaluators and practitioners must be transparent about the pros and cons of evaluation methods used to assess impact. For example, ROI analyses should be framed in the context of the plausibility of the asso-ciations between program participation and impact rather than cast as a simple cause and effect relationship. At the same time, it is fair to acknowl-edge how the strength of the associations between wellness programs and cost savings compare to other investments in human capital. This is where the relative value and utility of cost-effectiveness analysis become relevant.

Putting Wellness on Par with Other Human Capital Investments

Most business investments do not depend on evidence from sophisticated studies published in peer-reviewed scientific journals to merit an invest-ment. Accordingly, broadening the metrics used to assess the value of wellness programs and aligning these measures with those used for other business decisions should better support decisions on whether to invest in wellness. For example, a study by Fabius and colleagues compared stock market performance of companies with award-winning health and safety programs to the performance of the S&P 500 (Fabius et al., 2013). While this study did not compare the influence of various human capital invest-ments, it did demonstrate an association between companies that invest in employee well-being (one facet of human capital management) against an index that matters to business leaders. There are multiple benefits to providers and purchasers of wellness programs that are realized by broad-ening the metrics used to evaluate wellness and making room for a value on investment (VOI) approach in addition to the ROI approach presently used. Wellness ROI often relies on a cost–benefit calculation that compares healthcare dollars saved per dollar invested in programs. Conversely, VOI uses cost-effectiveness analysis, measuring how much total value is yielded by a given investment. ROI is a mathematical formula that compares the hard-dollar 'tangible' benefits against the investment needed to produce them. In contrast, VOI includes both the tangible and intangible benefits that result from the same investment (Norris et al., 2003; Cellini and Kee, 2010).

Elements of VOI

VOI recognizes that the value of health and well-being goes beyond the mere absence of illness or disability and related costs (Loeppke, 2008). Seligman identified five elements of well-being, including positive emotions or life satisfaction, engagement or the ability to become absorbed in the activities of life, positive relationships with people one cares about, connection to meaning or one's mission in life, and a sense of accomplishment or the achievement of a valued goal (Seligman, 2012). Programs designed to enhance these aspects of employee well-being inherently expand upon the traditional, narrow list of outcomes. VOI for wellness may include elements such as worker productivity, employee satisfaction and morale, recruitment and retention, quality of life, and corporate brand or image. The value proposition for wellness broadens even more when considering wellness programs as one part of a comprehensive set of benefits intended to attract and retain top talent, support innovation, reduce workplace injuries, improve performance at work, and optimize employee commitment to and engagement in organizational goals and objectives. In addition to increasing the organizational perception of value, these additional outcomes appeal to a broader constituency of stakeholders (NICHM Foundation, 2011). As wellness program evaluation encompasses such outcomes, the assessment of wellness as an expense that must be justified based solely on financial returns broadens to assessing wellness in comparison to other investments in human capital. VOI metrics will be valuable if they show how wellness programs help drive business success. Therefore, the focus of wellness program evaluation should be less about how high health risks drive higher long-term healthcare costs and more about how engagement in wellness relates to higher levels of morale, team cohesion, job satisfaction and improved business results.

VALUE CHAIN FROM HEALTH TO BUSINESS RESULTS

Broadening wellness metrics to enable a VOI approach involves developing and providing a broader catalogue of potential program outcomes that will appeal to more corporate C-suite stakeholders. To underscore the breadth and depth of a VOI value proposition, it is helpful to have a conceptual framework for how wellness programs may contribute to other outcomes of interest. Figure 14.1 provides such a guide to considering how health contributes to multiple business results that organizational leaders care about, including organizational profitability, revenue, market share, and customer loyalty, among others.

The left side of the diagram introduces two areas of influence that may directly and indirectly contribute to the intermediary human capital outcomes that drive positive business results. Employee-level influences focus on attributes of an individual including health and well-being, emotional intelligence, resilience, job satisfaction, knowledge, skills, self-efficacy, alignment with organizational mission, and empowerment. Best-practice wellness programs aim to have a direct impact on all of these attributes. These individual attributes can influence and be influenced by organizational factors including co-worker relationships, organizational support, work processes, team cohesion, work climate, organizational communication, leadership support, management styles, performance feedback, job demands, organizational policies, and team dynamics and processes. An additional contributor not included in the figure is the influence of that industry's marketplace, which could include economic climate, competitive environment, and the market need or desire for the products or services an organization produces. These broad market influences can contribute to both employee-level and organizational attributes.

Wellness-related employee and organizational attributes directly and indirectly influence human capital outcomes. Human capital outcomes are comprised of the outputs or products of human capital. Human capital has several definitions. From an organizational finance perspective, human capital represents 'the value that the employees of a business provide through the application of skills, know-how and expertise' (Maddocks and Beaney, 2002); while from a human resources (HR) perspective, human capital represents the capabilities and commitment of employees in an organization, which includes their current and potential capacity (Ceridian, 2007). Human capital outcomes are contributors to an organization's profit-and-loss bottom line, and investments in human capital intend to increase profit and help manage or reduce costs. While it requires a change in today's predominant mindset to view wellness programs within the context of human capital outcomes, there are plausible links between employee well-being and several of the listed outcomes.

Focusing first on the direct pathway, it is intuitive to link individual knowledge, skills, resourcefulness, and well-being to an employee's capacity to perform their job. The organizational pathway is similar to this

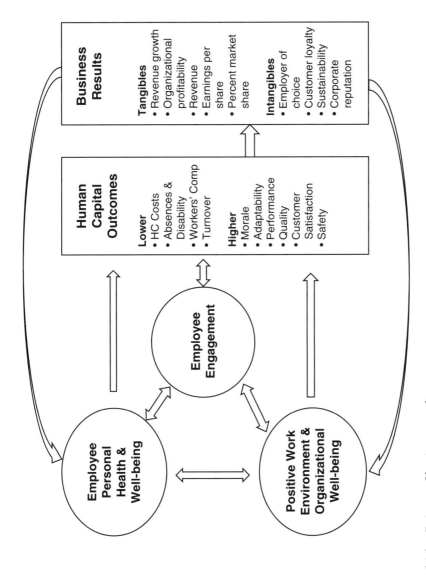

Figure 14.1　Drivers of business results

employee-level pathway. That is, the aggregation of individual attributes to collective team attributes clearly has an influence on team performance. Employee engagement with their work may operate as an indirect pathway to human capital outcomes, with employee-level and organizational attributes influencing employee engagement with work. For example, employee engagement may be influenced by how aligned an employee's values are with the values of the organization. A high degree of alignment may result in increased employee engagement with work, which is translated into higher levels of discretionary output by the employee. This analysis also applies to groups or teams. An organizational team or department with a strong sense of collective purpose aligned with high-level organizational goals is likely to have a strong degree of team cohesion and engagement around specific projects or tasks. This alignment translates into higher levels of team performance.

Human capital outcomes are the driver of business results like organizational profitability. Ideally, improvements in human capital outcomes, when growing in concert with organizational values and goals, will produce better business results. For example, reducing absence alone may not contribute to significant increases in organizational profitability if employees are not aligned with organizational goals while at work. However, reducing absence and turnover through strategies that increase engagement while at work are likely to improve profitability.

The diagram includes two-directional arrows suggesting business results may in turn influence employee and organizational well-being. At the employee level of well-being one of many plausible examples of this hypothesized flow is the relationship between an organization's reputation in the community and an employee's sense of pride in being associated with the organization or its accomplishments. At the organizational level of well-being, organizational reputation may influence team cohesion.

Although there is research supporting the relationships between the influencers on the left side of Figure 14.1 and many of the human capital outcomes and business results on the right side, this diagram is not intended to be a formal model representing known causal links between well-being and business results. Rather, the diagram in Figure 14.1 is put forward as a testable framework that can inform wellness program evaluation.

DEVELOPING A VOI APPROACH TO MEASUREMENT

Wellness programs aim to optimize employee and organizational well-being, so testing the plausibility of a wellness program's ability to influence human capital outcomes could start by measuring the influence of changes in well-being with changes in levels of engagement or changes in human capital outcomes. The most promising example of how to broaden the wellness value proposition beyond ROI based on healthcare cost containment comes from research showing the relationship between health improvement and productivity-related outcomes.

Wellness programs have been linked to improved employee productivity, reduced absence, and improved employee performance (Christensen et al., 2013; Mitchell et al., 2013; Sears et al., 2013; Shi et al., 2013), and there is reasonable evidence that the impact on productivity-related costs may exceed that on direct healthcare costs (Goetzel et al., 2001). Despite early studies demonstrating a link between lifestyle-related health risks and employee productivity (Burton et al., 1999, 2005; Wright et al., 2002; Boles et al., 2004), there is a paucity of research on the impact of wellness programs on productivity (Lerner et al., 2013). This represents an opportunity for wellness program evaluators and researchers to redouble their efforts to include productivity-related outcomes in their wellness program evaluation plan.

There is also a growing evidence base connecting individual health to cognitive function, particularly in the field of sports science (Ratey, 2008). Several school-based studies demonstrated that relatively short exercise sessions before the school day were linked to improvements in student academic performance. Application of this evidence to the workplace suggests physical activity may improve short-term levels of concentration, problem-solving, creativity, and innovation. Indeed, several studies have linked increased physical activity to improvements in mental recall (Hillman et al., 2003; Pereira et al., 2007), ability to process information more quickly (Hogervorst et al., 1996; McMorris and Graydon, 1997; Audiffren et al., 2008; Joyce et al., 2009), and other complex cognitive tasks such as planning and scheduling (Kramer et al., 1999). A review of scientific evidence connecting physical activity to improved cognitive function led Ratey and Loehr to conclude that while wellness programs do not typically include cognitive function as a measurable outcome, there is enough evidence to suggest that improving physical activity levels through the implementation of wellness programs will also improve cognitive performance among employees (Ratey and Loehr, 2011). Such research is the basis of corporate athlete programs that emerged in the adolescent years of worksite wellness programs (Groppel, 1999).

Another area of research with the potential to link employee health to human capital outcomes is in the area of employee engagement in their work. While no definitive definition of employee engagement exists, one review of the literature concluded that it is a 'construct that consists of cognitive, emotional, and behavioral components that are associated with individual role performance' (Saks, 2006). When the majority of a work-force is not engaged with their work, business productivity and profits suffer. Gallup researchers report that having more engaged workers is associated with less absence, lower turnover rates, fewer on-the-job acci-dents, and fewer quality defects, as well as higher customer satisfaction ratings and profitability (Harter et al., 2009). Additionally, employees under stress exhibit survival-based behaviors such as impatience, uncoop-erativeness, defensiveness, frustration, hyper-criticality, and pessimism. Such emotions decrease an employee's ability to perform effectively at work (Rath and Harter, 2010). Demonstrating that wellness programs can address the listed components is a first step in establishing a causal pathway that could explain and better establish the connection between employee wellness and performance. One indication of a positive asso-ciation between wellness and employee engagement comes from Gallup researchers, who showed that engaged employees are 21 percent more likely to participate in wellness programs than their disengaged counter-parts (Agrawal and Harter, 2009). A related study found employees with higher levels of well-being were more likely to remain with their company over the next year (Sears et al., 2013). The potential of wellness to support increased engagement suggests future research focusing on a bi-causal, interactive relationship between wellness and employee engagement.

An emerging area of interest in the wellness field involves assessing and intervening on organizational culture, including the evaluation and introduction of policies and environmental supports for healthy lifestyles. Most often referred to as building a 'culture of health', this work typically starts by using quantitative surveys or qualitative data collection methods for assessing organizational culture (Aldana et al., 2012). Surveys include assessment of structural components such as walking paths or availability of healthy choices, as well as health-supporting policies and social com-ponents such as supervisory support, employee perceptions, and norms. Several organizational health and work climate assessments have been developed and validated (Ribisl and Reischl, 1993; Basen-Engquist et al., 1998; Golaszewski et al., 2008; Centers for Disease Control and Prevention, 2012), but little research has been done to understand the influence of a healthy worksite culture on human capital outcomes (Aldana et al., 2012). This gap between the hypothesized importance of culture in driving health and the data supporting such a relationship represents another key area of opportunity for wellness program evaluation.

A literature review on engagement suggests that organizational factors affect engagement with one's job more strongly than individual factors (Simpson, 2009). Though there is little empirical evidence to show how culture changes improve health, some researchers have shown that organizational support for worker well-being is indeed correlated with successful wellness programs (Terry et al., 2008; CDC, 2012; Hoebbel et al., 2012; Sears et al., 2013; Shi et al., 2013). For example, Shi and colleagues examined well-being dimensions that included employee perceptions about their relationships with supervisors, their job's utilization of their strengths, and organizational support for employee well-being. Longitudinal tracking of a multi-employer pool of study participants indicated that a 5 percent reduction in well-being scores was significantly associated with lower worker perceptions of their on-the-job productivity (Shi et al., 2013).

While it may be daunting to consider adding VOI metrics to a wellness evaluation plan, exploring the measurement practices used in the aforementioned studies provides a promising start. In addition, many employers have employee engagement surveys that ask employees how they feel about their job and their role in the organization. A few questions could be added to determine the extent to which employees feel their employers support their health and well-being. When the provision of wellness programs and participation in programs can be linked to improved scores on employee engagement surveys, the value proposition for wellness may begin broadening from being perceived as a healthcare cost management initiative to being understood as an investment in human capital.

RECOMMENDATIONS FOR PRACTITIONERS

For organizations and practitioners steeped in the long-held view that the direct financial benefits of wellness programs must be 'proven' to justify their use at the workplace, expanding the value proposition from ROI to include VOI metrics may be especially challenging. Just as there are limitations to well-designed financial impact studies, there will also be limitations associated with non-financial measures of wellness program impact. Still, to focus on demonstrating a positive ROI effectively sets the standard for wellness much higher than that needed to support other investments in human capital such as employee training. For some purchasers this higher standard of evidence may continue to be a requirement for justifying investments in employee health management. Nevertheless, a positive ROI does not need to be the only justification for investment. A recommended first step to broadening the value proposition for wellness is to investigate how other human capital investments within the organization are being evaluated. For many employee benefits or human capital investments, it is enough for the intervention to demonstrate precisely what the program was designed to do. Examples of this pragmatic standard for evaluation include merit-based pay being shown to improve employee output or competency-based tests demonstrating that a new employee learning modality increased desired levels of execution of a business process.

In the case of wellness programs that focus on disease prevention and health promotion, their core function is to increase or maintain employee health. While health and health-related behaviors are recognized to be a root-cause contributor to chronic conditions, which then influence future use of the healthcare system, the etiology of disease is a long-term process. So, too, is the mitigation of that process. Organizations that need to demonstrate a short-term saving may be better served with healthcare consumerism programs and other policy-focused initiatives than with wellness programs (Lynch and Sherman, 2014). For example, it is much easier to document the short-term impact on health services utilization of programs that teach employees about self-limiting conditions and self-management of common acute health problems than of wellness programs that equip employees with chronic condition management skills intended to improve their health and lower consequent costs over a long-term time horizon (Terry et al., in press). Alternatively, those organizations with goals for containing both short-term and long-term costs are likely to be better served with a comprehensive approach that addresses short-term utilization dynamics while also investing in the long-term, upstream prevention strategy represented by well-designed wellness programs.

Table 14.1 provides a summary of the steps that might be taken to expand wellness program evaluation to a more comprehensive approach.

For organizations with the interest and wherewithal to explore and demonstrate the influence of wellness on other types of outcomes beyond health, which is most likely to be larger organizations with mature wellness offerings, the best place to start is an analysis of the metrics and evaluation approaches most accepted by and relevant to the decision-makers for that organization's human capital investments. This should include both leading and lagging indicators of program performance. The leading indicators are the primary outcomes the program aims to influence, while the lagging indicators are the secondary and tertiary outcomes that are likely to be derived from the primary outcomes. If the wellness program focus is broad enough in scope (for example, focuses on multi-faceted components of well-being), secondary outcomes may be associated with program exposure.

The next step subjects the list of desired metrics to a plausibility analysis to determine the extent to which the wellness program was designed to influence the primary or secondary outcomes of interest. In other words, there must be sufficient evidence from research, theory, or case studies that

Table 14.1 *Wellness evaluation plan development process*

	Primary Wellness Outcomes	Secondary Wellness Outcomes	Tertiary Wellness Outcomes
1. Identify measures of interest to stakeholders and assess beliefs about connection between wellness and outcomes	Self care Health risks Well-being Resilience Chronic conditions' severity and prevalence Incidence rates Health habits Clinical prevention practices Healthy environment components Perceived quality of life	Engagement Job satisfaction Team cohesion Creativity Energy Morale Time away from work Job performance Healthcare utilization Turnover Work quality Customer satisfaction	Healthcare costs as a percent of cost of goods sold Revenue per employee EBITDA[a] Percentage of market share Best places to work recognition Customer loyalty Profitability
2. Assess plausibility (i.e., is program designed to produce identified outcomes?)	Program design is supported by existing theories or research (program development was evidence based) Stakeholders intuitively believe program focus is tied to primary wellness outcomes Stakeholders intuitively believe primary wellness outcomes may be associated with human capital outcomes		
3. Assess feasibility of data collection	Which of the above measures are presently collected? Are there plans for adding metrics not yet collected? Is there budget available for added metrics? Are internal and industry benchmarks available? Can cohorts be identified with both wellness and capital outcomes measures? What are the sizes of the cohorts?		

Table 14.1 (continued)

	Primary Wellness Outcomes	Secondary Wellness Outcomes	Tertiary Wellness Outcomes
	Can changes in cohorts be monitored over three to five years? Can industry market trends affecting these outcomes be monitored?		
4. Identify acceptable measurement methods	Health risk assessment tools Biometric screenings Primary care visits Onsite clinic visits Wellness program award applications such as Koop Award (Goetzel, 2001)	Employee satisfaction surveys Employee focus groups Key informant interviews Leader/mgmt surveys Best places to work applications	ROI analysis Cost impact models Cost–benefit analysis Cost-effectiveness analysis VOI analysis Case studies
5. Identify evaluation approach/method that will be acceptable to stakeholders	How are other human capital investments evaluated? Are there internal capabilities for data analysis? What level of rigor is required to support the evaluation? Are external (third party) experts required to support evaluation? Is it desirable for the results to be publishable in peer-reviewed journals or will results be used to support industry recognition programs?		
6. Obtain leadership support for evaluation approach	Obtain necessary funding to support evaluation plan Executive leaders communicate to functional area leaders to ensure collaboration across organizational departments to integrate disparate data		
7. Set goals for key metrics based on available information	Published research Benchmarking Historical organizational trends Industry survey reports from consulting firms Vendor normative data		

8. Integrate wellness with organizational strategy	Internal stakeholder summit to identify needs, best practices, and capabilities
	Identify champions at different levels of leadership to serve as advisors
	Vendor summit to identify data collection, reporting, and analysis capabilities
	Strategic planning sessions with internal and external stakeholders to develop comprehensive evaluation plan
	Determine how evaluation plan and metrics support or align with broader organizational priorities:
	– Organizational mission and vision
	– Top organizational priorities
	– Measures of leadership performance
	– Industry recognition programs such as Baldridge, Working Mother, and Best Employers awards
	– Healthcare quality initiatives
	– Performance and work quality
	– Health and safety priorities
	– National policy initiatives important to the company

Note: a. Earnings before interest, taxes, depreciation and amortization.

313

similar programs were associated with the primary outcomes. This includes assessing what programmatic gaps would need to be filled to better align wellness offerings with primary measures of interest. If the wellness offerings are considered to be aligned with the outcome measures that matter to stakeholders, a feasibility assessment must be performed to determine if and how the desired metrics can be collected. In some cases, new data collection mechanisms may need to be developed. It is also important to consider what methods are needed to credibly associate the wellness program with the identified outcomes. The wellness program should not be held to different standards of performance or proof than other human capital investments. In some organizations business leaders are satisfied with directional analyses that are more cross-sectional or correlational, as opposed to a rigorously executed study with sophisticated statistical procedures that only outside experts may understand. For example, showing how changes in health or well-being status align directionally with changes in other outcomes may be preferable to an ROI study. At the same time, it is important to note that acknowledging wellness program impact might have been influenced by other human capital initiatives or policy changes also needs to be addressed (Lynch and Sherman, 2014). Once there is agreement about the core metrics to be included in the evaluation plan, it is essential to obtain executive leadership support for the evaluation plan. This includes ensuring staff, data integration, and analytic resources are in place to execute the approved plan, not to mention the funds needed to retain third party support for these activities. Further, leaders must communicate their support for the plan and engage lower levels of leaders in supporting the plan. The importance of this step should not be overlooked, as lack of functional leadership support may prove the biggest barrier to data integration. At this stage, it is appropriate to identify goals for the program outcomes being measured, which may require some initial baseline data to develop. The final step is to ensure the measures and measurement strategies are integrated with the overall wellness evaluation plan and presented in a way that resonates with decision-makers.

The utility of the process described above can be illustrated by showing how the steps recommended relate to employee engagement as one construct among many that can relate to the quality of work in the organization. Many senior leaders rely on enterprise-wide employee engagement surveys to inform their decisions about human capital investments. As discussed earlier in this chapter, it is quite plausible for a well-designed wellness program to influence employee engagement with work. This is particularly likely if the wellness program addresses employee stress by providing resiliency training both for leaders and employees and/or the wellness program is perceived as a fun, energizing set of activities that fosters workplace relationships and instills employee trust and belief in management support for their well-being. Once these measures are added, baseline analysis may be conducted to determine how levels of employee well-being are associated with levels of engagement and inform long-term goal setting.

More rigorous measurement may be desired, such as that obtained by linking individual well-being and employee engagement data so that changes in well-being can be associated with changes in engagement at both the organizational and individual levels. The results of such an evaluation will be most compelling when they are presented at the level of clarity and frequency desired by senior leaders. Communicating about employee engagement and the status of a company's human capital, if done well, should be no less impactful than reporting on profitability or market share. Accordingly, building an organized and persuasive case for interpreting wellness program evaluation findings and taking great care to communicate findings accurately to leaders cannot be overstated. Overly sophisticated language or multi-dimensional visual data displays can unnecessarily complicate the core message. It may be helpful to enlist the support of a champion on the senior leadership team who can provide guidance and support for development, execution, and reporting associated with the wellness program evaluation. While the general steps in the process should be transferable to many different kinds of organizations, the tactics and specifics of the evaluation plan will be unique to each organization.

Packaging wellness program reports and developing effective mechanisms for communicating the results is an important evaluation step that is often overlooked. There may be differences among groups of stakeholders best addressed by developing several different types of reports optimized to the needs and preferences of each respective group. Some business leaders prefer a scorecard approach while others require detailed tables that compare multiple metrics across different operating units of the company. Documenting the different stakeholder needs and preferences for information can be a helpful way to identify which measures are important to the largest cross-section of stakeholders.

CONCLUSION

When wellness practitioners focus on healthcare cost containment as the primary outcome of interest, the business case for wellness will be limited by an investment justification that starts and ends with the impact of the program on healthcare spending. This narrow focus on ROI has inadvertently undermined the recognition of the broader potential of wellness as both an instrument for long-term cost containment and a vehicle for enriching an organization's most valuable asset – its human capital. For organizations with a short-term cost containment objective, wellness programs alone (i.e., without the support of immediate cost savings through health benefit policy changes) may not be the right investment, since even disease management strategies targeted to those with costly chronic conditions have not generally been shown to deliver a significant net positive impact healthcare cost trends in the first few years after program launch (Nyman et al., 2012).

Broadening wellness program evaluation beyond ROI to include outcomes that demonstrate a more comprehensive value proposition will significantly strengthen the business case for wellness programs. This chapter offers guidelines for wellness practitioners and aims to assist in identifying other relevant human-capital-related outcomes that will strongly resonate with key corporate stakeholders. These outcomes may vary from one company to another depending on industry and will typically include outcomes that are not as readily associated with monetary returns as traditional wellness variables such as health risks. Once the desired outcomes are identified, wellness program practitioners must identify ways to link health metrics to outcomes and demonstrate how improved health influences these outcomes. Just as important as assessment and analysis of metrics, the packaging and presentation of the information is critical in most effectively supporting stakeholders.

The business result value chain introduced in this chapter provides a framework that identifies a conceptual and testable pathway from improved employee well-being to more effective human capital to better business results. Research is needed to assess the contribution of employee wellness alongside other influencers contributing to employee engagement with work and other human capital outcomes. Once the path from health to business results is better understood, wellness program evaluations will be able to focus on the more proximal leading indicators of improved health, increased employee engagement at work, and improved worker productivity. Although ROI may remain a relevant measure for organizations focused on long-term healthcare cost containment, being able to quantify these other presumably more short-term benefits of wellness will yield a broader and more compelling business case for wellness. In the end, a VOI approach to wellness program evaluation offers much more promise than the dubious real-world potential of developing a stronger short-term ROI business case. Moving beyond a narrow focus on ROI, broadening wellness program evaluation to include VOI metrics will also elevate wellness from a cost that must be justified to an investment in human capital that represents a potentially important driver of business results.

REFERENCES

Agrawal, S. and J.K. Harter (2009), 'Employee engagement influences involvement in wellness programs', Omaha, NE: Gallup, as cited in T. Rath and J. Harter (2010), *The Economics of Well-being*, Gallup, accessed 1 November 2013 at http://www.gallup.com/strategicconsulting/126908/Economics-Wellbeing.aspx.

Aldana, S.G., D.R. Anderson, T.B. Adams, R.W. Whitmer, R.M. Merrill, V. George and J. Noyce (2012), 'A review of the knowledge base on healthy worksite culture', *Journal of Occupational and Environmental Medicine*, **54**(4), 414–19.

Audiffren, M., P.D. Tomporowski and J. Zagrodnik (2008), 'Acute aerobic exercise and information processing: energizing motor processes during a choice reaction time task', *Acta Psychologica*, **129**(3), 410–19.

Baicker, K., D. Cutler and Z. Song (2010), 'Workplace wellness programs can generate savings', *Health Affairs*, **29**(2), 1–8.

Basen-Engquist, K., K.S. Hudmon, M. Tripp and R. Chamberlain (1998), 'Worksite health and safety climate: scale development and effects of a health promotion intervention', *Preventive Medicine*, **27**(1), 111–19.

Baxter, S., K. Sanderson, A.J. Venn, L. Blizzard, and A.J. Palmer (2014), 'The relationship between return on investment and quality of study methodology in workplace health promotion programs', *American Journal of Health Promotion*, **28**(6), 347–363.

Boles, M., B. Pelletier and W. Lynch (2004), 'The relationship between health risks and productivity', *Journal of Occupational and Environmental Medicine*, **46**(7), 737–45.

Burton, W.N., D.J. Conti, C. Chen, A.B. Schultz and D.W. Edington (1999), 'The role of health risk factors and disease on worker productivity', *Journal of Occupational and Environmental Medicine*, **41**(10), 863–77.

Burton, W.N., C.Y. Chen, D.J. Conti, A.B. Schultz, G. Pransky and D. Edington (2005), 'The association of health risks with on-the-job productivity', *Journal of Occupational and Environmental Medicine*, **47**(8), 769–77.

Caloyeras, J.P., H. Liu, E. Exum, M. Broderick and S. Mattke (2014), 'Managing manifest diseases, but not health risks, saved PepsiCo money over seven years', *Health Affairs*, **33**(1), 124–31.

Cellini, S.R. and J.E. Kee (2010), 'Cost-effectiveness and cost-benefit analysis', in J.S. Wholey, H.P. Hatry and K.E. Newcomer (eds), *Handbook of Practical Program Evaluation*, San Francisco, CA: Jossey-Bass, pp. 493–530.

Centers for Disease Control and Prevention (CDC) (2012), *The CDC Worksite Health ScoreCard: An Assessment Tool for Employers to Prevent Heart Disease, Stroke, and Related Health Conditions*, Atlanta, GA: US Department of Health and Human Services.

Ceridian (2007), *Human Capital Outcomes White Paper*, accessed 5 November 2013 at http://www.ceridian.co.uk/hr/downloads/HumanCapitalWhitePaper_2007_01_26.pdf.

Chenoweth, D.H. (2002), *Evaluating Worksite Health Promotion*, Champaign, IL: Human Kinetics.

Christensen, J.R., K. Overgaard, K. Hansen, K. Sogarrd and A. Holtermann (2013), 'Effects on presenteeism and absenteeism from a 1-year workplace randomized controlled trial among healthcare workers', *Journal of Occupational and Environmental Medicine*, **55**(10), 1186–90.

Fabius, R., R.D. Thayer, D.L. Konicki, C.M. Yarborough, K.W. Peterson, F. Isaac, R.R. Loeppke, B.S. Eisenberg and M. Dreger (2013), 'The link between workforce health and safety and the health of the bottom line', *Journal of Occupational and Environmental Medicine*, **55**(9), 993–1000.

Goetzel, R.Z. (2001), 'Survey of Koop Award winners: life-cycle insights', *Art of Health Promotion*, **15**(1), 1–8.

Goetzel, R.Z. (2013), 'On workplace wellness, don't throw the baby out with the bath water: a reply to Lewis and Khanna', accessed 24 November 2013 at http://healthaffairs.org/blog/2013/01/29/on-workplace-wellness-dont-throw-the-baby-out-with-the-bath-water-a-reply-to-lewis-and-khanna/.

Goetzel, R.Z., A.M. Guindon, I.J. Turshen and R.J. Ozminkowski (2001), 'Health and productivity management: establishing key performance measures, benchmarks, and best practices', *Journal of Occupational and Environmental Medicine*, **43**(1), 10–17.

Goetzel, R.Z., J.A. Schoenman, L.S. Chapman, R.J. Ozminkowski and G.M. Lindsay (2011), 'Strategies for strengthening the evidence base for employee health promotion programs', *American Journal of Health Promotion*, **26**(1), TAHP1–TAHP6.

Goetzel, R.Z., D. Shechter, R. Ozminkowski, P. Marmet, M. Tabrizi and E. Chung Roemer (2007), 'Promising practices in employer health and productivity management efforts: findings from a benchmarking study', *Journal of Occupational and Environmental Medicine*, **49**(2), 111–30.

Golaszewski, T., C. Hoebbel, J. Crossley, G. Foley and J. Dom (2008), 'The reliability and validity of an organizational health culture audit', *American Journal of Health Studies*, **23**(3), 116–23.

Gold, D.B. and B. Umland (2012), 'Relating the use of best practices to outcomes', *HERO EHM Best Practice Scorecard, in Collaboration with Mercer: Annual Report 2012*, accessed 25 October 2013 at http://www.the-hero.org/scorecard_folder/2012_annual_report.pdf.

Groppel, J. (1999), *The Corporate Athlete*, New York, NY: Wiley & Sons.

Grossmeier, J., P.E. Terry, D.R. Anderson and S. Wright (2012), 'Financial impact of population health management programs: reevaluating the literature', *Population Health Management*, **15**(3), 129–34.

Grossmeier, J., P.E. Terry, A. Cipriotti and J.E. Burtaine (2010), 'Best practices in evaluating worksite health promotion programs', *American Journal of Health Promotion*, **24**(3), TAHP1–TAHP9, iii.

Harter, J.K., F.L. Schmidt, E.A. Killham and S. Agrawal (2009), 'Gallup Q12 meta-analysis: the relationship between engagement at work and organizational outcomes', accessed 1 November 2013 at http://www.gallup.com/strategicconsulting/126806/q12-meta-analysis.aspx.

Health Enhancement Research Organization (HERO) (2013), *HERO Employee Health Management Best Practices Scorecard, in collaboration with Mercer Benchmark Report: June 30, 2013*, available upon request at www.the-hero.org.

Heinen, L. (2012), 'Take a measured approach to financial return expectations on wellness programs', *Business Insurance*, accessed 28 October 2012 at http://

www.businessinsurance.com/article/99999999/NEWS030104/120919898?tags=%
7C331%7C63%7C70%7C74%7C339%7C257#full_story.

Hillman, C.H, E.M. Snook and G.J. Jerome (2003), 'Acute cardiovascular exercise and executive control function', *International Journal of Psychophysiology*, **48**(3), 307–14.

Hoebbel, C., T. Golaszewski, M. Swanson and J. Dorn (2012), 'Associations between the worksite environment and perceived health culture', *American Journal of Health Promotion*, **26**(5), 301–4.

Hogervorst, E., W. Riedel, A. Jeukendrup and J. Jolles (1996), 'Cognitive performance after strenuous physical exercise', *Perceptual and Motor Skills*, **83**(2), 479–88.

Joyce, J., J. Graydon, T. McMorris and K. Davranche (2009), 'The time course effect of moderate intensity exercise on response execution and response inhibition', *Brain and Cognition*, **71**(1), 14–19.

Kramer, A.F., S. Hahn, N.J. Cohen, M.T. Banich, E. McAuley, C.R. Harrison, J. Chason, E. Vakil, L. Bardell, R.A. Boileu and A. Colcombc (1999) 'Ageing, fitness, and neurocognitive function', *Nature*, **400**(6743), 418–19.

Lerner, D., A.M. Rodday, J.T. Cohen and W.H. Rogers (2013), 'A systematic review of the evidence concerning the economic impact of employee-focused health promotion and wellness programs', *Journal of Occupational and Environmental Medicine*, **55**(2), 209–22.

Loeppke, R. (2008), 'The value of health and the power of prevention', *International Journal of Workplace Health Management*, **1**(2), 95–108.

Loeppke, R. and P.A. Hymel (2006), 'Good health is good business', *Journal of Occupational and Environmental Medicine*, **48**(5), 533–7.

Lynch, W.D. and B. Sherman (2014), 'Missing variables: how exclusion of human resources policy information confounds research connecting health and business outcomes', *Journal of Occupational and Environmental Medicine*, **56**(1), 28–34.

Lynch, W. and P.E. Terry (2014), 'Measures that matter: considering the stakes in assessing stakeholder's values', *American Journal of Health Promotion*, **28**(4), TAHP10–TAHP12.

Maddocks, J. and M. Beaney (2002), 'See the invisible and intangible', *Knowledge Management*, March, 16–17.

Mattke, S., H. Liu, J.P. Caloyeras, C.Y. Huang, K.R. van Busum, D. Khodyakov and V. Shier (2013), *Workplace Wellness Programs Study*, accessed 25 October 2013 at www.rand.org/content/dam/rand/pubs/research_reports/RR200/RR254/RAND_RR254.sum.pdf.

McMorris, T. and J. Graydon (1997), 'The effect of exercise on cognitive performance in soccer-specific tests', *Journal of Sports Sciences*, **15**(5), 459–68.

Mitchell, R.J., R.J. Ozminkowski and S. Serxner (2013), 'Improving employee productivity through improved health', *Journal of Occupational and Environmental Medicine*, **55**(10), 1142–8.

National Business Group on Health (NBGH) and Fidelity Investments (2013), *Employer Investments in Improving Employee Health: Results from the Fourth Annual NBGH/Fidelity Investments Benefits Consulting Survey*, Washington, DC: National Business Group on Health.

National Institute for Healthcare Management (NICHM Foundation) (2011), *Building a Stronger Evidence Base for Employee Wellness Programs: Meeting Brief*, accessed 25 October 2013 at http://www.nihcm.org/pdf/Wellness%20FINAL%20electonic%20version.pdf.

Norris, D.M., J. Mason and P. Lefrere (2003), *A Revolution in the Sharing of Knowledge: Transforming e-Knowledge*, Ann Arbor, MI: Society for College and University Planning.

Nyce, S., J. Grossmeier, D.A. Anderson, P.E. Terry and B. Kelley (2012), 'Association between changes in health risk status and changes in future healthcare costs', *Journal of Occupational and Environmental Medicine*, **54**(11), 1364–73.

Nyman, J.A., J.M. Abraham, M.M. Jeffery and N.A. Barleen (2012), 'The effectiveness of a health promotion program after 3 years: evidence from the University of Minnesota', *Journal of Occupational and Environmental Medicine*, **50**(9), 772–8.

O'Donnell, M.P. (2013), 'Does workplace health promotion work or not? Are you sure you really want to know the truth?', *American Journal of Health Promotion*, **28**(1), iv–vii.

O'Donnell, M.P., C. Bishop and K. Kaplan (1997), 'Benchmarking best practices in workplace health promotion', *Art of Health Promotion*, **1**(1), 1–8.

Oscilla, K.C., K. van Busum, C. Schnyer, J.W. Larkin, C. Eibner and S. Mattke (2012), 'Systematic review of the impact of worksite wellness programs', *American Journal of Managed Care*, **19**(2), e68–e81.

Pereira, A.C., D.E. Huddleston, A.M. Brickman, A.A. Sosunov, R. Hen, G.M. McKhann, R. Sloan, F.H. Gage, T.R. Brown and S.A. Small (2007), 'An in vivo correlate of exercise-induced neurogenesis in the adult dentate gyrus', *Proceedings of the National Academy of Sciences*, **104**(13), 5638–43.

Ratey, J.J. (2008), *Spark: The Revolutionary New Science of Exercise and the Brain*, New York: Little, Brown & Company.

Ratey, J.J. and J.E. Loehr (2011), 'The positive impact of physical activity on cognition during adulthood: a review of the underlying mechanisms, evidence, and recommendations', *Annual Review of Neuroscience*, **22**(2), 171–85.

Rath, T. and J. Harter (2010), *Wellbeing: The Five Essential Elements*, New York: Gallup Press.

Ribisl, K.M. and T.M. Reischl (1993), 'Measuring the climate for health at organizations', *Journal of Occupational Medicine*, **35**(8), 812–24.

Rose, G. (1990), 'British perspective on the U.S. preventive services task force guidelines', *Journal of Internal Medicine*, **5**(2), S128–S132.

Saks, A. (2006), 'Antecedents and consequences of employee engagement', *Journal of Managerial Psychology*, **21**(7), 600–19.

Sears, L.E., Y. Shi, C.R. Coberley and J.E. Pope (2013), 'Overall productivity as a predictor of healthcare, productivity, and retention outcomes in a large employer', *Population Health Management*, **16**(6), 397–405.

Seligman, M.E.P. (2012), *Flourish: A Visionary New Understanding of Happiness and Well-being*, New York: Free Press.

Serxner, S., S. Noeldner and D. Gold (2006), 'Best practices for an integrated population health management (PHM) program', *AJHP's The Art of Health Promotion*, **20**(5), 1–10.

Sherman, B.W. and W.D. Lynch (2014), 'Connecting the dots: examining the link between workforce health and business performance', *The American Journal of Managed Care*, **20**(2), 115–20.

Shi, Y., L.E. Sears, C.R. Coberley and J.E. Pope (2013), 'The association between modifiable well-being risks and productivity', *Journal of Occupational and Environmental Medicine*, **55**(4), 353–64.

Simpson, M.R. (2009), 'Engagement at work: a review of the literature', *International Journal of Nursing Studies*, **46**(7), 1012–24.

Soler, R.E., K.D. Leeks, S. Razi, D.P. Hopkins, M. Griffith, A. Aten, S.K. Chattopadhyay, S.C. Smith, N. Habarta, R.Z. Goetzel, N.P. Pronk, D.E. Richling, D.R. Bauer, L.R. Buchanan, C.S. Florence, L. Koonin, D. MacLean, A. Rosenthal, D.M. Koffman, J.V. Grizzell, A.M. Walker and the Task Force on Community Preventive Services (2010), 'A systematic review of selected interventions for worksite health promotion: the assessment of health risks with feedback', *American Journal of Preventive Medicine*, **38**(2S), S237–S262.

Terry, P.E., E.L.D. Seaverson and J. Hibbard (in press), 'Health decision support: health and medical decision support and chronic condition self management', in M.P. O'Donnell (ed.), *Health Promotion in the Workplace*, 4th edition, Troy, MI: American Journal of Health Promotion, Inc.

Terry, P.E., E.L.D. Seaverson, J. Grossmeier and D.R. Anderson (2008), 'Association between nine quality components and superior worksite health management program results', *Journal of Occupational and Environmental Medicine*, **50**(6), 633–41.

Woolf, S.H., C.G. Husten, L.S. Lewin, J.S. Marks, J.E. Fielding and E.J. Sanchez (2009), *The Economic Argument for Disease Prevention: Distinguishing Between Value and Savings*, Washington, DC: Partnership for Prevention.

Wright, D.W., M.J. Beard and D.W. Edington (2002), 'Association of health risks with the cost of time away from work', *Journal of Occupational and Environmental Medicine*, **44**(12), 1126–34.

15. The development, implementation, and evaluation of corporate wellness programs

Ronald J. Ozminkowski

INTRODUCTION

Corporate wellness programs are not just about saving money on medical care. As I wrote that sentence, I almost took the word 'just' out of it. The days of a sole focus on medical expenditures are numbered. As noted in a recent article by Matt Dunning from BusinessInsurance.com (2013b, p. 1), 13 percent of employers with fewer than 500 employees are thinking of moving from traditional health insurance plans to defined contribution plans. In a survey of larger firms that was completed recently by Aon Hewitt, 'about 28% reported a desire to move to a defined contribution approach over the next three to five years' (Aon Hewitt, 2013, p. 5). Taken to its logical extreme where medical care is eventually treated like defined contribution 401k plans, the corporate contribution toward medical care will be capped by a dollar amount, not defined in terms of the particular set of covered medical benefits people use. Thus, as we move forward, Brian Gifford from the Integrated Benefits Institute says the case for corporate wellness programs will be based less on the need to control medical expenditures and more on the program's 'impact on core business processes' (2012, p. 1).

With that in mind, this chapter offers some thoughts about the design, implementation, and evaluation of corporate wellness programs. Throughout the chapter, I use some interchangeable labels for these programs, including health promotion, health improvement programs, health and productivity management programs, and total population management programs. Those labels are interspersed throughout the literature and have overlapping constructs.

Writers may differ a bit about what they mean when they apply these labels, so let's start with a useful high-level definition from Michael O'Donnell's textbook entitled *Health Promotion in the Workplace* (2001,

p. 49). He says 'health promotion is the science and art of helping people change their lifestyle to move toward a state of optimal health'. This same definition applies no matter what label we give to corporate wellness programs that vary in scope.

IS YOUR COMPANY READY FOR A HEALTH IMPROVEMENT PROGRAM?

If not, stop here. If there is interest but uncertainty whether such a program will work, O'Donnell (2001, p. 52) advises that a feasibility study be conducted to answer the readiness question before moving forward. A feasibility study should address the company's goals and motives for the program, and it should find out what its employees and other potential program participants would want to accomplish by using these programs (Witherspoon, 2013, p. 2). A feasibility study should determine where financial and non-financial support for the program would come from, at all levels of management and non-management staff. A cost-effectiveness analysis to forecast the likely success of the program should also be completed (O'Donnell, 2001, p. 58).

If key stakeholders are already sold on the wellness program concept, O'Donnell (2001, p. 55) suggests conducting a needs assessment to figure out which program features are most likely to be useful. Some thoughts about how wellness programs should be designed are noted in the next section of this chapter.

As investments in corporate wellness programs are being contemplated, O'Donnell advises that realistic goals be set for the program. Quoting from page 51 of his text (but with my thoughts in brackets) he says: 'it is realistic to expect program participants to:

- achieve modest weight loss;
- stop smoking [this is probably the most difficult objective to obtain];
- improve cardiovascular condition, muscle tone, and flexibility;
- reduce stress levels; and
- develop more nutritious eating habits' [this is also a challenge to sustain in the long run].

He then says (p. 52) 'it is not realistic to:

- expect no relapses to current poor health behaviors;
- reverse significantly deteriorated health conditions in less than five years;

- expect major improvements in health conditions without major effort; or to
- expect health improvements to continue after a program is discontinued'.

Finally (p. 52), he notes that 'it is not realistic to:

- expect 100% participation in programs;
- see major reduction in healthcare expenditures within a few years without major investments in the programs;
- see absenteeism rates drop off immediately;
- see increased job output from all participants in the program; or
- expect organizational improvements to continue after a program is discontinued'.

Some writers suggest starting out by making small investments in wellness and then learning from that before investing more (Gyster, 2013, p. 2). O'Donnell (2001, p. 52), however, seems to be saying that small investments are likely to yield small returns. I would argue accordingly that the investment needs to be big enough to reach realistic goals you have in mind for the program. Wellness programming is not a lottery; a $1 ticket won't yield millions in savings. Think about what you want to accomplish with a wellness program and start by setting SMART goals for it. SMART goals are Specific, Measurable, Attainable, Relevant, and Time-bound. Use monthly, quarterly, and annual reporting and analytic approaches to learn whether those goals are being met, whether the program needs to be refined to meet those goals, or whether the goals should be more realistic.

PROGRAM DEVELOPMENT

A few years ago Dr. Ron Goetzel and I noted a rationale for health promotion programs that has five elements (Goetzel and Ozminkowski, 2006):

1. Many diseases, disorders, health risks are preventable.
2. Modifiable health risks lead to disease later.
3. Many risks are associated with higher costs and lower productivity.
4. Many risks can be reduced via participation in good programs.
5. Over time, these programs can help save money and improve productivity.

Risks don't always go down though. Some may go up (Lewis, 2012, pp. 78, 94) and the value of a program can be related to net risk change and associated cost, productivity, safety, and other impacts.

It is debatable whether the rationale for a wellness programs should include its financial performance, as we will see later. If financial returns are expected though, O'Donnell (2001) suggests these steps to determine if the program would be a good financial investment (p. 42):

1. Identify and quantify the areas affected by the health promotion program.
2. Estimate the cost ranges of the health promotion program.
3. Determine the percentage savings required in the areas to be affected in order to pay for the program.
4. Ask if it is reasonable to achieve the level of savings required to pay for the program.
5. Add other non-quantifiable benefits.
6. Compare program costs to other expenditures.

A good way to start is to talk to employees at all levels of your company to figure out what kinds of return they want from a program, financially and otherwise. Conversations with vendors can help estimate the associated costs that would be required to satisfy these wants. Information about how to craft those conversations can be based on the knowledge gained by completing the HERO (Health Enhancement Research Organization) scorecard – using this scorecard will motivate useful discussions about program goals and expectations, budgets, resources, and employee experience (HERO, 2013, pp. 1–3).

If financial returns are of keen interest, see Ozminkowski et al. (2004) and Goetzel et al. (2005); they describe methods that can be used to estimate how successful a program would have to be to at least break even within a reasonable period of time, and how much more can be saved over longer periods. The most important point though is the last one O'Donnell notes: define the notion of whether health promotion would be a good investment by comparing its likely costs and benefits to those obtained from all of your other corporate investments. More about that later.

As you think about program development, don't forget about the mental health issues faced by your workforce and their significant others. Research shows that these are among the most costly health risks (Goetzel et al., 1998, 2002, 2003; White et al., 2013).

Good pre-investment analytics can show you where most of your corporate health burden lies. Knowing your top ten most expensive physical and mental health conditions can help you figure out how to focus the design of a good program (Goetzel et al., 2003, 2004). However, keep in mind that the magnitude of the cost burden of a health risk or medical problem does not always correlate strongly with the likelihood that such burden can be removed. That is why one must have a solid understanding of what problems employees and their loved ones really want to solve – these may not be the most expensive ones, yet their motivation to solve them will be key to success.

SHOULD YOU BUY YOUR WELLNESS PROGRAM, BUILD IT, OR DO BOTH?

As I write this section I'm sitting in an office provided by one of the largest wellness program vendors in the industry, so you can imagine that my perspective on the build or buy question is that it is easier, faster, and more useful to buy rather than build it from scratch. I do believe that, and have done so since well before I started working at my current employer.

In previous stints as a program evaluator at companies not affiliated with any vendor, I saw enough fits and starts and wasted time and resources spent by company staff who first had to learn what many vendors already knew in order to build a good program. While some were successful, many were not and I came away from those experiences with a belief that buying with a critical and skeptical eye is probably better than trying to build one's own program from ground zero. Thus, it would be useful to spend the time suggested earlier to learn what your employees and their significant others want to accomplish with your program and then confer with multiple vendors to see which are most likely to achieve those goals. In my view, it would be worth spending the resources needed to build from scratch only if vendors cannot flex enough to meet your objectives.

In today's market most people buy from vendor organizations because significant data and operational infrastructures are needed to support the many different yet integrated types of activities that make up a great program. Even large organizations of healthcare providers are not likely to have the staff mix capable of this without significant investment. Most small and medium-sized firms are not likely to have it either.

Over time the employer client can work with their vendor to refine or build upon the program where needed. This requires an ongoing reassessment of needs to craft an understanding of environmental and other barriers to building a culture of health and productivity. Programs can then be tailored to address changing needs and continually improve the health of the population of interest.

IDENTIFYING THE RIGHT CANDIDATES FOR YOUR PROGRAM

As program operations commence, you will need to find the candidates who are most likely to benefit from participating in that program. Most vendors use predictive models to do this. In my view, the gold standard approach has two parts. One part of it would be to find people at very high risk for a bad health event such as a heart attack, stroke, a major surgery, a major workplace accident, or a series of emergency room visits, and to find them early enough so better health management can help avoid these events. The second part is to find those at lower risk and then offer program features to help them stay there.

Working together, your in-house analysts, external consultants, and potential wellness program vendors should conduct pre-sales analytics to help find the right program candidates. Ideally they should be able to take health assessment survey data and link those data to health plan enrollment and medical claims and pharmacy data. Eventually, these data also should be linked to data from your absenteeism, disability, family leave, safety programs, workers' compensation programs, or other benefit programs. This would be done to relate utilization in those programs to modifiable health risks. They should in turn be able to relate program activities to risk reduction, to give you an idea of how successful your program can be to reduce risks and expenditures in these areas.

It is admittedly a very tall order to use so many different types of data in the search for good program candidates, and most analysts, consultants, or vendors cannot do this yet because their experience is with just health plan data. Basing the initial search for candidates on just medical and pharmacy data is a good place to start. As you gain experience with your program over the years, consider buying the expertise required to add other types of data to the mix to find who might be the best program candidates. The more data types added to your predictive models, the more expensive and time consuming the modeling will be, so investment in this area will need to be offset by program successes down the road.

WHAT DOES IT TAKE TO DESIGN A GREAT TOTAL POPULATION MANAGEMENT PROGRAM?

O'Donnell (2001, p. 54) notes that the knowledge and expertise required to design a great program need to come from many areas. Specifically, he says that program staff should understand 'organizational theory,

group process, operations management, communication and marketing methods, motivation techniques, design process, health assessment,
fitness, nutrition, stress management, smoking cessation, medical self-
care, and social health'. Companies who want to build their program
from scratch may need to find consultants or hire staff to fill the gaps
they have in these areas. Good vendors should have expertise in all these
areas.

As perspectives from these disciplines are leveraged it will be possible
to design a program that benefits many types of people: (1) those who are
well, (2) those who are at moderate or high risk for chronic health conditions or bad health events such as heart attack, or stroke, but who have
not yet experienced those events, (3) people who have such conditions
and/or have experienced those events, and (4) those who have extremely
trying or life threatening conditions. Most employer populations will have
members in each group, and generally about 80 percent of them will fall
into the first two groups. A great health promotion program should be
able to serve all of them well. Programs designed to do so are called 'total
population management' programs.

The key to a great program is to help people understand the benefits of
reducing their health risks on their pocketbooks and their safety, productivity, and quality of life. A health assessment (HA), biometric information, and a personal healthcare cost calculator can be used to do this. A
calculator that helps people estimate the impact of their risks on their own
pocketbook is described in Bowen et al. (2009). The value of the HA and
biometric information is described below.

THE FOCUS OF A GREAT PROGRAM

Some companies focus program efforts only on employees, while others
offer program services to spouses and dependents too. The former
approach may be useful if most concerns relate to job safety and productivity. Even here though, keep in mind that an employee's safety and productivity may be related to the health of his or her spouse and dependents.
If there is high concern about medical expenditures as well, then it may
be useful to craft programs with a wider net that includes spouses and
dependents too.

The most successful programs will be those that are integrated into the
overall human capital strategy of the firm. To do this, make sure the incentives across all of your benefits and human resource programs are aligned
in ways that can enhance health, productivity, safety, corporate image,
social welfare, and other objectives you want to attain.

HOW DO GREAT PROGRAMS WORK?

The best programs promote awareness of health risks, the challenges that are related to worsening acute or chronic conditions, and other factors that influence productivity loss or worker safety (Goetzel et al., 2008). Great programs also help participants build and maintain skills to address these issues.

Great wellness programs are based in psychological or behavioral economic theory about how people make health-related decisions. Great programs motivate health, promote access to appropriate health enhancement technologies and processes, guide behavior change in ways that are tailored to the level of risk faced by the participant, help people live better lifestyles that will reduce their health risks, help them reach and maintain healthful behaviors, and steer them back toward those behaviors when recidivism occurs. The program should also guide those needing medical treatment to the right venue for that treatment and support good clinical management of chronic conditions.

For this to occur, the program should use secure and frequent modes of communication between program providers (nurses, health coaches, and others) and program participants. This process needs to be well coordinated. The process must help people understand where they are with regard to a healthful life, let them know how to get there, help them get there, and offer small yet frequent rewards or kudos throughout the process to help keep people on track.

Finally, the best programs garner very high participation levels due to the focus on meeting the perceived needs of program participants. Companies with the best programs also make significant investments in branding, marketing, and communication about their programs, just as they would for the products or services their companies make and sell.

TOOLS FOR SUCCESS: THE HEALTH ASSESSMENT AND PERIODIC BIOMETRIC INFORMATION

The health assessment is a tool to enhance awareness of risks that can lead to poor health. This knowledge helps guide individuals toward better health. The HA also provides aggregate health risk data from all program participants; such data are useful for program planners. With multiple applications over time individuals and program planners can see how health risks change, and these changes can be analyzed with respect to participation in wellness programs. Periodic evaluations of the HA should collect information about how useful the assessment seems to those who complete it; then the HA can be refined to make it better able to meet respondents' needs.

Health assessments inquire about multiple risks. A good HA will ask respondents about their exercise and nutrition habits, smoking status, sleep patterns, stress, and other correlates of physical and mental health. The HA may also include measures of happiness at home and at work, productivity at work, health-related absenteeism, and social and spiritual involvement. Readiness to address risks in these areas should be assessed via the HA and then prioritized as well. This information can be used to guide participants to program features that can help them manage or reduce their risks.

Separate biometric markers of physical health are often measured in wellness programs too. These include measures of blood sugar, cholesterol and triglyceride levels, blood pressure, and body mass index. People who are already being treated for diabetes, high cholesterol or high blood pressure are likely to know the values of these metrics and the program may not need to promote separate biometric monitoring for these people. Many others though will not be aware of their risks in these areas, and program designs that motivate the collection of this information will help identify those at moderate or high risk who did not know these risks were present. Confer with potential program providers, trusted consultants, or other outside experts to decide whom to offer biometric data collection services, and how frequently to do so. Lewis (2012) suggests that biometric screening be offered no more frequently or broadly than endorsed by the U.S. Preventive Services Task Force.

WHAT DO GREAT PROGRAMS OFFER?

Programs that address a wide variety of health risks and problems are likely to enhance engagement and lead to better long-term success (Smeltzer et al., 2011). Such programs have a moniker like 'total population management' or other similar titles. These programs may have features such as:

- utilization management for hospitalized members;
- immediate follow-up after hospital discharge to help avoid readmission;
- health risk measurement and biometric screening;
- disease management for those with chronic conditions (typically these disease management program features are offered for people with asthma, chronic obstructive pulmonary disease, coronary artery disease, diabetes and heart failure);

- management or coordination of services for other conditions too, such as back problems, high-risk pregnancy, bariatric surgery, cancer, serious kidney problems, stress/anxiety, and/or depression;
- exercise, nutrition, and weight management components;
- stress reduction features; decision support services to help those who want guidance about the most appropriate place to receive treatment for acute conditions they or their loved ones have;
- decision support services that offer guidance about where best to receive services for those who are considering care for conditions where lower-cost options may be just as (or more) effective as higher-cost options (such as for hip and knee problems);
- decision support services for frequent users of emergency room services; and
- lifestyle coaching or management activities, to help monitor and reduce health risks or prevent risks from worsening.

The best programs will tailor the above services to the particular needs of individuals, based upon their objectives for wellness, their risks and health conditions, and so on. (Serxner et al., 2006, p. 4). The best programs also allow the same staff members to provide most of the services noted above, minimizing the need to refer to other providers as participants move through the program process. Many of these activities can occur at the worksite and can be integrated with onsite health clinics.

Successful programs will also incorporate an audit of the physical structure and operations of the workplace, to determine if cafeteria offerings, stairway environments, parking lot location and lighting, and other features of the worksite are conducive to good health and safety. Workplace and human resources policies can also be audited to determine if they promote or reinforce healthful behaviors. See DeJoy et al (2008) for an example of how to audit the corporate environment.

SHOULD INCENTIVES BE USED TO MOTIVATE PROGRAM PARTICIPATION OR TO REACH WELLNESS

About 68 percent of the companies surveyed by Aon Hewitt in 2013 offer incentives to increase program participation, but there are different schools of thought about the effectiveness of incentives to maximize program engagement or to reach particular health goals (Lewis, 2012; Aon Hewitt, 2013; Dunning, 2013a; Singer, 2013). The empirical literature to date suggests that most incentives influence engagement but may not affect health outcomes (Serxner, 2013), but more work is being done to test this hypothesis.

Behavioral economic research about incentives is very limited in the health promotion space. Most work has taken place in other settings. Generally, the economic research shows that incentives are more useful if they are non-monetary, or monetary but small (less than $150 per participant per year – Serxner et al., 2006, p. 6). In either case the incentives should occur frequently throughout the time frame of program participation in order to be useful. There is still much to be learned about the impact of various incentive programs in the health improvement space.

PROGRAM IMPLEMENTATION

This section describes the general flow of members into and through a successful corporate wellness program. First, it is essential that aggressive branding and communication strategies be used to promote awareness and help drive participation.

Next, using solid predictive modeling and via direct referrals to the program from other sources, the program provider will find candidates who meet program inclusion criteria. Hopefully these will be the ones most likely to benefit from the program, but keep in mind that some of the ones in most need of help may be among the most difficult to engage or keep engaged.

Next, efforts will be made either to contact these members directly, or to motivate them to contact program providers for potential inclusion into the program. These efforts will be met with varying success.

Among those who are successfully reached, many will initially give a verbal commitment to enroll in the program. Most of these will actively engage in the program by trying to close health-related gaps. Closing those gaps would help reduce their risks and improve their health.

Some people will engage via web-based or smartphone-based options. Even in the best program, many will not become actively engaged, either because they are not interested in the program or because they have found other ways to reach their health goals. Still others may have insufficient time to participate in to the program.

Among those who actively engage in the program, many will complete it by closing all their gaps or reducing all the risks they decide to work on. Others may drop out before completion, or die.

Finally, the program provider may not be able to contact everyone who qualifies for a program, due to missing phone numbers, incorrect addresses, or other reasons. These members may be used as a comparison group when reporting and evaluation efforts are conducted.

For some program features (e.g., disease management and high-risk case management) the process described above typically occurs monthly. Each month health insurance claims and other data are processed to refresh the information about members and their health conditions. As time moves on those who previously dropped out of programs or who could not be reached to discuss program participation will be re-identified and the contact/enroll/engage process described above will occur again, hopefully with more success.

For other program features, health assessment, productivity, and safety-related data can be integrated into the process annually to help ensure that suitable candidates who are at high risk for future adverse events are not missed. While it is often the case that health assessments are used to help guide members to the right programs, it is still rare that other types of data are used. This means that many good candidates will not be identified for participation in useful programs. This lack of data also may prevent employers from understanding the full value of their programs.

PROGRAM REPORTING

The purpose of program reporting is to continually update program sponsors, operators, clients, and other stakeholders about the workings of and results obtained from the program (Ozminkowski and Serxner, 2012). Telling a believable story in the reporting process requires monthly, quarterly, or annual updating of metrics related to:

- who is served by the program (demographics, job type, employee/spouse/dependent status, location metrics, etc.);
- the health risks they have, based on health assessment and biometric data;
- the health conditions they have, based on insurance claims and HA data;
- safety, disability, absenteeism, productivity at work, overall happiness, or other issues that members state were problematic for them;
- program operating metrics related to engagement rates, modes of engagement, gaps in care or care coordination that are being addressed, what happens when engagement ends and why engagement ended;
- the quality of the medical care people receive to manage their conditions or reduce their risks;

- healthcare utilization and expenses;
- safety and productivity-related events;
- health and well-being; and
- program satisfaction.

Data on these issues will be available at different intervals. Metrics related to who is served and the conditions they have can be updated quarterly as the program grows and perhaps less frequently as it reaches a steady state. Health risks and other information taken from the HA are usually measured annually, while biometrics are either measured annually or every two or three years, depending on budget and/or other considerations. Quality of care can be measured roughly and indirectly using health insurance claims data to estimate evidence of adherence to clinical practice guidelines and the use of preventive care services; this information is typically available monthly or quarterly. Utilization and expenditures for healthcare are usually updated quarterly, but with an annual look, comparing the most recent 12 months to the previous 12-month period. Other measures of health, well-being, and satisfaction may be measured annually.

The most important feature of the reporting effort is to be clear about how metrics are defined and to agree with stakeholders about which metrics are most important to monitor and why. If this happens, the reports can be used to stimulate discussions about how to make the program better.

PROBLEM SOLVING

Solid program implementation requires structures and processes to help members resolve any problems that occur when using the program. Similarly, solid implementation requires support to resolve issues that affect the relationship between the vendor and the company client. Examples of these issues might be unforeseen data problems that delay implementation or that occur after implementation.

Issues or disputes should be identified, discussed, and resolved quickly (i.e., within a week), and to the satisfaction of the program sponsors and members, if possible. Methods for escalation/appeal should be incorporated that involve unbiased third-party reviews of disputes that cannot be resolved up front.

Implementation and ongoing program operation are likely to be smooth if the program staff members engage in frequent formal and informal team meetings. Annual vendor summit meetings may be useful if multiple vendors are used.

Implementation and ongoing operation will also be smooth if program staff members are highly trained in the areas mentioned above and are periodically retrained to keep abreast of developments in their fields. Annual audits can facilitate successful operation if the results of those audits are documented and discussed in open and free exchanges of viewpoints and if appropriate action plans are devised to address any problems raised in the audits.

PROGRAM EVALUATION

In Chapter 14, Grossmeier, Terry and Anderson made the case for moving beyond return on investment (ROI) metrics to focus more on the total value of corporate wellness programs. I will also offer some thoughts about how to estimate ROI using basic principles of cost–benefit and cost-effectiveness analysis that have stood the test of time.

I will incorporate some new thinking into this discussion that has been developed by Al Lewis, a critic of evaluation approaches offered by some vendors (2012). He suggests that plausibility tests be used to help interpret the ROI findings.

I will also describe how to leverage the dataset used for ROI analytics to perform 'propensity to succeed analyses', which can help assure that the best candidates for programs are found. The propensity to succeed analyses can also increase the likelihood that participants are served in ways that maximize the quality of their care, and that maximize savings for the company client.

First I will offer some thoughts about how to move forward in the ROI vein that helps clients better understand the benefits of corporate wellness programs, in the context of the other benefits they offer. Decisions about one benefit should be made with complete information about the impact of all benefits that are offered, to maximize returns across the board.

Let's start with a radical thought about this issue. Employers offer lots of benefits. Examples include health insurance, pensions, 401k, personal time off, family leave, adoption assistance, long-term care insurance, casual days, contraception and other lifestyle benefits (Viagra, etc.), legal assistance, sports team sponsorships, retiree medical, dental, vision, and maybe more. Each of these benefits has its own direct or indirect revenue and expenditure stream, and each may have its own non-monetary costs and consequences. A broad cost-effectiveness analysis can provide a much more complete understanding that the employer can use to make more informed decisions about all of their programs, including but not limited to their corporate wellness programs. Moreover, returns from many of these programs may be correlated, so doing well in one area might help them do well in another. Unless one looks, though, one may never know.

Using Plausibility Tests to Evaluate a Program

In a recent survey done by Willis North America Inc., '44% of employers said it is prohibitively difficult to determine their wellness program's influence on healthcare costs' (Business Insurance, 2013). In response to this complexity Lewis (2012, p. 7) argues that fourth or fifth grade math can go a long way toward understanding program impact. I think there is some value in this notion, but by themselves elementary school math concepts are not really enough to fully grasp the value of a corporate wellness program. The reason is that plausibility tests based on simple math are not sufficiently grounded in science. A much better understanding of program impact would come from applying the scientific method to determine if the program is reaching its goals. One can then use plausibility tests to help interpret the results obtained from the scientific approach and to guide subsequent program design and operating strategies.

Thus, one of the benefits of plausibility testing is that these tests can tell you whether the estimates of program value you are getting from program vendors or your internal operators seem to be in the right ballpark. In his recent book, Lewis (2012) offers many examples where basic math concepts were violated, resulting in unbelievable or impossible estimates of program impact. In these cases a good scientific process was not followed, and he suggests several rules of thumb to help check those results.

The italicized titles of these rules of thumb are quoted directly from his 2012 text, on pages 56 and 57. The descriptions that follow the titles are my paraphrases of his text material:

1. *The 100% Rule*. When declines in event rates are the desired program goals, it is mathematically impossible for any of those rates to decline by more than 100 percent.
2. *The Every Metric Cannot Improve Rule*. Every healthcare utilization or expenditure metric cannot decline; some should go up. Examples of the latter are the use of selected preventive services, numbers of covered days of pharmacotherapy, and some primary care visit rates. If these are going down they may not provide evidence of good program performance.
3. *The 50% Savings Rule*. Lewis says that declines in excess of 50 percent are not likely in voluntary programs, so such declines are more likely to represent poor savings estimation methods than better outcomes.

4. *The Nexus Rule.* There must be a theoretically or conceptually solid link between program design and outcomes, and savings metrics should reflect this link.

5. *The Quality Dose/Response Rule.* Lewis says that costs cannot decline faster or more than related utilization or other metrics improve. This is not a mathematical truism, but is probably good guidance anyway. It serves as a recommendation to peak under the hood when savings seem radically higher than changes in associated utilization or quality metrics.

6. *The Control Group Equivalency Rule.* Lewis says that control groups are useful only if selected before anyone is contacted and asked to participate in a program. I believe this rule is false because good quasi-experimental design and analytic techniques can avoid the selection bias he is concerned about if the control group is selected inappropri-ately. Nevertheless, he does raise an important issue because, in prac-tice, many control groups are improperly selected or their data are not analyzed appropriately. Unfortunately one cannot solve this problem by avoiding control groups entirely and it is easy to obtain bad results without using them. It is much better to figure out how to use control group data correctly. If needed, get help from a good applied statisti-cian at a local university or from someone with a strong record of peer-reviewed publications that demonstrate good empirical work in evaluation studies. One of the ways Lewis (2012, p. 101) suggests to avoid problems with control groups is to get information from a good benchmark source. He recommends checking into the Agency for Healthcare Research and Quality's Healthcare Cost and Utilization Project to get rough benchmark information about the utilization of many healthcare services that can be used for comparison. To do this, check out http://hcupnet.ahrq.gov/HCUPnet.jsp. Also see Musich et al. (2010) for benchmark information. Using published benchmarks will help a little, but conducting a sound scientific study would be better.

7. *The Multiple Violations Rule.* Finally, Lewis says that when any of the above rules are violated (except maybe Rules 5 and 6, for reasons I noted above), others are likely to be violated as well.

Use the Scientific Method to Generate Program Impact Estimates

The evaluation design you choose should be decided upon before your program is launched. This design should incorporate the scientific method. As you apply the scientific method to get accurate answers about the value of your program, evaluate its structure, process, and outcomes, not just outcomes alone (Ozminkowski et al., 2010; Goetzel et al., 2011).

The steps involved in the scientific method are noted in any good cost–benefit analysis textbook and are summarized with regard to corporate wellness programs in Ozminkowski and Goetzel (2001, pp. 289–95) and in Smeltzer et al. (2011). These include efforts to do the following:

1. Decide upon the financial and non-financial outcomes of interest to stakeholders (consider both, not just one or the other).
2. Specify hypotheses for each of these outcomes that are grounded in the conceptual model that underlies the program. (If the program is not grounded in a strong conceptual model that considers how people make health-related decisions, you are likely to be in trouble!)
3. Choose an evaluation design that is well suited to testing these hypotheses (this is probably the most important step, and where most evaluations fail).
4. Adjust for inflation before conducting any analyses of financial metrics.
5. Also adjust for the changing value of money over time that is not related to inflation by applying a suitable discount rate to program benefits and costs in out-years – this will assure that the value of each dollar is held constant over time.
6. Use solid statistical analyses to estimate program impact.
7. Conduct sensitivity analyses to learn how results vary according to key assumptions that must be made as the evaluation is conducted. Examples are criteria for study inclusion and exclusion, methods for designating program participation status, methods for addressing very high- and very low-cost outliers among the study sample, and techniques to adjust for selection bias and other validity threats.
8. Discuss all the above with key stakeholders and do this throughout the evaluation process from start to finish, not just after the analysis is done. Make refinements along the way to fully consider alternative viewpoints.
9. Recognize and describe the limitations of the analysis.
10. Disseminate your findings, and deal with critics and accolades accordingly.

Using the scientific process will provide the most accurate estimates of program benefits you can get. The level of rigor for each of the above steps can vary according to your interests and budget, but every step should be followed.

WHAT IS A GOOD RETURN ON INVESTMENT FROM YOUR WELLNESS PROGRAM?

What return on investment should you expect from your wellness programs? I believe the answer is 'As high as you are getting with your other investments'. If the answer comes in lower try to find out why.

Keep in mind that all return on investment figures are *average* figures. For example, an ROI ratio of 1 to 1 means that, on average, every dollar you spend on these programs yields a dollar in benefits. Since ROI values are averages, many people are likely to be served by the program in ways that yield lower than average savings, and many will yield higher than average savings. With this in mind, try to find the answers to these two questions: (1) What percentage of program participants were served in such a way that their savings were higher than it cost to serve them? Expecting this to be greater than or equal to 50 percent seems reasonable, and observing anything less than, say, 90 percent means there are opportunities for improvement or reconfiguration of the program. (2) What characteristics of program participants are associated with higher savings? Your evaluation can tell you this, and if you want to maximize future savings you can use this information to focus your ongoing search for appropriate program participants. This is what I referred to earlier as a 'propensity to succeed analysis'.

Do not keep or kill a program based solely on the average ROI value. Using the average ROI value as the sole metric to keep a program as it is if the ROI is high, or to kill it if the ROI value is too low, are both likely to be counterproductive. Use the information about pockets of success that can be identified by answering the two questions above to figure out how to make that average as high as it can be in the future. First try to serve those who are most likely to benefit from the program. Then figure out alternative ways to serve those who are less likely to benefit from it.

If you expand your evaluation strategy to account for other relevant outcome metrics too (not just dollars), then the answers to the two questions above can be cast in terms of those outcomes as well. This will help you search for the best candidates for your programs no matter what metric of success you choose.

For those of you who are stuck with a primary focus on savings as your success metric though, let's return one last time to the question of how big should the ROI be. Many people in the wellness industry and many clients expect savings to be two or more times as high as program costs. This is much higher than returns from other corporate investments and may not be realistic, especially in the first two or three years of the program.

Think about returns in light of your other investments. In a good year, investments in stocks and bonds would be about 10 percent, which corresponds to an ROI ratio of just $1.10 in savings per dollar spent on those investments. Over three years that ROI turns out to be 1.10 to the third power, or 1.33. Investments in other policy areas of national interest (e.g., education policy) tend to be even lower.

Why should expectations for wellness program ROI be so out of whack compared to other investments? Why not just compare the wellness ROI to ROIs from all of your other investments, then refine the wellness program as suggested above to maximize its return? Do the same for all of your investments. Really large ROI expectations are not likely to be satisfied by any investment.

THE MOTIVATION QUESTION

Finally, many skeptics wonder if program savings are due just to the supposed facts that only highly motivated people participate in corporate wellness programs and that motivation is not measurable. I use the word 'supposed' here deliberately, for several reasons:

- First, motivation in and of itself is not sufficient for making changes in lifestyle that reduce health risks and yield other good outcomes. As any detective will tell you, means and opportunity are needed as well. Even highly motivated people need to find an opportunity (i.e., a program or another activity set) that will help them make these changes. They also have to have the means (i.e., the ability and venue) to carry out these activities. Motivation alone is not sufficient to guarantee success.
- Second, many people who participate are not very motivated. They may participate to achieve some sort of incentive, such as reduced premiums for healthcare benefits or to avoid fines for not becoming recognized program participants. Their success will be limited unless the program staff can help improve their motivation levels.
- Third, motivation changes over time. Psychological studies indicate that situational factors influence motivation and behavior (Antonides, 1996, pp. 26, 113). As these change, so can motivation; and in either direction. Thus, the assumption that program participants are highly motivated often corresponds to an erroneous assumption that program participants are always highly motivated to care for themselves. The error here may be evidenced by the fact that many people who quit smoking restart, and that many people who lose weight gain much of it back.

- Finally, some aspects of motivation are measurable. An example is when recent very bad events occur, such as unplanned hospitalizations, emergency room visits, or other indicators of bad health. These often scare people, at least for a while, and accounting for this in the measurement process can help account for motivational factors. Another example is the use of preventive health services. It should be easy to find evidence of the utilization of various screening tests or other preventive services, prior to program participation. People with a history of getting these tests and services are likely to be more motivated to properly manage their health status over the coming year (Williams et al., 2010). A good health assessment survey can also provide information about readiness to engage in health improvement activities, and about the use of health improvement activities that were utilized prior to and outside the program being evaluated. Accounting for these activities will help reduce motivation as a validity threat when savings are estimated.

There is still a legitimate concern about motivation though, and it must be accounted for when savings are estimated, to get accurate results. Fortunately, there are sound statistical techniques that can account for unmeasured aspects of motivation when program impact estimates are generated. Examples of these techniques are offered by James J. Heckman, who won the Nobel Prize in Economics in 2000 for his work on selection bias due to unmeasurable factors such as some aspects of motivation. His seminal paper in this area was published in 1976 and he has published scores of papers on selection bias since then. Recent advances have been offered by Terza et al. (2008) as well. Random effects models can also be used to avoid selection bias due to factors that do not change much over time, as shown by Nyman et al. (2009).

CONCLUSIONS

A great wellness program can be targeted to everyone to who works for your company and their significant others. These programs should address physical and mental health, safety, productivity, and quality of life (Goetzel and Ozminkowski, 2000; Witherspoon, 2013). In addition to generating improvements in these areas, a great wellness program is also likely to enhance engagement in other aspects of corporate life. Measure its impact in all of these areas.

Factors associated with wellness program success are noted in Goetzel et al. (2007). These include:

- integrating programs into the organization's operations;
- simultaneously addressing individual, environmental, policy, and cultural factors affecting health and productivity;
- targeting several health issues and risks;
- tailoring programs to address specific needs;
- attaining high participation;
- rigorously evaluating programs; and
- communicating successful outcomes to key stakeholders.

Additional 'pillars' of a successful program are noted by Berry et al. (2010). They say that the best programs create program leadership opportunities for all levels of corporate staff. They mention the need to align program content with corporate goals, and with the needs of likely participants. They suggest that participation be offered for free or at very low cost, and that there should be an active partnership between company staff, program vendors, and program participants in all program activities. Ongoing communication between all of these people is a key to success.

As you design your program, keep in mind that what your employees want from a wellness program is likely to be influenced by new consumer responsibilities arising in our US economy. Workers may need help choosing insurance programs offered by their employers or via federal or state health exchanges. These programs will vary in terms of how much consumers have to pay out of their own pockets for healthcare. Insurance programs may incorporate varying incentives about where to receive good healthcare. These structural issues will influence their ability to get and stay healthy and will therefore influence the utility they may gain from wellness programs. Align the wellness program with other activities that people use to select their health benefits, manage the money they devote to healthcare now and in the future, manage their health risks and chronic conditions, and generally improve their health, productivity, and safety.

Many people suggest crafting programs in light of the company's vision for a healthy workforce. Success is more likely to occur and may occur faster if that vision for a healthy workforce is tied directly to the company's vision for success in other areas such as with regard to revenues, profits, image, social welfare and so on. Vision statements for all of these should be aligned.

Success is more likely if managers and employees at all levels understand their roles in producing a healthy and productive company culture and their roles in maximizing their own health and productivity. The best corporate wellness programs will target everyone in the employer's population, but in reality everyone will not participate. Make participation fun and make it seem relevant to people's needs. Vary the program interventions to keep things interesting. These activities will help improve participation.

Sustaining high engagement in wellness programs is difficult but is probably the most important key to success. Motivation to take better care of oneself will ebb and flow. With continuous quality improvement efforts dedicated to finding out how your employees perceive the costs and benefits of wellness programming, you can continue to refine program content so it always meets their needs.

Report periodically on all facets of the program, from who it is targeted toward to who engages and why, and what happens to them as they participate. Find out what people say about the program in their water cooler conversations. Conduct rigorous evaluations of program impact either annually or every couple of years, and use the results from all of these efforts to tailor the program to your ever-changing needs.

Get skilled evaluation research professionals who have peer-reviewed publication experience to help conduct the evaluation of your program if need be (O'Donnell, 2013). Plausibility test results can help you interpret their findings. If you use all this information in ongoing discussions meant to improve the wellness of those you care about, the likelihood of success will be high. Good luck!

ACKNOWLEDGMENTS

My work on this chapter has benefited greatly from reviews by Stephen Hartley, Rohit Kichlu, Shirley Musich, Erin Ratelis, Michael Rosen, Seth Serxner, Sue Willman, and Jan Wuorenma. Any remaining errors are mine. The opinions expressed in this chapter are mine and do not necessarily represent the opinions of Optum or UnitedHealth Group.

REFERENCES

Aon Hewitt (2013), *2013 Healthcare Survey*, Chicago, IL: Aon Hewitt.
Antonides, G. (1996), *Psychology in Economics and Business*, 2nd revised edition, Boston, MA: Kluwer Academic Publishers.
Berry L., A. Mirabito and W. Baun (2010), 'What's the hard return on employee wellness programs?', *Harvard Business Review*, December, accessed 5 November 2013 at http://hbr.org/2010/12/whats-the-hard-return-on-employee-wellness-programs/ar/1.
Bowen, J., R. Goetzel, G. Lenhart, R. Ozminkowski, K. Babamoto and J. Portale

(2009), 'Using a personal health calculator to estimate future expenditures based on individual health risks', *Journal of Occupational and Environmental Medicine*, **51**(4), 449–55.

Business Insurance (2013), 'Midsize firms struggle to implement effective wellness programs: panel', accessed 28 May 2013 at http://www.businessinsurance.com/article/20130528/NEWS05/130529848.

DeJoy, D., M. Wilson, R. Goetzel, R. Ozminkowski, S. Wang, K. Baker, H. Bowen and K. Tully (2008), 'Development of the Environmental Assessment Tool (EAT) to measure organizational physical and social support for work-site obesity prevention programs', *Journal of Occupational and Environmental Medicine*, **50**(2), 126–37.

Dunning, M. (2013a), '22% of employers penalize workers not taking part in well-ness programs', 26 September, *Business Insurance*, accessed 27 September 2013 at http://www.businessinsurance.com/article/20130926/NEWS03/130929864.

Dunning, M. (2013b), 'Employers mull defined contribution model for employee benefits', *Business Insurance*, accessed 29 September 2013 at http://www.businessinsurance.com/article/20130911/NEWS03/130919950?tags=|307|70|74|305.

Gifford, B. (2012), 'What's the question for employers? "What does illness cost us", or "What does health buy us?"', *IBI Research Highlights*, 1–5.

Goetzel, R. and R. Ozminkowski (2000), 'Disease management as a part of total health and productivity management', *Disease Management and Health Outcomes*, **8**(3), 121–8.

Goetzel, R. and R. Ozminkowski (2006), 'What's holding you back: why should (or shouldn't) employers invest in health promotion programs?', *North Caroline Medical Journal*, **67**(6), 428–30.

Goetzel, R., K. Hawkins, R. Ozminkowski and S. Wang (2003), 'The health and productivity cost burden of the "top 10" physical and mental health condi-tions affecting six large U.S. employers in 1999', *Journal of Occupational and Environmental Medicine*, **45**(1), 5–14.

Goetzel, R., R. Ozminkowski, C. Baase and G. Billotti (2005), 'Estimating the return on investment from changes in employee health risks on the Dow Chemical Company's healthcare costs', *Journal of Occupational and Environmental Medicine*, **47**(8), 759–68.

Goetzel, R., R. Ozminkowski, J. Bowen and M. Tabrizi (2008), 'Employer integra-tion of health promotion and health protection programs', *International Journal of Workplace Health Management*, **1**(2), 109–22.

Goetzel, R., R. Ozminkowski, L. Sederer and T. Mark (2002), 'The business case for quality mental health services: why employers should care about the mental health and well-being of their employees', *Journal of Occupational and Environmental Medicine*, **44**(4), 320–30.

Goetzel, R., J. Schoenman, L. Chapman, R. Ozminkowski and G. Lindsay (2011), 'Strategies for strengthening the evidence base for employee health promotion programs', *The Art of Health Promotion*, **26**(1), TAHP-1–TAHP-6.

Goetzel, R., S. Long, R. Ozminkowski, K. Hawkins, S. Wang and W. Lynch (2004), 'Health, absence, disability, and presenteeism cost estimates of certain physical and mental health conditions affecting U.S. employers', *Journal of Occupational and Environmental Medicine*, **46**(4), 398–412.

Goetzel, R., D. Anderson, R. Whitmer, R. Ozminkowski, R. Dunn, J. Wasserman and the Health Enhancement Research Organization Research Committee

(1998), 'The relationship between modifiable health risks and healthcare expenditures', *Journal of Occupational and Environmental Medicine*, **40**(10), 843–54.

Goetzel, R. D. Shechter, R. Ozminkowski, P. Marmet, M. Tabrizi and E. Chung Roemer (2007), 'Promising practices in employer health and productivity management efforts: findings from a benchmarking study', *Journal of Occupational and Environmental Medicine*, **49**(2), 111–30.

Gyster, V. (2013), 'A faster, cheaper way to wellness programs that work', *Employee Benefit News*, accessed 10 September 2013 at http://www.benefitnews.com/news/faster-cheaper-way-to-wellness-programs-that-work-2735879–1.html.

Heckman, J. (1976), 'The common structure of statistical models of truncation, sample selection and limited dependent variables, and a simple estimator for such models', *Annals of Economic and Social Measurement*, **5**(4), 475–92.

HERO (2013), *HERO Employee Health Management (EHM) Best Practices Scorecard in Collaboration with Mercer*, accessed 10 October 2013 at http://www.the-hero.org/scorecard.

Lewis, A. (2012), *Why Nobody Believes the Numbers: Distinguishing Fact from Fiction in Population Health Management*, Hoboken, NJ: John Wiley & Sons, Inc.

Musich, S., R. Ozminkowski and F. Battone Jr. (2010), 'Benchmarking wellness programs: how does your program measure up?', *Corporate Wellness Magazine*, accessed 9 November 2010 at http://www.corporatewellnessmagazine.com/issue-16/features-issue-16/benchmarking-wellness-programs/.

Nyman, J., N. Barleen and B. Dowd (2009), 'A return-on-investment analysis of the health promotion program at the University of Minnesota', *Journal of Occupational and Environmental Medicine*, **51**(1), 54–65.

O'Donnell, M. (2001), *Health Promotion in the Workplace*, 3rd edition, Clifton Park, NY: Delmar Cengage Learning.

O'Donnell, M. (2013), 'Does workplace health promotion work or not? Are you sure you really want to know?', *American Journal of Health Promotion*, **28**(1), iv–vi.

Ozminkowski, R. and R. Goetzel (2001), 'Getting closer to the truth: overcoming research challenges when estimating the financial impact of worksite health promotion programs', *American Journal of Health Promotion*, **15**(5), 289–95.

Ozminkowski, R. and S. Serxner (2012), 'Tell the right story with your program reporting processes', *Corporate Wellness Magazine*, accessed 7 June 2013 at http://www.corporatewellnessmagazine.com/issue-35/column-issue-35/tell-the-right-story-with-your/.

Ozminkowski, R., S. Musich, K. Hawkins and F. Bottone Jr. (2010), 'Evaluating the effectiveness of your health and productivity management program', *Corporate Wellness Magazine*, accessed 10 July 2014 at http://www.corporatewellnessmagazine.com/issue-10/features-issue-10/evaluating-the-effectiveness-of-your-health/.

Ozminkowski, R., R. Goetzel, J. Santoro, B.-J. Saenz, C. Eley and B. Gorsky (2004), 'Estimating risk reduction required to break even in a health promotion program', *American Journal of Health Promotion*, **18**(4), 316–25.

Serxner, S. (2013), 'A different approach to population health and behavior change: moving from incentives to a motivation-based approach', *The Art of Health Promotion*, **27**(4), TAHP-4–TAHP-7.

Serxner, S., S.P. Noeldner and D. Gold (2006), 'Best practices for an integrated population health management (PHM) program', *The Art of Health Promotion*, **21**(3), 1–10.

Singer, N. (2013), 'Rules sought for workplace wellness questionnaires', accessed 25 September 2013 at http://www.nytimes.com/2013/09/25/business/rules-sought-for-workplace-wellness-questionnaires.html?_r=0.

Smeltzer, P., R. Ozminkowski and S. Musich (2011), 'Applying best practices to evaluate and study the impact of health promotion programs' benefit costs, health, and productivity', *Corporate Wellness Magazine*, 29 January, accessed 10 June 2013 at http://www.corporatewellnessmagazine.com/issue-20/economics-issue-20/impact-of-health-promotion/.

Terza, R., A. Basu and P. Rathouz (2008), 'Two-stage residual inclusion estimation: addressing endogeneity in health econometric modeling', *Journal of Health Economics*, **27**(3), 531–43.

White, J., S. Hartley, S. Musich, K. Hawkins and R. Ozminkowski (2013), 'A more generalizable method to evaluate the association between commonly reported health risks and healthcare expenditures among employers of all sizes', *Journal of Occupational and Environmental Medicine*, **55**(10), 1179–85.

Williams, B., P. Diehr and J. LoGerfo (2010), 'Evaluating a preventive services index to adjust for healthy behaviors in observational studies of older adults', *Preventing Chronic Disease: Public Health Research, Practice, and Policy*, **7**(5), 1–7.

Witherspoon, D. (2013), 'Winning at workplace wellness: why quality matters more than ROI', accessed 16 September 2013 at http://www.hesonline.com/blog/wellnesssolutionsarchive/599-qol-matters-more-than-roi.

PART V

Best practices in implementing corporate
wellness programs

16. Corporate wellness programs: a summary of best practices and effectiveness*

Astrid M. Richardsen and Ronald J. Burke

The previous chapters make it apparent that workplace wellness programs are popular and widespread, and workplace health promotion is well established, especially in the United States. European countries lag behind in both providing programs and in evaluating such programs. More than 60 percent of Americans get their health insurance coverage through an employment-based plan (Baicker et al., 2010), and companies are therefore looking for ways to reduce healthcare costs and health insurance premiums. Sickness absence and poor health are also costing companies in terms of productivity losses and ultimately bottom line results. It has been estimated that as much as two-thirds of the US adult population are overweight, which is associated with a host of chronic health conditions (Goetzel et al., 2010). Also, the health of today's workforce is changing – there is a higher percentage of older workers, and with increasing age comes increased risk and prevalence of chronic health conditions, associated with higher medical and workers' compensation costs (Kelly and Carter, Chapter 9 this volume). Thus, investing in improving the health of workers can bring about significant cost reductions and increase organizational effectiveness. The increased interest in workplace wellness programs is reflected in statistics, especially for large employers. Baicker et al. (2010) reported that in 2006, 19 percent of companies with 500 or more employees reported offering wellness programs, and a survey of large manufacturing companies in 2008 indicated that 77 percent offered some form of health and wellness programs.

While the most commonly cited reason why such programs have gained popularity is the potential for reductions in healthcare costs, offering employee wellness programs is also motivated by concern over population health problems and the effect this has on worker productivity and consequently the organization's bottom line. In addition, such programs may improve the employer's image, as showing concern for employees' health and well-being will be highly valued. Wellness programs may help companies to appear as an employer of choice, which will enhance the company's ability to hire the best people, improving person–job fit, and increase employee morale and job commitment, which again may result in less absenteeism and improved productivity, and ultimately less turnover (Baun et al., 1986; Berry et al., 2010; Campbell, Chapter 12 this volume).

There is a need to integrate as well as encourage research and writing across disciplines and boundaries. Ballard (Chapter 3 this volume) documents initiatives undertaken by the National Institute for Occupational Safety and Health and the American Psychological Association to foster employee, safety, health and well-being, going back almost 20 years. There is also a need to foster integration of US and European work on employee health and well-being (Kok, Zijlstra and Ruiter, Chapter 2 this volume). While the context and motivations for enhancing employee health and well-being are clearly different in different countries, common features are the role played by work and organizations as well as the individual's role in lifestyle and physical well-being and why improving working conditions benefits multiple stakeholders (Burke, Chapter 1 this volume).

Early work and organization research was targeted at negative workplace experiences such as job dissatisfaction, burnout, job stress, depression, anxiety and intention to quit. The recently emerging and growing field of positive psychology and positive organizational behavior has put the focus on concepts such as self-efficacy, hope, optimism and resilience. Dawkins and Martin (Chapter 4 this volume) show how an intervention focused on these well-being and work-related benefits can bring about desired improvements.

A number of studies have established the relationship between participation in wellness programs and increases in productivity (Pelletier et al., 2004; Burton et al., 2005; Goetzel et al., 2010; Dollard and Neser, 2013; Mitchell et al., 2013). For example, a longitudinal study of 500 wellness program participants indicated that reductions in health risks were associated with positive changes in work productivity (Pelletier et al., 2004). Burton et al. (2005) studied over 28 000 employees in a national company and found that ten out of 12 health risk factors were significantly associated with four self-reported work limitations: time, physical, mental and output. As the number of health risks increased for individuals, so did their on-the-job productivity loss. Risk factors such as low life satisfaction, poor physical health, job dissatisfaction and high stress showed some of the highest productivity loss estimates by employees. The annual cost of productivity loss was estimated at between $99 and $185 million (Burton et al., 2005). Such findings strengthen the expectation that investments in a healthy workforce such as workplace health and wellness programs can result in important behavior change, improved health and consequently productivity, as well as may improve quality of life and create a healthy culture (Kelly and Carter, Chapter 9 this volume).

A workplace wellness program has been defined as 'an organized, employer-sponsored program that is designed to support employees (and sometimes their families) as they adopt and sustain behaviors that reduce health risks, improve quality of life, enhance personal effectiveness, and benefit the organization's bottom line' (Berry et al., 2010). However, as demonstrated from the previous chapters in this book, corporate wellness programs are diverse in scope, targets and objectives. Programs may vary from focusing on specific targets, such as smoking cessation (Goetzel et al., 2002), weight loss and/or physical fitness (Baker et al., 2008); through programs with educational focus, such as health risk assessments, and lunch-and-learn lectures (Campbell, Chapter 12 this volume); programs combining both individual and organizational strategies designed to shape healthier on the job habits, such as healthy cafeteria food, company picnics with healthy food choices (Campbell, Chapter 12 this volume); to multi-disciplinary, comprehensive programs focusing on education and health promotion for individuals, families, the organization and the community (Kelly and Carter, Chapter 9 this volume). Also, programs may be contracted through external healthcare providers (Campbell, Chapter 12 this volume; Ozminkowski, Chapter 15 this volume) or may be using internal resources, as, for example, the WellBAMA program described by Kelly and Carter.

In a review of the literature on worker health promotion programs between 2000 and 2010, Lerner et al. (2013) identified seven types of programs based on main emphasis: (1) health promotion and disease prevention, (2) fitness/exercise programs, (3) disease management programs, (4) combination programs (wellness, disease management and demand management), (5) employee assistance and behavioral health programs, (6) worksite medical clinics, and (7) disability management programs.

Baicker et al. (2010) in their meta-analysis of employee wellness programs found that more than 60 percent of the programs focused on weight loss and fitness, and smoking cessation. The remaining programs focused on various risk factors, for example, stress management, back care, nutrition, alcohol consumption, and blood pressure.

What is associated with program success? What are best practices to ensure that programs reach their objectives? This chapter will outline some of the key factors necessary for program success, despite scope and objectives.

THE IMPORTANCE OF PLANNING

Program planning is essential for the success of any worksite health promotion effort (Baun and Pronk, 2006). If the planning of programs is less than optimal, the chances of success are diminished. Baun and Pronk (2006) estimated that it takes up to three months to complete the preparation for implementing a successful program. Using a physical fitness program as an example, the authors outline the steps necessary for designing a good program. First, there are a number of issues to consider, such as the major purpose and the need for the program, as well as the potential benefits and the major program goals (ibid.). The program plan should include detailed descriptions of program content, which includes the scope of the program (the variety of services to be implemented), the goals and objectives, the metrics for evaluation, marketing ideas, and delivery and implementation plans.

Other key factors essential to program planning include alignment between the health promotion and the company's vision for success and overall business strategy (Goetzel et al., 2001), interdisciplinary team focus (Kelly and Carter, Chapter 9 this volume; Campbell, Chapter 12 this volume; Goetzel et al., 2008), a team of champions for the program, senior and middle management support (Della et al., 2008; Nielsen and Randall, 2009), involvement of employees at all organizational levels in the planning and implementation of the program (Nielsen and Randall, 2012), emphasis on quality-of-life improvements (not just cutting costs), and communication directed throughout the organization (Goetzel et al., 2001, 2007; Grossmeier et al., 2010). The implementation of wellness interventions is likely to fail if one does not adequately address the organizational context, employee ownership of the project, and the design of the intervention in the planning (Biron et al., 2010).

Goetzel and Pronk (2010) summarized what the evidence from literature reviews really show about the effectiveness of worksite health promotion programs. They concluded that promising programs often include six best practice features: organizational commitment, incentives for employees to participate, effective screening and triage, state-of-the-art theory- and evidence-based interventions, effective implementation, and ongoing program evaluation. The previous chapters (Kelly and Carter, Chapter 9, Kaufman, Chapter 11, Campbell, Chapter 12, Holland, Chapter 13 and Ozminkowski, Chapter 15) provide many practical guidelines and examples of some of these planning principles.

One of the most important aspects of planning a program is identifying the right candidates for the program. Ideally a health promotion program should be able to serve a variety of employee groups – both those who are well and those with risk. In order for any wellness program to achieve its desired population level outcomes, a significant level of participation is required. According to Kaufman (Chapter 11 this volume), successfully recruiting of individuals to participate in wellness programs requires careful planning and outreach strategy. Since wellness programs generally attempt to change individual behaviors, participation and engagement are often directly related as a prerequisite to success at both behavior change at the individual level and program success at the organizational level (ibid.).

Morris and Morris (Chapter 10 this volume) review what is known about bringing about successful individual behavior change in corporate wellness programs. Workplaces provide excellent opportunities to promote healthy habits such as smoking cessation, improved diets and increased exercise.

THE IMPORTANCE OF PARTICIPATION

The key question is to motivate employees to participate in worksite wellness programs, as program participation is a key driver for subsequent results (Grossmeier et al., 2010). Ozminkowski (Chapter 15 this volume) states that it is important to consider that motivation in and of itself is not sufficient for making changes in lifestyle, means and opportunity are needed as well. The issue is complicated because many people who do participate are not highly motivated, and in addition, motivation may change over time. In a study by Person et al. (2010) the results showed that important barriers to participation in a worksite wellness program were insufficient incentives, inconvenient locations, time limitations, schedule, marketing, health beliefs, and either not being interested in the topics presented or not being interested in the program. The study by Baicker et al. (2010) found that over 30 percent of programs used incentives such as bonuses and reimbursements to motivate for program participation.

One of the keys to high participation is that the program meets the perceived needs of program participants. This can be achieved by, for example, focusing on a definable and modifiable risk factor that is of importance to the specific worker group. Effective program interventions may therefore vary from one occupational context to another. The best corporate wellness programs will target everyone in the employer's population, but in reality everyone will not participate (Ozminkowski, Chapter 15 this volume). As Campbell (Chapter 12 this volume) notes, even in the best programs, many will not become actively engaged, either because they are not interested in the program or because they have found other ways to reach their health goals. Still others may have insufficient time to participate in the program.

Another approach is to increase motivation to participate through higher awareness. Health assessment is a tool to enhance awareness of risks that can lead to poor health (Holland, Chapter 13 this volume). Health risk assessment, which has the objective to assess individual health status, estimate the level of individual health risk, and through feedback motivate individuals to change their behavior to reduce identified risks, is by far the most common methodology used by organizations. The best programs promote awareness of health risks and the challenges that are related to worsening acute or chronic conditions (Goetzel and Ozmlnkowski, 2008). However, health risk assessments are often based on self-reported information, and therefore can be of limited value to both individuals and the organization (Holland, Chapter 13 this volume). Also, many organizations use the health risk assessment as a stand-alone intervention, which does not in itself promote health behavior change. In order for health risk assessment to be reliable and valid, it needs to include objective measures such as physical screening (e.g., blood pressure, cholesterol) and create incentives that ensure a high level of self-responsibility and participation in wellness programs, for example, high deductible health plans (ibid.). According to Ozminkowski (Chapter 15 this volume), great programs help participants build and maintain skills to address these issues, through the use of psychological or behavioral economic theory about motivation and how people make health-related decisions.

Sustaining high engagement and participation in wellness programs is difficult. It requires aggressive branding and communication strategies in order to promote awareness and help drive participation (Campbell, Chapter 12 this volume). Through screening and direct referrals to the program from other sources, it is possible to find potential candidates who meet program inclusion criteria. These may then be contacted directly or motivated to contact program coordinators for inclusion in the program. These efforts will be met with varying success (ibid.).

According to Kaufman (Chapter 11 this volume), wellness program outreach and recruiting should follow the best practices of other marketing campaigns and rigorously consider the population, the outreach channels, and the messages. The five distinct steps that are considered best practices in terms of developing a strategy for program recruitment are (1) to make a situation assessment to understand and document the goals of the program and the target population; (2) to explore and define the points of contact with the desired participants, for example 'direct channels' such as email, print, online advertising, and social media; and 'indirect strategies' such as HR departments or healthcare providers; (3) to define an outreach strategy to generate interest, attention and awareness and move target participants to action; (4) to tailor communication elements to reflect prospective participants' attitudes, beliefs, values and perceptions; and (5) to actually deploy the strategy. According to Kaufman, wellness programs have become more sophisticated in understanding the demographics of the target user population, and increasingly apply modern direct marketing approaches to wellness program recruiting, for example, sophisticated population segmentation, digital outreach through email and online, and ongoing analytics and campaign optimization. While these approaches are just evolving, early evidence shows that they more cost-effectively drive participation and program engagement (ibid.).

Campbell (Chapter 12 this volume) also emphasizes the importance of making participation fun and making it seem relevant to people's needs. She recommends varying the program interventions to keep things interesting and never to underestimate the power of being creative for pure silliness. If the wellness program can help provide fun and laughter and promote behavior change – all the better. These activities will help improve participation.

EVALUATION OF PROGRAMS

Because of the widespread use of wellness programs in the United States, the majority of evaluation studies are American. While there seems to be a consensus among researchers in this area that program evaluation is a key component for program success (Kaufman, Chapter 11 this volume; Campbell, Chapter 12 this volume; Grossmeier et al., Chapter 14 this volume), the literature indicates that it is difficult to determine effectiveness due to a number of methodological issues. One of the methodological problems is the selection bias, that is, the participants choose whether or not to participate, they are not randomly assigned, which may lead to motivational differences between the groups (Grossmeier et al., Chapter 14 this volume).

Many studies have focused on economic analyses of worksite health promotion programs to establish the effects on healthcare costs and return on investment (ROI) (Goetzel et al., 2005; Baker et al., 2008; Naydeck et al., 2008; Baicker et al., 2010; Berry et al., 2010). However, conclusions are hampered by the use of different measurement methods, varying categories of economic variables used for measuring economic return, and the use of alternative designs and statistical tests (Chapman, 2012). In addition, the literature is based principally on naturalistic studies that have serious methodological flaws, ranging from little standardization of the type of program tested, lack of randomization, lack of control groups, differences in the testing methods applied and outcome metrics, and not taking advantage of developments in emerging research methods in the field of comparative effectiveness research (Lerner et al., 2013). For example, the review done by Lerner et al. (2013) found over 2000 studies investigating the economic impact of employer-focused health promotion and wellness programs, but only 44 of these met the inclusion criteria. In a meta-analysis of organizational wellness programs between 1980 and 2005 measuring improvements in absenteeism and job satisfaction (Parks and Steelman, 2008), just under 200 studies were identified, of which 17 studies met the inclusion criteria. The conclusion to be drawn from this body of literature is that higher-quality research is needed to demonstrate program effectiveness.

Despite these methodological flaws, several studies have indicated that worksite wellness programs are associated with substantial saving for organizations. Baker et al. (2008) estimated that the outcomes from an obesity management worksite health promotion program resulted in reductions in healthcare expenditures and improvements in productivity, which represented a considerable return on investment. Goetzel et al. (2001) studied health and productivity management costs from 43 companies with almost 1 million workers. The results indicated substantial opportunities for savings in major areas through effective coordination and management of health and productivity management programs.

Several recent meta-analyses and reviews have also indicated that wellness programs are associated with cost savings. Lerner et al. (2013) did a systematic review of peer-reviewed studies on worker health promotion programs in the USA between 2000 and 2010. Inclusion criteria were the use of an experimental or quasi-experimental design and analyzing direct and/or indirect costs. Key study outcomes were medical and pharmacy costs, work performance/productivity loss, and disability claims. Seventy-three percent reported one or more favorable results, and 27 percent reported unfavorable, mixed or no results (Lerner et al., 2013). Chapman (2012) conducted a meta-analysis resulting in findings that employee health programs demonstrate a 25 percent reduction in sick leave, health plan costs, workers' compensation and disability insurance costs.

Using more sophisticated statistical techniques, Baicker et al. (2010) did a meta-analysis of peer-reviewed studies on the financial impact of employee wellness programs limited to health plan cost savings and sick leave absenteeism savings. Data from 22 studies indicated that for each dollar spent on employee health and wellness programs, medical costs dropped by approximately $3.27, and costs related to absenteeism were reduced by approximately $2.73. The results suggested that employer-based wellness programs improve employee health and productivity and result in substantial savings for companies in terms of healthcare and workers' compensation.

The results from the Baicker et al. (2010) study showed more modest return on investment than some earlier studies. Also, because it may take several years for most wellness programs to produce a statistically significant impact on healthcare cost, many will be skeptical of the research findings on ROI (Grossmeier et al. 2010). As a consequence of inconsistent findings, there is a certain skepticism regarding the robustness of evidence on return of investment. Ozminkowski (Chapter 15 this volume) argues that the return on investment one should expect from wellness programs should be as high as what is expected with other investments. In a good year, return on investments in stocks and bonds tends to be modest, so why should expectations for wellness programs be different? One should just compare the return on investments for wellness programs to that of all other investments, and realize that really large return on investment expectations are not likely to be satisfied by any investment (ibid.).

Fewer studies have looked at non-financial outcomes, such as employees' quality of life, health behaviors, risk factors and clinical measures, as well as process-related research questions, such as the role of financial incentives and various program implementation strategies (Goetzel et al., 2011). Also, organizations rarely evaluate whether these programs reach their goals of lowering absenteeism rates or measure job satisfaction (Parks and Steelman, 2008), even though it is assumed that job satisfaction will increase as a result of feeling more organizational support from employers who provide wellness programs. Parks and Steelman (2008) did a meta-analysis of on- or off-site services to promote good health or to identify and correct potential health-related problems. They looked at programs that were fitness only or comprehensive, defined as including a fitness and an educational component (ibid.). The meta-analysis involved 17 studies of organizational wellness programs conducted during 1980–2005. Criteria for inclusion were inclusion of measures of absenteeism and/or job satisfaction, control group, and the necessary empirical data. The results from the meta-analysis showed that those who participated in organizational wellness programs were associated with lower absenteeism rates and higher job satisfaction than non-participants. The data suggested that comprehensive programs were slightly better in terms of reducing absenteeism, but program type did not moderate the relationship between participation in wellness programs and job satisfaction. The authors concluded that the existence of a wellness program may signal that the organization supports employees, and thus be associated with job satisfaction. Also, wellness programs may be valuable recruiting and retention tools, because they are attractive to employees valuing physical fitness. Wellness programs also reduce stress levels, which in turn affect personal well-being and job satisfaction (ibid.).

While many authors have called for better and more standardized methods for evaluating cost-effectiveness of employee health promotion interventions, there is some evidence that studies of interventions are becoming increasingly sophisticated (LaMontagne et al., 2007). In a study of the job stress intervention literature between 1990 and 2005, organizationally focused high-rated systems-approach interventions represented a growing proportion of studies, and in addition, these high-rated interventions had favorable impacts at both the individual and organizational level. The observed growth in high- and moderate-rated studies evaluating job stress interventions probably reflect a growing application of such approaches in practice internationally (ibid.).

Grossmeier, Terry and Anderson (Chapter 14 this volume) distinguish between process evaluation, which involves the use of data collection instruments and methods that help practitioners understand if the program is operating as intended, and impact evaluation methods, which are those that assess the extent to which a program achieves its goals and objectives. These include measures such as increased awareness about health risks, changes in relevant knowledge or skills, and improvements in targeted behaviors such as increased physical activity and reduced fat, sugar or sodium consumption, as well as reductions in risk factors such as overweight/obesity, blood pressure, and cholesterol.

Biron and Karanika-Murray (2014) present the emerging field of intervention process evaluation (IPE), which may enhance our understanding of why organizational interventions succeed or fail. Organizational interventions presumably focus on prevention, that is, reducing or eliminating stressful or harmful aspects of the workplace, and should therefore be more effective than individual-level interventions, which mainly focus on improving the individual's ability to cope with stress (ibid.). Since researchers have mainly focused on whether such interventions work, and not how, when and why they work, the knowledge of process and context variables in intervention success is rather sparse (Nielsen and Randall, 2013; Biron and Karanika-Murray, 2014). Some authors recommend that 'intervention studies should include a process evaluation that includes a close examination of the psychological and organizational mechanisms that hinder and facilitate desired intervention outcomes' (Nielsen and Randall, 2013). Including such measures will greatly strengthen the evidence base for employee health programs (Goetzel et al., 2011). Kaufman (Chapter 11 this volume) also points out that it is critical to ensure that program effectiveness is measured alongside outcome metrics, so that program tactics can be reviewed and altered based on success.

Baun and Pronk (2006) point out that it is important to ensure that program evaluation measures areas for improvement as well as program success. It is also important to build program evaluation into the program plan, as evaluation is often the first process eliminated in a busy workday. While it is important to focus on outcome data for comparison purposes, most programs fail because of derailed programming or implementation details (ibid.).

CREATING A WELLNESS CULTURE AT WORK

The question is whether you want to achieve just ROI or whether the health improvement would be a valuable investment in and of itself. Aldana et al. (2012) conducted a summary of literature of workplace health culture on Fortune 500 companies, resulting in the determination that a healthy culture was linked to both a highly supportive leadership and a positive work environment that included policies supporting a workplace health culture.

Kelly and Carter (Chapter 9 this volume) present a model of employee health that includes five keys for the design of a healthy workplace: (1) leadership commitment and engagement, (2) involve workers and their representatives, (3) business ethics and legality, (4) use a systematic, comprehensive process to ensure effectiveness and continual improvement, and (5) sustainability and integration. These five keys provide an opportunity for organizations to further define their strategic plan for employee health (ibid.).

The health promotion program at the University of Alabama is a model comprehensive program (ibid.). The office directs wellness efforts all over the university with the involvement of numerous staff, research activities and continuous evaluation. The WellBAMA Rewards program involves four steps: (1) personal health screening, (2) opportunity for participants to set goals, (3) focus for participants to create a plan to achieve their goals, and (4) an opportunity for participants to receive annual incentives (VISA reward card). The program addresses individuals, families, campus environment, policies addressing health, health benefits as well as the larger community in order to create a healthy culture with sustained behavioral change.

While there is some evidence that worksite health promotion programs give adequate ROI, Grossmeier et al. (Chapter 14 this volume) make the point of broadening the value proposition for wellness from ROI to the value of investment (VOI). The methods and rigor of studies reporting ROI vary widely, although reviews show that on average, the medical cost savings per dollar invested in wellness programs are considerable. Many companies do not include ROI measures at all, and certainly not over time, and so the evidence on the financial impact of wellness programs is imperfect. Accordingly, Grossmeier et al. argue that the metrics used to assess the value of wellness programs should be broadened to make room for a value-on-investment approach in addition to the ROI approach.

According to Grossmeier et al., VOI for wellness may include elements such as worker productivity, employee satisfaction and morale, recruitment and retention, quality of life, and corporate brand or image. In this sense, wellness programs may be seen as one part of a comprehensive set of benefits intended to attract and retain top talent, support innovation, reduce workplace injuries, improve performance at work, and optimize employee commitment to and engagement in organizational goals and objectives. Thus, successful wellness programs will improve employee health and well-being, which in turn may contribute to the organization's bottom line, not only in terms of tangible (revenue growth, organizational profitability, percentage market share) business results, but also intangible (employer of choice, customer loyalty, corporate reputation) business results. These may in turn influence employee and organizational well-being, creating a positive spiral of benefits to both individuals and organizations (Grossmeier et al., Chapter 14 this volume).

Caouette, Paradis and Biron (Chapter 6 this volume) describe how several countries (e.g., Canada, UK, France) are considering or have already developed standards to create healthy workplaces. In Quebec, a voluntary health and well-being standard has been adopted by the 'Bureau de normalisation du Québec' (BNQ: Standards Bureau of Quebec). The standard implies the implementation of individual and organizational interventions, which can be categorized within four spheres. One of these spheres is the adoption of healthy management practices by managers. Management practices are specifically aimed at reducing employees' exposure to psychosocial risks, and are known to be a particularly difficult area of intervention. The project aims to clarify and identify key markers that can predict successful implementation of the 'Healthy Enterprise' standard. In their chapter, they present a research project currently conducted in organizations that have been certified as 'Healthy Enterprises'. More specifically, they describe the standard and the pertinence of considering psychosocial safety climate and readiness for change as key predictors for the implementation of healthy management practices.

In a similar vein, Bailey, Pignata and Dollard (Chapter 5 this volume) look at risk factors at work that may have detrimental effects on employee health, engagement and/or productivity. A holistic approach to interventions aimed at improving worker well-being is preferred because such interventions address both the causes of stress and the consequences for the individual. They advocate the psychosocial safety climate framework to establish psychosocial risk factors and develop effective stress prevention interventions. The literature on organizational interventions for stress remains underdeveloped in terms of the theoretical foundations for change, what interventions work and when they are effective.

Bailey et al. (ibid.) recommend using a holistic approach to promoting worker well-being that includes primary, secondary and tertiary interventions. Including all three levels of interventions will address both the causes of ill health and the consequences on the worker. Research has shown that intervention programs that include all three levels of interventions were effective in improving both individual and organizational outcomes (LaMontagne et al., 2007). However, some reviews (Briner and Reynolds, 1999; Richardson and Rothstein, 2008) have found a lack of empirical evidence to draw conclusions on the effectiveness of organizational-level interventions. The literature demonstrates clearly that work stress programs are predominantly reactive (i.e., secondary or tertiary approaches) strategies directed at individuals.

In a review of prominent European methods that describe systematic approaches to improving employee health and well-being, Nielsen et al. (2010) found that the methods all consisted of a five-phase process in which there were considerable similarities. The phases were: (1) preparation phase, consisting of components such as establishment of a steering group, addressing employee and organizational readiness for change, senior management support, communication, and drivers of change; (2) screening phase, including selection of methods of risk assessment, audit of existing methods, and determining methods of feedback to employees; (3) action planning phase, including developing activities and participatory workshops; (4) implementation phase, which includes monitoring of intervention activities, using middle managers as drivers of change, and communication; and (5) evaluation phase, including effect evaluation, but also process evaluation, that is, evaluation of the impact of context, how interventions have been implemented, and how intervention activities have been received by participants (Randall et al., 2009; Nielsen et al., 2010). A central part in all the approaches to organizational-level health interventions was the emphasis on employee participation to optimize the fit of the intervention to the organizational culture and context and to smooth the change process and increase exposure to the intervention. Also, these approaches to creating a wellness culture recognized the importance of employee participation as an intervention in its own right, increasing perceived control and responsibility for ensuring a good working environment (Nielsen et al., 2010). The study illustrates best practices in bringing about sustainable improvements in the psychosocial work environment and creating a wellness culture, but also points to the complexity of such interventions and highlights some gaps in the research evidence for intervention effectiveness.

The trend in the literature over the past years is clearly toward more comprehensive programs, organizational-level interventions and more stringent criteria for evaluation. Still, there are issues that need to be addressed to increase our knowledge. These include issues of what should be the goal of interventions (reducing risks or improving employee development) (Nielsen et al., 2010), the importance of employee participation (e.g., why and when participation works) (Nielsen and Randall, 2012), how to conduct risk assessments (Holland, Chapter 13 this volume), the links between occupational health and performance (Nielsen et al., 2010), and the use of better methodology in evaluating effectiveness of program interventions (LaMontagne et al., 2007; Grossmeier et al., 2010).

Many of the authors in this volume have addressed these questions from theoretical as well as practical perspectives. We hope this volume improves both the nature of corporate wellness programs and related workplace health and well-being interventions and their effectiveness.

NOTE

* Preparation of this chapter was supported in part by the BI Norwegian Business School and York University.

REFERENCES

Aldana, S.G., D.R. Anderson, T.B. Adams, R.W. Whitmer, R.M. Merrill, V. George and J. Noyce (2012), 'A review of the knowledge base on healthy worksite culture', *Journal of Occupational and Environmental Medicine*, **54**(4), 414–19.
Baicker, K., D. Cutler and Z.R. Song (2010), 'Workplace wellness programs can generate savings', *Health Affairs*, **29**(2), 304–11.
Baker, K.M., R.Z. Goetzel, X.F. Pei, A.J. Weiss, J. Bowen, M.J. Tabrizi, C.F. Nelson, R.D. Metz and K.R. Pelletier (2008), 'Using a return-on-investment estimation model to evaluate outcomes from an obesity management worksite health promotion program', *Journal of Occupational and Environmental Medicine*, **50**(9), 981–90.
Baun, W.B. and N.P. Pronk (2006), 'Good programs don't just happen – they're planned!', *ACSM's Health and Fitness Journal*, **10**(3), 40–43.

Baun, W.B., E.J. Bernacki and S.P. Tsai (1986), 'A preliminary investigation: effect of a corporate fitness program on absenteeism and healthcare cost', *Journal of Occupational Medicine*, **28**(1), 18–22.

Berry, L.L., A.M. Mirabito and W.B. Baun (2010), 'What's the hard return on employee wellness programs?', *Harvard Business Review*, **88**(12), 104–12.

Biron, C. and M. Karanika-Murray (2014), 'Process evaluation for organizational stress and well-being interventions: implications for theory, method, and practice', *International Journal of Stress Management*, **21**(1), 85–111.

Biron, C., C. Gatrell and C.L. Cooper (2010), 'Autopsy of a failure: evaluating process and contextual issues in an organizational-level work stress intervention', *International Journal of Stress Management*, **17**(2), 135–58.

Briner, R.B. and S. Reynolds (1999), 'The costs, benefits, and limitations of organizational level stress interventions', *Journal of Organizational Behavior*, **20**(5), 647–64.

Burton, W.N., C.Y. Chen, D.J. Conti, A.B. Schultz, G. Pransky and D.W. Edington (2005), 'The association of health risks with on-the-job productivity', *Journal of Occupational and Environmental Medicine*, **47**(8), 769–77.

Chapman, L.S. (2012), 'Meta-evaluation of worksite health promotion economic return studies: 2012 update', *American Journal of Health Promotion*, **26**(4), TAHP-1–TAHP-12.

Della, L.J., D.M. DeJoy, R.Z. Goetzel, R.J. Ozminkowski and M.G. Wilson (2008), 'Assessing management support for worksite health promotion: psychometric analysis of the leading by example (LBE) instrument', *American Journal of Health Promotion*, **22**(5), 359–67.

Dollard, M.F. and D.Y. Neser (2013), 'Worker health is good for the economy: union density and psychosocial safety climate as determinants of country differences in worker health and productivity in 31 European countries', *Social Science and Medicine*, **92**, 114–23.

Goetzel, R.Z. and R.J. Ozminkowski (2008), 'The health and cost benefits of worksite health-promotion programs', *Annual Review of Public Health*, **29**(1), 303–23.

Goetzel, R.Z. and N.P. Pronk (2010), 'Worksite health promotion: how much do we really know about what works?' *American Journal of Preventive Medicine*, **38**(2), S223–S225.

Goetzel, R.Z., A.M. Guindon, I.J. Turshen and R.J. Ozminkowski (2001), 'Health and productivity management: establishing key performance measures, benchmarks, and best practices', *Journal of Occupational and Environmental Medicine*, **43**(1), 10–17.

Goetzel, R.Z., R.J. Ozminkowski, C.M. Baase and G.M. Billotti (2005), 'Estimating the return-on-investment from changes in employee health risks on the Dow Chemical Company's healthcare costs', *Journal of Occupational and Environmental Medicine*, **47**(8), 759–68.

Goetzel, R.Z., R.J. Ozminkowski, J. Bowen and M.J. Tabrizi (2008), 'Employer integration of health promotion and health protection programs', *International Journal of Workplace Health Management*, **1**(2), 109–22.

Goetzel, R.Z., J.A. Schoenman, L.S. Chapman, R.J. Ozminkowski and G.M. Lindsay (2011), 'Strategies for strengthening the evidence base for employee health promotion programs', *American Journal of Health Promotion*, **26**(1), TAHP1–TAHP6.

Goetzel, R.Z., R.J. Ozminkowski, J.A. Bruno, K.R. Rutter, F. Isaac and

S.H. Wang (2002), 'The long-term impact of Johnson & Johnson's health and wellness program on employee health risks', *Journal of Occupational and Environmental Medicine*, **44**(5), 417–24.

Goetzel, R.Z., D. Shechter, R.J. Ozminkowski, P.F. Marmet, M.J. Tabrizi and E.C. Roemer (2007), 'Promising practices in employer health and productivity management efforts: findings from a benchmarking study', *Journal of Occupational and Environmental Medicine*, **49**(2), 111–30.

Goetzel, R.Z., T.B. Gibson, M.E. Short, B.C. Chu, J. Waddell, J. Bowen, J., S.C.Lemon, I.D. Fernandez, R. Ozminkowski, M. Wilson and D.M. DeJoy (2010), 'A multi-worksite analysis of the relationships among body mass index, medical utilization, and worker productivity', *Journal of Occupational and Environmental Medicine*, **52**(1), S52–S58.

Grossmeier, J., P.E. Terry, A. Cipriotti and J.E. Burtaine (2010), 'Best practices in evaluating worksite health promotion programs', *American Journal of Health Promotion*, **24**(3), TAHP1–TAHP9.

LaMontagne, A.D., T. Keegel, A.M. Louie, A. Ostry and P.A. Landsbergis (2007), 'A systematic review of the job-stress intervention evaluation literature, 1990–2005', *International Journal of Occupational and Environmental Health*, **13**(3), 268–80.

Lerner, D., A.M. Rodday, J.T. Cohen and W.H. Rogers (2013), 'A systematic review of the evidence concerning the economic impact of employee-focused health promotion and wellness programs', *Journal of Occupational and Environmental Medicine*, **55**(2), 209–22.

Mitchell, R.J., R.J. Ozminkowski and S. Serxner (2013), 'Improving employee productivity through improved health', *Journal of Occupational and Environmental Medicine*, **55**(10), 1142–8.

Naydeck, B.L., J.A. Pearson, R.J. Ozminkowski, B.T. Day and R.Z. Goetzel (2008), 'The impact of the Highmark Employee Wellness Programs on 4-year healthcare costs', *Journal of Occupational and Environmental Medicine*, **50**(1), 146–56.

Nielsen, K. and R. Randall (2009), 'Managers' active support when implementing teams: the impact on employee well-being', *Applied Psychology – Health and Well Being*, **1**(3), 374–90.

Nielsen, K. and R. Randall (2012), 'The importance of employee participation and perceptions of changes in procedures in a teamworking intervention', *Work and Stress*, **26**(2), 91–111.

Nielsen, K. and R. Randall (2013), 'Opening the black box: presenting a model for evaluating organizational-level interventions', *European Journal of Work and Organizational Psychology*, **22**(5), 601–17.

Nielsen, K., R. Randall, A.L. Holten and E.R. Gonzalez (2010), 'Conducting organizational-level occupational health interventions: what works?' *Work and Stress*, **24**(3), 234–59.

Parks, K.M. and L.A. Steelman (2008), 'Organizational wellness programs: a meta-analysis', *Journal of Occupational Health Psychology*, **13**(1), 58–68.

Pelletier, B., M. Boles and M.D. Lynch (2004), 'Change in health risks and work productivity over time', *Journal of Environmental Medicine*, **46**(7), 746–54.

Person, A.L., S.E. Colby, J.A. Bulova and J.W. Eubanks (2010), 'Barriers to participation in a worksite wellness program', *Nutrition Research and Practice*, **4**(2), 149–54.

Randall, R., K. Nielsen and S.D. Tvedt (2009), 'The development of five scales to

measure employees' appraisals of organizational-level stress management interventions', *Work and Stress*, **23**(1), 1–23.
Richardson, K.M. and H.R. Rothstein (2008), 'Effects of occupational stress
management intervention programs: a meta-analysis', *Journal of Occupational
Health Psychology*, **13**(1), 69–93.

Index

and employee growth and
development 64, 66–7, 71–2
and employee involvement 64–5, 71
and employee recognition 64, 69–70,
72
and health and safety 64, 65–6, 71
and public health models 70
and work–life balance 64, 68–9, 72
psychosocial risk
and 'Healthy Enterprise' standard
123, 133–9
and healthy work environments
108–11
and psychosocial safety climate 101,
107–8, 111–14, 123, 125–8,
130
and Quebec survey 120–21
and readiness for change 131, 132
'psychosocial risk literacy' 136
public health models 70

'Quality Dose/Response Rule' (in
plausibility tests) 337
quality transparency 156
questionnaires (health risk assessment
element) 279
Quick, J. C. 70

Randall, R. 129, 131–2
Ratey, J. J. 307
Ratzan, S. C. 13
RCT (randomized controlled trial) 299,
300–301
reasoned action approach 31–2
recruitment
content experience 254–5
dLife case study 241, 242, 249–53,
254
DPS Health case study 241, 242,
247–9, 254
and employee participation 241,
242–7, 255–6
and expertise/partnerships 254
sophisticated technology
infrastructure 255
reduction in status differences (human
resource management strategy) 3
referent-shift approach 89–90
'relapse' 221
removing barriers 210–11

reporting (health risk assessment
element) 279
'resilience' 80, 82, 83, 84, 87–8
resource assessment 262–4
results-per-condition 151–2
Reynolds, S. 104
RFC (readiness for change) 123, 124,
125–6, 130–39
Richardson, K. M. 104–5
risk computation (health risk
assessment element) 279
'risk perception' 32
ROI (return on investment)
and building the business case 12
and employee health management
programs 278
and evaluating programs 298–303,
309, 314, 315–16, 335–6,
339–40, 357
and health improvement programs
193
and health insurance 8
and healthcare costs 359–60
and psychological capital 85, 92
research evidence examples 16, 17
and success of corporate wellness
programs 215–16
Rose, G. 300, 301–2
Rothstein, H. R. 104–5

'salesperson' role 264
SAS Institute 17
Schein, Edward 170
scientific method 337–8
scope, relevance and quality (as pillar
of corporate wellness program
success) 11
SDT (self-determination theory) 220
secondary interventions 103, 104
'selection bias' 299
selective hiring (human resource
management strategy) 3
self-efficacy 80, 82, 83, 84, 87–8, 89–90,
225–6
self-funding 282, 283, 287
'self-liberation' 223
self-managed teams and
decentralization (human resource
management strategy) 3
'self-reevaluation' 223